NEW TESTAMENT
THEOLOGY

NEW TESTAMENT
THEOLOGY

COMMUNION
AND
COMMUNITY

PHILIP F. ESLER

SPCK

NEW TESTAMENT THEOLOGY
Communion and Community

First published in Great Britain in 2005

Society for Promoting Christian Knowledge
36 Causton Street
London SW1P 4ST

Cover image: Three disciples of Jesus. © Erich Lessing / Art Resource, NY.
Cover design: Laurie Ingram
Book design: James Korsmo

British Library Cataloguing-in-Publication Data
A catalogue record for this book is available from the British Library.

ISBN 0–281–05758–3

10 9 8 7 6 5 4 3 2 1

Printed in the United States of America

In Memory of Anthony Stephen Esler

15 November 1985–12 March 2002

ἐνδημεῖ πρὸς τὸν Κύριον

CONTENTS

PREFACE

This book represents the culmination of reflection over many years. Some of the ideas in it go back to the time of my doctoral studies in Oxford in the early 1980s—especially my conviction that the *historical* investigation of what messages the New Testament authors conveyed to their original audiences must have *theological* significance when the texts are read in a Christian context today. Yet this work has reached its present form as a result of research I have conducted in the last few years. I was able to expose the germ of my thesis in the form of the Manson Memorial Lecture I delivered in the University of Manchester on 25 October 2001. The warm reception and helpful feedback I received on that occasion encouraged me to press on and I am most grateful for the invitation to present the lecture. The bulk of the manuscript was written during a full year's research leave in 2002–3 that was made possible by a generous grant from the UK Arts and Humanities Research Board.

I have incurred many debts while thinking about or writing this book, of which I will mention a few in particular. Robert Morgan of Linacre College, Oxford, provoked my initial thoughts on New Testament theology back in my Oxford days and in the years since his writings have continued to stimulate my reflections; this year he has also offered detailed comments on some draft chapters. Alan Torrance of the University of St. Andrews was most helpful when I was formulating my model of socio-theological communion (chapter 2). Bruce Malina of Creighton University, Omaha, has assisted me with several points. I have also profited from responses to some aspects of this project by Richard Bauckham from St. Andrews and Werner Jeanrond of the University of Lund. While I am most grateful to all of these, they bear no responsibility for the views here expressed.

I am also grateful for the encouragement and assistance I have received from the staff of Fortress, especially K. C. Hanson and James Korsmo, in the process of producing this book.

The circumstances of the dedication of this book to the memory of my nephew, Anthony Stephen Esler (15 November 1985–12 March 2002), appear in chapter 10. The Greek is based on 2 Cor 5:8: "He is at home with the Lord."

St. Mary's College, St. Andrews
11 April 2005

ABBREVIATIONS

BibInt	*Biblical Interpretation*
BTB	*Biblical Theology Bulletin*
CBQ	*Catholic Biblical Quarterly*
CJT	*Canadian Journal of Theology*
CRINT	Compendia Rerum Iudaicarum ad Novum Testamentum
EvQ	*Evangelical Quarterly*
ExpT	*Expository Times*
HBT	*Horizons in Biblical Theology*
HNT	Handbuch zum Neuen Testament
HTR	*Harvard Theological Review*
HTS	Harvard Theological Studies
IDB	*Interpreter's Dictionary of the Bible*. Edited by G. A. Buttrick. 4 vols. Nashville: Abingdon, 1962.
Int	*Interpretation*
JBL	*Journal of Biblical Literature*
JCCP	*Journal of Cross-Cultural Psychology*
JR	*Journal of Religion*
JSNT	*Journal for the Study of the New Testament*
JSNTSup	Journal for the Study of the New Testament Supplement Series
JTS	*Journal of Theological Studies*
LXX	Septuagint
Neot	*Neotestamentica*
NovTSup	Novum Testamentum Supplements
NTS	*New Testament Studies*

OTL	Old Testament Library
OTP	*Old Testament Pseudepigrapha.* Edited by J. H. Charlesworth. 2 vols. New York: Doubleday, 1983
RB	*Revue biblique*
RSV	Revised Standard Version
SBLDS	Society of Biblical Literature Dissertation Series
SBT	Studies in Biblical Theology
SHR	Studies in the History of Religion
SJT	*Scottish Journal of Theology*
SNTSMS	Society for New Testament Studies Monograph Series
SwJT	*Southwestern Journal of Theology*
TDNT	*Theological Dictionary of the New Testament.* 10 vols. Edited by Gerhard Kittel and Gerhard Friedrickson. Translated by Geoffrey W. Bromiley
VTSup	Vetus Testamentum Supplements
WUNT	Wissenschaftliche Untersuchungen zum Neuen Testament
ZNW	*Zeitschrift für die neutestamentliche Wissenschaft*

THE NEW TESTAMENT AND CONTEMPORARY CHRISTIANITY

The motivation for writing this book is my belief that the New Testament *is* a fundamental resource for the maintenance of Christian life. While the precise role and status of the New Testament are variously construed among different Christian denominations, all will agree with this. All Christians find in its pages information concerning God's intervention in the world through Jesus Christ and the immediate aftermath of that intervention that speaks directly to the character of their current life and identity and of their ultimate destiny. In this book, I aim to make a particular proposal on how we should read or listen to the New Testament so as to maximize the impact that its twenty-seven constituent documents will have on contemporary Christian existence under God.

From this it is clear that my intention in writing is an avowedly theological one. I wish to promote a specifically Christian rationale for reading the New Testament that is related to its role in speaking of God's ongoing relationship with human beings and with the cosmos.

Taking this line, however, neither entails denying that there are other ways of approaching this work nor denigrating the results of such approaches. Many critics (some Christian and some not) are solely preoccupied with the historical question of what the documents that comprise the New Testament meant when they were first published. Unlike some, I see nothing whatever wrong with this. Much of my own biblical research has been and will continue to be historical in character. Similarly, it is possible to interpret the New Testament documents as literary texts in a way quite divorced from their role in sustaining contemporary Christian life and reflection. Again, I regard that as an entirely valid mode of inquiry. The fact, moreover, that some critics are working on the New Testament outside of a Christian context (for example, within a religious studies framework) should be a cause of celebration, not of anxiety and regret. While the

New Testament makes particular demands on practicing Christians, they do not own it.

Nevertheless, this book is expressly devoted to the question of how, and how best, we might interpret the New Testament so that its pages are applied to the challenges of contemporary Christian life, experience, and identity. How should we read or listen to the New Testament so that it continues to have a vital role in telling us what it means to be a Christian in the twenty-first century after Christ? As eminent an authority as Heikki Räisänen has recently attacked the idea of exegesis serving the church. In a post-Christian society, he thinks, exegesis should be oriented to the concerns of wider society.[1] While I agree that Christianity should be outward-looking and actively involved with the world, where there are upsurges of great good as well as of great evil, I cannot see a problem in occasionally recalling that the relationship Christians have with the New Testament is necessarily different from that of non-Christians. It speaks to their inmost selves in a way that it does not speak to others and there must be times when we explore more fully what this means. Outlining a particular line of such exploration is my task in this book.

Yet although the proposal that I will make in this book is "theological" in the sense outlined above, I will not be advocating the need for a "theology of the New Testament" in its currently understood sense, let alone suggesting what such a construct might look like. I wish to propose an entirely different model for New Testament theology. Biblical theology, of which the various New Testament theologies constitute a subcategory, was first theorized by Johann Philipp Gabler in 1787 and is still the subject of much attention over two centuries later. Its central idea, as I will explain in chapter 1, is that it is possible for biblical scholars to analyze the Bible historically in order to isolate the key "theological" ideas that (on most but not all views) are then available for use by systematic or dogmatic theologians. This results in "biblical theology," while the process applied to the Old or New Testaments produces "Old Testament theology" or "New Testament theology," respectively. The key aspects of this approach should be underlined. An individual scholar applies historical analysis to the texts and derives certain theological ideas from them. Usually this process involves according a central role to some of the material (most commonly the prophets in the Old Testament and Paul or John in the New) and then arranging the ideas hierarchically, thus setting the "more important" ideas above the "less important." Thus a "theology" is produced.[2] All of this continues an approach Gabler inaugurated in 1787.

The thesis of this book is that the time has come to propose an entirely different way of bringing the results of the historical investigation of the New

Testament into connection with contemporary Christian belief, practice, and identity. It is not part of my aim to criticize the numerous New Testament theologies that exist along the lines just mentioned or the enterprise of producing them. Nevertheless, I will argue that they represent an unnecessarily limited way of relating the New Testament—investigated historically—to present-day Christianity. To illustrate the issue and to set out some of my reasons for charting a different course, it will be useful to consider a recent essay by Robert Morgan, one of the leading authorities on New Testament theology, entitled "Can the Critical Study of Scripture Provide a Doctrinal Norm?"

This essay argues for one way in which New Testament theology can define the shape of Christian belief. Morgan correctly states that biblical and New Testament theology "have their origins and rationale in the assumption that scripture is in some sense normative for Christian belief and practice." Although he does not consider that Christian Scripture yields "a normative theology," he proposes, "it is possible to draw from Christian scripture one simple norm by which all subsequent Christian theologies can be tested for their faithfulness to the Christian claim to a decisive revelation of God."[3] Morgan finds his criterion in the divinity of Jesus. He suggests that every New Testament writer shared the conviction that "in having to do with the crucified and risen Lord Jesus Messiah they have to do with God, the one God of Israel who loves the world as its Creator, Redeemer, life-giver." He then proceeds to suggest that this doctrinal criterion of Christianity is classically summarized in the four words of the Chalcedonian definition that assert that Jesus is "truly God, truly a human being" (*vere Deus vere homo*).[4] Morgan finds John's Gospel to be the center of New Testament theology from the perspective of this doctrinal norm, against the view of many others who have marginalized or neglected the theological witness of this Gospel.[5]

I have no difficulty with the norm Morgan articulates to represent the heart of the New Testament's theological reflection. His advocacy of a fairly high Christology at an early period coheres with the research of others (myself included), even if to some Paul might seem as useful a source here as John.[6] And he and I are totally at one in the overall aim of bringing the New Testament into fruitful encounter with contemporary Christianity. My problem lies in the *utility* of Morgan's procedure for achieving this end.

Let us recall that he is looking for the historical exploration of Scripture to provide "normative" guidance for Christian belief and practice. Clearly, a "norm" of the sort he has in mind here is equivalent to what he also calls "a measuring rod or canon of truth."[7] Another way of describing the type of norm in question is as a credal or doctrinal formula.[8] But is there a good reason to stipulate a norm/canon of truth/credal or doctrinal formula derived from Scripture? Something of an answer is given in his observation that the "doctrinal shape of Christianity is vital because it affects belief, worship, and moral practice."[9] On a number of occasions in the essay he raises the importance of theology for Christian identity. Thus he claims "doctrinal formulae have served as badges of Christian identity and guidelines for Christian interpretation of scripture."[10] At one point he even suggests that, in mediating between biblical study and systematic theology, "New Testament theology does not give arguments for the truth of Christianity, as was once expected, but rather helps to clarify its identity."[11] Perhaps the nearest he comes to explaining what he means by this last remark is when he states that if it is "the heart and center of the New Testament and traditional Christian faith" to insist that, in having to do with Jesus, Christians have to do with God, then "the task of theological interpretation is *to make it plain*."[12]

I will grant that the clarification of Christian identity, the elucidation of whom we really are when we call ourselves Christians, is of critical importance. It has been at the center of my own thinking about the New Testament for a decade. Yet we must still ask whether, and, if so, in what sense, the "making plain" (which I take to mean the exposition and declaration) of *vere Deus vere homo*, the foundational theological truth to be discerned in the New Testament, can clarify that identity. Unfortunately, Morgan does not explain what he means by "identity." It does seem, however, to embrace "belief, worship and moral practice."[13]

That it is possible, however, to have a rich view of the identity shared by members of a group without much interest in beliefs held by the members can be seen in the analogy with social identity theory. This is a branch of social psychology Henri Tajfel, John Turner, and others developed at the University of Bristol in the late 1970s and early 1980s and which flourishes still in the United Kingdom, Europe, and Australasia. It focuses on that aspect of an individual's identity that he or she derives from belonging to a particular group (= "social identity"), especially in relation to out-groups to which he or she does not belong. The theory highlights three dimensions of group belonging: the "cognitive" (the fact of belonging), the "emotional" (how one felt about belonging), and the "evaluative" (how one rated oneself in relation to members, other groups). Yet this rich theory of identity persisted for twenty years before one of its exponents suggested the possible importance of "group beliefs" as an expression of group identity. This research, by Daniel Bar-Tal, represents a step beyond the theories of Tajfel and Turner in the direction of recognizing that social identity is not based solely on the mere fact of categorization, but that "group beliefs" held by the members also provide a rationale and character to group existence. Such beliefs are additional to the fundamental belief, namely, that the group *is* a group, and give a particular character to "we-ness and uniqueness" experienced by the members.[14]

Plainly, the scriptural norm Morgan has identified would qualify as a "group belief" of this kind, one that tells the members something fundamentally important about who they are if they belong to this group. Yet, just as there is a lot more to social identity than group beliefs, so too there is much more to being a Christian than holding this belief (*vere Deus vere homo*). First, there are other beliefs that are important, such as how the cosmos and human beings originated, the manner in which they should interact, and the ultimate destiny for the cosmos and humanity. Second, and perhaps more important, there are behavioral patterns that are presented as Christian, often exemplified in great figures like Francis of Assisi, Oscar Romero, or Martin Luther King Jr. These patterns include a relationship with God expressed in prayer and ways of relating to other people. Third, for some Christians, there is the continuous annual cycle of Christian liturgy. Fourth, there are the emotional and evaluative dimensions of being a Christian at a time when various denominations are experiencing turmoil centering on matters such as sexual abuse by priests and ministers, the status of homosexuals, the suppressing of prophetic theological voices by centralized ecclesial authority, the involvement of religious in the genocide in Rwanda in 1994, the possibility that traditional Christian views on creation have legitimated an exploitative approach to the environment, and so on.

In view of these various elements of Christian identity (to select only the more obvious candidates), how would one describe a theological interpretation of the New Testament devoted to clearly stating that in having to do with Jesus, Christians have to do with God? Probably as true, but as too foundational to have an immediate bearing on the crises just identified. In these circumstances, emphasizing the divinity of Jesus would appear reductionist. One would be taking all of the rich data in the New Testament and reducing them to this particular doctrinal formula when the contemporary situation might be calling for an infusion of biblical ideas and experience in other and more specific areas. While Morgan could say, as noted above, that he is not giving arguments for the truth of this assertion but rather simply propounding it as true, this would not allow him to escape the charge of reductionism in its use.

Let us situate the issue in a firmer context by trying out Morgan's approach on an imaginary Christian congregation in church one Sunday morning. Assuming they all participate in the four dimensions of Christian experience mentioned above, we inform them that in consequence of our historical research into the New Testament we have discovered that theological core to this collection of texts—that Jesus is truly God and truly a human being. Most will probably say, "That is good to hear. But we already believe that. Is the assertion of this truth to which we have long subscribed all that the historical interpretation of the New Testament has to offer us in leading our lives before God? In telling us who we are as Christians?" This imaginary scenario brings out the underappreciated fact that while theologians agonize about the truth claims of their religion (indeed, their identity depends on them and their continued fascination!), either asserting them or defending them, for most laypeople they are not hot topics. They are simply assumed. Regular churchgoers would not normally repeat a creed week after week if its central assertions were something about which they entertained severe doubts. The everyday fabric of Christian life is not normally disturbed by radical reconsideration of the fundamental beliefs of Christianity. On the other hand, there may be transitional periods in the lives of believers where this does happen. Adolescence, or tragedy suffered by oneself or one's relative or friend, may trigger off this process. Nevertheless, a person who eventually denies a central belief is likely to sever his or her ties with the religious group, even though it is possible that someone who denies that the belief in question is true might maintain his or her allegiance in spite of this.

But there is a more worrying side to the reductionism inherent in "New Testament theology" than the fact that any attempt by a single scholar to generate a central theological norm or a fully fledged theology from a historical investigation of the New Testament will isolate phenomena that are almost exclusively of interest to the theologically trained but not necessarily to the rest of the faithful. This is that the whole process involves nonchalance toward the original form and communicative intentions of the constituent documents of the New Testament. Theologies of the New Testament (but far less so Morgan's attempt to isolate a norm) usually proceed by propounding certain themes that are claimed to be foundational. Data from various parts of certain of the twenty-seven documents are gathered together to support the case being made. Some of the writings are invariably prioritized as affording a richer yield of the data needed (Paul's letters are often the favorites). Yet since the interest lies in a particular theme identified as significant by the interpreter in question, the intention of the biblical author, the original communicative impact of the text, and data irrelevant to the exercise are sometimes treated with indifference. The whole process is like a mining operation. Areas with a rich lode of the right ore (passages containing the theological concepts prioritized by the exegete) are dynamited and excavated (the act of exegesis) and the minerals separated (the act of interpreting the exegetical results) from the rock (the text under discussion), thus leaving nasty scars on the landscape (the text) and desolate heaps of tailings (the remnants of texts thought irrelevant).

Is there a way to avoid these consequences? Are we able to bring the results of the historical investigation of the New Testament to bear on contemporary Christian identity in a manner that matches and addresses its rich and variegated character *and* that does not violate the original form and message of the texts? The aim of this book is to propose a method of New Testament interpretation that achieves this result.

From the above critique of the current model of New Testament theology, it is clear that pursuing the "normative" will lead to precisely these problems: ignoring the intention of the original author, the effects of the text on its original audience, and the neglect of many texts and exegetical data. Seeking to extract from the New Testament a single theological norm or a set of related norms (a "theology") will always result in these problems. After two centuries of exegetical effort since Gabler, it is surely time to try something different.

The condition that philosophical ethics found itself in some forty years ago is closely and instructively parallel to the contemporary attempts to erect a theology of the New Testament. For many years, Kantian and utilitarian ethics dominated the field. Both of these aimed to establish normative ethical principles that could be applied in difficult moral dilemmas. Kantian ethics looked to the nature of the act in itself, stressing what one should do in a certain case, regardless of the consequences. Utilitarian ethics demanded that one look to the consequences of an action and seek to produce the greatest happiness for the greatest number and generated rules to put this principle into effect. The endeavors of biblical critics to detect normative principles in Scripture are closely cognate with this enterprise of stipulating ethical rules for particular situations.

In the last forty years, however, an entirely new approach to philosophical ethics has become popular—one that builds on Aristotelian philosophy especially to propose an ethics of virtue, character, and the good life. Here the interest is not in difficult moral dilemmas, that most of us, by good fortune, encounter only rarely, but in everyday human experience and how to make it flourish. The aim is to lead a good life and the means to achieve this by developing character through practicing virtues.[15] In this ethics the emphasis falls on the *formative*, not the *normative*, although claims that it has no place for normativeness are unfounded. Virtue ethics does not teach moral behavior by postulating norms to be obeyed, but by holding up virtuous persons ("saints and heroes") to be emulated.[16] In consequence, this form of ethics more closely engages human life in all its richness than Kantian or utilitarian ethics, which seek to develop abstract norms and then impose them on behavior. For these reasons, the movement from rule-oriented ethics to an ethics of the good life and of character and virtue offers an arresting possibility for a similar transition in theological interpretation of the New Testament.

This analogy suggests that contemporary Christians can find resources for maintaining and developing their identity by attending to the diverse ways of having faith in Jesus as the Messiah, which covers all of the dimensions of religious life mentioned above and which a historical investigation of the New Testament has the capacity to disclose. Rather than concentrating on what the early Christians believed, the analogy with virtue ethics prompts us to determine how such beliefs were manifested and maintained in the totality of their experience in particular contexts, some hostile to this new movement, in cities around the Mediterranean.

In pursuing this path we immediately come up against the form our evidence takes, twenty-seven distinct documents, most of them epistolary in form, but the bulk of the corpus comprising six narrative texts: the four Gospels, the Acts of the Apostles, and Revelation. The author of each document (some of whom are known but most unknown) has sought to communicate a message or messages to Christ-followers of the primordial period, the great majority of whom were illiterate, that would cement their allegiance to the new faith and the new identity that came with it.

For reasons that will become apparent later, these messages must have been read aloud at meetings; that is, their meanings were communicated orally and accessed aurally. It is therefore reasonable to regard our twenty-seven canonical texts as scripts for oral performance delivered within a setting of face-to-face dialogue concerning their contents at the movement's (probably noisy) meetings. The oral and dialogical character of communication among the first Christ-followers will be a continual theme in what follows. The approach I will propose in this volume is that modern Christians join in this dialogue and engage with the authors of these texts on an interpersonal and intersubjective basis that involves hearing their voices as much as reading their words.

I must immediately acknowledge that taking this route is rather at odds with modern methods of encountering the New Testament as text. The omnipresence of printed text in our lives as a result of Gutenberg's fifteenth-century invention of the printing press represents quite an obstacle to our understanding and benefiting from these communications in a manner that accords with their original and oral and interpersonal nature. Marshall McLuhan once said, "as the Gutenberg typography filled the world the human voice closed down. People began to read silently and passively as consumers."[17] This did not happen overnight. While the Reformation promoted the spread of vernacular literacy and habits of reading, the old oral ways were not displaced immediately.[18] Nevertheless, displaced they were. Silent, often solitary, reading by individuals seems to have become dominant with the advent of widespread literacy in much of Western Europe, which was largely achieved during the nineteenth century.[19] Communication as a process of interpersonal exchange in a face-to-face setting became less and less significant.

Accordingly, there is a great chasm in communication, not so much between literate and nonliterate societies as between those that have the printing press and those that do not. There is a huge "gulf between our own modern Western, post-Enlightenment world of the printed page and *all* past cultures (including our own predecessors in the West), as well as most contemporary ones."[20] It is essential to be cognizant of this if we are to avoid ethnocentrism or anachronism in our understanding of other cultures and eras.[21] But in addition to this, the dominance (especially since the Reformation) of the model of the solitary reader with the Bible in hand is one reason perhaps why there has been so little interest in the type of interpersonal approach proposed here.

The course of my argument is as follows: Chapter 1 will consider the state of the debate on using the fruits of historical criticism of the New Testament in Christian theology beginning with Gabler in 1787. In chapter 2, I will set out a model of persons in communion that embodies the social and theological presuppositions underlying my argument. In chapter 3, I defend the possibility of obtaining reliable knowledge of the past, including that of the New Testament period, in the face of recent skepticism. In chapter 4, I argue that the New Testament texts are nonliterary in character and that it is appropriate when interpreting them to pay attention to the communicative intentions of their authors. Chapter 5 proposes Friedrich Schleiermacher's hermeneutics as a powerful model for interpreting the New Testament in a way that does justice to its oral and interpersonal origins. The chapter also defends his ideas in this area against the false and stereotyped manner in which they have been portrayed. In chapter 6, I argue that face-to-face communion was characteristic of the first generations of the Christ-movement, using 1 Corinthians 10–14 as a test case. Chapter 7 argues for the minimal effect of writing in the early Christian period, suggesting that writing was primarily a means to maintain personal presence over distance. Chapter 8 is the first of three chapters devoted to the meaning of "the communion of saints," as a way of maintaining the presence of the deceased New Testament authors among modern Christians; here I essay its origins and development. In chapter 9, I explore models for giving meaning to the idea of communion between Christians living and dead that do not depend upon those who have died in Christ having any form of postmortem existence. In chapter 10, however, I do proceed to an understanding of the communion of saints predicated upon the survival of the faithful Christian in some way after death that can be found in certain parts of the New Testament (Hebrews especially) and in highly developed form in various early Christian texts from the early second century CE onwards. Chapter 11 seeks to makes sense of the canon in a way that is consonant with the interpersonal hermeneutics put forward in the earlier chapters. Lastly, in chapter 12, in order to illustrate what my method looks like in practice, I will outline the conjunction of history, hermeneutics, and communion in relation to a specific New Testament text, Paul's letter to the Romans. To keep the size of this book within manageable proportions, this last chapter is necessarily brief. Nevertheless, it should be sufficient to indicate the potential in the new approach to New Testament theology that I propose in this volume.

I

THE NEW TESTAMENT, HISTORY, AND THEOLOGY

THE STATE OF THE DEBATE

The aim of this book, as noted in the introduction, is to outline an approach to interpreting the New Testament that is directed toward its continuing to maintain and foster Christian life and reflection. For nearly two millennia Christians have regarded the New Testament as a unique resource in understanding the meaning of God's intervention in the world through Jesus Christ and, just as important, in trying to live in accordance with the new possibilities for existence and the new hope thus unveiled. As Robert Morgan has noted, it is this vital role that the New Testament plays in relation to the Christian faithful—for which he insists "theological" is an appropriate designation and "New Testament theology" an appropriate pursuit—that is the motivating force for much research into its pages:

> The word "theology" in the phrase ([namely,] "New Testament theology") is no accident. Most people's interest in the New Testament, including their historical interest in it, has been engendered by its significance for Christian faith. The discipline has been developed in the interests of traditional Christian faith and also out of hostility to it, but not with indifference to it.[1]

For over two centuries, indeed, the efforts of biblical scholars to bring the fruits of the (largely historical) interpretation of the texts of the Bible into the service of the Christian community have been encapsulated in the concepts of "biblical theology" or, more specifically, "Old Testament theology" and "New Testament theology." These concepts might seem, at the outset, to be broad and powerful enough to deliver the results sought, namely, the biblical or New Testament enrichment of Christian beliefs and practices. Yet while one must applaud the energy that generations of scholars have devoted to this task, a critical examination of "biblical" or "New Testament theology" from its origins to the present discloses certain systemic problems that have always stood in the road of its achieving this end and continue to bedevil the discussion in ways to be examined later. Our first task, accordingly, must be to assess the nature of biblical theology from its beginnings onwards, both to establish the context and also to justify proposing an entirely different approach to the problem.

GABLER'S BIBLICAL THEOLOGY
CRITICALLY ASSESSED

Because we are all subject to the ethnocentric temptation to imagine that our world is the whole world, that our microcosm is the macrocosm, it is useful to begin with a recognition of the very circumscribed Christian context in which biblical theology was born. "Only among followers of the Reformation," Gerhard Ebeling has observed, "could the concept 'biblical theology' have been coined at all."[2] He could, in fact, have described its progenitors with greater precision as "theologically expert Lutheran and Calvinist followers of the Reformation in Europe." For as he and Hendrikus Boers have shown, biblical theology only emerged as a response to a major problem among the intellectual elite of Protestant orthodoxy in Europe in the seventeenth and eighteenth centuries.

The Reformers had sought to establish the authority of the Bible as the basis and norm for judging and correcting abuses of the contemporary church and for renewing Christendom. But whereas in medieval Christianity the Bible had been taken as an integral, almost contemporary part of the religion, the Reformers' move inevitably meant to some extent separating the Bible form the life of the church in which it had previously been embedded. In time this separation also came to encompass a sense of the historical distance between the Bible and post-Reformation Christianity. Luther and Calvin both managed to prevent the rift from opening too wide by their writing commentaries that related biblical thought to the contemporary life of the church. In due course, however, Lutheran and Calvinist orthodoxies began to erect dogmatic systems of theology.[3] The result was that "Reformation theology, like medieval scholasticism, also developed into a scholastic system."[4] Theology in the strict sense became the total explication of Christian doctrine; it proceeded by systematic method and was normative for exegesis. Protestant scholasticism even resorted to use of Aristotelian philosophy in spite of Luther's struggle against the dominance of Aristotle in theology.[5]

Such developments invited negative reactions, naturally enough in the reassertion of the Bible in relation to these elaborate dogmatic structures, and these began to appear as early as the first half of the seventeenth century. This process took a fairly modest form in the first extant work bearing the title *Theologica biblica*, published by H. A. Diest in 1643. Here passages from both Testaments were collected under the names of central doctrines.[6] More negative was the response of the German Pietists. In 1675 we find one of them, P. J. Spener, claiming in his *Pia Desideria* that Scholastic theology had been thrown out the front door by Luther, but let in again through the back door by orthodox theologians, only to be thrown out again by the pietist churches.[7] Spener wanted theology brought back to its original simplicity. His was not an attack on Protestant orthodoxy, but a demand that its systematic theology be reformed.[8]

The Pietists failed to realize that by their formal critique of orthodox Protestant scholasticism they were actually raising a fundamental problem of its theological methodology—the extent to which theology should draw upon philosophy. This realization only dawned with the Enlightenment, when theologians influenced by it and rallying under the biblical banner launched a frontal assault on the use of scholastic philosophy in theology. A. F. Büsching raised this flag in a work published in 1758 that asserted the superiority of "biblical-dogmatic theology" over old and new forms of scholasticism. Thus he advocated a biblical dogmatics that stood out against scholastic dogmatics by accounting for Christian doctrine in a manner that could disregard the confessional statements of the Reformation and rest its claims solely on biblical texts. In 1771, Gotthilf Zachariä (1729–77) published his *Biblische Theologie* (Biblical Theology) which presented biblical arguments for theological doctrines as a means of criticizing dogmatic theology.[9] The vital next step, of removing dogmatics entirely from the work of biblical theology, was taken by Johann Philipp Gabler.

Before considering Gabler's innovation, however, we must remind ourselves again of the context. The issue was not the very general one that has always affected all Christians—Roman Catholics, Christians of the various autocephalous Orthodox churches, and members of the various Protestant and Reformed churches and denominations—of how the Bible, and the New Testament in particular, might inform and enrich Christian life and reflection. Rather, it was the very particular problem of the proper relationship between the Bible and the dogmatic theology of early modern European Protestantism. Although in later centuries the issue has widened out to embrace, at least potentially, the connection between biblical data and the dogmatic theologies of other Christian denominations, this notable and historically contingent limitation of the discussion to dogma that attended its birth has continued to accompany it. One of the most remarkable features of this subject is the rarity with which this obvious point is made. While, as we will see, there is great variety in the various models proposed for exploring the biblical side to the relationship, it is very difficult indeed to find anyone challenging the idea that the partner on the other side must be dogmatic or systematic theology, rather than some broader domain of Christian existence.

From a sociological point of view, this curious phenomenon is probably explicable in terms of the champions for various positions within this debate being either systematic theologians or exegetes defining themselves, often negatively, in relation to the theologians. Here the professional interests of the participants determine the game that is played.

This is not to deny for one moment that it is essential that the theological elites of every Christian denomination continue to bring their minds to bear systematically on the meaning of their faith (this entailing concern with the status of its "truth claims") and struggle with the role that Scripture should play in their formulations. The question is simply—Why is this the only game in town? Why has the immense effort since Gabler to understand the role of Scripture—examined historically—in relation to dogmatic theology not been matched by an effort of at least equal intellectual seriousness to bring the Bible—examined historically—into contact with the broader reaches of Christian life and identity?

It is submitted that the answer to this puzzle lies partly in the sociological explanation just mentioned. In addition, however, there is the further factor that the initial task which historical analysis of the Bible set itself was not generally to determine what biblical texts, as communicative discourses, meant when they were first published. Rather, historical criticism, with the occasional exception such as John Locke (1632–1704),[10] set about discriminating between historical and non-historical elements (the latter frequently labeled as "mythological") in the texts. Pre-eminent in this regard was *The Life of Jesus Critically Examined* of David Friedrich Strauss (1808–74), first published in German in 1835,[11] with three more editions appearing by 1840. Strauss's *Life of Jesus* became available to the English-speaking world as early as 1846 in the form of a translation of remarkably high quality of the 1840 fourth edition in three volumes by none other than the novelist George Eliot.[12] This approach tended to rouse the suspicions of many Christians, especially lay people, toward the whole process of historical analysis. We will return to this issue later in this chapter. For the moment, however, we must turn to Johann Gabler, who inaugurated the process that has led to the historical analysis of the texts to discern their theological outlooks being engaged solely with dogmatic theology. We will also look briefly at some of the developments after Gabler.

In describing what Gabler had to say on this matter it is important not to exaggerate his significance. Although he initiated a particular approach to biblical theology, his reception in the nineteenth century was patchy and often diverged from his own intent. Nevertheless, it is worthwhile to scrutinize the *fons et origo* of a phenomenon whatever may have been its fate thereafter. Moreover, Heikki Räisänen has recently explained and commended Gabler's proposal in his own significant volume *Beyond New Testament Theology*.[13] Gabler's ideas offer a useful contrast with the very different ends pursued in this volume.

Gabler set out his understanding of the distinction between biblical theology and dogmatic theology and the specific objectives of each in his inaugural lecture of that title as a professor of theology in Altdorf, Germany, on 30 March 1787.[14] This lecture is generally regarded as instituting biblical theology as a separate discipline. It is worthy of close scrutiny.

Gabler acknowledges debts to several previous scholars. Three of these were particularly important.[15] From Johann Semler (1725–91) he gained the idea that the word of God was to be found in Scripture, but was not identical with it (which freed the Bible for critical investigation without denying that it was inspired).[16] From Semler, but especially from C. C. Tittmann, he learned that religion and theology were distinct.[17] From Gotthilf Zachariä (1729–77) he drew the idea that some theological conceptions to be found in the Bible were subject to the contingencies of history, while others transcended such contingencies, and only the latter provided material for a biblical theology.[18]

It is worth quoting some of what Gabler said on the difference between religion and theology:

> Religion is passed on by the doctrine in the Scriptures, teaching what each Christian ought to know and believe and do in order to secure happiness in this life and in the life to come. Religion then, is every-day, transparently clear knowledge; but theology is subtle, learned knowledge, surrounded by a retinue of many disciplines, and by the same token derived not only from the sacred Scripture but also from elsewhere, especially from the domain of philosophy and history. It is therefore a field elaborated by human discipline and ingenuity. . . But religion for the common man has nothing to do with this abundance of literature and history.[19]

Today we are very aware that religion embraces far more than "knowledge," since *experience* is central to all religion. Yet Gabler's now-dated limitation of religion to knowledge makes all the more noticeable the fact that it was the form of knowledge represented by theology—the realm of those capable of subtlety, learning, and ingenuity, not the knowledge of the religion for the "common man"— that exclusively engaged his attention.

How did he distinguish biblical and dogmatic theology? On the one hand, he says:

there is truly a biblical theology, of historical origin, conveying what the holy writers felt about divine matters; on the other hand there is a dogmatic theology of didactic origin, teaching what each theologian philosophises rationally about divine things, according to the measure of his ability or of the times, age, place, sect, school, and other similar factors.[20]

There was a stability about biblical theology that was quite lacking in dogmatic theology, which was subject to a multiplicity of change, even among the followers of Luther.[21]

Inspired by Zachariä, he advocated that biblical theology should proceed by separating "those things which in the sacred books refer most immediately to their own times and to the men of those times from those pure notions which divine providence wished to be characteristic of all times and places,"[22] with the latter "pure" notions to constitute its actual substance. "These passages will show with unambiguous words," he adds later, "the form of faith that is truly divine; the *dicta classica* ["proof texts"] properly so called, which can then be laid out as the fundamental basis for a more subtle dogmatic scrutiny. For only from these methods can those certain and universal undoubted ideas be singled out, those ideas which alone are useful in dogmatic theology."[23] In time Gabler further developed this approach by dividing biblical theology into a first stage that systematically set out biblical religion as it appeared conditioned by its original historical particularities (which he rather unhelpfully called *wahre* ["true"] biblical theology) and a second stage (just noted) where he isolated the universal truths in this historical shell (which he called *reine* ["pure"] biblical theology).[24] Räisänen refers to these two stages as "historical" and "normative" biblical theology.[25]

Gabler's biblical theology was historical in the sense that its subject matter was a fixed body of material from the past, namely, biblical revelation, even if it was possible through critical analysis to distinguish historically contingent ideas from universal truths in that material. To this extent its methodology differentiated it from dogmatic theology, which remained dependent upon philosophical thought.

Gabler, however, regarded biblical theology and dogmatic theology as distinct yet closely connected. As Boers accurately notes, "Biblical theology was intended for a specific purpose, that is, to serve dogmatic theology by providing it with an independent base. With regard to its purpose, thus, biblical theology was not independent of dogmatic theology."[26] In this aim Gabler was motivated by an attempt to understand the theological task as a whole.[27] After Gabler, however, it was entirely predictable that other scholars would establish historical analysis of the biblical texts as a discipline completely independent of dogmatics.[28] That is, in time, precisely what occurred, with consequences I will return to below.

TWO IMPLICATIONS OF GABLER'S PROPOSAL

Before pressing on to Gabler's successors, however, we should tease out two implications of his proposal of distinguishing biblical and dogmatic theology that he so confidently announced. The *first* concerns his entire assumption that historical analysis of the Bible (or of the Old and New Testaments, since he was properly appreciative of the very different type of religion represented in each)[29] that is directed to generating a biblical theology has as its end the provision of biblical truths for dogmatic theology. *Why*, we must ask (although finding a precedent for the question is surprisingly difficult), *did Gabler limit the historical investigation of the theology of Scripture, in the pursuit of both contingent historical details and universal truths, to the provision of ideas for dogmatic theology?* He subscribed, after all, to the view that religion and dogmatic theology were both types of knowledge, the former being the ordinary and plain understanding of the common man and the latter the subtle and highly sophisticated understanding of the theological intellectual elite. Why did it not occur to him that knowledge for the sake of religion was just as capable of being enriched by biblical truth as knowledge for the sake of dogmatic theology? In particular, why did he not realize that the delineation of biblical truths that were universal would find just as warm a welcome in the religion of the common man as in the elaborate philosophical structures of the dogmaticians?

It is most unlikely that Gabler foresaw that historical criticism, as it developed, would prove as unpalatable to so many Christians as it eventually did. Admittedly, English Deism, beginning especially with John Locke's 1695 work *The Reasonableness of Christianity, as Delivered in the Scriptures,* had established a strong current of rationalistic thought inimical to dogmatic interpretation of Scripture and that insisted upon viewing the biblical texts as witnesses from the past to be understood in their original contexts.[30] In the previous decade, moreover, from 1774 to 1778, Gotthold Lessing (1729-81) had published the *Fragments* of Reimarus, with their radical attack on the historicity of aspects of Jesus's life and of his resurrection. Yet it is most unlikely that anyone could have known before David Friedrich Strauss published his *Life of Jesus Critically Examined* just how radical and alarming to Christian orthodoxy historical criticism would become. *There is certainly no mention of any such concern in Gabler's lecture.*

Most probably the reason for Gabler's directing biblical theology exclusively to dogmatics was that he himself was a Lutheran theologian of his time. He had been socialized, accordingly, to believe that the critical issue was the mess into which Protestant orthodoxy in Europe had got itself with the development of a theological scholasticism that was perceived to be almost as oppressive as that of medieval Catholicism. And all this in spite of Luther, and within a century or two of his death.

So it is easy to see why Gabler brought biblical theology into conjunction with dogmatic theology. This probably seemed to represent the reassertion of the Lutheran heritage at a time when it was in danger of being overwhelmed. Yet this explanation cannot disguise the fatal limitation in Gabler's proposal, or the serious consequences of both biblical and dogmatic scholars having been fixated on this way of formulating the relationship between historical research into the Bible and the contemporary demands of the Christian faith these past two-hundred-twenty years. This is not to suggest, as already noted, that there is anything wrong with an interest in the relation between Scripture historically examined and dogmatics, but only to insist that there is more to Christianity than dogmatics. It is most unfortunate that Gabler, the pioneer of the approach to biblical theological that was to become the dominant model, failed to pursue the consequences of his distinction between religion and theology. It is equally unfortunate that he failed to conceive the thought that historically elicited biblical data and truth could just as easily enrich the knowledge (to use his term) configured as everyday Christian religion as the knowledge represented in dogmatic theology. If he had done so, the subsequent course of biblical scholarship and its relationship with the Christian faithful might have been entirely different. When we expand the scope of religion beyond Gabler's "knowledge" to embrace dimensions such as experience and identity (as we must, given our modern understanding of religion), the potential for the results of historical biblical interpretation to enrich contemporary Christian life becomes even greater.

But Gabler did not have that thought. Instead, he initiated the idea that historical research into the Old and New Testaments could only be brought to bear upon the present experience and beliefs of Christians via the link with dogmatic theology (a link which was to become increasingly tenuous as the decades rolled on). The main exception to this was to come in the occasional, opportunistic context of the homily for ministers game enough to try out on congregations the results of historical research with which the latter were almost completely unacquainted. The possibility of a systematic application of the fruits of biblical investigation to the ongoing life of Christians was strangled at birth.

So it happened that as historical criticism of the Bible took hold in the late eighteenth and nineteenth centuries, there was a lamentable failure to implement any systematic effort to apply its results in a creative way to everyday Christian existence, coupled with the production of increasingly radical views by its practitioners, whose historical research seemed to imperil popular beliefs in the inerrancy and infallibility of Scripture—a phenomenon itself fostered by the fact that no one, partially thanks to Gabler, was urging a positive role for their historical investigations in Christian life. Not surprisingly, therefore, the combination of these factors produced an excessively negative misunderstanding of the character of historical criticism and a suspicion toward it among ordinary Christians. This suspicion culminated in the widespread anxiety that it was inimical to faith. Historical criticism was cast as a dangerous threat, not as a golden opportunity. It is for all of these reasons that one can say with some justice that 30 March 1787, widely regarded as the birthday of modern biblical theology, was actually a black day for Christianity.

The *second* implication of Gabler's proposal concerns his distinction between the contingent historical features of Scripture and its universal truths, only the latter of which could be injected into dogmatic theology. Some features of Scripture, such as the laws in Leviticus that few indeed would claim have application to Christians, seem to demand a distinction of this kind. Yet there is still a mischief to it. Gabler is suggesting that *all* features of the Bible that relate to the historical particularities of the ancient times and places in which its constituent works were written have no role in the theological task, for only the universal truths that can be distilled from the texts by historical analysis can serve that function.

Ten years earlier Lessing had written, "accidental truths of history can never become the proof of necessary truths of reason."[31] In saying this he was heavily influenced by the philosophers Leibniz and Spinoza, who had distinguished historical knowledge from the necessary truths of reason (Leibniz) or natural divine law (Spinoza), and had argued that the former could not lead to the latter.[32] Lessing famously encapsulated his resistance to the idea that the fact of the resurrection of Jesus Christ in the past could prove that he *is* the Son of God *now* in the statement "That, then, is the ugly, broad ditch which I cannot get across, however often and however earnestly I have tried to make the leap."[33] This type of view seems to have appealed to Gabler.

Robert Morgan (utilizing Clifford Geertz's notion of religion as a cultural system of interconnected symbols) has commented on this aspect of Gabler's program as follows:

> Sketching the bare outline of the Christian symbol-system in isolation
> from its successive social contexts can only have a regulative function. The

biblical witness may have more purchase on contemporary reality when seen in its own historically conditioned reality.[34]

The point can be put more brutally than this by observing that Gabler's view entails the frankly nonsensical notion that modern Christians, struggling to do God's will and to hold on to their identity in their own epoch, are incapable of deriving valuable assistance from considering how the first people who followed Christ did God's will and held on to their new identity in the particular circumstances of their times.

Although Gabler unnecessarily and tragically confined the contemporary Christian realm to benefit from biblical theology to dogmatics, it is difficult to see that he would have taken any different view if he had also wanted to introduce the results of historical biblical research into the "knowledge" represented by everyday Christian religion. It would have been universal truths, not contingent historical features that he employed.

We may sharpen this point by suggesting that the problem with Gabler's approach is that it would have entailed the erasure of the otherness from the biblical data used in this task. To seek "universal truth" applicable to two sets of experience—that of the Bible and those who wrote and first received its various writings, on the one hand, and that of contemporary Christians, on the other—is to shun differences between the two situations and to pursue commonality. The possibility of learning from the other by the very fact of his or her otherness, of shaping one's own experience and understanding in the encounter with someone culturally unlike oneself, disappears in such a process.

No doubt it is artificial to charge Gabler with missing a potential obstacle on a journey he (unfortunately) never chose to make. Nevertheless, by conducting this modest mental experiment we are alerted to a question of fundamental importance if we do initiate the task that he left in abeyance, namely, the use of the results of historical research into the New Testament to strengthen and enrich the beliefs, experience, and identity of Christians in the present. And that issue is precisely what the current volume is about.

TWO RADICAL SUCCESSORS OF GABLER: STRAUSS AND WREDE

Although the work of Johann Semler (1725–91) and Johann Michaelis (1717–91) during the period 1770 to 1790 had given the historical criticism of the Bible a decisive stimulus, consistent historical analysis came with the work of David Strauss and Ferdinand Baur from the 1830s onward.[35] As already noted, in 1835 David Strauss, then only twenty seven years old, published *The Life of Jesus Critically Examined*. With Strauss we encounter a rejection of the idea that history can be useful for theology. Whereas Gabler had proposed that the historical analysis of the Bible to discern its theological notions could lay the foundations for dogmatics, Strauss wanted, as he said, to "annul the life of Jesus as history" and then "re-establish dogmatically what had been destroyed."[36] Thus, Strauss had both a negative and a positive aim, which can be identified respectively with his interests in myth on the one hand and in an aspect of Hegelian philosophy on the other. The fact that Strauss does not cite Gabler in *The Life of Jesus* may reflect the gulf between them on their attitude to history.[37]

During the years 1821–1825 Strauss was a student at the seminary at Blaubeuren in the state of Württemberg, where one of his teachers was Ferdinand Baur. At that time Baur was already insisting on the role of philosophy to give meaning to history, but he did so via the idealist philosophy of Friedrich Schelling (1775–1854), since he had not yet been exposed to Hegel.[38] Central to Baur's appropriation of idealist ideas was the notion of history as "a continuous, gradually self-disclosing revelation of the absolute," which represented a fruitful alternative to the then current but tired approaches of naturalism and supernaturalism.[39] During those years Baur also worked and taught on myth and symbolism in antiquity, including to Strauss.[40] Here again Schelling was useful, in his notion "that philosophical myths present ideas in visual, palpable form, and hence are not expected to be taken at face value as factual history, but are expected to persuade one of their truth."[41]

In 1825 Strauss moved to Tübingen. He began to interest himself in romanticism, and read Friedrich Schelling avidly, especially for his philosophy of nature. Strauss and his friends also became involved in the spiritualist side of romanticism. In 1826 Baur also moved to Tübingen, to fill a vacant post. At that time, Hegel (1770–1831) was virtually unknown in Tübingen. In the winter of 1828–1829 a tutor in the evangelical faculty, recently returned from Berlin, began lecturing on his thought. In the winter of that year Strauss and some friends began an intensive study of Hegel. Strauss continued working on the Hegel in the years that followed.[42] One aspect of Hegel's thought proved particularly appealing to him. Hegel had distinguished between *Vorstellung* (= religious imagery) and *Begriff* (= philosophical concept). Strauss utilized this distinction in developing his own theological and philosophical views. Hegel had claimed that *Begriff* transcended *Vorstellung*, raising its meaning to a higher and more adequate level. Strauss's particular contribution was to equate *Vorstellung* with theology and *Begriff* with philosophy. It was not a big step for Strauss to argue that the heart of Christian theology, the Gospel story of Jesus, was *Vorstellung*, a story representing a truth that could be better expressed in philosophical concepts.[43] In 1830 Strauss even conceded to a colleague that the use of images (*Vorstellungen*) or ("myths")—which for ordinary Christians were often the content of the faith—instead of concepts could well be "dishonest" and "self-contradictory."[44]

When he came to write his *Life of Jesus*, accordingly, Strauss was working with the idealist idea of myth as expressing an idea and the Hegelian proposal of the concept as transcending the representation, even if the extent to which both stimuli were reconciled in his mind can be debated.[45] So he worked through the Gospel accounts of Jesus, demolishing supernaturalist and naturalist explanations and interpreting the various phenomena as myth. Räisänen has rightly observed that "[n]ot only did Strauss demand a historical exegesis independent of dogmatics; he also carried out the task—with ruthless efficiency."[46]

Yet at the end of this vast critical exercise Strauss made a positive proposal, that appeared as a short concluding chapter on the "Dogmatic Import of the Life of Jesus." The core of this proposal was his conviction that "the central truth of Christianity was the divine incarnation in humanity as a whole, not in a single historical figure."[47] Strauss expressed this view in the concluding chapter of the fourth edition as follows:

> Is not the idea of the unity of the divine and human natures a real one in a far higher sense, when I regard the whole race of mankind as its realization, than when I single out one man as such a realization? Is not an incarnation of God from eternity, a truer one than an incarnation limited to a particular point of time.[48]

Hodgson reasonably suggests that the philosophical perspective here is one of monistic pantheism.[49]

Whereas Gabler had thought that New Testament theological ideas (of universal application) could be won using historical analysis to serve as a foundation for a systematic theology that could also draw on philosophy, Strauss saw no role for history in his theology. With William Wrede, on the other hand, we find a re-assertion of history, but arguably at the expense of theology.

The publication by William Wrede (1859–1906) of the short monograph "The Tasks and Methods of So-called 'New Testament Theology'" in 1897 represented a potent argument for finally severing the connection between biblical theology that was conducted historically and dogmatic theology.[50]

Thus we find Wrede near the start of the work insisting that his comments "presuppose the strictly historical character of New Testament theology."[51] For Wrede the task of New Testament theology was "to lay out the history of early Christian religion and theology." This entailed, at the least, knowing *"what was believed, thought, hoped, required and striven for* in the earliest period of Christianity, not what certain writings say about faith, doctrine, hope, etc."[52]

Allied to this was his view that *"the writers' personalities and the writings as such are not important, but very subsidiary matters."*[53] Wrede argued that in relation to 1 Peter, the Lukan writings, Mark and Matthew, *1 Clement*, James, the *Didache*, the Pastoral Epistles, and many others we know nothing or virtually nothing of the authors of these documents. None of them shows signs of an individual mind that one could class "epoch-making." None of them advances an idea that became normative. However edifying, they contain only "average Christianity." This meant "that these writings and their authors are of no interest to New Testament theology" and setting out their content is just the preliminary work for New Testament theology, the gathering of raw material.[54] He granted that there was a place for accounts of each New Testament writing, even these rather ordinary ones, in commentaries and New Testament introductions.[55] Wrede found epoch-making ideas only in the preaching of Jesus and in the writings of Paul and John and offered an extensive sketch of what a New Testament theology focusing on the works of these three figures might embrace.[56]

Toward the end of the work, Wrede considered how this discipline should be designated. He suggested that "the name New Testament theology is wrong in both its terms. The New Testament is not concerned merely with theology, but is in fact more concerned with religion." Rather, he proposed that the appropriate name for it was "early Christian history of religion, or rather: the history of early Christian religion and theology." He then, rather adventurously in the circumstances, proceeded to say, "If anyone protests that this is no longer a New Testament theology, that is a strange objection. The name is obviously controlled by the subject-matter, not vice versa."[57]

Yet it is, in spite of this disavowal, very difficult to see any sense in which Wrede's enterprise can be described as "theology." It does not acknowledge the reality of God, nor does it exhibit any interest in the influence of the New Testament on the existence and identity of Christians contemporary with its exercise, both of which must be a minimal requirement for the description "theology" or "theological."[58] Wrede's is a purely historical account of early Christian religion and theology that is expressly disconnected from any service to the Christian church. As Morgan has observed, it has to be said against

Wrede "that New Testament theology does involve theology."[59] Morgan him-self has proposed a theological function for Wrede's historical project: "It pro-vides a criterion against which all theological interpretations must be tested. If these conflict with what historians say about the sources, they cannot be accepted."[60] But this is a minimalist and essentially negative role for history.

Yet Wrede did not merely reject the relationship of biblical theology to dogmatics, he went further and strongly denied that it had any duty "to serve the church." This notion was either "utterly untenable or utterly devoid of content." His reasons for this view require noting, since they constitute an argument against the whole thesis of this volume:

> The service to be rendered to the church would still have to be either the results of research or the way in which the material is treated or the tasks which are set. Striving to serve the church says absolutely nothing about results or method. Both are determined solely by the nature of the his-torical object. The tasks set also come in the main from the subject-matter. The questions and needs of the church can be a legitimate influence only in a limited sense—and probably least of all in the biblical field. On the whole it is not within the historical researcher's power to serve the church through his work.

From this Wrede concluded that "*[t]he theologian who obeys the historical object as his master is not in a position to serve the church through his properly scientific-historical work, even if he were personally interested in doing so*" (emphasis added). The same applies to the whole business of investigating historical truth (that is, beyond the work of any individual researcher) in relation to the church: "the church rests on history, but historical reality cannot escape investigation, and this investiga-tion of historical reality has its own laws." His final statement on this subject reveals with absolute clarity that Wrede's whole position on history not serv-ing the church rests on the fear that this will inevitably do violence to the historical investigation:

> It is, then, impossible to make the special value placed on the New Testament by the church of the past or the present, or any other account of its special historical importance, into a reason for a particular delineation of biblical theology, if this contradicts the nature of the subject-matter.[61]

Wrede must have thought that the condition in the last clause would be satisfied in every case. Although by his time it had become crystal clear that modern Christians could not continue to use the Bible in the same way as their premodern ancestors in faith, since that would conflict with their modern, historically conditioned consciousness of truth, Wrede seems to go beyond this. Historical accuracy, he implies, would always be violated in any context of service to the church.

Lying behind Wrede's skepticism on this point was no doubt the long, sorry story of the hostility which historical research into the New Testament had aroused among many Christians during the nineteenth century. The specter of Strauss's onslaught on the numerous "mythological" features of the Jesus tradition in the Gospels and of the work of those who followed him continued to haunt the Christian consciousness. History was thought to be inimical to the supernatural dimensions of the texts. Much historical research was aimed at what lay "behind" the New Testament accounts.[62] In such a context Wrede's attitude becomes understandable.

But what if historical investigation were to pursue a different aim, not what lies "behind" the texts, but simply what they communicated to their original audiences?

A CONSERVATIVE SUCCESSOR TO GABLER: ADOLF SCHLATTER

Whereas Wrede represented the radically critical wing of New Testament scholarship, Adolf Schlatter (1852–1938) stood for the very best in conservative scholarship. He was very much a theologian and consciously rejected the methodological atheism of modern historiography as applied to the Bible.[63] His *New Testament Theology* was published in 1909–10. Shortly after, in 1911, he published *Das christliche Dogma* (*Christian Dogma*), thus producing two separate works, one historical and one dogmatic in character, in the spirit of Gabler. The conservative aspect to Schlatter's enterprise is revealed in his view that all the New Testament documents were authentic, except for 2 Peter, and his belief in Matthean priority. Yet he still believed in and practiced historical method, even while insisting that his theism was bound to affect how he did so. At the same time, while the fact that many of his historical views about the New Testament (such as those just cited) are not widely accepted has a negative impact on his theological opinions, he does strongly defend the view that history and theology can be integrated. At one point he wrote:

> God does his work of grace and judgment not outside man and so, too, not beyond history, but in it and through it. So the New Testament utterly repudiates the thesis that revelation and history cannot be united, and this

at the same time destroys the view that historical research is a denial of revelation.[64]

To this extent there is some parallel between Schlatter's vision and the thesis to be argued in this book, even though the manner in which historical research and theology are to be combined is very different from what Schlatter had in mind.

SUBSEQUENT DEVELOPMENTS: BULTMANN, STENDAHL, MORGAN, RÄISÄNEN, AND WATSON

Rather than attempting an exhaustive summary of the development of biblical theology since Schlatter, I will now briefly analyze five major contributions, from Rudolf Bultmann, Krister Stendahl, Robert Morgan, Heikki Räisänen, and Francis Watson.

My aim will be to highlight certain critical issues of the debate with which I will engage, often but not always critically, as I unfold the very different approach to bringing the results of historical criticism into connection with contemporary Christian experience, reflection, and identity outlined in this volume.

Rudolf Bultmann

There is no doubt that the most successful attempt to create a New Testament theology in the twentieth century, even if its time has now passed, was that of Rudolf Bultmann (1884–1976). During the 1920s and 1930s, aided by existentialist ideas he derived from the phenomenologist philosopher Martin Heidegger, he developed a powerful and distinctive theology of the New Testament that focused on what it has to say about human existence when confronted by God. He found this theology primarily in Paul and in John and expressed it most extensively in his *Theology of the New Testament* and *The Gospel of John: A Commentary*.[65]

Bultmann provided a succinct summary of his approach in the Epilogue to his *Theology of the New Testament*.[66] He was adamant that theology as the outworking of faith take precedence over theology as the product of systematization largely detached from human subjectivity. "It is of decisive importance," he wrote, "that *the theological thoughts be conceived and explicated as thoughts of faith*, that is: *as thoughts in which faith's understanding of God, the world, and man is unfolding itself*—not as products of free speculation or of a scientific mastering of the problems involved in 'God,' 'the world,' and 'man' carried out by the objectifying kind of thinking."[67] These thoughts, in fact, "grew out of one's new self-understanding." By "understanding" he did not mean that produced by "a scientific anthropology which objectifies man into a phenomenon of the world." No, Bultmann meant:

> an existential understanding of myself which is at one with and inseparable from my understanding of God and the world. For I am I, of course, not as an isolable and objectifiable world-phenomenon but I am I in my particular existence inseparably bound up with God and the world.

For Bultmann, faith is not a form of self-understanding arising naturally from our human nature, but is "an understanding made possible by God." He goes on:

> Faith is not choosing to understand one's self in one of several possible ways that are universally available to man but is man's response to God's word which encounters him in the proclamation of Jesus Christ. It is *faith in the kerygma* [the "gospel message"], which tells of God's dealing in the man Jesus of Nazareth.[68]

A little later he encapsulates his position as follows:

> faith can be nothing else but the response to the kerygma, and . . . the kerygma is nothing else than God's word addressing man as a questioning and promising word, a condemning and forgiving word. As such a word, it does not offer itself to critical thought but speaks into one's concrete existence . . . the statements of the kerygma are not universal truths but are personal address in a concrete situation. Hence they can appear only in a form molded by an individual's understanding of his own existence or by his interpretation of that understanding. And correspondingly they are understandable only to him who is able to recognize the kerygma as a word addressed to him in his situation—to recognize it immediately only as a question asked him, a demand made of him.[69]

I have quoted Bultmann at some length because for many his way of conceiving New Testament theology, if ultimately open to criticism, was the most significant effort of its kind in the twentieth century.

Bultmann's project, "though unsurpassed in the grandeur of its vision," attracted and attracts much criticism and now seems rather dated.[70] The fact that his focus on self-understanding found far more responsive data in Paul's letters and the Fourth Gospel than elsewhere in the corpus led to these texts receiving far more attention than the others. As Stendahl has noted, this gave "his New Testament theology a strikingly uneven character."[71]

The feature of Bultmann's theology that needs emphasizing to provide a contrast for what will be proposed in this volume is its monadic picture of the human person. Bultmann was preoccupied with the self-understanding of the individual before God. The *individual* of faith hears the kerygma in the particular circumstances of his or her life and must respond appropriately. Other human beings are largely irrelevant to this process, except to the extent they constitute the field in which the response is played out. For Bultmann, interpersonal relationships were not part of the central dynamic between human beings and God.

There is an extreme contrast between Bultmann's thoroughgoing individualism and the interpersonal nature of the Christ-movement that is evident, for example, on virtually every page of Paul's letters. I will cite one example. In Romans 5 Paul describes how God's love (*agapē*) for us is poured into our hearts through the Holy Spirit that has been given to us (5:5; see 15:30).[72] God had previously shown his love (*agapē*) for us in that while we were still sinners Christ died for us (5:8). In powerful passage at the end of Romans 8 Paul asserts that nothing can separate us from the love of Christ and the love of God, using *agapē* in each case (8:35, 38). Having thus described the divine *agapē* for us as involving God, Christ, and the Holy Spirit, Paul uses the same word later to epitomize how Christ-followers should relate to one another. In Rom 12:9-21 he illustrates the meaning of *agapē* between people with a rich series of thirty statements,[73] and reiterates its importance in this sense in two significant places later (13:10; 14:15).

Bultmann's straitened model of what it means to be a Christian is something he did not get from the New Testament but developed under the influence of modern philosophical thought, that of Martin Heidegger in particular. This was an unfortunate move on his part. Although for a period the sheer brilliance with which he assimilated Heidegger could hardly fail to impress, this type of synthesis ultimately failed to win acceptance. I will now suggest a particular reason for this failure. As we will see in the next chapter, in 1939 Martin Buber acutely diagnosed a central problem in Heidegger's thought, by suggesting that for Heidegger a human being of "real existence" is not the person who lives with another person, but someone who can no longer live with another, a person "who now knows a real life only in communication with himself." In short, Heidegger "absolutizes the temporally conditioned situation of the radically solitary man."[74]

Bultmann did not go quite so far. His solitary man (more like Kierkegaard perhaps, as we will observe in chapter 2) at least had God for company. Yet in the fundamental decisions of such a man before God, other human beings are marginalized or absent altogether. Such an understanding of the Christian is irreconcilable with Paul's vision of life in Christ, where those with faith in Christ receive love from God, Christ, and the Holy Spirit and love others in turn. It is central to Paul's gospel that the disposition—of *agapē*—with which God acted in sending his son for our salvation must be replicated in how we treat others.

Krister Stendahl

In 1962 Krister Stendahl published an essay on the subject of contemporary biblical theology that has since achieved classic status.[75] Stendahl made a strong case for what he described as the "descriptive task" in biblical theology. He dated the possibility of such an approach to the development of the "history-of-religions school" (*religionsgeschichtliche Schule*), in the late nineteenth and early twentieth century. The exponents of this form of research, by comparing biblical data more thoroughly with comparable phenomena in the ancient Near East and the Greco-Roman world, brought into sharp focus just how different biblical social and religious features were from those familiar to the modern world. Important examples were the publications by Johannes Weiss (*Jesus' Teaching on the Kingdom of God*, 1892) and Albert Schweitzer (*The Quest of the Historical Jesus*, 1906) that extracted Jesus from the comfortable ethical frameworks of liberal Christianity and "made a forceful plea for a most abstruse and appalling eschatology as the actual setting for Jesus and his followers." Such work emphasized the difference between biblical and modern times and forced scholars wishing to explore the biblical texts in this way to creep out of their "Western and twentieth-century skin" and identify themselves "with the feelings and thought patterns of the past."[76] The descriptive task simply meant spelling out the meaning of a biblical phenomenon "with the highest degree of perception in its own terms."[77]

Above all, the results of the history-of-religions school made clear much more surely than had been the case before that the meaning of a biblical text was now split up in two tenses: "'What *did* it mean?' and 'What *does* it mean?'"[78] Stendahl showed how initial distaste for the findings of the history-of-religions school on account of its disregard for theological meaning and relevance gradually gave way to considered responses by figures such as Karl Barth, Rudolf Bultmann, and Oscar Cullmann aimed at confronting the distance between ancient and modern sensibilities. He observed that when "the biblical theologian becomes primarily concerned with the present meaning, he implicitly (Barth) or explicitly (Bultmann) loses his enthusiasm or ultimate respect for the descriptive task." In Bultmann's case, Stendahl reasonably suggests that his plea for demythologizing, which entails stripping kernels of universal truth from the ancient husk in which they were lodged, meant a certain dehistoricizing of the New Testament.[79]

Stendahl proposed that there were three stages necessary "for the Bible to exert the maximum of influence on theology, church life, and culture." The first was the descriptive task, the second was the clarification of the hermeneutic principles involved, and the third was the determination of answers to the question of the meaning here and now. He raised the possibility that teamwork with the disciplines of philosophy and theology might be necessary.[80] He was adamant that the distinction between the three aspects was essential:

> The distinction between the descriptive function as the core of all biblical theology on the one hand, and the hermeneutics and up-to-date biblical translation on the other, must be upheld if there is to be any chance for the original to act creatively on the minds of theologians and believers of our time.[81]

The foundation for Stendahl's view was the sheer value inherent in the distance of the biblical material from us:

> For the life of the church such a consistent descriptive approach is a great and promising asset which enables the church, its teaching and preaching ministry, to be exposed to the Bible in its original intention and intensity, as an ever new challenge to thought, faith, and response.[82]

It is worth noting, lastly, that this 1962 essay does *not*, in spite of the suggestion to the contrary by Ben Ollenburger, use the word "normative" to denote the theological phase, of determining what the biblical texts mean, as an antithesis to the descriptive phase.[83]

How useful will this approach of Stendahl be for the argument of this book? At one point Stendahl suggested that by a descriptive investigation we were ushered "right into the world of biblical thought which deserves the name 'theology' just as much as do the thoughts of Augustine, Thomas, Calvin, and Schleiermacher."[84] To the extent that he thinks that the results of historical interpretation of the Bible directed to its theology produce "thoughts," we must ask whether this is not an unfortunately ideational emphasis to the neglect of other areas of the biblical data, especially experience. The specter of Gabler's unfortunate preoccupation with religion as knowledge rises before us.

Yet elsewhere Stendahl offers many more useful insights that are capable of development here. He proposes two possible ways of mediating the distance between our biblical ancestors and ourselves. The first is a radical, ahistorical, or even antihistorical translation of the biblical material (as represented by Bultmann). The second, which he obviously prefers, is a systematic theology that depends on the historical framework of biblical thought (again, the stress on thought alone is unfortunate) being retained and considers that "the bridge between the centuries of biblical events and our own time" was to be found "in the actual history of the church as still ongoing history of God's people." A moment later he adds:

> Such a theology would conceive of the Christian existence as a life by the fruits of God's acts in Jesus Christ, rather than as a faith according to concepts deduced from the teaching of the prophets, Jesus, and Paul regarding God's acts.

In sum, "*A theology which retains history as a theologically charged category finds in its ecclesiology the overarching principles of interpretation and meaning.*" Such a theology, moreover, "does not permit its ecclesiology to be transferred to the second last chapter in its systematic works, followed by that on an equally inactivated eschatology."[85] Stendahl went on to insist that once we move from the descriptive phase to theological considerations of this sort, the question of the canon of Scripture assumed critical importance. I will return to the canon in chapter 11.

Robert Morgan

In 1988 Robert Morgan acutely analyzed the troubled relationship between history and theology in contemporary biblical interpretation. For Morgan a critical issue was that the Bible had come to be interpreted within contrasting frameworks—that of the believer on the one hand and the historian on the other. This meant that the biblical texts were subjected to the (often conflicting) claims of both reason and faith. Since older syntheses of history and theology (such as Rudolf Bultmann's) had fallen out of favor, our culture had become ever more secular and (with the exception of Germany) the number of biblical scholars active in pastoral work had declined, the existence of a thriving historical criticism of the Bible located outside an ecclesial context had become more obvious and troubling.

Morgan allowed only a limited and largely negative role for history. The problem of the falsifiability of Christian belief posed by Reimarus required a historical answer; interpreters' use of historical method allowed them to reach beyond the Christian ghetto to the public square; and historical research was a useful device for ruling out arbitrary or even irrational interpretations. He mentioned Krister Stendahl's view in his 1962 essay (just discussed) that the church at times needs to hear the biblical message in all its strangeness, "its cutting edge not blunted by the familiarity of hallowed religious expectations," but did not much develop it.[86] Räisänen summarizes Morgan to be of the view that "[t]heology cannot be built on historical work, but theological constructions can be assessed and criticized from a historical perspective."[87]

On the other hand, in the same year as the work by Morgan appeared, 1988, William Countryman published his *Dirt, Greed, and Sex: Sexual Ethics in the New Testament and Their Implications for Today,* which contained a powerful plea for the use of history to determine how the biblical authors expressed themselves in terms of their own religious traditions, not as an end in itself, but to show how "the inevitably alien past that is canonized in the Bible breaks our present open and directs us to new opportunities of faithfulness in the future."[88]

Morgan's answer to the dilemma he had identified was to have a thoroughgoing theological interpretation of the Bible, not tacked onto the end of a work of historical interpretation, a pattern they deprecated, but developed before the execution of historical research, with the latter informing it.

Heikki Räisänen

Much of Räisänen's monograph *Beyond New Testament Theology* (1990) is taken up with an analysis of the history of "New Testament theology" as a discipline from a methodological perspective. A central theme of his analysis is that New Testament scholarship made a fatal mistake after the First World War when it "turned its back on the liberals and the history-of-religions school and succumbed to the rhetorical-theological appeal of dialectical theology."[89] His interest is really in reviving ideas that were sidelined by this development, especially those of Gabler and Wrede. Thus he considers that Gabler's distinction between historical and theoretical interpretation of the Bible, assigning the tasks to two different stages, was helpful, but has not been followed up. Wrede made a similar proposal, but his early death prevented him from pursuing his ideas. Bultmann's attempt was impressive, although he limited New

Testament theology to Paul and John (both understood in existential terms) and everything else that has happened since has been in Bultmann's shadow.[90]

He ultimately adopts Wrede's proposal in modified form: "biblical studies are to serve society and mankind within their own limited resources, but not the church in particular. The task is not proclamatory, but informative and understanding. The material has to be treated impartially, with no distinction between 'orthodox' and 'heterodox' views." Räisänen is really proposing a history of early Christian thought. He is aiming at early Christian thought directed to serving society and humankind, not the church in particular. Scholars of the church, on the other hand, can outline New Testament theologies.[91] Not surprisingly, Räisänen is basically in agreement with Stendahl's 1962 essay.[92]

Only in the final, brief chapter, however, does Räisänen hint at the desirability of exegetes also engaging in "a theological (or philosophical, or some other type or critically actualizing) interpretation of their historical work." For Räisänen is insistent that "[i]t is quite impossible to build a theology on the Bible alone."[93] This is probably correct, if by "theology" is meant "systematic theology." Yet it leaves unanswered the question whether the Bible may function theologically (understood in the broad sense I am employing in this volume) through the interaction of the messages it communicates in their historical particularity and contemporary Christian life and identity without the involvement of a structured systematic theology.

Räisänen agrees with the widespread appreciation that early Christian religion included experience and not just thought, but still favors retaining "theology" to refer to religious thought for the reason that a comprehensive history of early Christian religion, covering cult, rite, myth, and communality, would be too immense an undertaking.[94] This means that he is content to live with the unsatisfactory limitation that Gabler imposed on the subject in 1787. It is for this reason that Räisänen, for all the acuity of his analysis, has possibly blunted his chances of making a decisive new advance in this area.

Francis Watson

The scholar who has probably moved farthest in the direction outlined by Morgan is Francis Watson, now Professor of New Testament at the University of Aberdeen. Beginning with a gentle sketching of the theme in a collection he edited in 1993, he has now produced four major works of explicitly theological biblical interpretation in 1994, 1997, 2000, and 2004[95] that are characterized by a powerful grip on contemporary theological and hermeneutical debates, fine analytic and synthetic abilities, elegant style, and a strongly expressed distaste for history. By "history" I mean the attempt to understand the meanings of biblical texts when they first appeared in relation to their original context, understood in its fullest sense, using all the available literary, epigraphic, and archaeological evidence, which, unlike him, I consider exists in sufficient abundance to make the exercise a worthwhile one.

I will briefly set out aspects of his views on history in this sense, which are, at least in part, similar to those of Brevard Childs (whom we will return to in chapter 11). As opposed to his concern for the "final text" of the biblical works, by which he means "the form we now encounter it on the printed page," Watson bluntly asserts in his 1994 text *Text, Church, and World* that it "has been agreed that the primary task of biblical scholarship is to reconstruct the diachronic historical processes underlying the text as it now stands."[96] But there is no such agreement. While a consensus along these lines may have existed in the heydays of source and form criticism, since the inception of redaction criticism in 1948 with Günther Bornkamm's essay on the stilling of the storm in Matthew's Gospel,[97] there has been intense interest in the meaning conveyed by the Gospels to their original audiences, whatever the prehistory of the traditions they deployed. More recently, this interest in the meaning of a text when it was published has been strengthened by the rise of social-scientific interpretation, which generally builds on the sociolinguistic insight that texts have meaning in particular contexts, and by the development of socio-rhetorical criticism by Vernon Robbins and its recent use by Gerd Theissen.[98] This flourishing type of New Testament criticism, therefore, explores what the texts meant when they appeared in particular first-century contexts.

Watson's *Agape, Eros, Gender* (2000) probably represents one of the most pervasively theological interpretations of biblical texts, in this case certain Pauline epistles, currently available. It illustrates brilliantly what theological interpretation might look like, what someone fully responding to the challenge posed by Morgan and Barton might produce. Yet the question that remains is what has happened to history in this project.

Watson rejects the idea that interpretation should be controlled by a hypothetical "background" reconstructed by the interpreter working with historical-critical method.[99] In other words, he turns his face against investigating the first-century context of Paul's writings, using a full panoply of historical techniques. Thus, the main evidence from Paul's setting that Watson employs to interpret 1 Corinthians is other biblical texts, although he sometimes also cites Greco-Roman texts. One instructive exception to his disinclination to dig into the historical context is a note on ancient Greek and Roman male haircutting practices—but then only through the (safe?) filter of a quotation from Calvin's commentary on 1 Corinthians.[100]

THE NEW TESTAMENT, HISTORY, AND THEOLOGY

Nevertheless, Watson still insists that the "canonical" approach, which he favors, does not involve treating such a text as a "timeless theological tractate" or "overlooking the historical particularities that are here ([namely,] ... in Rom 1:1–7) given a canonical role."[101] The problem with such assertions is to find what part, if any, the contingent historical details of Paul's first-century setting play in his reading. While Watson may not regard the Pauline letters as "timeless" tractates, it is difficult to discern any sense in which the first century CE is for him a relevant, let alone an important, period. He is, after all, explicitly opposed to what he calls the "hermeneutics of historicism."[102] To this extent his interpretation of Paul is a notably dehistoricized one. In all this Watson exemplifies Stendahl's observation, noted above, that when biblical theologians become primarily concerned with the present meaning, they lose their enthusiasm or respect for the descriptive task.

THE WAY FORWARD

Where do we go from here? I am entirely in agreement with Morgan on the desirability of the fruits of historical biblical criticism feeding into contemporary Christian experience and identity. This is a perfectly appropriate aim for someone wishing to speak to the Christian faithful and Wrede's attempt (repristinated by Räisänen) to excise "theology" from New Testament theology misses the importance of this particular audience and its need continually to reconnect with its sources of identity and access to divine truth. Certainly there are other perfectly legitimate audiences, but there is nothing to prevent us limiting ourselves, for present purposes, to this one.

My difficulty is that none of the writers whose works I have considered seem to me to offer a reasonable means to achieve the result of the New Testament fertilizing contemporary Christian experience, although Stendahl comes the closest.

The main obstacle remains just as Gabler—whose project Räisänen has recently given significant support—left it, when he divided religion into the everyday knowledge of the ordinary Christian and the subtle, elaborated knowledge of the systematic theologian and directed that biblical theology could only be infused into the latter. There is an almost universal acceptance that in this context the theological dimension of the enterprise—the recognition that in the gospel of Christ we are dealing with a reality God offers us and with claims he makes on us—refers only to systematic theology. The notion that it might embrace the religious experience of Christians who are not theologians remains strangely unthinkable. Räisänen actually

entertained widening the project beyond theological ideas to embrace experience but rejected it as impractical.

The route proposed by Morgan and Watson, following in a line of thought
going back to Lessing as well as Gabler (although with major transformations
since), does not only entail the advocacy of a theological perspective adopted
in advance of the historical interpretation of the Bible, it also involves ascribing to history an inadequate function. Morgan's role for history is rather
attenuated, while Watson seems positively to devalue it.

The primary objective, therefore, must be the valorization of what
Stendahl called the descriptive task. This means the investigation of aspects of
New Testament texts that have a bearing on the relationship between the first
believers in Christ that brings out their original meaning. Such an exploration does not require some digging "under" or inspection "behind" the text,
but simply seeks to determine what those texts meant in their original contexts when they first appeared. Nothing more, nothing less.

This book is written in the belief that the results of such historical investigation are, *in and of themselves*, the bearers of theological truth. They speak of how
those who first had faith in Jesus as the Christ generated a distinctive identity
around that conviction and how that identity and the experience that produced it still have power to tell us who we are vis-à-vis God and one another.
The importance of experience in the life of the first Christ-followers in relation to baptism, charismatic phenomena like glossolalia, and shared meals,
and the connection of that experience to the crucified and risen Messiah has
been persuasively affirmed by Luke Johnson.[103] There is no reason why such
primordial Christ-oriented experience, understood in its own terms, cannot
enrich contemporary Christian experience and identity within the model of
socio-theological communion argued for in this volume. The notion that the
truth of God's dealing with humanity and the cosmos in his son can only have
a "theological" impact if it is mediated through the structures of systematic
theology was untenable in 1787 and it is today.

The alternative to Gabler and those who follow this path is, as Stendahl
suggested, to advocate a theology "which retains history as a theologically
charged category." Such a theology finds in its *ecclesiology* the principles of
interpretation and meaning. It does not relegate ecclesiology to the penultimate chapter of the complete presentation, moreover, but brings it to the
forefront. This suggests a way forward. "A theological awareness of sacred history," writes Stendahl, "seems to imply by inner necessity a growing recognition of the church as something beyond an organization for the promotion of
evangelism and theology." In the next chapter I will take up this challenge by
presenting a socio-theological model of persons in communion as the central

feature of an ecclesiology tailored to present requirements. The aim will be to propose a model of dialogue and communion, necessarily intercultural and critical, between those first Christ-followers who composed the twenty-seven documents of the New Testament and ourselves. This model will then form the theoretical foundation for the chapters that follow. It will be apparent that this model is theological. Yet it is one that accepts the absolute necessity of seeking to understand our biblical forebears in all their historical particularity. It is not a body of systematic theological truth that can only be fed by breaking up or ignoring the historical distinctiveness of the New Testament writings. Rather, it is a way of rendering articulate the theological foundations of what we are doing when we seek to understand the original meanings of the New Testament as composed by persons who, like us, belonged (or belong?) to the body of Christ and experienced the same Holy Spirit in spite of the cultural chasm between us and them.

2

PERSONS IN COMMUNION

A Socio-Theological Model

The aim of this volume, as indicated in the introduction, is explicitly theological. For my intention is to set out an approach to reading the New Testament historically that will assist Christians in understanding and responding to the reality God offers them and the claims he makes on them here and now through the life, death, and resurrection of his son, Jesus Christ. Yet the arena I have chosen for promoting the role of historical criticism is not the dogmatic or systematic theology that is normally selected for this task. Rather, my plan is to show how historical New Testament research can be brought into contact with everyday Christian life, experience, and identity. As we saw in the preceding chapter, since 1787 when Gabler first articulated his notion of New Testament theology linked to dogmatic theology, the dominant paradigm in this area ever since, the alternative approach to the theological application of historical New Testament research I am advocating here has existed in potential only. Now is the time to bring it to life.

I noted in the preceding chapter Krister Stendahl's view that "[a] theology which retains history as a theologically charged category finds in its ecclesiology the overarching principles of interpretation and meaning."[1] The use of a word such as "ecclesiology" can obstruct as much as assist meaning. However, if we convert Stendahl's statement into an assertion that the theological gains derived from historical investigation of the New Testament reside in a clearer understanding of the relationships between the members of the church under God rather than in the structured cognitive propositions of a systematic theology, we will find his insight abundantly confirmed in what follows. Furthermore, since I share his dissatisfaction with the demotion of this area in works of systematic theology to the penultimate chapter, I will cover it now, as the foundation of the thesis I propound in this volume.

PRESUPPOSITIONS AND
AN AUTOBIOGRAPHICAL NOTE

I must first lay my cards on the table. Although I do not come to this task with an agenda derived from dogmatic theology (since that would be inimical to the entire project), I am most certainly undertaking it on the basis of certain social and theological presuppositions. This chapter's purpose is to organize the most important of these presuppositions in the form of a model.

The dominant attitude that has shaped my view of Scripture and has prompted the thesis of this volume is that all of the canonical documents of the two Testaments are the product of actual people who have responded to the experience of God in their lives and have sought to communicate that experience to others. I am struck by the extent to which the various writings of both Testaments represent a cooperative enterprise between the Holy Spirit and flesh-and-blood human beings who once walked this earth. I am committed to the notion that in reading these works we should not forget the persons who produced them hoping to include others in the circle of understanding resulting from their having been touched by God in the multifarious circumstances of their lives. This is so even when, as is usually the case, we do not know their names. There is a personal dimension to the works of the Old and New Testaments that I find impossible to ignore. This attitude makes me unsympathetic, for example, to claims that the intentions of those who composed these works are of no consequence, that once they were published they became entirely disconnected from their authors, or that when we read them we are at complete liberty to impute or create meaning rather than attending carefully to the meanings these works conveyed to their original audiences. Needless to say there are many biblical critics who do not share my views on these issues. My aim at this point is not to argue that my fundamental attitude to Scripture is superior to others, but merely to unveil it as the motivation for the argument to come. Later on, however, I will argue that this conviction does induce me to take positions on particular points that stand up well in the face of opposing ideas.

When I seek to articulate this fundamental conviction more fully, the line of development that seems most natural to me consists of notions, both social and theological, of interpersonal dialogue and relationship. One of the main discoveries I made while writing this book was that an interest in this dimension of human experience had also motivated Friedrich Schleiermacher's hermeneutics. I will attempt to retrieve Schleiermacher's theory of interpretation from the miasma of misunderstanding that surrounds it in chapter 5.

Let us assume that New Testament texts were written to create new believers or strengthen the conviction of existing believers. This means that we are treating the texts as invitations to dialogue and relationship. True, we must understand these concepts in particular ways, for these communicators are all long dead. They can speak to us but—subject to the possibility of a high theology of the communion of saints that I will consider in chapter 11—we cannot speak to them.

Nevertheless, those of us who listen regularly, say, to particular broadcasters on radio will know that it is possible to learn quite a lot about people and the views they hold even when we do not reply to them in person. We may, quite possibly, be responding in a partial way, by vocalizing our responses as we listen: "You can't mean that, John," or "You've got him on the run now," and so on. We also know how such broadcasts can affect our views and even, at times, our behavior. This applies even more convincingly when the material transmitted relates directly to our membership in a strongly circumscribed group, as when the radio station is serving a small rural town. The words of the broadcaster may strengthen our sense of belonging to a particular community that embraces, to use the language of social identity theory,[2] our *cognitive* understanding of the nature of the group, the *emotional* capital we have invested in belonging to it, and the *evaluative* dimension, how we rate ourselves by belonging to this group rather than to others. If we now imagine that a particular broadcaster has died, but that the station continues to broadcast classic shows he or she produced while alive, we will have a reasonable analogy to what happens when we read New Testament texts. Nor should we forget that sometimes dialogue can occur through silence as well as through speech. For example, two people who have a very close relationship are sitting next to one another on a park bench and communicate in silence.

To cite a different analogy, assume that we possess a letter that our grandfather wrote home to his wife and children shortly before his death on active wartime service. In the letter he sought to express his love for them and what it meant to belong to a family such as this that had been blessed in so many ways. A spouse, children, and grandchildren fortunate enough to possess such a letter would most probably have a very strong sense of the continued presence of their husband, father, and grandfather. In such a case, it is not too much to speak of a dialogue and relationship between the living and the dead. We may go further and suggest, by introducing a concept to be developed shortly, that it is even appropriate in these circumstances to use the word that designates interrelationships of an optimal kind, so that we speak of *communion* between the living and the dead (*communio inter vivos et mortuos*). In such a case, the contents of the letter are vital, yet so is the context of interpersonal relationship in which these contents are communicated. When Christians read the writings of the New Testament, is their experience fundamentally different from this?

We will see in chapters 10 and 11 that there are several ways to understand the character and processes of this type of communion. Clearly, the forces of human remembrance and acknowledgment of the past play a vital role. Does it matter that many of the authors of the New Testament writings are unknown to us by name and that we know nothing about them except the fact that they composed the work in question, the Gospels most notably? There is good precedent suggesting that it does not. In Sirach 44 the author begins with the exhortation "Next let us praise illustrious men, our ancestors in their successive generations."[3] He goes on to say that the Lord has created reputations and displayed his greatness from earliest times in figures of various types. Some were kings, some offered advice, some spoke in prophecy, while "Others directed the people by their advice, by their understanding of the popular mind, and by the wise words of their teaching" (44:4). Some of them left a name behind so that they are still praised, "While others have left no memory, and disappeared as though they had not existed, they are now as though they had never been" (44:8-9). The author then lists "generous men whose good works have not been forgotten" (44:10), named figures from Israel's past. The names of the authors of many of the New Testament documents have not survived, but they have certainly not "disappeared as though they had not existed," since "their advice," "their understanding of the popular mind," and the "wise words of their teaching" have not.

In chapter 7 I will also argue that early Christian tradition went to great lengths to retain a sense of the persons who had written the four Gospels and other works in the biblical corpus, even where the actual authors were no longer known.

COMMUNICATION ACROSS CULTURAL DIFFERENCE

Yet there is one aspect of this enterprise of reading New Testament texts within a framework of communion with their authors that must never be forgotten. This is that they were in so many ways different from us! There is a profound cultural distance between the inhabitants of the Mediterranean world of the first century CE responsible for the New Testament and ourselves, wherever on planet Earth we find ourselves in the first part of the twenty-first century—in the north or south, east or west, in an industrial-izing or a postindustrial society. This is significant for our investigation, first because it makes understanding inhabitants of the ancient Mediterranean world a challenging business. Communication between or across cultures is certainly possible, as we will soon see, but the factors operative in such a process need to be taken into account. Second, the existence of cultural dis-tance reminds us that at times we will need to be *critical* of what our biblical ancestors are saying.[4]

When I reflect upon what it means to be in communication with our ancestors in faith who produced the New Testament—both convinced of its possibility and alive to its difficulties and risks—I find that my position has been indelibly marked by an aspect of my own life. In the interests of disclos-ing one of the bases of my pre-understanding in this area, but also to perhaps illustrate some of the aspects of this type of communion, I will now narrate an autobiographical detail. No doubt it will also testify to the power of mem-ory to shape how we see the world.

On several occasions in my youth my late mother told me a story from her own childhood. In the 1920s she was a young girl living with her parents, brothers, and sisters in Maroubra, a seaside suburb of Sydney. Her father was a permanent officer in the Australian army. He had served on the Hindenburg Line in the First World War, where he survived a dose of mustard gas (for-tunately living on into the 1960s, so that I got to know him well). He was of Irish descent, as his name Michael Flannery might suggest. Out of the blue a young Irishman, a cousin, turned up to stay with them. He was a Republican who had to flee Ireland for his own safety around the time of the Irish civil war in 1922–23.

It was wonderful to have him. He brought family news, tales of Irish poli-tics and the Roman Catholic Church, and sang Irish songs with the family. There was only one problem, however. He often rebuked my grandfather for being an officer in the "British army." "I'm in the Australian army, not the British," my grandfather would insist. But the Irishman would reply, "Oh, come on, now, Mick, you fought with them on the Western Front, didn't you? What's the difference?" After some months of this, my grandfather was not all that sorry to accompany his cousin on the old, wooden-seated tram that used to rattle along Anzac Parade from the coast to Circular Quay in the city, from where he took a steamer back to Europe.

What point do I draw from this? Simply that the Irishman was ours but he was awkward. He reminded my family of who they were in all sorts of ways, yet there was a critical, cultural distance between them. For many years this episode of family history has shaped the way I envisage the relationship of the New Testament to contemporary Christians. I take the New Testament personally. I look back on the real people who produced and first listened to its various documents, my biblical ancestors in faith, in much the same way as my mother's family regarded their Irish cousin then in person and as I do now in memory. Our biblical ancestors were greatly different from us, awkward perhaps, but still our ancestors in the faith, and the progenitors of an identity we share. When we read the New Testament documents, we encounter them in similarity and in difference, but still we encounter them.

These considerations propel me to suggest that what is needed fully to express my presuppositions is a model of interpersonal communion. It will need to embrace both the psychological and the social dimensions of human relationships, including the element of cultural difference. But this model will also have a theological component, since the communion in question is the result of God's intervention in the world and, I will argue, partakes of the trinitarian character of the divine nature. If asked why I find my model appealing, I can only answer that it comes from some deep part of how I see the world that is rooted in my upbringing. In proceeding to develop a model of interpersonal communion in this chapter, I am therefore articulating my instincts as much as simply choosing a promising theory for its logical, intellectual force. Although unsure whether that will make the model more or less attractive, I will push on regardless.

In subsequent chapters I will rely on this model to critique scholarship that would argue against the proposal I am making here (chapters 3 and 4) and also to lay the foundation of its positive aspects (chapters 5 to 12).

PSYCHOLOGICAL AND SOCIAL ASPECTS OF INTERPERSONAL COMMUNION

The Foundation of the Model: Martin Buber's "I and You"

THE CENTRAL IDEA

Martin Buber's 1923 work *Ich und Du* (I and You) and his other writings on the centrality of interhuman relationships to humanity's very character provide the initial insights for the model outlined above. Buber was concerned with relationships between persons and their relationship with God, so his ideas embrace social and theological aspects of human experience. In the present section, however, we will consider what he has to say on the person-to-person relationship and return to the theological dimension of his position in the next major section of this chapter. A full discussion of his thought, such as offered by Maurice Friedman,[5] is not needed here, since my interest lies in Buber's contributions to a socio-theological model of persons in communion.

Buber drew a sharp distinction between our attitude to other persons and our attitude to things. In the former, one human subject, "I," confronts another, "You," whereas in the latter a person contemplates and experiences an object. When "I" encounters "You," a meeting occurs that goes to the heart of our shared humanity: "The basic word I-You can only be spoken with one's whole being. The basic word I-It can never be spoken with one's whole being."[6] The other person is a reality "given to me, but it is not bounded by me."[7] Buber's position is well expressed in this statement: "[E]very It borders on other Its; It is only by virtue of bordering on others. But where You is said there is no something. You has no borders. Whoever says You does not have something; he has nothing. But he stands in relation."[8] Later he says, "The basic word I-You establishes the world of relation."[9] Relations are foundational for our humanity. Only in relation to other persons do we truly become ourselves: "Man becomes an I through a You."[10] Or again: "Egos appear by setting themselves apart from other egos. Persons appear by entering into relation to other persons. One is the spiritual form of natural differentiation, the other that of natural association."[11]

Something of the distinctiveness and (let me say at once) appeal of Buber's position emerges in the criticism he levels against Kierkegaard and Heidegger in an essay published in 1939 entitled "What Is Man?" (*Was ist der Mensch?*).[12] Kierkegaard had famously broken off his engagement with his fiancée to allow him to concentrate on God as the only other of significance. This meant that his was an open system with respect to interpersonal relationships, even if it was only open to God.[13] Heidegger, on the other hand, took a very different view. Buber suggested, with good reason, that for Heidegger a human being of "real existence," who in Heidegger's view was the goal of life, is not the person who lives with and relates to another person, but a person who can no longer live with another, a person "who now knows a real life only in communication with himself." Heidegger "absolutizes the temporally conditioned situation of the radically solitary man, and wants to derive the essence of human existence from the experience of a nightmare."[14] Heidegger's self is "*a closed system*" as far as interpersonal relationships are concerned: "Existence is completed in self-being; there is no way beyond this for Heidegger."[15] As opposed to this, Buber proposes a model in which human existence is completed in the relation between two subjects.

Language and Dialogue

In *I and You* Buber touched at times on the importance of language. Such a relation, he said at one point, "enters language." There is a much fuller development of his thoughts on dialogue elsewhere, however, especially in the essay of this name (in German, *Zwiesprache*) that he published in 1929 and another essay, "Distance and Relation," that appeared initially in 1951.[16] In "Dialogue," Buber described "genuine dialogue" as occurring when "each of the participants really has in mind the other or others in their present and particular being and turns to them with the intention of establishing a living mutual relation between himself and them."[17] By virtue of this character, genuine dialogue is to be distinguished from a debate, conversation, friendly chat, or lovers' talk. Those who engage in dialogue experience a strong sense of reciprocity; those who engage in monologue exist in a solitude where they never manage to grope beyond the outlines of the self. Dialogue is not the same as love, but there is no real love without genuine dialogue.[18] It is important to note that Buber considered that genuine dialogue could actually occur through silence as well as through spoken discourse.[19]

Moreover, beyond language lies our relation to God, "the eternal you," the ultimate "you." In "every You we address the eternal You," and in "every sphere, through everything that becomes present to us, we gaze toward the train of the eternal You."[20]

Community and Communion: The Presence of Disagreement

Buber did not, however, restrict his gaze to the dyadic relationship between isolated pairs of I and You. He knew such pairs could come together in a larger collectivity where their relationships would be vital but not the whole story. For this reason he proposes that there are two essential features of a true community:

> True community does not come into being because people have feelings for each other (though that is required, too), but rather on two accounts: all of them have to stand in a living, reciprocal relationship to a single living center, and they have to stand in a living, reciprocal relationship to one another.[21]

Nevertheless, community structures derive their life "from the fullness of the relational force that permeates their members."[22]

In his essay "Dialogue" he distinguishes community from collectivity, with the latter being a bundling, not a binding together. In community we are not just side by side with a multitude of other persons, we are *with* them, *connected* to them. "And this multitude," he adds, "though it also moves towards one goal, yet experiences everywhere a turning to, a dynamic facing of, the other, a flowing from I to Thou." Community is based on the "increase and confirmation in life lived towards one another."[23]

It is fundamental to Buber's understanding of community that those who comprise it do not need to agree on everything. A recognition of otherness, that others are different from oneself, lies at the heart of the I-You relation that is necessary for community: "Only men who are truly capable of saying *Thou* to one another can truly say *We* to one another."[24] Furthermore, by "*We*" Buber meant "a community of several independent persons, who have reached a self and self-responsibility, the community resting on the basis of this self and self-responsibility, and being made possible by them."[25]

There are very significant expressions of similar ideas in "Distance and Relation." His fundamental insight is that "Genuine conversation, and therefore every actual fulfilment of relation between men, means acceptance of otherness." The critical factor is the disposition that the participants have toward one another. He then goes on to give a particular example, where the individual views expressed pale into insignificance beside the interpersonal framework of their discussion:

> When two men inform one another of their basically different views about an object, each aiming to convince the other of the rightness of his own way of looking at the matter, everything depends so far as human life is concerned, on whether each thinks of the other as the one he is, whether each, that is, with all his desire to influence the other, nevertheless unreservedly accepts and confirms him in his being this man in his being made in this particular way.[26]

It is noteworthy that Buber does not set up the example as one aimed at reaching agreement, but rather one where each participant is trying to have his or her view prevail. But it would not matter if one did not manage to change the other's view, since the point is how the participants regard one another. Gudykunst and Kim accurately interpret Buber to mean that in dialogues, the feelings of control and ownership of the participants are minimized: "each participant confirms the other, even when conflict occurs."[27]

Maurice Friedman usefully develops Buber's thought by positing a contrast between a "community of affinity" and a "community of otherness." A "community of affinity" is a community of like-mindedness where people huddle together for security; this is really a form of false community, one that makes its members secure because they are afraid of conflict and opposition.

A "community of otherness," on the other hand, is in accord with Buber's notions of the centrality of otherness in the I-You relation. Such a community recognizes that there are as many points of view as there are members. "The community of otherness is not one where people are alike but where they have a common concern, where they share in a common situation that they approach and respond to in different ways."[28]

The recognition of difference in human relations lies at the basis of Buber's insistence that we must retain a critical attitude in relation to the views of others. He states that the true turning of one person to another includes the acceptance and confirmation of that other, but then immediately adds, "Of course, such a confirmation does not mean approval; but no matter in what I am against the other, by accepting him as my partner in genuine dialogue I have affirmed him as a person."[29]

Buber's approach easily accommodates itself to the fundamental issue of the cultural distance that exists between us and the New Testament authors and our need to retain a critical attitude toward them. To the dynamics of intercultural communication we must now turn.

The Intercultural Dimension of the Model

From what has been said above, it is essential that our model apply to communication between people from different cultures. The primary issue here is the two thousand years that have elapsed since certain of our ancestors in faith composed the works that now comprise the New Testament. This means they were culturally different from anyone alive today.

In addition, however, we must factor in the vast differences that exist between cultures today, from postindustrial societies at one extreme to agrarian and even hunter-gatherer peoples at the other. This raises the significant possibility that some cultures might be closer to those of the first-century Mediterranean world than others. To use the useful macro-sociological model of Gerhard and Jean Lenski,[30] the Greco-Roman world existed at the "advanced agrarian" stage of socioeconomic development. This means that agriculture was the dominant mode of production and was largely conducted by peasants[31] who lived their lives in villages in face-to-face contact with their neighbors. Their iron-tipped ploughs not only provided subsistence for them and their families but also produced a surplus that local elites acquired through rent and taxation. Cultures today that have not fully industrialized and are still heavily agrarian are likely to be closer to our New Testament forebears than are the postindustrial societies of the West. This also has the consequence that Christians who have been raised in agrarian or industrializing cultures today may respond differently to the New Testament and to the authors of its twenty-seven constituent documents. The present volume is aimed at readers from a wide range of cultural settings, from the industrialized West to the developing Two-Thirds World. All these considerations reinforce the extent to which an approach to hearing or reading the New Testament that focuses on the interpersonal dynamics involved must necessarily have at its heart the question of intercultural communication.

There is nothing new in the notion of intercultural communication, although we will see in chapter 3 that some writers on New Testament hermeneutics proceed as if it could not and does not exist! Every day across the world there are people who are setting off to spend extended periods of time in cultures very different from their own. They include aid workers, diplomats, health professionals, businesspeople, volunteers abroad, emigrants, and students, to name only a few. They all face the probability of "culture shock" when they arrive at their destination—the painful realization that their own culturally ingrained ways of thinking, feeling, and behaving are substantially different to those of the locals, thus exposing them to feelings of awkwardness and inadequacy.[32] If they are fortunate, they may have taken part in a program before they left home aimed at alerting them to the difficulties of coping in a foreign setting and how they might go about understanding and communicating with others in this foreign culture.

There is, indeed, a vast literature on intercultural communication that offers assistance to people in this predicament. Particularly useful, because of its integration of theoretical ideas and empirical data, is the work by William B. Gudykunst and Young Yun Kim.[33] The relevance of this area of inquiry, as I have sought to explain elsewhere,[34] lies in the fact that the cultural distance between us and our ancestors in faith is similar to that encountered by any person who immerses himself or herself in a foreign culture today. The good news, from scholars such as Gudykunst and Kim, is that representatives of very different cultures can learn to sensitize themselves to the other so as to allow significant communication and even interdependence.

Fundamental to the fact and character of intercultural communication is the nature of communication and the cultural contexts in which it occurs. Contemporary research into communication recognizes two principal schools of thought.[35]

The first school treats communication as the transmission of messages whereby one person affects or attempts to affect the behavior or state of mind of another. Its proponents focus on the way in which the sender formulates his or her message, the channels and media of communication, and how the receiver makes sense of the message. On this view, someone wishing to communicate with someone else first formulates his or her message for transmission ("encoding"), transmits it using available media/channels of communication (the spoken voice, telephone, radio, letter, e-mail, to name only a few) to a receiver, who must then make sense of it ("decodes" the message). It is important to note that this approach envisages communication as an interpersonal activity; it is a means by which a person (or persons) conveys a message to another person (or persons). This approach, the "process" school of communication, fully recognizes that errors can occur at any one of these three stages: the sender may not say precisely what he or she intended, the message may get garbled during the course of transmission, and the receiver may make mistakes in reading and understanding it. Nevertheless, in spite of these hazards, messages get through. It is possible to locate this model in a context of cultural difference. This essentially means examining what communication looks like when the sender and the receiver come from different cultures. It is readily apparent that here greater errors in meaning occur than when the sender and the receiver belong to the same culture. But this just means it is harder to communicate, not that communication becomes impossible.

The second school of communication theory stems especially from the work of the Swiss linguist Ferdinand de Saussure and analyzes communication as the production and exchange of meaning. It is concerned with how messages, texts especially, interact with people to produce meanings. Its principal mode of analysis is semiotics, the study of signs and meanings, and this is a convenient word by which to describe it. This school prefers the term "reader" to "receiver," since this denotes the greater degree of activity required by this approach. Whereas the process school envisages communication as interpersonal, semiotics proposes a single person working with a text, since the text's author or creator is largely or completely irrelevant to its interpretation. While the process school is interested in communicative *acts*, the semiotics school is interested in communicative *works*. Intercultural communication assumes the approach taken by the process school. It makes little sense in terms of semiotics.

Culture is a notoriously difficult concept to define. In 1952 A. Krober and C. Kluckhohn came up with over one hundred definitions.[36] Culture in its broadest sense includes everything that is human-made, material and immaterial. In this book, I am interested in the immaterial aspects of culture and find most useful the notion of culture as the implicit theories held by members of a particular society as to how it operates, their taken-for-granted knowledge of the "games" played in that society. This can be seen as the "software of the mind" which the members of any culture acquire through socialization.[37] These ingrained theories tell them how to communicate with others and how to interpret their behavior. Those involved may not give much conscious thought to the rules, but they act as though they were in agreement concerning them.[38]

We should be careful, however, not to interpret culture as being deterministically imposed on us. Individuals sometimes deviate from their cultural conditioning and manipulate its features to their own advantage. Nevertheless, although individuals are able to diverge from culturally expected responses, very often they do not. Thus, while the vagaries of human nature and the demands of human freedom preclude the possibility of social laws, one still observes regularities of behavior among members of particular cultures. Yet we must clarify what we mean here. Long ago Max Weber, having noted that it was customary to refer to various "sociological generalizations" as "scientific laws," corrected this by insisting that: "These are in fact typical probabilities confirmed by observation to the effect that under certain given conditions an expected course of social action will occur, which is understandable in terms of the typical motives and typical subjective intentions of the actors."[39] When Weber uses the expression "typical probabilities" he is not making an indefensible assertion of the existence of social laws governing human behavior, for there are no such laws. Nor is he guilty of reifying culture, of considering the abstraction "culture" as a physical reality. He is simply making the commonsense observation that patterns of difference can be observed among human groups in ways that are statistically significant and that can be confirmed empirically.[40]

This means that it is possible to generalize about cultures. This idea may not be particularly palatable to those who see all generalizations about cultures as illicit metanarratives, unsustainable reifications, the imposition of positivist nomistic patterns on the diversity of human experience, grabs for power, or (in the present context) a "racist" species of "orientalism" directed toward the peoples of the Mediterranean, and so forth, but it is true nevertheless.

A most significant milestone in the measurement of typical probabilities across the globe (as explained by Weber) has been Dutch social scientist Geert Hofstede's classic 1980 study of 117,000 IBM employees in sixty-six countries, *Culture's Consequences: International Differences in Work-Related Values*.[41] Hofstede set the measurement of cultural difference around the world on a firm basis by developing a set of defined variables capable of profiling the distinctiveness of various national groups. Perhaps the most useful cultural variable, judging by subsequent research, has been that between collectivism and individualism. According to Hofstede, "*Individualism* pertains to societies in which the ties between individuals are loose: Everyone is expected to look after himself or herself and his or her immediate family." On the other hand, "*Collectivism* as its opposite pertains to societies in which people from birth onwards are integrated into strong, cohesive in-groups, which throughout people's lifetime continue to protect them in exchange for unquestioning loyalty."[42] The research of American psychologist Harry Triandis and his collaborators (from around the world) has vindicated the usefulness of this distinction and its power to produce generalizations applicable to cultures as suggested by Weber.[43]

Cultural differences can cause dramatic misunderstandings between people (thus we may interpret a wink as an invitation to a pleasant liaison, while for some other groups it may be a warning against closer contact). Nevertheless, the fact that regularities susceptible of generalized description exist means that we can seek to take them into account in order to achieve successful cross-cultural communication.

Applying Intercultural Communication to the New Testament

How does this intercultural communication aspect of the model apply to the New Testament? The first point to make is that we are dealing with a collection of twenty-seven documents for which someone, an author or perhaps a redactor, has been responsible for their present textual form. While I defer until chapter 4 discussing the full implications of this, it is enough for the present to note that I assume that each author or redactor wrote the work with the intention of communicating with certain persons living in the first- (or, in one or two cases, the second-) century CE Mediterranean region. Both the senders and the receivers of the messages had been socialized into cultural patterns unfamiliar to us. When we read these works, which is similar to overhearing a conversation between members of another cultural group today, we must attempt to penetrate the different cultural script in which the messages are expressed.

In 1981 Bruce Malina published *The New Testament World: Insights from Cultural Anthropology*, which drew upon recent anthropological research to model Mediterranean culture. Malina was really focusing on "typical probabilities" of behavior, to use Weber's phrase, to be expected of first-century Mediterranean people, especially in areas such as honor and shame, group-oriented personality, limited good, patron and client relations, and concern with purity issues. He described his model at a fairly high level of abstraction. One always needs to be ready for specific local cultures to diverge from the expected pattern. Those of us who originate in cultures of or from northern

Europe or North America have been socialized in, have internalized, very different cultural patterns. We do not rate personal and group honor nearly so highly (although they still matter to us); we tend to be individualistic rather than group-oriented (as seen in our desire to leave home as soon as possible upon attaining adulthood); we think that hiring should be done on the basis of rational selection criteria and not the fact that the candidate is a relative; we strongly favor innovation rather than the traditional way of doing things; and so on. The fact of these differences means that we must make a real effort to be aware of them, both to ensure that we really understand what our ancestors in faith were saying and to remind ourselves of the cultural distance between our world and theirs. This may be very important for maintaining a critical attitude to their messages.

The Positive Nature of the Communication

The model must also deal with how persons relate to one another positively. We are not interested in communications that serve purely functional purposes or in the bare fact of social coexistence, but in conversations (and their consequences) characterized by successful communication, or true understanding, in a setting of mutual regard and interpersonal warmth. Where such conversations are habitual we are usually dealing with relationships. It is useful to describe such relationships as "communal." Mills and Clark contrast communal relations (such as those found in families among first-degree relatives), on the one hand, and exchange relationships (such as commercial transactions), on the other. Communal relationships are characterized by a greater concern for the welfare of the other, by equality of affect (meaning the sharing of emotions), by high rates of responding to one another's needs, by the exchange of benefits without attention to their size or temporal contiguity (a phenomenon referred to as generalized reciprocity), by relationships that can vary in strength, and by an expectation that interactions will continue over the long term.[44] In addition, the interpersonal state in such a communal relationship is usefully described as "communion." "Communion" is frequently applied to a relationship marked by a strong element of interdependence that leads to a high degree of mutual understanding, trust, and loyalty and promotes the full realization of the personhood of those involved.[45]

While the fullest expression of communion is probably to be found in functional families within a particular culture, other (if less intense) expressions may also occur in various groups marked by personal interaction: one's workplace, classroom, church, sports team, civic organization, and so on. Communal relationships are also found in the context of what T. R. Gurr has described as "communal groups." These are groups that are more persistent than social or sporting associations but lack precise political or social bounds. In essence, they are psychological communities, groups whose core members share a distinctive and collective identity based on cultural traits and lifeways that matter to them and to others with whom they interact.[46] We can integrate some of these perspectives to conceptualize a communal group whose members straddle different cultures and, indeed, different periods of time.[47] It is possible to envisage the early Christ-movement as a communal group. Paul's letters (Romans and Galatians especially) provide abundant evidence that some of the movement's constituent congregations disregarded Judean ethnic exclusivity by embracing both Judeans and non-Judeans.[48]

Yet in speaking about communal relationships, communal groups, and communion we must not forget the impact of the varying cultural contexts involved. It is likely that in cultures typified by collectivism, rather than individualism, there will be a greater incidence of the strong measures of personal interdependence necessary for communion.[49] Research conducted by M. H. Bond and others offered some support to this hypothesis but also revealed that the picture was variegated and complex.[50] Triandis has done much to provide the necessary nuances. He uses the words "idiocentric" and "allocentric" to refer to orientations adopted by individuals that correspond to individualist and collectivist cultures. This terminology allows him to acknowledge the existence of the idiocentric (who selects mostly individualist solutions) in collectivist cultures and the allocentric (who selects mostly collectivist solutions) in individualist cultures. Such individuals are countercultural, but nevertheless very real.[51] He considers that the essential advance upon Hofstede's (1980) formulation is the realization that "we are both allocentric and idiocentric, and we *sample* cognitive elements that correspond to these relational modes differently in different situations." However, in some cultures more sample situations are allocentric; these are collectivist cultures. In other cultures more sample situations are idiocentric; these are individualist cultures.[52] Even in individualist cultures, however, communion between persons still regularly occurs.

The essential point is that in speaking about communion between persons, especially in a communal group, we need to bear in mind whether we are speaking of a group that exists in a collectivist or individualistic culture or includes members from both cultural settings. The character of the communication and communion within the group will differ depending on which type we are considering. Thus, the New Testament texts were written within the collectivist cultures of the first- (and perhaps early second-) century CE Mediterranean world. They are now being listened to and read by people from a wide range of contemporary societies, some individualistic and some collectivist. But even the contemporary collectivist cultures are different from those out of which the New Testament emerged. This affects the character of the intercultural communication and communion possible between these first-century Christ-followers and contemporary Christians.

It is necessary to insist, initially on the basis of the analysis of Martin Buber's thought set out above, that communion and agreement are not synonymous. It is a commonplace feature of human relationships that strong, positive ties can exist between persons in spite of their disagreeing on certain issues. Most happily married couples, for example, will recognize this phenomenon. At times a relationship can even be strengthened when the parties resolve to live with some point of difference between them. This is one facet of communion between persons that does not entail erasing their individuality. Communion represents a balance between similarity and difference. This brings us to the theological dimensions of this model of interpersonal communion.

THE THEOLOGICAL DIMENSION OF INTERPERSONAL COMMUNION

Since I write this book in the belief that God has intervened in reality through Jesus Christ and with the intent to explain how the New Testament witness to that event contributes to contemporary Christian identity, it is necessary that I develop my model of communion between persons within the theological arena.[53] I am not merely concerned with the social dimension of human existence, but also with the relationship of human beings to God. Accordingly, I must develop our model of communion between persons so as to include God in the process. In traditional theological parlance, this brings us to "ecclesiology." It is fortunate, therefore, that one of the hot spots in recent Christian theology has been the meaning of the human person. Even more helpful, the major result of this discussion has been a transition from monadic notions of human personhood to relational ones. The advantages of this for the present discussion will soon become apparent.

Augustine of Hippo (354–430 CE) and Boethius (ca. 480–ca. 525 CE) laid the foundations of a monadic understanding of the human person in Christian theology. In his *Confessions*, written in 397 CE, with their probing examination of his personal and spiritual development, Augustine had pioneered a new approach to the human person based on his or her psychological experience and consciousness. Krister Stendahl has discerned in this text the inauguration of the "introspective conscience of the West."[54] Boethius famously defined a person as "an individual substance with a rational nature."[55] This definition of the person as rational individuality became normative for the subsequent philosophical tradition. It suppressed any understanding of the word "person" as role, face, or mask, and maintained its position in the face of medieval attempts by writers such as Abelard and Duns Scotus to propose a relational meaning based on the model of the Trinity. The definition of the self proposed by Descartes (1596–1650) as a "thinking thing" and the tendency of modern idealist philosophies to define a person in terms of self-consciousness are both directly indebted to Boethius.[56] Alan Torrance has detected a threefold tendency in the widespread and persistent Western interpretations of the person that reflect the Boethian legacy: (a) The person has been construed as an essentially self-contained, monadic entity (an *individuum*); (b) the person has been conceived of in static terms as possessing a fixed nature paralleling other things or entities; and (c) the defining characteristic of persons has been thought or reason.[57]

It would be possible to investigate a variety of factors in the social, religious, economic, political, and cultural development of Europe in the last thousand years that paralleled and perhaps contributed to this valorization of the individual among philosophers and theologians. Prominent factors would include the twelfth-century appearance of courtly love poetry in France with its emphasis on the anguished I-voice,[58] the Reformation with its stress on the conscience of the individual (and the growth of the practice of solitary Bible reading), Romanticism, the industrial revolution (and the associated movement from *Gemeinschaft* [integrated, face-to-face rural community built on kinship and neighborhood] to *Gesellschaft* [atomized, anonymous, contractual association]) plotted by Ferdinand Tönnies, the works of Freud and Jung, and so on. Much of the story has been well told by Charles Taylor.[59]

The last century, however, has witnessed a powerful reaction against this whole individualistic approach to the person among theologians. Wolfhart Pannenberg summarizes what has happened in this way: "Since the end of the nineteenth century there has been a growing desire to avoid taking as the starting point of thought either the isolated subject or an abstract, supra-individual subject which exists only in the form of individual subjects but which is asserted to be the basis of all experience."[60] Such a development actually represents a theological reaction against individualistic construals of the person that not only have been widespread among theologians and philosophers but also have been dominant in many northern European and North American cultures.

Pannenberg diagnoses the transition among theologians and philosophers in a section in his major treatment of theological anthropology entitled "The Constitution of the Ego by Its Relation to the Thou."[61] The answer to rational individualism as characterizing the person has been found not to lie in ideologies that subordinate the individual to society, such as Marxism. Rather, the social constitution of individuals emerges in their relationship to another individual, the Thou or person to whom they are related in their everyday lives. "This is the basic idea of 'dialogical personalism,' which Ferdinand Ebner and Franz Rosenzweig, working along different lines, founded after World War I and which Martin Buber made familiar to a wide circle of readers."[62] Buber's *Ich und Du* (*I and You*) appeared in 1923 and was discussed above.[63]

As already noted, in *I and You* Buber proposed that there is a radical difference between a person's attitude to other people and to things. In the former a person confronts another subject, and in the latter he or she confronts an object. The full realization of our humanity is only possible if we meet the other as a "you," as a subject, not as an "it," as an object. "Community" consisted of persons being together in mutual relation and treating one another as a subject, as a "you." God is the ultimate You. Buber's emphasis on the mutual relation of human subjects severely challenged construals of the person that focused on the contemplation and actions of one subject.

Pannenberg observes that both Ebner and Buber have been criticized because their notion of I-You is so closely patterned on the contrast with I-It that it is essentially a negative concept with very little positive import. While Buber's largely atemporal understanding of the I-You relationship clearly left room for development, such criticism seems rather overblown for a work that did so much to insist on human relations as the focus of our humanity. In any event, Rosenzweig (1886–1929) steered a very different route. In his major work, *The Star of Redemption,* he generated a new model for the I-You relationship that eschewed the atemporality that had characterized Buber's presentation and chose instead to build on the temporal nature of speech between persons.[64] Rosenzweig described the "wholly real employment of language" as the centerpiece of the entire book.[65] That is, he understood the meaning of persons and their reality in the world fundamentally in relation to speech and dialogue: "For speech is truly mankind's morning gift from the Creator, and yet at the same time it is the common property of all the children of men, in which each has his particular share and, finally, it is the seal of humanity in man." For "man became man when he first spoke," and "language makes human." Language as the "organon of revelation" is the "thread running through everything human."[66]

It must be stressed that by "language" Rosenzweig primarily had in mind the spoken, rather than the written, word. In 1925 Rosenzweig and Buber launched jointly upon a unique translation of the Bible. In essays, written by them in connection with this venture, the extent to which both men privileged speaking over writing becomes abundantly apparent. The deep underlying reason for this view was perhaps the central role that relation between persons actually present to one another had in their thinking. In one of these essays, from 1930, Buber explained that he had "come long before the beginning of our work to the conviction that in translating the Bible one had to go behind the *writtenness* of the word, and had then to return to its *spokenness*—a spokenness at once original and made anew in every genuine reading aloud of the text." This meant dividing the text of the translation into natural speech units, in accordance with the requirements of breathing: "Each unit was to be an easily speakable, easily perceptible and thus rhythmically ordered unity—as indeed all early oral tradition works towards what is easily speakable and easily perceptible, and thus works by the formation of rhythms."[67] Buber commented that Rosenzweig had readily fallen in with this approach and made it his own, as seen in his essay "Scripture and the Word," written late in 1925. Given the prominent role Rosenzweig had already accorded to the spoken word in *The Star of Redemption* in 1921, it is not surprising that he quickly reached agreement with Buber on this point. We will return to their views on the oral dimension of biblical discourse in more detail later.

Rosenzweig exhibits a nuanced understanding of the processes of dialogue. Dialogue does not merely involve alternate bouts of speaking and listening by those taking part. In the course of dialogue, for example, someone who listens may also "speak," not by uttering words, but by conjuring nonverbal "words" to the current speaker in the form of facial expressions of assent or dissent.[68] Thus Rosenzweig emphasizes the significance of listening. On the one hand, when someone is speaking to a group, the members present may give the speaker his cue "by agreement and displeasure, by interjections and general restlessness, and by the conflicting moods it forces him to parry at every moment." On the other hand, when a scriptural passage is read to a congregation, for example, the unanimity of its hearing those words provides a firm foundation for entire unanimity among the congregation.[69]

Yet Rosenzweig is also very much alive to the extent to which *silences* contribute to oral communication. In the tragedies of Aeschylus, for example, he notes that the tragic hero "has only one language which completely corresponds to him: precisely keeping silent." By keeping silent, "the hero breaks down the bridges which connect him with God and the world, and elevates himself out of the fields of personality, delimiting itself and individualizing itself from others in speech, into the icy solitude of the self."[70] Yet silence is equally central to communion. "In eternity," he writes, "the spoken word fades away into the silence of perfect togetherness—for union occurs in silence only; the word unites, but those who are united fall silent."[71] The same phenomenon figures in this-worldly experience: two people newly in love will speak enthusiastically and passionately to one another face-to-face, whereas more established couples may sit side by side in silent communion.

So speech unites persons, yet the resulting communion is silent. But for Rosenzweig that is not the end of the story. Silent listening is not the permanent and final state of a community but must itself give way to the renewal, even re-creation of its bodily life—and this happens in the course of a meal: "Even for the individual, eating and drinking constitute re-birth for the body. For the community, the meal taken in common is the action through which it is reborn to conscious life." For the "sweet, fully ripened fruit of humanity craves the community of man with man in the very act of renewing the life of the body."[72]

Meals, moreover, are regularly the occasion for dialogue. At meals "the guests become acquainted, in the talk which springs from sitting at table together." When they leave, "they are no longer strangers to one another. They greet one another when they meet again." Yet even here Rosenzweig insists on the role of silence: "such greeting is the loftiest symbol of silence. They are silent because they know one another." This silent greeting becomes an expression of community: "the all-embracing common unity where everyone knows everyone else and greets him wordlessly—face-to-face."[73]

Yet Rosenzweig insists, however, that such a meal is not the final stage:

> The common life as represented by the common meal is, of course, not the ultimate experience; it is no more ultimate than the common listening. But on the road of education to the ultimate experience of common silence this is the second station, just as common listening is the first.[74]

With this comment we confront his interest in the future orientation of human persons. For his was also a model that had room for a variety of ways in which God's future for all persons might impact on the present. "The World is not yet finished."[75] Of the kingdom he writes:

> It is always yet to come—but to come it is always. It is always already in existence and at the same time still to come. It is not yet in existence once and for all. It is eternally coming. Eternity is not a very long time; it is a Tomorrow that could as well be Today. Eternity is a future which, without ceasing to be future, is nonetheless present. Eternity is a Today which is, however, conscious of being more than Today.[76]

Pannenberg accurately summarizes Rosenzweig's position in these words: "In the temporality of dialogue the eschaton of the world is anticipated at every moment, and yet is also opened to the future of the 'kingdom.'"[77] Pannenberg has suggested that Rosenzweig's thinking on language with its thematization of time opens up a new way of looking at the person, even though it left room for considerable development.[78] We must now consider more recent attempts to understand the self relationally.

A clear example of the impetus toward this outlook in the area of philosophy can be seen in John MacMurray's Gifford lectures in 1953–54 entitled *The Form of the Personal*. Here MacMurray (1891–1976), a Scottish philosopher of a theistic persuasion, mounted a vigorous philosophical attack on the notion of the person as a thinking subject (usually accompanied by a pronounced mind-body dualism). In the first part, *The Self as Agent*,[79] he argued that what was fundamentally characteristic of the human self was not its rationality but its capacity to act in the world as an agent. This entailed asserting the primacy of the practical over the theoretical. He was concerned to present the self as a doer, not as an event of self-consciousness and self-absorption. It is possible, however, that in making this point he drew too sharp a distinction between rationality and action, since it is characteristic of human beings to act in a way that is thought-rich, especially as seen in the rich tool use by Homo sapiens and other hominids hundreds of thousands of years ago.

In the second part, *Persons in Relation*, he argued that human persons are only persons in relation to others: "'I' need 'you' in order to be myself."[80] He argued that mutuality was the hallmark of personal identity. In this work MacMurray also considered the role of God. He saw God as: "a personal Other who stands in the same mutual relation to every member of the community. Without the idea of such a universal and personal Other it is impossible to represent the unity of a community of persons, each in personal relationship with all the others. In its full development, the idea of a universal personal Other is the idea of God."[81]

In the last few decades John Zizioulas has been an influential voice in the reassessment of the nature of the human person in relation to the person of God. In an important essay published in 1975 he outlined a strongly relational position. His first move was against the Augustinian and Boethian tradition: "Man's personhood should not be understood in terms of 'personality,' i.e. of a complex of natural, psychological or moral qualities which are in some way 'possessed' by or 'contained' in the human *individuum*.

He then proceeded to outline his own view:

On the contrary, being a person is basically different from being an individual or "personality" in that the person can not be conceived in itself as a static entity, but only as it *relates to*. Thus personhood implies the "openness of being," and even more than that, the *ek-stasis* of being, i.e. a movement towards communion which leads to a transcendence of the boundaries of the "self" and thus to *freedom*.

In addition, "the person in its ekstatic character reveals its being in a catholic, i.e. integral and undivided, way, and thus in its being ekstatic it becomes hypostatic, the bearer of its nature in its totality."[82] He notes that the circumstance we see in every human person not part, but the totality of human nature, is essential to the biblical picture of "Adam," both the first and the last (Christ), a notion that illustrates the idea of "corporate personality," as first enunciated by H. Wheeler Robinson.[83] For Zizioulas, *ekstasis* and *hypostasis* represent two basic aspects of personhood. Originally, *hypostasis* had meant "substance" (*ousia*), but in the fourth century CE, with the cross-fertilization of Greek and biblical thought, it ceased to have this meaning and came to denote "person." Yet ontology continues to be an important theme for Zizioulas. Since hypostasis is identified not with substance but with personhood, the ontological status of a person is not settled by pointing to the "self-existent," that is, to an entity determined by its own boundaries, "but to a being which in its ekstasis breaks through these boundaries in a movement of communion."[84]

In 1975 Zizioulas had only very briefly sketched out the relationship of his idea of personhood to the personhood of God, noting especially that God was characterized by his *ekstasis* of communion constituted in Trinity and love.[85] He had suggested that the notion of the person was "perhaps the only notion that can be applied to God without the danger of anthropomorphism."[86] He returned to the origins and nature of the communion he placed at the center of personhood ten years later in his work *Being as Communion*.[87] The critical question, as noted by Alan Torrance, is whether and how we may conceive of a unified interpretation of the being of God and of the created order, in particular. Further, if we can offer such an interpretation, how is there continuity between the communion of the Trinity and the communion that exists among human beings, either within or outside of the body of Christ?[88]

The important theological positions on the Trinity taken by both Karl Barth and Karl Rahner are problematic precisely in relation to the issue of communion between Father, Son, and Holy Spirit, as Alan Torrance has shown. Barth's view is heavily dependent on notions of God's lordship and encounter with human beings but is problematic for the reason that his conception of unity fails to take due cognizance of "the extent to which the New Testament accounts make it difficult to avoid affirming that God is a Thou to himself and an I in relation to himself, and that this eternal mutuality is opened to the world so that we are brought into communion *within* the union not *a* 'we' but of *the* one, eternal and primordial We—'The Father and I (i.e., "we") are one.'"[89]

Karl Rahner presents the problem even more starkly. Having claimed at one point in his work on the Trinity that "within the Trinity there is no reciprocal 'Thou,'" when he is later explaining how he understands the concept of "person" in relation to the triune God, he actually goes so far as to state that "there is properly no mutual love between Father and Son, for this would presuppose two acts."[90] It is hard to avoid the conclusion that his underlying philosophy of the person has here carried him too far from the New Testament wellsprings of Christian thought, especially the mutual love between Father and Son that is such a prominent theme in the Fourth Gospel.[91] While Rahner effectively sets out a theology of the interaction of the Trinity with human beings and the world (the "economic" aspect of the Trinity), there seems less life in his understanding of the relationship of persons of the Trinity among themselves (the "immanent" aspect of the Trinity). This leads Torrance to question "how seriously he is committed *in practice* to the two-way identification of the immanent and economic Trinities and what the hypostatic union specifically involves with respect to the unique *hypostasis* of the Son."[92] What is needed is an explanation in which the "divine dealings with humankind find realization and consummation in God's relations to himself interpreted in a trinitarian way." Here we are able to understand the New Testament notion of human participation in the divine economy as *koinōnia* in sharp contrast to the Platonic notion of *methexis*.[93] It is precisely in this area that John Zizioulas has made a decisive and positive contribution.

The thesis maintained by Zizioulas runs like this. The ancient Greek understanding of ontology had been fundamentally monistic: the being, or the essence, of the world and the being, or the essence, of God formed an unbreakable unity. Biblical faith, on the other hand, proclaimed God to be absolutely free in relation to the world, its creator in fact. What Christianity needed was a conception of God that avoided Greek monism but also the radical gulf between God and the material world espoused by Gnostics. The answer came from pastoral theologians such as Ignatius of Antioch and Irenaeus who approached the being of God through the experience of the ecclesial community, of *ecclesial being*, especially as it was embodied in eucharistic practice. They realized that the being of God could only be known through personal relationships and personal love, in other words, through communion. Athanasius and the Cappadocian Fathers (Basil the Great, Gregory of Nazianzus, and Gregory of Nyssa) formulated the results of this approach. They argued that the being of God is a relational being; without the concept of communion it would be impossible to speak of God's being. To speak of the divine communion is to speak of the Holy Trinity. This is a primordial ontological concept and not something merely added to the divine substance. Thus communion became an ontological idea in patristic thought.[94]

Moreover, God is a free person who loves freely, that is, freely affirms his identity through an event of communion with other persons. This means that the only way freedom can be exercised in an ontological manner is love. "The expression 'God is love' (1 John 4:16) signifies that God 'subsists' as Trinity, that is, as person and not as substance." Love is not an emanation or property of the substance of God but constitutive of this substance.[95]

This construal of the Trinity was the foundation of a general theology of the person that specified that communion is an ontological category; there is no true being without it. Communion which does not derive from a hypostasis (meaning a free and concrete person) is not an "image" of the being of God.[96] The result of this approach was "an integrated conception of the communion of God and human participation in the life of God which gave ontological grounds to ecclesial being and the eucharistic experience."[97] This seems to answer the problem, noted above, that is inherent in the trinitarian formulations of Barth and Rahner.

How does the reality of death relate to this vision of personhood? This is an area that Zizioulas leaves rather unexplored. Nevertheless, for him, the "eternal survival of the person as a unique, unrepeatable and free 'hypostasis,' as loving and being loved, constitutes the quintessence of salvation, the bringing of the Gospel to man." The Greek fathers called this process "divinization" (*theōsis*). To push this further, he explains that patristic theology sees human beings in the light of two modes of existence, which he calls the *hypostasis of biological existence* and the *hypostasis of ecclesial existence*. The first refers to the existence of a person as resulting from an act of passion, as developing as a separate individual, generating other such hypostases, and then dying. The second is constituted by the new birth of a person, by baptism, and expressed in relationships beyond those of kin in the context of the church, paradigmatically in the eucharist. For the eucharist is "first of all an assembly (*synaxis*), a community, a network of relations, in which man 'subsists' in a manner different from the biological as a member of a body that transcends every exclusiveness of a biological or social kind."[98] The ecclesial hypostasis also has an eschatological dimension; it entails that the human beings involved are oriented to the future, are even images of the future. It is a pledge of the final victory that human beings will have over death.[99]

Yet there some difficulties with the general approach taken by Zizioulas. The first one, very relevant to the New Testament data we are soon to consider, is that the type of communion he has in mind depends upon one individual person moving beyond the boundaries of his or her selfhood to reach out to others. The conditions for such *ekstasis* can, however, be satisfied in a dyadic context, where one person reaches to one other. Although if both persons are members of one community, this type of engagement may have a salutary effect upon it, that is not its inevitable result. The benefits of the relationship may remain localized in the lives of the two individuals concerned. To ensure that communion between members does extend to making a community more unified it is necessary to address the characteristic social and institutional issues that obtain in any group. The key insight of that branch of social psychology known as social identity theory is that a group is much more than the sum of its individual members.[100] As soon as two or more persons form a group, processes begin to come into play that are distinct and separable from the members. This means that to build communion within a group it is necessary to take action at the level of the group as a whole; it is not enough to focus upon the quality of dyadic relationships among the members.

The second area in which it is necessary to challenge Zizioulas is his neglect of what we might call the "downside" of the experience of the human person and how God has acted to address this. There seems little place in his scheme for the suffering and alienation that afflict human beings, or for the status of those outside the ecclesial communion in Christ. Alan Torrance, using Alan Lewis's eloquent words, critiques Zizioulas at this point in that an adequate account of the grace of God must speak of that "unheard-of immanence: God's presence, incarnate and unseen, in that godless world, among its criminals and cripples, its villains and victims, beside whom and as whom Jesus lived and died and was interred."[101] Lewis, indeed, taxes Zizioulas with his reluctance to acknowledge the death of Jesus as significant for God's being.[102] Too much resurrection and too little cross? Lewis also criticizes Zizioulas for his interpretation of the resurrection as the persistence or survival of being. This view, arguably, makes the cross a failed attempt to suppress being, thus "presupposing an ontology in which God swamps non-being with the power of being, rather than receiving non-being into himself and thus going beyond it."[103]

The third problem with Zizioulas's approach lies in his understanding of the Trinity. At one point he notes that the communion of the Trinity is not a relationship to be understood as existing for its own sake. It is the

Father who is the cause of it, he insists, taking his cue in this respect from the Cappadocian Fathers.[104] The principal concern with this view is that the endorsement of Cappadocian notions of the Father as cause imperils his understanding of being and communion, since under it the hypostases of the Son and Spirit become contingent and derivative.[105] Thomas Torrance has, in fact, argued precisely against this aspect of the Cappadocians' thought. Their attempt to preserve the oneness of God by referring the three persons to the Principle (*archē*) or Cause (*aitia*) in the Father could only be achieved "at the expense of a damaging distinction between the deity of the Father as wholly underived or "uncaused," and the deity of the Son and of the Spirit as eternally derived or "caused."[106] In other words, Zizioulas must be subordinating the Son to the Father (even if he is not suggesting that that Son was created). Zizioulas adopted the Cappadocian view partially for the reason that it allowed him to avoid the view that the ultimate ontological category was a "structure of communion existing by itself."[107] Yet this seems to be precisely the position in which his understanding leaves us and it is very difficult to see what is wrong with it![108] In the patristic period, Cyril of Alexandria offered, as noted by Thomas Torrance, a far more satisfactory explanation: "Cyril's conception of the interrelation of the three perfect, coequal, coeternal, enhypostatic Persons through their wholly reciprocal indwelling and containing of one another, in which they are inconfusedly united and inseparably distinguished, was very different [from the Cappadocian proposal], for it carried within it the combined notion of μία οὐσία [one being] and μία ἀρχή [one being]."[109]

The final contribution to the developing understanding of personhood as relational to be considered here is that of Catherine LaCugna in her important 1992 monograph *God for Us: The Trinity and Christian Life*. Under the primary influence of Zizioulas, and also to a lesser extent in positive response to MacMurray, feminist and liberation theologies, and Catholic and Orthodox moral theologies, LaCugna presents a powerful case for an ontology that privileges persons-in-communion, the persons in question comprising the three persons of the Trinity and human beings. The thesis of her book is that the doctrine of the Trinity is a practical doctrine with radical consequences for Christian life. At the heart of her case is the argument that there is the closest connection between *oikonomia* (meaning the economy of salvation that subsists in the self-communication of God to human beings in the person of Christ and the activity of the Spirit) or "the economic Trinity," and *theologia* (meaning the mystery of God as such) or the "immanent Trinity."[110] Critics suggest that she has gone too far in her advocacy of the connection between the two, thus in effect collapsing the immanent Trinity into the economic.[111] Whether that be the case or not, her book contains a compelling vision of communion between the three persons of God and human beings. It is also a vision closely concerned with the social and political ramifications of trinitarian theologies.[112]

For LaCugna, person, not substance, is the ultimate ontological category. And persons are fundamentally interpersonal and intersubjective. In relation to God this means that "God's way of being in relationship *with us*—which is God's personhood—is a perfect expression of God's being as God."[113] As for human beings, persons living in right relationship, in communion, constitute the meaning of salvation and the Christian faith: "God is interactive, neither solitary nor isolated. Human beings are created in the image of the relational God and gradually are being perfected in that image (*theōsis*), making more and more real the communion of all creatures with one another."[114] The Spirit of God is the animating power of this communion, making God's will and work known and realized in Jesus Christ, most notably in baptism and the eucharist. Yet this is a communion of a particular type: "The communion of persons in the Spirit does not entail a leveling to the lowest common denominator. *Koinōnia* does not swallow up the individual, nor obscure his or her uniqueness and unique contribution, nor take away individual freedom by assimilating it to the collective will."[115] With this insistence on the Spirit as the force animating this communion, we have developed our model as far as is necessary for the purposes of this volume.

CONCLUSION

In the course of this chapter I have set out the social and theological bases for my commitment to the communion between persons as a central hermeneutical requirement in order to take seriously the historicity of the New Testament texts. I have now completed that task by formulating a model that encompasses the psychological, social, intercultural, and theological dimensions of communion.

In this chapter I have set out a social and theological model of persons in communion. Now the time has come to begin applying this model to interpreting the New Testament documents within a Christian context. My overall aim in this volume is to propose that such interpretation involves communion between modern Christians and the people who wrote these texts in various parts of the Mediterranean world ca. 50–150 CE.

But first we must address two areas that some might think pose obstacles to the whole enterprise. This task will occupy the next two chapters of this volume. The first potential obstacle is the extent to which we can comprehend messages from the past when they originated in a setting remote from us in culture and time. The second potential obstacle is how their embodiment in authored texts, some of which arguably have literary characteristics, affects our reception of these messages. Whereas the first obstacle centers on the more fundamental question of whether people from the past are knowable at all, the second takes up the particular problem relating to the authors (or addressees) of texts that have come down to us. Having covered these issues, I will then proceed, in chapters 5 to 12, to a positive application of my thesis.

3

KNOWING AND UNDERSTANDING THE MESSAGE OF OUR ANCESTORS IN THE FAITH

One aspect of the model advanced in the preceding chapter is that normally we enter into interpersonal communion with people of whom we have some knowledge. While it is possible to envisage, as Benedict Anderson does,[1] a form of imagined communion with members of our group whom we have never met and do not know (except as members of our group), the richest possibilities for communion, that is, for actual communion, exist when we have some knowledge of the individuals concerned. Face-to-face meeting and dialogue is certainly the most promising route to such communion, but are there other ways of achieving it? If there were not, how could we know the people who wrote the various writings of the New Testament, who lived and died in various parts of the Mediterranean world some nineteen hundred years ago, or understand their communications? Two major obstacles exist to such communion with our New Testament ancestors in faith.

First, there is the sheer fact that these authors belong to the past and that we cannot have direct knowledge of them. One aspect of this problem, that they can speak to us but we cannot reply to them, I have already dealt with in chapter 2. This is not as large an issue as it might seem. Many of us frequently listen to the regular announcers of radio programs or the hosts of television shows and consider that we gain some knowledge of their personalities even though we may never speak to them. There is no difference in principle between this situation and that of our having access to our biblical ancestors in faith only through their writings.

Second, there is the problem that, even if we could meet our ancestors in faith face-to-face, we would encounter a cultural distance at least as great as that which exists today between people from the societies of northern Europe and North America and those of the Middle East. This cultural disjunction does not merely constitute a hindrance to our understanding our ancestors in faith, but also entails that we are likely to differ from them in relation to our respective beliefs, attitudes, and practices. Such a divergence will project before us a fresh vision in these areas where our ancestors in faith seem to have insights that we do not, an important point made by Krister Stendahl in his 1962 *Interpreter's Dictionary of the Bible* essay discussed in chapter 1. On the other hand, they may also manifest beliefs or attitudes or engage in behavior that we feel impelled to criticize. To this extent, when faced with such differences, we may well wish to learn from our ancestors in some areas, while maintaining a critical distance in others. We have seen in the preceding chapter that agreement is not a necessary condition for communion between persons.

I will argue in the following two sections of this chapter that each of these obstacles can be surmounted.

DEFENDING HISTORY AGAINST ITS CULTURED DESPISERS

An awareness of the past is an inescapable aspect of human experience, except where precluded by infancy, illness, or trauma. At various points in every day of our lives, events or personalities from the past come to mind.

At times these recollections are outside our personal experience: the Spanish Armada, Martin Luther, the Boston Tea Party, the construction of the railways in Victorian England, Abraham Lincoln, the Boer War, or the Gallipoli campaign in 1915. While we may have a variable understanding of these events or figures and be aware of differences of opinion as to their significance, few of us would doubt that these events occurred or that these people lived. We assume that evidence for their existence is available for consultation in archives and libraries.

At other times, however, we bring to mind aspects of the past lying within our own personal experience. We recall events in which we were involved or people we know or knew. Thus, we all retain memories of relatives and friends who have died. Most of us, moreover, remember being told stories by these people of people they met or who affected them but whom we have never known. We do not normally doubt the previous existence of our deceased family members or friends, nor do we usually question the existence of people who were significant in their lives but whom we have never known. My own mother, Evelyn, died on 18 March 1995. On a number of occasions in my childhood she related to me certain events—described in the preceding chapter—concerning what happened when an Irish cousin of hers, Republican in sympathies, who had fled Ireland around the time of the civil war, lived with her family in Sydney in the 1920s. I did not doubt the existence of the young man or his visit when my mother told me about it, nor do I now, even though I have no documentary evidence to that effect. Even though we are all aware that our memory can sometimes play tricks on us, we live our lives on the understanding that the memories we have of the past are generally based on events that actually happened and people who actually lived.

These reflections demonstrate the importance of memory in maintaining our sense of the past. Sometimes we remember events, both trivial and weighty, within our own personal experience. On other occasions we remember phenomena that we have learned about from sources such as teachers, books, visual media, travel, and so on. Yet, as just noted, we assume that data about such phenomena exist, especially in the form of documents contemporaneous with the events or persons in question. We further assume that if we consulted such data they would provide evidence for what we have heard about these phenomena. We are accustomed to apply the words "history" and "historical" to those aspects of human activity in the past that are susceptible to such investigation. There is a lively discussion at present concerning the relationship between history and memory. In the current chapter I am concerned mainly with this former issue, the existence of evidence for past phenomena apart from our memory of them. I will return to the extent to which our memories are socially constructed and the significance of this for our communion with the New Testament authors in chapter 9.

This awareness of the past almost always plays a dominant role in our identity, our sense of who we are. Perhaps the past as personally experienced intrudes more directly into our self-understanding than the past as the history of groups and nations with whom we may not be closely connected. Nevertheless, in either case we accept that supporting our sense of the past are actual occurrences and real people.

Most historical writing represents the academic embodiment of this assumption. British historian Richard Evans, for example, has stated: "A historical fact is something that happened in history and can be verified as such through the traces history has left behind. Whether or not a historian has actually carried out the act of verification is irrelevant to its factuality: it really is there entirely independently of the historian."[2] This view, with which many historians would still agree in spite of doubts we are about to consider, probably also accords with how most nonspecialists see the matter.

In spite of the apparent plausibility of the idea that facts from the past are knowable and can be ascertained by examination of the surviving evidence for them, in the last few decades some thinkers, especially Jacques Derrida and his supporters, have mounted an intense challenge against this position. At the level of everyday experience, we would probably find any suggestion that the past is of its very nature unknowable as hardly worth serious consideration. But among historians and others professionally interested in the debate, including literary theorists and biblical critics, this radical challenge to the knowability of the past (and the sheer number of scholars involved) requires consideration. In addition, scholars such as Hans-Georg Gadamer and his supporters have posed a further challenge to the view, exemplified by Evans above, by insisting that even if the past is knowable, the only access we have to it is via a tradition that embraces both itself and us. On this view, understanding the past on its own terms as a reality removed from us is not possible.

Some works on biblical interpretation have given great prominence to opinions such as those of Derrida and Gadamer. To cite two examples, Gadamer heavily influenced Anthony Thiselton's significant hermeneutical text, *The Two Horizons*,[3] while in 1998 Kevin Vanhoozer published a book that is nearly five hundred pages long, and in a small font, in which Derrida is his main sparring partner.[4]

In the argument to follow I will analyze and reject claims that the past is unknowable or that it is knowable but only as embedded in a tradition including us. In mounting this defense of a past that can be known and, to certain extent, on its own terms, against more and less radical forms of attack, I draw inspiration from the book published by Friedrich Schleiermacher in 1799—*On Religion: Speeches to Its Cultured Despisers*.[5]

Jacques Derrida and the Past as a Play of Signifiers

The Swiss linguist Ferdinand de Saussure argued early in the twentieth century that the relation of words to their meanings was completely arbitrary and that words, which he called "signifiers," were defined not by their relation to the things they denoted but by their relation to one another.[6] He regarded language as a system of differentiation, a set of contrasts between certain key elements in a discourse, constructed from signs, where the signifiers were related to one another in a logical way. In 1968 the French linguistic theorist Roland Barthes, under the influence of Saussure's notion of signifiers, rejected the claim of historians to be reconstructing past reality as a pretense. The history that historians produced was "an inscription on the past pretending to a likeness of it, a parade of signifiers masquerading as a collection of facts." Objectivity was "the product of what might be called the referential illusion."[7]

The French philosopher Jacques Derrida has gone further than Saussure and even Barthes. He announced the broad outlines of his project, which has come to be known as deconstruction and which forms an important strand in postmodernist thought, at a literary conference at Johns Hopkins University in 1966.[8] Although the character of Derrida's writing is such that summarizing his thought is not easy, it is clear that even at this early stage he was announcing (in language that is portentous and rather breathless) that reality was affected by a major transformation in which it had become decentered:

> This was the moment when language invaded the universal problematic, the moment when, in the absence of a center or origin, everything became discourse . . . that is to say, a system in which the central signified, the original or transcendental signified, is never absolutely present outside a system of differences. The absence of the transcendental signified extends the domain and the play of signification infinitely.[9]

What does this all boil down to? Of central importance is the difference between "signifiers" and "signified." For Derrida each time a word, a signifier, is uttered, the relationship between it and other words changes. Thus language becomes an infinite play of significations. In the quotation just given, Derrida seems to be saying that there is no reality apart from language. There is no "transcendental signified." This is coming perilously close to asserting that everything is merely an arrangement of words and that nothing exists outside language—a view that Richard Evans does indeed attribute to him.[10] Such suspicions are supported by Derrida's frequently cited saying "There is nothing outside the text."[11] Vanhoozer, who takes extraordinary pains to present Derrida's position accurately, clarifies this dictum: "Some commentators discredit Derrida by offering the perfunctory suggestion that he means that things such as oak trees or Ford Escorts do not exist. Such a reading is ludicrous." He insists that Derrida's point is really that everything forms part of a signifying system, so that even natural objects are "written," meaning that they are classified by some language system or other: "What Derrida denies is that there is any presence, any kind of being or determinate reality outside the play of signs. There is no original ground or 'home' of meaning beyond particular and contingent language systems, and therefore nothing to keep meaning centered, stable, and determinate."[12] Yet in trying to salvage Derrida, Vanhoozer thus sinks him. How can one take seriously the idea that there is no ground of meaning beyond particular language systems, that the world does not exist except by grace of the human capacity to name it and in the act of so doing? Far more plausible is the view that "Language and grammar are in fact not completely arbitrary signifiers, but have evolved through contact with the real world in an attempt to name real things."[13] In other words, the signifiers are not just playing among themselves; they play over and among real objects.

Derrida's view that there is nothing outside the text constitutes the assumed and uninvestigated foundation of his whole theory and is enunciated with a quasi-religious conviction. The picture in Genesis, on the other hand, is of a world with living things in it that God permits man to name (Gen 2:19-20) and this accords with the reality of the case. Derrida's view installs an anthropocentric hegemony over the created order and all that is in it. It pushes to an extreme and unconvincing conclusion our very reasonable excitement over the flexibility of human language systems to name the features of the natural and human realms. Considered sociologically, his position (and probably that of those who espouse his views) is explicable as the product of a creative Western intellectual full of enthusiasm for the books and other written materials he spends much of his time poring over. The limited reality of his office or study becomes a totalizing reality projected onto the world at large.

One related aspect of Derrida's thought is his antipathy toward the spoken word and the personal presence that it entails (a phenomenon he castigates as "logocentrism") and his preference for writing and absence.[14] That is to say, Derrida is challenging what he sees as a priority given to speech since it requires the presence of at least two human speakers, real selves who are the origin of what is said, over writing that can be received in the absence of its producer. Derrida considered that the notion of "presence" has been dominant in Western philosophy since Plato and his own textual strategy of deconstruction was aimed at opposing it.

What are the consequences for history of Derrida's insistence that there is nothing outside the text? The main result, as Richard Evans observes, is that "meaning cannot be found in the past; it is merely put there, each time differently, and with equal validity, by different historians."[15] "If there is nothing outside the text," Lawrence Stone comments, "then history as we have known it collapses altogether, and fact and fiction become indistinguishable from one another."[16]

The consequence of Derrida's theory has become a central plank in postmodernist construals of historiography. Hayden White has proposed that researching and writing a book of history was much the same as writing a novel. He also argued that the only bases for choosing between rival views of the past are moral or aesthetic.[17] For some postmodernist theorists, like Keith Jenkins, the proper study is not the past but other historians, while Frank Ankersmit claims that differences between historians are matters of style, of aesthetics.[18]

How are we to understand and respond to views such as these? In answering, it is worth noting initially that there is one habit of thought that typifies the writings of Derrida and many other postmodernist historians and literary critics. This is the idea, as Derrida puts it, that "when a distinction cannot be rigorous or precise, it is not a distinction at all."[19] Thus a concept has a conceptual purity which excludes all marginal cases. This notion is the foundation of the pervasive dichotomizing practiced by Derrida and postmodernist thinkers. Everything is either A or B; there is no middle ground. As far as history is concerned, for example, this means that whereas traditional historians (allegedly) work with the idea that the historical text has a completely fixed and unalterable meaning installed there by its author, the postmodernists prefer the complete opposite—historical sources are capable of an infinite number of meanings as historians imagine them. Whereas traditional historians (allegedly) gaze through historical documents without interference to the historical reality that lies behind them, they assert that it is impossible to do so. Thus they erect "a set of binary opposites and polarized extremes."[20]

In spite of postmodernist fascination with absolute dichotomies, everyday experience is replete with distinctions that allow exceptions and marginal cases. Did Derrida never pass through the border zone between two countries? Or notice a gradual transition from one style of vegetation to another as he ascended a mountain? In addition, however, this recognition that many boundaries are gradated and not sharply defined is firmly embedded in the philosophy of language. As John Searle notes:

> most concepts and distinctions are rough at the edges and do not have sharp
> boundaries. The distinctions between fat and thin, rich and poor, democracy and authoritarianism, for example, do not have sharp boundaries . . .
> the distinctions between literal and metaphorical, serious and nonserious,
> fiction and nonfiction and, yes, even true and false, admit of degrees and all
> apply *more or less*.[21]

Searle pointed out in debate with Derrida that an acceptance of the fuzziness of boundaries is universal among philosophers of language, but Derrida refused to recant his untenable belief in the opposite view.[22]

In relation to history, therefore (the role of the author is discussed in the next chapter of this volume), the fact that boundaries are not necessarily rigorous or precise requires that we eschew the postmodernist dichotomy between texts with a wholly authorially derived fixed meaning and texts capable of an infinite number of meanings constructed by the historian/novelist. It is, in fact, not easy to name historians, at least in the last two or three centuries, who have thought that they could simply gaze through historical documents to the historical facts behind the documents. This caution emerges most clearly in the long-accepted need to be alert to the bias of the various sources. The historian who believes that the past can be known with 100 percent certainty and objectivity is a scholar of straw erected by deconstructionists and postmodernists like Derrida to give their opposing position a veneer of respectability. Nevertheless, while we cannot recover a single, unalterably true meaning from a document, neither can we impose any meaning we want on it either. We are limited by the words it contains, which are not, in spite of postmodernist protestations, capable of an infinity of meanings.[23]

In order to illustrate and undermine the postmodernist rejection of the reality of the past, it has become customary to cite the Holocaust. The reason for this is clearly made by Richard Evans, a specialist in modern German history, who testified in a defamation suit in London brought (unsuccessfully, in the result) by David Irving against the American scholar Deborah Lipstadt and her publisher, Penguin Books, on the basis that she had accused him of being a Holocaust denier in a book she had written.[24] Judgment was given against Irving by Mr. Justice Gray on 11 April 2000. Evans states that "[h]ere is an issue where evidence really counts, and can be used to establish the essential facts. Auschwitz was not a discourse. It trivializes mass murder to see it as a text. The gas chambers were not a piece of rhetoric."[25] The consequences of the Holocaust for postmodernist history were considered in a 1992 collection of essays entitled *Probing the Limits of Postmodernism: Nazism and the "Final Solution."*[26] Yet what is true of the Holocaust must also be true to some degree of other past events, people, and institutions. It simply brings home most graphically the irresponsibility of the postmodernist denial of the reality of the past. Evans observes with justifiable severity that "the postmodernist concentration on words diverts attention away from real suffering and oppression and towards the kinds of secondary intellectual issues that matter in the physically comfortable world of academia."[27]

A particular instance of the relevance of the Holocaust focuses on the controversy concerning Paul de Man that erupted in 1987 and which has been the subject of a number of books.[28] Paul de Man was born and grew up in Belgium before emigrating to the United States after the war. He became a professor at Yale and was one of the leading deconstructionists and postmodernists and a friend of Derrida. He died in 1983. In 1987 a young Belgian scholar discovered that during the German occupation of Belgium from 1940 to 1942, de Man had written some 180 articles for a Nazi-controlled newspaper in Brussels, *Le Soir*. The focus of the articles was cultural but in some of them de Man attacked the contribution of Jews to European culture in the twentieth century as mediocre and of no lasting value. In one article he suggested that if the Jews were deported to a Jewish colony outside Europe, European culture would not suffer a great loss.[29] He never mentioned this to colleagues in the United States and always denied collaborationist activity during the war. When the storm broke, it seemed to the critics of deconstruction and postmodernism that de Man's assertion of the irrelevance of authorial intention and the infinite possibilities of textual interpretation was a way of denying authorial responsibility and thus of exculpating himself for his own wartime writing. Deconstructionists and postmodernists, including Jacques Derrida, sprang to his defense. But, as Richard Evans has noted:

> Like much postmodernist writing, the defence of de Man by the deconstructionists was riddled with contradictions. On the one hand, Derrida and his supporters insisted theoretically on the infinite possibilities of textual interpretation; on the other, they argued in practice that to interpret de Man's early writings as collaborationist or antisemitic was just plain wrong. On the one hand, the author himself theoretically had no control over the meaning of what he wrote; on the other, Derrida denounced in the most polemical terms those he thought were wilfully misunderstanding what he said in de Man's defence.[30]

From this discussion we conclude that the attack launched by Derrida, and the postmodernist historians influenced by him, on our very ability to know the past fails. This is not to say that historians can ever attain to absolute, objective truth in what they are writing; very few, if any, think they do. Rather, they aim at learning the truth about the past, following accepted procedures for investigating the evidence, as a matter of probability. To this extent, their practice corroborates the view of nonspecialists that we can know the past, either because we remember our own past experience or because it is accessible in the texts and artifacts that have survived.

This means that Derrida and postmodernist historians do not provide a reason for shaking our confidence that we can derive knowledge, acceptable to the (perfectly adequate) standard of probable truth, concerning our ancestors in faith who wrote the New Testament documents and who first heard or read them. But what of the further problem that even if we can know these figures from the past, we are only able to do so in the context of a tradition that embraces both them and us and that unmediated knowledge of them is impossible? Thus we come to Hans-Georg Gadamer. While his writings have been highly influential in New Testament hermeneutics, it will be necessary to expose a fundamental flaw in his argument. It is, in fact, time to take a close and critical view at the warm welcome his views have generally received among New Testament interpreters and the powerful influence he has had on New Testament interpretation. I will suggest after the discussion below that Gadamer has obscured rather than illuminated the nature of the task.

Hans-Georg Gadamer and the Fusion of Horizons

Gadamer's thought offers a challenging answer to the problem of our distance from the biblical past that was first starkly revealed by the history-of-religions school in the late nineteenth and early twentieth centuries. He attacks historicism's "naïve assumption" that the temporal distance between the people in the past and ourselves was something that had to be overcome by setting ourselves within the spirit of that age, thinking with its ideas and thoughts, and "thus advance towards historical objectivity." Basing himself on the thought of Martin Heidegger, Gadamer favors the view that time was no longer primarily a gulf to be bridged but was actually "the supportive ground of process in which the present is rooted."[31] Gadamer insists on the priority of the viewpoint of the person reading a historical text: "Every age has to understand a transmitted text in its own way, for the text is part of the whole of the tradition in which the age takes an objective interest and in which it seeks to understand itself."[32] Thiselton accurately interprets Gadamer to mean by this statement that we "cannot, as it were, leave the present to go back into the past and to view the past solely on its own terms," since the "very meaning which the text has for us is partly shaped by the our own place in a tradition which reaches the present."[33] Thus Gadamer can say, "True historical thinking must take account of its own historicality."[34]

To illustrate his point Gadamer employs the metaphor of the merging or fusion of two horizons. For Gadamer a "horizon" is "the range of vision that includes everything that can be seen from a particular vantage point" and allows one to see beyond a particular place or state.[35] He notes that when doing history we refer to "horizons," especially when we are attempting to see the past on its own terms, "not in terms of contemporary criteria and prejudices," but then he immediately challenges this notion. The basis for his challenge, using conversation as an analogy, is very revealing, both to the extent that it indicates the source and foundation of his thinking and also because it lays bare the fatal flaw in his thought.

GADAMER AND THE NATURE OF HUMAN CONVERSATION
Gadamer poses the example of when we have a conversation with someone "simply in order to get to know him, i.e. to discover his standpoint and horizon,"

and continues as follows: "This is not a true conversation, in the sense that we not *seeking agreement concerning an object* [emphasis added], but the specific contents of the conversation are only a means to get to know the horizon of the other person. Examples are oral examinations, or some kinds of conversation between doctor and patient." For Gadamer the only true conversation is when we are "seeking agreement concerning an object." What is wrong with this? Simply that it excludes important kinds of conversations (apart from the technical cases mentioned by Gadamer) where the aim is not necessarily to reach an agreement. A common example is conversations directed simply to understanding the other's point of view, even though the conversation partners may strongly disagree. Martin Buber expressed the truth of the matter when he stated, as already noted in chapter 2, that "Genuine conversation, and therefore every actual fulfilment of relation between men, means acceptance of otherness." Even if one party wants to persuade another of the correctness of his or her view, that is not the defining quality of a genuine conversation. Rather, the defining quality resides in the circumstance that each conversation partner unreservedly accepts and confirms the other.[36]

On one view, Gadamer's model of conversation rests on the *sentimental* notion that we are only truly speaking to one another if we are trying to reach agreement. Interpreted a little more bleakly, however, he is actually opposing the mutual coexistence of different views and is indefensibly advocating the *hegemonic* assertion of sameness over difference. In other words, "You're only free to agree."

We saw in the preceding chapter, moreover, that there is ample scope for the meaning of communion between persons to embrace dialogue that respectfully listens to and understands their respective, divergent points of view. Ephesians 4:15 theologically expresses this reality in the powerful phrase *alētheuontes en agapē*, "being truthful in love."[37] It is an everyday human experience that we can love those with whom we disagree and in the very process of such disagreement. This confirms the truth of Buber's insight that the essential hallmark of genuine conversation and dialogue is that those involved accept one another as persons. This means listening to one another with respect while seeking to understand the other's point of view. Meaningful communion between persons frequently occurs in such a context. Sometimes such a conversation may have the aim of securing an agreement, but that is only one subset of a larger category and most certainly cannot exclude genuine dialogue.

Sadly misled by his failure to appreciate the realities of conversation, Gadamer then builds on his error by applying the analogy to historical investigation: "Just as in a conversation, when we have discovered the standpoint and horizon of the other person, his ideas become intelligible, without our necessarily having to agree with him, the person who thinks historically comes to understand the meaning of what has been handed down, without necessarily agreeing with it, or seeing himself in it." For Buber, and rightly, this would be close to the ideal of human conversation. But for Gadamer this is a bad thing, since it involves withdrawing from the possibility of reaching agreement! Even more extraordinary is Gadamer's claim that a text or person thus understood in its or his or her otherness and with which or whom we do not agree cannot be speaking the truth! "The text that is understood historically," he alleges, "is forced to abandon its claim that it is uttering something true." When we seek to understand the past from its historical standpoint, "we have given up any claim to find, in the past, any truth valid and intelligible for ourselves." Or, again, "this acknowledgement of the otherness of the other, which makes him the object of objective knowledge, involves the fundamental suspension of his claim to truth."[38]

When one briefly considers what is entailed in this perspective, the fundamentally flawed character of Gadamer's proposal quickly reveals itself. Assume Mary and Jennifer are having a conversation with one another. They are not trying to reach an agreement, but rather they have the greatest respect and affection for one another and are simply seeking to clarify each other's divergent positions. On Gadamer's view, both Mary and Jennifer are precluded from the *very* beginning from believing that what the other says is true. Both of them must be 100 percent confident of the truth of their position and consider that they have nothing to gain from the dialogue. They must assume that from it they will learn no "truth valid and intelligible" for themselves. Only if they are aiming at reaching an agreement, presumably a compromise combining elements from each of their positions, could that be the result. In short, for Gadamer true conversation only occurs where both parties manage to impose their view on the other so as to produce an agreed position. His vision is ultimately reducible to a politics of discourse where the other matters if and only if I can successfully enforce my will during the dialogue by persuading him or her to agree with me. It is difficult to see how such an attitude could be consonant with a genuine respect for the other, who, by definition, is unable to contribute a truth with which I agree.

What preposterous confidence in the infallibility and indefectibility of one's own opinion could generate such beliefs? And yet, as we will soon see, they form the foundation of Gadamer's whole notion of the fusion of horizons that hermeneutics scholars have so warmly received. Has Gadamer never had a conversation with someone with whom he disagreed and yet come away thinking the other person was a bearer of truth? Has he never encountered someone who uttered a truth for his or her own situation if not for Gadamer's? Or, above all, has he never entered a conversation where he expected to explore disagreements and discovered that he was in the wrong and must completely and unqualifiedly adopt the other's point of view?

The Confusion of Horizons

Gadamer's (unsustainable) insistence on the necessity of agreement in a true conversation provides the foundation of his "fusion of horizons" (*Horizontverschmelzung*). Not surprisingly, he deprecates the idea that there are two horizons, the horizon in which the person lives and the historical horizon within which the person places himself or herself. For Gadamer, these would represent "closed horizons." Instead, the "historical movement of human life consists in the fact that it is never utterly bound to any one standpoint, and hence can never be a truly closed horizon. The horizon is, rather, something into which we move and that moves with us." There is, in fact, "a single horizon that embraces everything contained in historical consciousness."[39] A little later he asserts, "Understanding, rather, is always the fusion of these horizons which we imagine to exist by themselves." Nevertheless, he refrains from speaking of a single horizon to preserve a sense of the tension between the past and the present. He wants to retain a historical horizon different from the horizon of the present. The former, however, is "only a phase in the process of understanding, and does not become solidified into the self-alienation of a past consciousness, but is overtaken by our own present horizon of understanding. In the process of understanding there takes place a real fusion of horizons, which means that as the historical horizon is projected, it is simultaneously removed."[40] The hegemonic dimension to Gadamer's position, the extent to which it entails one's own position assuming dominance over the other, emerges here with crystal clarity.

This notion of fusion of horizon refers in essence to an agreement between our current understanding and that of the past period that we have under consideration. Since it presupposes the indefensible view that we can only gain truth from someone with whom we reach a measure of agreement, it must be rejected. It is desirable to offer a more appropriate metaphor for what actually happens in many conversations and in many historical investigations. I will select a very ancient one from Heraclitus. To express the idea of a unity that depends upon a balanced tension between opposites, Heraclitus once asserted: "There is a back-stretched connection, as in the bow and the lyre" (*palintonos harmoniē, hokōsper toxou kai lurōs*).[41] The appeal of this dictum is that here we have an entity with two constituent elements which together produce a unity but without losing their distinctive respective identities. This reflects the reality of a conversation or a historical inquiry in that both parties to the procedure are likely to be at least partial bearers of truth whether or not agreement exists between him or her. There is no doubt that we come to any phenomenon within a particular tradition and framework of understanding (our presuppositions); to that extent at least Gadamer is correct. Yet while we engage in a conversation or undertake a historical exploration from within our own unique personality and social setting, this does not displace the reality of our capacity to enter into genuine dialogue with other people. Neither does this displace our ability to derive truth from our conversation partner, whether our aim is to agree with them or not.

It now remains to consider other problematic aspects of Gadamer's approach that are linked with his broad thesis on how we understand the past from both within a tradition and within the fusion of horizons. In making the obvious point that we cannot understand the past solely on its own terms, Gadamer also suggests that we cannot understand the past even partly on its own terms. Consider the following: "The true historical object is not an object at all, but the unity of the one and the other, a relationship in which exist both the reality of history and the reality of historical understanding."[42] Stanford quotes this and then immediately continues: "Meanings, are, therefore, partly constituted by the percipient and his or her historicity. But, it is important to note, only in part."[43] While Stanford is certainly correct on this, he fails to note that Gadamer himself does not make this point. In Gadamer the objective reality of the past has disappeared, for it "is overtaken by our own present horizon of understanding."[44] It cannot be known in and of itself but has been replaced by a sentimental and hegemonic notion of "fusion" where two different perspectives (the past-mediated-through-history and the present) merge, or rather, the former is subjugated to the latter.

Stanford also seeks to defend Gadamer against the charge of imprisoning interpretations in tradition and hence in this or that ideology. "His reply is that hermeneutics, by searching out every meaning, is just the thing to free us from bondage to ideology."[45] But one could just as easily accuse Gadamer of imprisoning *the past* in tradition. Stanford returns to this issue a few pages later:

After all this one might be forgiven for supposing that Gadamer's ideas have enmired us in total relativism. Must the historian give up all hope, all pretence, of truth or objectivity? Gadamer does not think so. His position is that our prejudices (often unexamined) bind us into a tradition. This confines us to one road, as it were. Hermeneutics causes us to . . . see that there are many roads. This is an advance on seeing only one road. It does not, however, tell us which is the right direction.[46]

Oddly, Stanford still defends Gadamer on the basis that by his "'fusion of horizons' idea both participants can expand their understanding. From this process we learn which roads are the more and which the less likely to lead to knowledge." He then gives the game away by acknowledging, "Whether or not Gadamer explicitly states this, the answer is implicit in his thinking."[47] This is most unsatisfactory. Gadamer offers no criterion for differentiating between better and worse roads. Gadamer does not have such a thought, nor could he, since it is alien to his whole position. Stanford himself well appreciates that some measure of objectivity is possible in relation to the past just as it is with respect to contemporary foreign cultures, as we will now see. Yet he does not follow the logic of his argument with respect to Gadamer and criticize him, as he should, for failing to appreciate the problem caused by Gadamer's denial of the knowability of the past on its own terms.

THE PAST AS NOT ONTICALLY ALIEN

Central to Gadamer's argument is the idea that the past is ontically alien to us, that is, its reality is completely unknown and foreign to us. In a work better known for asserting the importance of authorial intention in interpreting a text, E. D. Hirsch exposed Gadamer to searching scrutiny on this point. While insisting upon the limitations of knowledge that affect every interpreter of an old text, Hirsch is nevertheless critical of the "radical historicism" that holds that the meanings of the past are intrinsically alien to us and that we have no "authentic" access to those meanings and can therefore never "truly" understand them.[48] He suggests that from Dilthey's conception that human consciousness was constituted by its historical givens it was not a very long step to Heidegger's "conception of the temporality and historicity of human being." There was a transition from the notion of each culture's individuality to the idea that it was impossible to study cultures in their own right. Thus, the "past became 'ontically alien' to us."[49] He argues powerfully against this conclusion.

Hirsch acutely observes that one of the most vulnerable conceptions in radical historicism is the rather sentimental belief that "only our own cultural entities have 'authentic' immediacy for us." For this reason, "we cannot 'truly' understand the texts of the past, such 'true' understanding being reserved for contemporary texts, and all understanding of the past being 'abstract' and 'constructed.'" Hirsch contradicts this view by insisting that "in

fact, all understanding of cultural entities past or present is 'constructed.'"
He states: "There is no immediacy in understanding either a contemporary
or a predecessor, and there is no certainty. In all cases, what we understand is
a construction, and if the construction happens to be unthinking and automatic, it is not necessarily more vital or authentic for that."[50] There is no fundamental difference in understanding a text from the past and one from the
present.[51] As Hirsch also says, "For it is merely arbitrary . . . to hold that a
meaning fifty years old is ontologically alien while one three years or three
minutes old is not . . . The ontical character of time does not in itself require
the arbitrary slicing up of time into homogeneous periods."[52]

Stanford has expressed a very similar view when he notes that one or two
philosophers, believing that we cannot have any knowledge of an independently real past, conclude that the past is what historians construct in their
narratives and descriptions. One of the assumptions upon which such theories depend is that the past has no reality and therefore cannot be known. He
insists that the first assumption is implausible:

> Since no limitation is placed on the word, "the past" must include events
> of five minutes or five seconds ago. Can it be argued that the breath I drew
> a few seconds past and have not yet expelled is not real? Is reality confined
> to the present minute, second, nanosecond? Then what is the present? How
> long is it? The theory is reduced to absurdity. Nor can we escape by sug-
> gesting that the assumption applies only to the historical past, for then we
> must ask at what point the historical past ceased and the present began. At
> which point did unreality give place to reality?[53]

This argument could be strengthened with reference to Augustine's discussion of time—how the present is a very fragile moment existing between
the past and the future that disappears as we touch it.[54] Every document (perhaps excepting movie subtitles and television captions that we experience
simultaneously with the living voice they accompany) we peruse belongs, *by
necessity*, to the past.

The real issue is that the character of the evidence differs for past and present
phenomena. With present phenomena we (sometimes) have the opportunity
for actual discourse or other forms of interaction with our research subjects.
But sometimes not (as when modern scholars of international relations refuse
to talk to "terrorists").[55] Very often we will depend on written material to study
the present. In this case, it is hard to see what the difference is between the
study of past texts and present texts, except that we have more information (or
the capacity to obtain it) about "present" texts than "past" texts.

GADAMER'S DISINCLINATION TO UNDERSTAND THE CULTURALLY DIFFERENT OTHER

We have now reached the final problem with Gadamer's theory. Why does Gadamer assume that because we are enculturated in certain traditions we are incapable of setting those traditions aside when it comes to understanding people, events, and facts from the past? Plainly such a claim attacks our very capacity to know about the past. And why does Thiselton—following Gadamer on this issue as on many others—seek to illustrate this point by quoting with approval Palmer's metaphor that we are immersed in the medium of our own tradition that is transparent to us, and therefore as invisible to us, as water to a fish.[56]

For reasons that escape the understanding of the present writer, Gadamer, Thiselton, and Lundin (another Gadamer enthusiast)[57] ignore, or are non-cognizant of, the possibility that people raised and socialized in one culture and tradition can communicate with representatives of another culture by actively taking steps to overcome the effects of their cultural conditioning. Gadamer and Thiselton give the impression that the notion that someone could put aside his or her enculturated traditions, or simply make the effort to be consciously aware of them, is both unheard of and impossible to achieve. In doing so they manifest a notable disconnection from human experience. Here this experience is represented most visibly in the considerable pedagogic enterprise that prepares those who will work in foreign cultures: aid workers, volunteers abroad, doctors, diplomats, businesspeople, or others.

There is, in fact, as we saw in the preceding chapter, a body of literature aimed at inculcating techniques for intercultural understanding.[58] Typically this involves helping the would-be expatriates appreciate the cultural baggage they bear from their own upbringing that they need to recognize and perhaps consciously discard when they communicate with people abroad. In this enterprise of intercultural communication (for that is what it is), social-scientific ideas and perspectives have proved particularly useful in reminding the participants of their own cultural presuppositions that they must consciously try to shed upon moving into another culture. What Gadamer and Thiselton (admittedly in 1979 and 1980, respectively) simply assumed was impossible is the stuff of numerous "entry shock" courses delivered across the world every day to professionals about to move to foreign cultures.

Emilio Betti very accurately outlined notable deficiencies in Gadamer's theory in 1962, in a pamphlet published only two years after the appearance of the first German edition of *Truth and Method*. The core of Betti's complaint was similar to my above critique. Gadamer had jeopardized the legitimacy of ascribing objective status to the objects of interpretation and had thus raised a question over the objectivity of interpretation itself. Betti did not for a moment deny that the interpreter's subjectivity is engaged in every act of interpretation. For him, understanding another is always a process that involves the interpreter's own experience in the world.[59] Nevertheless, he insisted that, whatever the subjective dimension to interpretation, the object remains an object and one could strive for and even obtain an objectively valid interpretation.[60] One may cite an analogy from any contact we have with people from a different culture. While we cannot escape the fact that we have been socialized differently from them, these people exist and they have something to say. What they say we will filter through our mind's cultural software just as our words will filter through theirs. Yet, at a pragmatic level (one quite sufficient for the purpose), communication will occur.

None of this is to deny that we need to be realistic about the extent to which or manner in which we can know people from past or present cultures different from our own. Stanford agrees that we can have understanding of human society and human actions in the past. But he disagrees that we need empathy to do it. Empathy is defined in the *Shorter Oxford English Dictionary* as "the power of projecting one's personality into, and so fully understanding, the object of contemplation." In his view: "We do not, as holders of the empathy theory require, have to project our personality into another. Is this possible even with contemporaries, let alone with people far into the past? Nor are we ever likely to attain 'full understanding' of another. For most purposes it suffices to have an acquaintance with the springs (most emotional) and the resourcefulness (most rational) of human action." No doubt, Stanford continues, it is true, as L. P. Hartley says at the beginning of his novel *The Go-Between*, "The past is another country. They do things differently there." But it is wrong to exaggerate this truth: "If you make the effort to acknowledge the differences, it is not too difficult to adjust to life in a foreign country; millions do it every day. Similar efforts enable us to enjoy the literature of societies separated from us by hundreds, even thousands, of years and many thousand miles."[61] This statement accurately assesses our ability to know the past.

NEGOTIATING THE CULTURAL DISTANCE BETWEEN US AND OUR ANCESTORS IN FAITH

We will now briefly consider the second obstacle to communion with our ancestors in faith—the cultural distance between us. As we noted earlier, there are two dimensions to this problem: First, how we can overcome this distance so as to understand what they are saying? Second, it is necessary that we preserve our critical faculties when we encounter our ancestors in faith;

while we fully expect to learn from them, we must also be ready to see their shortcomings. Our model of communion incorporates both the possibility of dissent and assent when interacting with our ancestors in faith.

Understanding Our Ancestors in Faith

To recapitulate briefly the model proposed in this book, I favor the theory that sees communication as the transmission of a message. (I find unhelpful the theory that communication is the production of meaning). Errors of meaning can occur at any step in the communication process.

As I have noted above in criticizing the views of Gadamer and Thiselton, the project of facilitating intercultural communication is a mature area of pedagogy. Numerous courses and books are available to assist people about to move to a foreign culture to understand its inhabitants and communicate with them.[62] I will briefly summarize these studies here and then relate my discussion specifically to the concerns of this volume.

William Gudykunst and Young Yun Kim, authors of a leading text in the field, isolate four factors as central to the context of intercultural communication: culture, groups and social roles, the individual, and the environment. By "culture" they mean the patterns of feeling, thinking, valuing, and potential action into which we are socialized by being brought up in a particular social setting. Socialization occurs in the family, at school, and in the workplace—to name what are probably the main contexts. Culture may be seen as "software of the mind and heart." Max Weber observed: "These are in fact typical probabilities confirmed by observation to the effect that under certain conditions an expected course of social action will occur, which is understandable in terms of the typical motives and typical subjective intentions of the actors."[63] In short, Weber rightly considered it possible to generalize about cultures. Such generalization does not reify culture; it merely and realistically acknowledges that it was more likely that when faced with situation A, a statistically significant percentage of the members of a particular culture would react in mode X rather than mode Y.

The second influence on culture is the set of groups we belong to. While the family is usually the most important group, ethnicity, religion, school, athletic team, town, and employer (to name only a few) can all be very prominent for certain people. Our membership in such groups lends a certain character to our attitudes and behavior that emerges in our interactions with others.

The third influence is our own distinctive individuality. No two members of a family, not even identical twins, are exactly the same. Our distinctive and unique personality inevitably means that we interact with others in a manner stamped by that personality. It is necessary to bear in mind, however, as Hofstede has shown by careful empirical research, that individualism is more prominent in some cultures than in others. This does not mean that individualistic persons do not occur in modern group-oriented cultures or that group-oriented people are not to be found in individualistic cultures; the point is that statistically, some cultures are more of one type than the other.

The fourth and last feature enumerated by Gudykunst and Kim is the environment. Geographic location, climate, architecture, and other physical aspects of a lifestyle all condition the way in which we create and express messages to others. Environmental features also condition the way in which we understand the messages we receive from others.

Applying This Communication Model to the New Testament Writings

All of the above factors are relevant when we interpret a New Testament document. As to the first and second factors, there is now a sophisticated body of research, beginning with Bruce Malina's pioneering 1981 text *The New Testament World*,[64] that uses the findings of anthropologists working in the contemporary Mediterranean to develop a setting of realistic social scenarios for interpreting the biblical texts. This work highlights issues such as honor and shame, group-oriented personality, patron and client relations, limited good, and purity concerns as central to understanding this culture. Yet this approach is heuristic, requiring close attention to the primary data and alert to the tremendous amount of cultural variation around the ancient Mediterranean. P. Horden and N. Purcell have recently subjected environmental issues, the fourth factor, to a major treatment.[65] Nor can we ignore the individuality of the communicators. For some New Testament texts, however, the Gospels for example, we know nothing, or next to nothing, about the individuality of the authors, even if we may be able to hypothesize about certain views they might have held because they belonged to particular groups. I will argue in chapters 4 and 5 that close attention to authorial intention does not entail deep psychological investigation of an author's personality.

CONCLUSION

In this chapter I have argued for the knowability of the past, in this case the biblical past. Yet such knowledge must take into account the cultural differences between the New Testament authors and us. To comprehend what they communicated to their original audiences is an exercise in intercultural understanding. We wish to understand them in their otherness, perceiving their horizon to be situated where it should be, separate from ours, with a separation that persists in spite of our conversation. To use Martin Buber's formulation, for an "I" to dialogue with a "You" entails a respect for the alterity, the radical otherness, of the other; there is no need to try to reach agreement. It is our attitude to the other that produces genuine dialogue and communion.

Yet the others that we know in this sense were the authors of texts and we know the messages they were communicating only by interpreting what they wrote. We now turn to the question of authors and authorial intention as a guide to understanding the New Testament texts.

4

THE PLACE OF NEW TESTAMENT AUTHORS IN INTERPRETATION

In the preceding chapter I argued that it was possible to understand the messages contained in the twenty-seven books of the New Testament in spite of their antiquity and their origins in a culture substantially different from ours. This brings us to the second major obstacle to communion with our ancestors in faith: these messages are embodied in the form of authored texts that arguably have literary characteristics.

Why should this matter? My aim in this book is to advocate personal interaction between the people who produced the New Testament writings and the modern readers or hearers of those works as the central and defining characteristic of specifically Christian New Testament interpretation. This requires maintaining a close link between the authors of the New Testament books and the writings themselves.

This project runs headlong against a central interest of much modern literary criticism in minimizing, or jettisoning altogether, any role for the author or authorial intention in ascertaining the meaning of a text. The most extreme exponents of this approach proclaim "the death of the author" and propound a model of reading in which the reader, and the reader alone, constructs the meaning of a text utterly indifferent to whatever meaning its author might have intended. Within such a perspective, the notion that our ancestors in faith produced the New Testament writings and that we enter into a relationship with them when we read what they wrote can have no place whatsoever.

Another reason why literary-critical modes of investigating the New Testament jar against an emphasis on the real people who wrote these documents lies in the justified interest of literary critics in the extent to which works of literature create their own quasi-autonomous imaginative worlds. Approaching a text from this perspective inevitably means reducing, and in some cases entirely eliminating, the significance of its connection with the actual world in which it was written, including both the author's intention in writing it and its impact on its first, ancient audience. To focus upon a text as having an independent existence in the realm of the imagination is to move in the direction of dehistoricizing the text and severing its connections to its creator.

Literary-critical opposition to authorial intention that derives from, especially, the dehistoricizing of texts is often found in close association with a denial that the past can yield determinate or reasonable meanings (as discussed in the preceding chapter). The reason for this is that examining documents from the past (such as New Testament texts) using the techniques of historical analysis involves attending to the meanings their authors communicated to their original audiences. This interest runs counter to literary-critical proclamations of the death of the author and the birth of the (modern) reader as the creator of textual meaning. Nevertheless, the two issues are conceptually distinct and that is why I earlier dealt with the more fundamental of the two—whether the past is knowable (a question that encompasses all sources of surviving information, including nontextual artifacts)—before now proceeding to the second question of authorial intention and the alleged character of the New Testament as literature.

It is necessary to recall that this book is oriented primarily to the way in which the New Testament can enrich contemporary Christian life, identity, and reflection, since some of my arguments have far less application outside such a framework.

My overall aim in this chapter is to argue that, when interpreted within a Christian framework, the New Testament writings are best construed as "nonliterary" rather than "literary" texts. It is, accordingly, necessary to pay close attention to the messages their authors intended to communicate in them. I certainly do not wish, however, to deny that literary interpretation of biblical texts could do service in bringing them to life for contemporary Christians. I will let others maintain that view.[1] In addition, there is clearly nothing wrong with interpreting the Bible as literature outside a context of Christian faith. My argument here is that construing the New Testament as "literary" (at least in the meaning of that term canvased in this chapter) is at odds with the model of a socio-theological communion between persons aimed at an expressly Christian use of the New Testament for which I am arguing in this volume. There are five sections to the argument. In the first section I propose that it is possible to distinguish between literary and nonliterary texts (such as the New Testament) and that the role of the author and of authorial intention is far more prominent in the latter. In particular, after having raised a question mark over the Bible's status as a "literary" text, I will discuss the debate among literary critics as to whether it is possible to distinguish literary from nonliterary texts. I then consider Wimsatt and Beardsley's seminal essay that strongly defended a definable place for the "literary" and offer a theory about the special character of the "literary" drawn from the aesthetics of Hans Georg-Gadamer, which rests on a firmer basis than his historiography. Lastly, I will introduce the views of Wolfgang Iser that corroborate and develop my construal of the literary/nonliterary distinction and conclude, in light of these arguments, by defining the character of New Testament writings as nonliterary.

In the second section I propose another approach to the literary/nonliterary distinction using the concepts "performative utterances" and "speech acts" derived from the philosophy of language. I initially set out the theory, explaining its application to literary texts, then outline its relevance to the New Testament writings.

The third section presents a critical response to two prominent exponents of the view that the author and authorial intention are irrelevant to the interpretation of texts: Roland Barthes and, in much more detail, Paul Ricoeur. I indicate generally how this critique bears upon the positive argument in subsequent chapters relating to the centrality of the voice of the New Testament's actual authors and the fact that they set down their words in written discourse.

In the fourth section I outline the reading process used to read the New Testament as a collection of nonliterary texts, but still meaningful complex structures, written in a foreign culture and therefore hard to comprehend.

I state my conclusions in the fifth section.

THE ROLE OF THE AUTHOR AND AUTHORIAL INTENTION IN LITERARY AND NONLITERARY TEXTS

The Notion That the Bible Is Literature

The notion that the Old and New Testaments constitute "literature" and are "literary" works is widespread in contemporary biblical criticism. It is an idea that is usually just assumed rather than defended or demonstrated. Thus, in his lengthy and thoughtful 1998 work on biblical interpretation, Kevin Vanhoozer assumes throughout that "*literary* knowledge [emphasis added]" of the Bible can be attained, even though on one occasion he cites a saying of

C. S. Lewis which conveys a warning against automatically reading the Bible as "literature."[2]

In part, I will critique the extent to which biblical interpreters have enthusiastically adopted literary-critical ideas and applied them to the New Testament texts without adequately considering whether these documents were actually the type of "literature" that the literary critics had in mind. Heikki Räisänen's 1990 comments on the "story world" of Mark's Gospel anticipate my discussion and conclusions: "For it will hardly be enough for the scholarly community or for the larger public to be provided with splendid analyses of NT writing as pieces of literature, each having its own story world. It is as religious documents, not as literature, that they have carried the day and come down to us."[3]

Distinguishing between Literary and Nonliterary Texts

On the one hand, two literary critics, Richard Freadman and Seumas Miller, are confident that the distinction between literary and nonliterary texts is viable:

> Clearly, there is a good deal of confusion—and indeed debate—about the term "literary"; but in practice people are generally intuitively able to identify as literary texts things like novels, poems and so on, as opposed to . . . bus tickets, railway timetables, reports of a royal commission and so on. Such acts of identification make use of a wide variety of criteria including genre, aesthetic value and so on.[4]

On the other hand, E. D. Hirsch, reacting strongly against antipathy to authorial intention in discourse properly designated "literary," asserts: "The literary text (in spite of the semimystical claims made for its uniqueness) does not have a special ontological status which somehow absolves the reader from the demands universally imposed by all linguistic texts of every description."[5] Hirsch is probably correct in insisting that *all* texts impose certain demands on readers (the need, for example, that we make an effort to understand what we are reading). Nevertheless, Freadman and Miller's insight that people are able intuitively and, one might add, pragmatically to distinguish literary texts from the other types of discourse they recognize does have the benefit of according with our everyday practice.

Yet if there is something inherently plausible about insisting that there is a difference between the process of following a recipe to bake a cake and reading a novel, what is the nature of the difference? Is it possible to suggest that there is some quality characteristic of a literary text? I will pursue this discussion by considering an essay that has come to be regarded as the clearest, classic expression of the irrelevance of authorial intention to interpreting a "literary" work.

Wimsatt and Beardsley on "The Intentional Fallacy"

In what was virtually a manifesto for the American New Criticism of the 1930s and 1940s, W. K. Wimsatt and Monroe Beardsley argued in their famous essay, "The Intentional Fallacy" (first published in 1946 but frequently reprinted), that an author's intended meaning is irrelevant to the meaning of his or her text.[6] It may be the case, as E. D. Hirsch observed, that subsequent critics have overly simplified Wimsatt and Beardsley's argument.[7] Nevertheless, their endorsement of a view that "the design or intention of the author is neither available nor desirable as a standard of judging the success of a work of literary art" certainly opened the door to those determined to apply their views systematically to the question of the author's role.[8] J. Timothy Bagwell has argued that, in retrospect, the debate this essay fomented about authorial intention is more a debate about whether there is or is not a uniquely "literary" form of expression, with Wimsatt and Beardsley being cited as prominent advocates that there is.[9] The reasonableness of this view, coupled with the suggestion that the Bible *is not* to be regarded as a "literary" text when read within an explicitly Christian context, will emerge in the ensuing argument.

There is one caveat in citing this essay: the only literary works Wimsatt and Beardsley discussed were poems. This limitation is significant in view of the exceptional nature of a poem and its evaluation as they describe it: "Judging a poem is like judging a pudding or a machine. One demands that it work. It is only because an artifact works that we infer the intention of an artificer. 'A poem should not mean but be.' A poem can only *be* through its *meaning*—since its medium is words—yet it *is*, simply *is*, in the sense that we have no excuse for inquiring what part is intended or meant."[10] In their view, poems dwell in a highly unusual world of signification divorced from both intention and meaning.

Many critics have refused to accept the idea that a poem was to be understood and interpreted in a mode divorced both from the author's intention in writing it and in relation to the poem's original historical context. The author's intention in writing as a guide to meaning has found an ardent advocate in E. D. Hirsch, while the importance of historical context for criticism is asserted in some quarters of the (admittedly diverse) movement known as the "new historicism."[11] Although Hirsch has come under heavy fire for his defense of authorial intention,[12] it is important to note the relatively modest nature of the case he makes. Hirsch does not claim access to the author's mental processes, and he emphatically denies that a text represents the author's subjective stance. Rather, the interpreter adopts a stance to make sense of the text and does the best he or she can to ensure that the stance adopted is, in all probability, the author's. Accordingly, even when a text is anonymous and we know nothing about the specific individual who produced it, "the interpreter simply makes his psychological reconstruction on the basis of fewer data." His point is especially seen in the case of a dispute about what is the most valid interpretation of a literary work; to resolve such a conflict Hirsch proposes using all available evidence to determine what the author probably intended.[13] We will see in the next chapter that this view is quite close to Schleiermacher's.

It is fortunate, however, that we can ignore this particular conundrum in modern literary theory by virtue of what Wimsatt and Beardsley said in their essay. Their statement, quoted above, concerning the character of poetry suggests that nonpoetic written discourse retains the ties to human intentionality. Although the fact is often overlooked,[14] Wimsatt and Beardsley themselves make precisely this point: "In this respect poetry differs from practical messages, which are successful if and only if we correctly infer the intention."[15] Therefore, even the most renowned opponents of the intentional fallacy grant that (authorial) intention is essential to understanding a practical message. But what does "practical" mean in such a context? The distinction between a poem and a practical message reveals Wimsatt and Beardsley's interest in firmly distinguishing between literary and nonliterary discourse. The fundamental question for this book is whether the New Testament documents are "practical messages" in this sense, where authorial intention is indispensable for the determination of meaning. Or are they poems or (expanding beyond Wimsatt and Beardsley's strictures), works of literary art which also simply *are* rather than *intending* or *meaning*. If we decide that the New Testament texts are "practical messages," Wimsatt and Beardsley's argument actually makes authorial intention indispensable. Given the cavalier way in which they are frequently cited for the contrary view, this is a rather surprising result. But what does "practical messages" mean? And is this distinction between literary and nonliterary language a valid one?

Asking the fundamental aesthetic question of whether there is something distinctive and unique about encountering a work of art, specifically a literary work of art, will guide our discussion.

Hans-Georg Gadamer on the Nature of Art and Literature

To characterize the distinctive character of the experience of a work of art, Hans-Georg Gadamer helpfully fixes on the idea of play. In play, "all those purposive relations which determine active and caring existence have not simply disappeared, but in a curious way acquire a different quality."[16] This means that play "fulfils its function only if the player loses himself in play."[17] The game is what "holds the player in its spell, draws him into play, and keeps him there."[18] He notes "the characteristic lightness and sense of relief which we find in the attitude of play" that depends on the particular character of the task set by the game and that comes from solving it.[19] On the other hand, there is a seriousness to the nature of play: someone who does not take the game seriously is a spoilsport.[20]

According to Gadamer, representation is central to the nature of play. From the huge range of examples, one thinks of the children's game "Doctors and Nurses." Just as one can say that performing a task successfully "represents" it, so also one can say "this all the more when it is a question of a game, for here the fulfilment of the task does not point to any *purposive context* [emphasis added]. Play is really limited to representing itself. Thus its mode of being is self-representation." The isolation of play, its function of allowing the players for the period of the game to enter a realm separate from the purposes and obligations of everyday life, means that one can speak of "the closed world of play." Yet since all representation is potentially representation for someone, at times play will be seen by others, as with a theatrical performance. Here the closed world, as it were, lets down one of its walls. This type of play, characteristic of all art, points beyond itself to the audience that is sharing it.[21] Thus "openness towards the spectator is part of the closedness of the play. The audience only completes what the play as such is."[22]

Gadamer calls the development in which human play finds its true perfection "art," where play is transformed into "structures" such as drama, paintings, or symphonies. It is important to note, however, that Gadamer develops his notions of play and representation as central to art by insisting upon the ontic status of all art forms and all experience of them. As Richard Palmer has pointed out, Gadamer is not suggesting that these structures that are works of art represent any form of escape from reality. "[W]hen we see a great work of art and enter its world, we do not leave home so much as 'come home.' We say at once: truly it is so! The artist has said what is . . . The legitimation of art is not that it gives aesthetic pleasure but that it reveals being."[23] "In the representation of play," writes Gadamer, "what is emerges."[24]

Or again, "From this viewpoint 'reality' is defined as what is untransformed, and art as the raising up of this reality into its truth."[25]

All this reflects Gadamer's fierce opposition to the notion of the experience of art as the gaining of aesthetic pleasure.[26] While I will return to this aspect of his theory shortly, it is enough to note that one may proffer notions of play and mimesis as central to the phenomenon of art without this ontological dimension to which Gadamer is committed. Since the time of Parmenides, philosophers have been captivated by the question of Being (*to on*).[27] Gadamer is no exception and, not surprisingly, his theory of art emphasizes the encounter with Being itself. On the other hand, other philosophers, such as Plato, have subscribed to a mimetic explanation of art without connecting art to Being. Indeed, the whole basis of Plato's dissatisfaction with art and the mimesis it embodied was precisely that it carried one too far away from the Real.[28]

Let us now return to the status of literary texts. Is Gadamer's theory, which focuses on play and representation, applicable to them? Possibly weighing against such a conclusion is that with literature "apparently there is no representation that could claim an ontological value of its own. Reading is a wholly internal event. In it there seems to be a complete detachment from all occasion and contingency, as in, for example, public reading or performance."[29] But Gadamer has a reasonable answer to this, namely, that literary art, such as a novel, has its original existence in being read as much as an epic has in being declaimed by a rhapsodist or a picture being viewed by a spectator. Accordingly, to "be read is an essential part of the literary work of art, like a public reading or a performance."[30]

When we read a poem or a novel, it is the case, just as with play (as described by Gadamer), that "all those purposive relations which determine active and caring existence have not simply disappeared, but in a curious way acquire a different quality."[31] There is clearly a transformation of the everyday world of experience of action and obligation into a mimetic form (the literary text) that draws upon those realities yet transmutes them into an entity of a different character. Being immersed in a novel, for example, does bear strong similarities to the experience of being temporarily withdrawn from the mundane world of purpose and responsibility that characterizes play or the time during which one gazes upon an accomplished painting or sculpture.

Here we have, therefore, a useful guide to the nature of a literary work of art. Literature takes those who read or hear it out of the purposive context of their everyday lives and places them firmly in an imaginative and self-contained realm where their experience will be the same as or similar to that of play. None of this is to deny that literature (just like a game such as

"Doctors and Nurses") feeds on real experience and represents some aspects of it. Nevertheless, those dimensions of actual experience that are in some way reflected in a literary work are thoroughly transformed and integrated into a new and entirely different entity. By contrast, returning to Wimsatt and Beardsley's terminology, all other forms of written discourse constitute "practical messages."

Yet one dimension of Gadamer's approach to literary works of art does not readily secure assent. This is his suggestion that "[l]iterature as an art-form can be understood only from the ontology of the work of art, and not from the aesthetic experiences that occur in the course of the reading."[32] This view, which again reflects the philosopher Gadamer's valorization of Being in his approach to art, is indefensible as a statement applicable to all artistic works, including literary texts. While some artistic productions do have the effect of inducing in their viewers a sense that they have touched the springs of ultimate reality, this is not a universally valid generalization. In particular, Gadamer's opposition to aesthetic consciousness and, indeed, to the notion of escape from reality is inappropriate in the case of many forms of art, such as light operettas and many novels, for example. Does anyone really believe that, when we attend a fine performance of Franz Lehar's *The Merry Widow* or read a Sherlock Holmes detective novel, we enter the domain of Being itself, come face-to-face with *to on*?

Wolfgang Iser on the Literary/Nonliterary Distinction

Other literary-critical theorists have expressed similar views about the differences between literary and nonliterary texts. Thus Wolfgang Iser, in a widely accepted formulation, encapsulates the uniqueness of "literary" texts by suggesting that they "do not correspond to any objective reality outside themselves."[33] He argues that the sentences of a literary work come together to produce a particular world.[34] Developing his views (derived from Husserl's phenomenology) based on an understanding of a person's inner consciousness of time, Iser argues that as a reader encounters the sentences in a literary work the reader forms an expectation of what is to come. But the work continually forces the reader to modify these expectations. Literary works continually surprise rather than confirm expectations. This leads him to suggest:

> Strangely enough, we feel that any confirmative effect—such as we implic-
> itly demand of expository texts, as we refer to the objects they are meant to
> present—is a defect in a literary text. For the more a text individualizes or
> confirms an expectation it has initially aroused, the more aware we become

of its didactic purpose, so that at best we can only accept or reject the thesis forced upon us. More often than not, the very clarity of such texts will make us want to free ourselves from their clutches.[35]

Iser's formulation suggests a further way to encapsulate the literary/nonliterary distinction. Nonliterary texts are expository and didactic, and seek to maintain a particular a thesis. Literary texts, on the other hand, are not didactic and do not seek to offer persuasive reasons for a particular thesis; rather, they create a particular world with horizons that are continually modified as they develop. Admittedly, some literary works, for example, novels such as Charles Dickens's *Hard Times* or John Steinbeck's *The Grapes of Wrath*, draw upon, and alert their readers to, larger social and political problems of pressing importance. Yet in such cases the novel is not just a veneer for what is really a pamphlet by the author pressing his or her readers to accept a particular point of view on these problems. If this were the case, as Iser has said, we would soon wish to free ourselves from the clutches of such a "novel." A novel like *The Grapes of Wrath* will exist and, hopefully, succeed as a novel, to be judged as such, not as a vehicle for the transmission of a didactic purpose or program. Nonliterary texts, on the other hand, plainly point to issues beyond their pages and seek to impel their readers toward them, either by providing information or by arguing a case. This is the very reason for their existence. Such nonliterary texts, again, seem to be very similar to the "practical messages" spoken of by Wimsatt and Beardsley, which are inevitably caught up in human intentionality.

At this point it is worth bringing the concept of fiction into the picture. Clearly, there is a distinction between literature and fiction. That not all literature is fictional is revealed in the existence of works such as James Boswell's *Life of Johnson* or Samuel Pepys's *Diaries*. One could also envisage a piece of fiction of such poor quality as not to achieve the status of literature. The defining characteristic of literature is that it possesses certain kinds of aesthetic qualities, not that it is fictional. In spite of all this, fictional works constitute a central (perhaps the central) category of literature.[36] Literary works that are fictional most fully exemplify the exposition of literature given above as producing a mode of experience fundamentally separated from mundane existence.

The New Testament Writings as Nonliterary Texts

On the basis of the above arguments, one can mount a strong case for the "nonliterary" nature of the New Testament writings when one reads them as contributing to Christian life and reflection. We must initially acknowledge the diversity of genres in this corpus, while noting that the epistolary form is by far the best represented, comprising twenty-one of the twenty-seven documents and about one-third of its total length. Thus, there are seven letters universally agreed to be by Paul (Romans, 1 and 2 Corinthians, Galatians, Philippians, 1 Thessalonians, and Philemon) and six more attributed (probably wrongly) to him but certainly written by other first- or early-second-century Christ-followers (Ephesians, Colossians, 2 Thessalonians, 1 and 2 Timothy, and Titus). There is a letter attributed to a certain James; two attributed to Peter; three to John; one to a certain Jude (the brother of one James); and a document loosely in letter form (Hebrews). In addition there are four Gospels (Matthew, Mark, Luke, and John), a historical narrative (the Acts of the Apostles), and an apocalypse (the book of Revelation). I will return to this issue in more detail in chapter 7. I will now further develop the idea that the New Testament documents are nonliterary texts by using the concepts "performative utterances" and "speech act theory" derived from the philosophy of language.

THE LITERARY AND THE NONLITERARY IN LIGHT OF PERFORMATIVE UTTERANCES AND SPEECH ACT THEORY

As stated above in relation to the views of Wimsatt and Beardsley on the meaning of "literary," one can posit a class of texts that are "nonliterary," in which discerning authorial intention is essential to understanding their meaning. What is the exact nature of "nonliterary" texts? It was suggested above that these texts differ from literary texts in not providing an experience removed from the actual conditions of life and in not providing a sense of lightness and relief characteristic of play. Rather, they correspond and refer to some object of reality outside themselves, which they either explain or argue a particular thesis about; thus they are "expository" or "didactic." We can now develop these insights by discussing the theory of speech acts, a theory that highlights the way language can achieve particular effects.

J. L. Austin's Speech Act Theory

It is only in the last half century that philosophers and other theorists of language have begun paying adequate attention to the fact that written statements do more than simply describe a state of affairs, or state some fact (either truly or falsely). Some statements actually *do* something, they *effect a result*, they *perform an act*. Recognition of the importance of such statements dates back to British philosopher J. L. Austin's series of lectures given at Harvard University in 1955 and published posthumously in 1962.

Austin called statements that did something "performatives" and statements that merely stated something "constatives." As typical performatives he offered cases such as: "I do take this woman to be my lawful wedded wife" (uttered in the course of a valid ceremony of marriage); "I name this ship *Queen Elizabeth*" (uttered when smashing a bottle of champagne against the bow); "I give and bequeath this watch to my brother" (in a will); and "I bet you sixpence it will rain tomorrow."[37]

Yet the class of performatives is much broader than these specific examples. Although it is difficult to produce an economical definition of performative statements, Austin identified a number of factors that usually characterized them. Quite commonly, for example, there is something that is *"at the moment of uttering being done by the person uttering* [Austin's emphasis]."[38] In addition, performatives are reducible to a verb in the first person singular present indicative active; thus the word "Guilty" is equivalent to "I deem, pronounce you guilty."[39] Examples of such performatives include: I thank, I apologize, I criticize, I censure, I approve, I bid you welcome, and I congratulate.[40] Other examples include utterances that constitute advice, urgings, warnings, orders, proclamations, or undertakings.[41]

One type of performative, particularly important to this book's argument, is what Austin calls the "expositive" performative. "Here the main body of an utterance has generally or often the straightforward form of a 'statement,' but there is an explicit performative at its head which shows how the 'statement' is to be fitted into the context of conversation, interlocution, dialogue, or in general of exposition." He supplies a number of examples, including "I argue (or urge) that there is no backside to the moon" and "I conclude (or infer) that there is no backside to the moon."[42] This means that, for example, a statement, within a story, that indicates the story is told to a make certain point or produce a certain result is a performative. Anticipating my argument below, the following statement from John's Gospel is an explicit expositive performative and indicates that his Gospel has a performative purpose: "but these things are written that you may believe that Jesus is the Christ, the Son of God, and that believing you may have life in his name" (20:31; RSV). Another example from the Gospels is Luke 1:1-4.

Austin argues that the words in performative statements must be spoken seriously and taken seriously. Thus someone who utters one "must not be joking, for example, nor writing a poem."[43] Residing in this observation is the recognition that poems are, by nature, nonperformative. In addition, performative utterances are to be understood as issued in ordinary circumstances. A performative statement employed by an actor in a soliloquy or in a poem would be hollow or void. Such an utterance is not used seriously but is parasitic upon normal use—it represents an etiolation, an enfeeblement of language.[44] Elsewhere he notes that such etiolation occurs when we use speech "in acting, fiction and poetry, quotation and recitation."[45]

Austin further categorized speech acts. He referred to the mere act *of* saying something with a certain sense and reference as the performance of a "locutionary act."[46] But when a statement had the additional force of being the performance of an act *in* saying something, he described it as an "illocutionary act."[47] Performative statements are thus subsumed under the category "illocutionary." When, third, a statement produced certain effects upon the feelings, thoughts, or actions of the audience, and the statement's effects were intentional, he classified it as a "perlocutionary act."[48]

He further notes that an illocutionary act will not be happily or successfully performed unless a certain effect has been achieved.[49] "I cannot be said to have warned an audience unless it hears what I say and takes what I say in a certain sense."[50] Austin distinguishes a number of types of illocutionary effects, of which two are especially pertinent. The first amounts to ensuring that the audience understands the meaning and force of the locution; a result Austin describes as "the securing of uptake." The second consists of inviting a response. The consequences of a statement beyond these effects are perlocutionary. A perlocutionary act may be either the achievement of a "perlocutionary object" (such as convincing or persuading) or the production of a "perlocutionary sequel." Thus an act of warning may be understood by an audience (illocutionary act), who are alerted in consequence (perlocutionary object) or even alarmed (perlocutionary sequel).[51]

A significant problem with Austin's methodology was that he sometimes developed his terms so finely that they lost any distinctive meaning, typically because the exceptions he discovered tended to swallow the normative class, and he had to abandon them.[52] One example is that Austin came to regard all utterances as performative. Nevertheless, G. J. Warnock has defended Austin against himself in this regard, by accurately pointing out that while there is a sense in which all utterances are performative, this does not mean that the special character of Austin's original sense of "performative statements" has been lost. Austin was not thinking at first of linguistic acts. Austin's original performatives were those where to make the utterance was to *do* something, in virtue of *conventions*, which meant that *to say* certain things was *to do* them. No such convention exists in relation to all speech acts generally.[53] I argue that, within the framework of early Christian writing, such a convention is announced in the words of John 20:31: "But these things are written that you may believe that Jesus is the Christ, the Son of God, and that believing you may have life in his name." There was a convention in force among the leaders of the early Christ-movement that they spoke or inscribed their speech within an accepted and conventional socioreligious framework where these speech acts were meant to produce or maintain faith in their audiences—and no doubt very often did. That is: "If the evangelist says Christ is the Son of God, and you believe, then you will have life in his name."

John Searle's Elaboration of Speech Act Theory

During the course of his 1955 Harvard lectures Austin also used the expression "speech act" as a general designation for his theory of language and its uses. [54] Others, John Searle in particular, have further developed this theory under the rubric of "speech acts." [55] Two aspects of Searle's development of the theory require comment in relation to the argument to follow.

First, Searle reduced the scope of the language that Austin classified as "constative" by insisting that making a statement was "as much performing an illocutionary act as making a promise, a bet, a warning or what have you." This led him to opine: "Any utterance will consist in performing one or more illocutionary acts." [56] On its face, this seems to make the category of "illocutionary" so broad as to denude it of meaning; the "constative" aspect of language seems to disappear and sometimes, as we will see below, Searle himself falls into this trap. Searle is in danger of losing sight of Austin's original insight that (as Warnock has noted) sometimes there are conventions in force that turn an utterance into an action. However, by "statement" Searle mainly intends that form of utterance that he calls *assertive*. The point of this type of utterance is "to commit the speaker (in varying degrees) to something's being the case, to the truth of the expressed proposition." [57] It serves to "tell people how things are." [58] Assertives are either true or false. Such an utterance does indeed do something—it establishes a link between the speaker and a particular state of affairs. Searle notes that assertives like this actually include the utterances that Austin referred to as "expositives," such as "conclude" and "deduce," since words like this involve the speaker stating a view (which is either true or false) on the rest of an utterance's character.

Second, Searle's taxonomy of illocutionary acts is generally more developed than Austin's. In addition to assertives, Searle distinguished a number of other categories. He defines *directives* as attempts by the speaker to get the hearer to do or not do something, which covers the initiation and avoidance of action and the adoption or abandonment of a particular view (as indicated by verbs such as "ask," "order," "command," "request," "beg," "plead," "pray," "entreat," and also "invite," "permit" and "advise," "dare," "defy," and "challenge"). *Commissives* commit the speaker to some future course of action; examples are "promise," "pledge," and "vow." *Expressives* are speech acts expressing a psychological condition in relation to a state of affairs and included verbs such as "thank," "congratulate," "apologize," "condole," "deplore," and "welcome." *Declarations* are speech acts that brought about some alteration in the status or condition of the object referred to solely by the successful performance of the utterance; they included "You're fired" and "I resign."[59]

Armed with this theory of performative utterances, we now return to the "practical," "didactic," and "expository" character of nonliterary discourse. Although this theory has been formulated primarily in relation to spoken discourse, it applies equally to written discourse. From this point onwards we will mainly be concerned with written texts. Based on the above discussion, we now state the following pair of theses:

a.   Nonliterary texts are predominantly performative, illocutionary, and perlocutionary in character; and

b.   Literary texts are predominantly nonperformative and locutionary in character.

The basic rationale for this proposal is that nonliterary texts maintain various types of direct relationship with the actual world of lived experience. As we have seen above, Austin himself recognized that performative utterances embodied a particular kind of seriousness in relation to the world of everyday experience and routine (by way of contrast to poems, which represented the etiolation of language).

Whether the text consists of an assertive (stating something true or false about some state of affairs), a directive (seeking to get the addressees of the text to do something), a commissive (whereby the author promises or vows to do something), an expressive (where the author expresses some psychological state in connection with a statement to certain existing persons), a declaration (where the author changes some state of affairs merely by a written statement), or some combination of any or all of the above, it has a direct link with real people (either as authors or audience) and the real world beyond its pages. In many, if not most, cases performative writing of this type will be successful if it produces a perlocutionary sequel. It is difficult, moreover, to conceive of a performative utterance that is not an expression of someone's purpose and intention. All of these cases, therefore, appear to be "practical messages," some expository, some didactic.

When we now confront literary texts, we can suggest that their character, transporting their readers from the world of everyday experience to the continually surprising and imagined realms they create, is encapsulated in the concepts of the nonperformative and the locutionary. We recall that Wimsatt and Beardsley characterized a poem as something that simply *is*. A poem is not an instrument for doing something else. Let us consider the opening stanza of W. B. Yeats's poem "The Wild Swans at Coole":

> The trees are in their autumn beauty,
> The woodland paths are dry,
> Under the October twilight the water
> Mirrors a still sky;
> Upon the brimming water among the stones
> Are nine-and-fifty swans.

There is no assertive here, for it is a matter of no consequence whether the poet has described a real scene or not. Nor does the poem contain a directive (a speech act urging the reader to do or avoid doing something, to subscribe to a view or lay one aside). Nor does it harbor a commissive, an expressive, or a declaration. Even if Yeats had never visited Coole Park, or even if it and its swans had never existed, this would make no difference to the status and integrity of this poem. The poem exists in an imaginary universe separated from daily life, with its cluster of human purposes and intentions. It is purely constative, purely locutionary, purely nonperformative.

Although this case is best made in relation to lyric poems, the same position obtains in respect to a novel. It is not in the nature of a novel to be a means by which the novelist does something else with respect to the real world, such as arguing a thesis. Like a poem, a novel simply is. When we read a novel, we enter its imagined and autonomous literary universe and enjoy an aesthetic experience that has strong affinities with play, even if the novelist has drawn upon, and reminds the reader of, particularly painful aspects of social life in creating that literary universe, as Steinbeck does in *The Grapes of Wrath*.

In a frequently cited essay, "The Logical Status of Fictional Discourse," John Searle argues unconvincingly how fiction and speech act theory overlap.[60] He begins by saying: "I believe that speaking or writing in a language consists in performing speech acts of a quite specific kind called 'illocutionary acts.'"[61] Here we observe his worrying tendency to discover illocutionary acts in every utterance. Accordingly, when he confronts the question of the status of fictional discourse, he simply assumes that it, too, is illocutionary. He then seeks to find some way of resolving the "paradox" that although we usually accept the truth of statements about how things are ("assertives"), in fiction such statements are not "true" because the characters they refer to are nonexistent. His answer, largely accepted by Richard Freadman and Seumas Miller, is that these statements are just *pretended* and not *actually asserted*.[62] Yet Searle's theory really rests on a false premise, namely, that a work of fiction is itself illocutionary. This would mean that a novelist writing a novel was setting out to achieve one or more of the illocutionary acts that Searle has helpfully taxonomized. Yet the only plausible candidate is an assertive, consisting of a statement about how things actually are, that is either true or false. But fiction, by definition, cannot have such a quality. It is a work of imagination, not a description of the real world. That is to say, fiction, of its very nature, is constative and locutionary. The novelist is not seeking to *do* something by writing a novel; like a poem, a novel *is*. Thus Searle has been led into an entirely false dilemma and is concerned with a paradox that does not exist.

Richard Ohmann has set out a much more satisfactory integration of speech acts and literature. He aims to define a "literary work," by which he means works of "imaginative literature": novels, plays, and poems in particular. He assumes that the concept of literature is reasonably sharp and "that there are necessary conditions, at least of a loose sort, associated with it."[63] His proposal is quite close to Austin's idea that poetry is an etiolated form of language. He defines (imaginative) literature in this way: "[A] *literary work is a discourse abstracted, or detached, from the circumstances and conditions which make illocutionary acts possible; hence it is a discourse without illocutionary force.*"[64] He then further develops this definition by introducing the element of pretense and mimesis. The author "pretends to report discourse, and the reader accepts the pretense": "*A literary work is a discourse whose sentences lack the illocutionary forces that would normally attach to them. Its illocutionary force is* mimetic. By 'mimetic,' I mean purportedly imitative. Specifically, a literary work *purportedly imitates* (or reports) a series of speech acts, which in fact have no other existence."[65] By this definition Ohmann is also able to account for and incorporate, among others, the two definitions of literature discussed above. First, literature is play. The various sentences in a literary work lack their usual force. "A literary work is a series of acts without consequences, and a release from the tension that normally attends speech acts . . . In this sense, he [the reader] comes to the work with esthetic detachment." Second, literature is autonomous, meaning that it "has an exemption from the normal connections between discourse and the world outside discourse."[66]

Ohmann's proposal has two advantages: It sticks closely to the original insight involved in Austin's distinction between language that actually *did* something in the real world and language that did not. It also produces an economical approach to the question consonant with other ways of characterizing literature. In these respects his position compares favorably with Mary Louise Pratt's alternative theory, which is heavily critical of Ohmann.[67] One of Pratt's criticisms is that Ohmann's proposal reduces "literature" to "fiction." Given the prominence of fiction, however, this still gives Ohmann's theory a wealth of material to work with. Although "literature" does cover other types of writing, such as high-quality biographies, fiction does comprise a large proportion of literature.

What bearing does Ohmann's integration of speech act theory and literature have on biblical interpretation? In 1988 Hugh White edited an issue of *Semeia* devoted to precisely this question.[68] The closest any of the contributors came to the connection I make here was White's statement in response to Ohmann: "This approach to literature might reveal why Biblical narrative seems never completely at home within the category of literature, since the act of writing sacred scripture cannot be understood as mimetic in this sense. Speech acts such as the promise of land, or the Sinai covenant, claim to be real world speech acts, in some sense, and not parasitic."[69]

Yet there is a more fundamental way of applying Ohmann's formulation of literature and speech act theory to the Bible, the New Testament in particular—our focus in this volume. Put simply, the authors responsible for the New Testament were trying to *do* something with their writings. While there are various ways of putting this, it is probably enough to say that they were all trying to encourage their readers to adopt a particular stance to God's irruption into the world that they believed had taken place in the life, death, and resurrection of Jesus Christ. The New Testament writers were all trying to persuade their audiences, mostly listeners, to have faith in Jesus as the Christ, God's anointed for the salvation of the world. Such is the case whether they wrote letters, where this appears most clearly, or Gospels, where it appears explicitly (Luke 1:1-4 and John 20:31) or by necessary implication (Mark and Matthew). Their authorial intention gave their compositions an unambiguous illocutionary and even perlocutionary character. In particular, all of these documents constitute what Searle calls "assertives" and Austin referred to as "expositives," meaning that the speaker is stating a view (here asserted to be true) concerning the character of the rest of an utterance. By whatever form of utterance employed, its purpose was to do something, namely, to encourage its recipients to have faith in Jesus Christ as the exalted Lord. Therefore, the biblical texts do not constitute literature as defined by Ohmann. Their illocutionary force is not mimetic but real. Plainly, however, this reality is more readily acceptable when someone reads these texts within a Christian framework.

THE DEATH OF THE AUTHOR?

Roland Barthes and the Death of the Reader

During the 1960s and 1970s structuralism became a significant mode of inquiry, mainly in linguistics, literary criticism, and anthropology, and especially at the hands of French theorists. Its proponents advocated and sought to discover the "deep structures" that underlie and generate observable phenomena. This focus of structuralism excluded the conscious and purposive actions of individuals and social groups as a means to explain human behavior. It is helpful to situate Roland Barthes within this wider context of structuralism. Brian Stock has made the following observation:

> An important principle in structuralism, emphasized by Barthes, is the separation of the author and authorial intentions from the text that results from the act of writing. The text may thus be seen to have a set of depersonalized relations with other texts, and all texts, including historical ones, are placed on an equal footing. In semiotics, a similar goal is achieved by a different route, since there is no valid way of distinguishing between the historical and literary use of signs.[70]

Later he adds that "structuralism desubjectivized literary experience."[71] Yet this had the following result: "[B]y demoting authorship, structuralism also weakened the tentatively established connections between literature and society and took the entire debate one step away from the living world of utterance, discourse, and action." He attributes this move in France to a the perceived failure of the Marxist sociology of knowledge during the 1950s. "The leading proponents seemed to say: if social relations cannot be revealed through texts, then we will study the properties of texts for their own sake and pretend we are studying society."[72]

Perhaps one can situate the common notion of "the death of the author" in the distinction between artistic/literary and nonartistic/nonliterary texts. Thus Roland Barthes begins a frequently cited essay, "The Death of the Author," by citing a statement concerning a character that appears in a story by Balzac and then asking, "Who is speaking thus?" meaning in what sense can the statement be Balzac's. He views the question as unanswerable: "We shall never know, for the good reason that writing is the destruction of every voice, of every point of origin. Writing is that neutral, composite oblique space where our subject slips away, the negative where all identity is lost, starting with the very identity of the body writing." A little further on he states that as soon as a fact is narrated "this disconnection occurs, the voice loses its origin, the author enters into his own death, writing begins."[73] One's initial reaction to this might be the thought that there is no generalization so hyperbolic, so absurd, but that some modern critic will be found to give it utterance in a form that is both gnomic and even elegant. On reflection, however, it appears that Barthes's pronouncement is restricted to the authors of novels and poems. Perhaps in texts such as these we find "a multi-dimensional space in which a variety of writings, none of them original, blend and clash."[74] Once the author is removed, the notion that one could decipher a text becomes futile. "In the multiplicity of writing, everything is to be disentangled, nothing deciphered."[75] For a text "is made of multiple writings, drawn from many cultures and entering into mutual relations of dialogue, parody, contestation, but there is one place where this multiplicity is focused and that place is the reader, not, as was hitherto said, the author."[76] That this view applies even to fiction has been strongly disputed by Freadman and Miller.[77] Yet how can it be thought to apply to nonfictional works? Did Barthes, for example, seriously expect and look forward to the readers of this essay treating whatever he intended by it with the same insouciance to authorial intention as he celebrated in the novel? Did he really apply such disciplined thought to the subject merely so as to provide fodder for a frenzy of postulations of meaning by multiple and competing readers disconnected from his own intentions? Hardly.

Paul Ricoeur: Interpretation as Depersonalization

THE SUPPLANTED AUTHOR

In an essay entitled "Language as Discourse" in his 1976 work *Interpretation Theory: Discourse and the Surplus of Meaning*, Paul Ricoeur argued that all texts inevitably became detached from the author and the author's meaning by time and distance.[78] If Ricoeur was correct, it would be difficult to maintain the thesis of this book that construes New Testament interpretation—within a Christian perspective—as tied to an encounter with the real people who composed the twenty-seven writings in the corpus, twenty-one of which are letters or written in epistolary form. Although the ideas in this book have been widely influential, Ricoeur's position is fundamentally flawed. By critiquing it here,

I will both answer an objection to my case and develop it further in dialogue with Ricoeur's challenging proposal.[79]

Ricoeur builds upon the fundamental distinction drawn by Ferdinand de Saussure in *Cours de linguistique général* between *langue* (the synchronic structural system of language) and *parole* (a linguistic event utilizing that system).[80] Then he suggests that discourse is the *event* of language.[81] He argues that there is a dialectical relation between event and meaning. All discourse is event, since it represents an occasion on which "our linguistic competence actualizes itself in performance." By "meaning" he has in mind that in one and the same sentence we have an intertwining and interplay between the functions of identification (the subject of the sentence) and predication.[82] This allows him to propose: "*If all discourse is actualized as an event, all discourse is understood as meaning* [Ricoeur's emphasis]."[83]

This formulation is the device by which Ricoeur seeks to eliminate the speaker from his or her discourse. For to mean is both what the speaker means (= utterer's meaning) and what the sentence means (= utterance meaning). The event is somebody speaking.[84] But we must avoid reducing the utterer's meaning to a mere psychological intention. Since the meaning can only be found in the utterance itself, "the utterer's meaning has its mark in the utterance meaning."[85] Then Ricoeur asks, How does this occur? In effect, he treats the speaker as a fiction of the discourse. Any personal pronouns "have no objective meaning" and an "I" in the discourse is not a concept: "It has a new meaning each time it is used and each time it refers to a singular subject. 'I' is the one who in speaking applies to himself the word 'I' which appears in the sentence as a logical subject." By this he means that the reader of a piece of discourse in first person singular must displace the original referent of the "I" as intended by the speaker. The result is that "we are able to give a nonpsychological, because purely semantic, definition of the utterer's meaning. No mental entity need be hypothesized or hypostasized."[86] Thus every subsequent reader simply supplants the author from having any role in the "I" voice of his or her discourse. Ricoeur is running a theory of reading as colonization.

While the notion that readers displace and disenfranchise authors has ethical implications, it is also necessary to see if Ricoeur's theory does accurately describe what happens; in other words, it must be tested against various types of discourse. We will begin with the most promising type for Ricoeur, the lyric poem. This was, after all, the literary form relied upon by Wimsatt and Beardsley to substantiate their point about the irrelevance of the author and of authorial meaning and intention in the interpretation of literature. To test the worth of Ricoeur's view we need a lyric poem delivered in the first person singular. Accordingly, let us return to Yeats's "The Wild Swans at Coole." An "I" voice appears in the second line of the second stanza and continues in the third (to reappear in the last stanza):

> The nineteenth autumn has come upon me
> Since I first made my count;
> I saw, before I had well finished,
> All suddenly mount
> And scatter wheeling in great broken rings
> Upon their clamorous wings.
>
> I have looked upon those brilliant creatures,
> And now my heart is sore.
> All's changed since I, hearing at twilight,
> The first time on this shore,
> The bell-beat of their wings above my head,
> Trod with a lighter tread.

It is arguably possible to interpret the "I" voice in these stanzas as Ricoeur suggests, so that the "I" is "the one who in speaking applies to himself the word 'I.'" If those reading the poem knew nothing at all about Yeats, perhaps they would take it that way, and read the poem as containing a universal message about the transience and sadness of human life set against the unchanging beauty and energy of the natural world. Or would they? Is it not artificial to suppose that anyone reading this poem could totally appropriate the "I" voice and ignore the signs of a real person's actual experience that presses with such power against the language? In this case, the reader would step into the "I" voice knowing that this process was only possible because real human experience prompted the poem's creation. We can make this point even more strongly if we assume that someone setting out to read the poem did know the basic details of Yeats's biography within the larger tragedy of Ireland in the first quarter of the twentieth century. How could such a reader entirely remove the poet from the "I" voice in this poem, given the probable references to his life contained in it? In this case, the reader steps into the "I" voice, but only in the company of the remarkable person who composed the poem. Since we nearly always know the identity and something of the life of lyric poets, this experience of sharing the "I" voice with the poet is the most common mode of reading lyric poetry, from the early Greek lyric poet Archilochus (seventh century BCE) onwards.

This brief analysis reveals that Ricoeur's theory is fundamentally flawed in relation to the form of discourse that seemed most compatible to it. And

I could have made things a lot harder for him by choosing a lyric poem where the autobiographical sense is more present than in "The Wild Swans at Coole." Thomas Wyatt's "They fle from me that sometyme did me seke," for example! But what if the discourse in question has some other character?

Let us assume, for example, that it is an actual letter, inscribed with its date and place of composition, from a real, named person to other real, named persons requesting them to do something—as from a young man at university to his parents seeking an urgent infusion of funds. In such a case, it is untenable, even absurd, to maintain that the "I"-voice in the letter has no objective meaning, that it changes each time the letter is read, or that no mental entity need be hypothesized or hypostasized. This applies to the first time the young man's parents read the letter, but also to any subsequent occasion of reading, since anyone reading it would be struck by its indelible stamp of a real individual facing a real dilemma.[87] Thus, not only does Ricoeur's vision of reading as a process wherein the reader supplants the "I" voice installed in the text by the author falter before its most promising example, lyric poetry, but it fails entirely when confronted with so typical a feature of human discourse as a letter.

The subsequent parts of this chapter confirm the extent to which Ricoeur is bent on depersonalizing the act of interpretation. Toward the end of his essay, he expresses his aim as being to release hermeneutics from its "psychological and existential prejudices." He is against understanding interpretation as being the task "to understand an author better than he understood himself."[88] Although he cites no source for that dictum, his immediately prior reference to Schleiermacher and Dilthey makes clear that they are the alleged bearers of such a view, a point expressly made by Vanhoozer about Schleiermacher.[89] As we will see in the next chapter, however, Schleiermacher has been profoundly misunderstood. Ricoeur here perpetuates a myth that Schleiermacher proposed that we understand a text by getting inside the mind of the author. This is, indeed, the charge leveled against all "Romantic hermeneutics" with a frequency inversely proportional to attempts to justify it in relation to primary sources. We will see in the next chapter how alien this notion was to the hermeneutics of Schleiermacher, who was interested in what an utterance meant, not what was happening in the subjective consciousness or unconsciousness of the person who produced it.

The extent of Ricoeur's efforts to depersonalize interpretation also emerges in his remarkably bleak understanding of the nature of writing, to which we now turn.

Writing as the Dehumanization of Discourse

A central part of Ricoeur's argument is the distinction he claims exists between speaking and writing.[90] The "problem of writing," he asserts, "is identical to that of the fixation of discourse in some exterior bearer, whether it be stone, papyrus, or paper, which is other than the human voice. This inscription, substituted for the immediate vocal, physiognomic, or gestural expression, is in itself a tremendous cultural achievement. *The human fact disappears* [Ricoeur's emphasis]. Now material 'marks' convey the message."[91]

It is not easy to see how anyone could seriously entertain such a view. Ricoeur is proposing that *the human dimension of a discourse is not conveyed by its contents!* A single example will suffice to reveal its implausibility. If Ricoeur were correct on this, it would follow that the "human fact" is present in a young woman saying to a young man, "I love you," but has disappeared in a letter she sends him bearing exactly the same words! Sometimes, indeed, as in the case of a love letter, the effect of writing may be to intensify the personal dimension (which is why couples whose relationship seems to be flagging are often advised to write love letters to one another). Ricoeur wants to say that merely consigning a message to writing depersonalizes its contents, even though it quite obviously does no such thing. Here, then, we have a major objection to this theory. Flying in the face of reality, Ricoeur construes (and celebrates?) writing as a technology for the dehumanization and hence depersonalization of discourse.

Equally problematic is his notion that what writing actually fixes "is the noema of the act of speaking, the meaning of the speech event, not the event as event."[92] This is unpersuasive for the reason that much written discourse is eloquent about the circumstances that helped produce it, both the event and what was said and done.

Ricoeur further suggests that the situation of message and speaker is radically altered when writing intrudes on the scene. This is allegedly because in spoken discourse "the speaker belongs to the situation of interlocution . . . the subjective intention of the speaker and the discourse's meaning overlap each other in such a way that it is the same thing to understand what the speaker means and what his discourse means . . . With written discourse, however, the author's intention and the meaning of the text cease to coincide."[93] Once again, the view is implausible in its unrealistic dichotomization of spoken and written discourse. Ricoeur seems to have forgotten how often *speakers* fail to say what they mean or are misheard or misunderstood by their audience—as in the Sermon on the Mount scene in the film *The Life of Brian*, where someone at the back of the crowd mishears Jesus to say "Blessed are the cheese-makers." There is no basis here for drawing a sharp distinction between spoken and written discourse.

There is also no evidence whatever offered for the last statement: "With written discourse, however, the author's intention and the meaning of the text cease to coincide." To the extent that this depends on his previous argument, we have seen that this does not work even for lyric poetry, and has no application at all for letters.

The dizzy sense of unreality that accompanies Ricoeur's understanding of all written discourse becomes even more pronounced in the following statement:

> Inscription becomes synonymous with the semantic autonomy of the text, which results from the disconnection of the mental intention of the author from the verbal meaning of the text, of what the author meant and what the text means. The text's career escapes the finite horizon lived by its author. What the text means now matters more than what the author meant when he wrote it.[94]

While a text may certainly acquire new meanings in new situations, the extent to which it has escaped from the horizon of its creator is not answered by a totalizing theory such as this about the almost miraculous effects of writing (from which Ricoeur would no doubt exempt his own works). Instead one must consider the type of text it was in the first place. Many texts will stubbornly carry with them the markings of their origin, purpose, and intention and that dimension of their meaning, where later readers pay attention to it, necessarily intrudes upon how they are interpreted.

"Whereas spoken discourse," Ricoeur tells us, "is addressed to someone who is determined in advance by the dialogical situation—it is addressed to you, the second person—a written text is addressed to an unknown reader and potentially to whoever knows how to read." He describes this as "the universalization of the audience" and says that by it "discourse is liberated from the narrowness of the face-to-face situation."[95]

I will note merely in passing that Ricoeur's suggestion that face-to-face discourse represents a form of "narrowness" suggests he harbors fundamental views about the nature of the person that are light-years away from Martin Buber's centrality of the I-You relationship to the experience of being human. The "face-to-face" situation is not narrow; it is, as explained in chapter 2, the dynamic where we discover and express our humanity. At a more pragmatic level of argument, it is clear that only some texts (in particular, literary ones, like poems and novels) are addressed to unknown readers. Many others, letters especially, are addressed to known persons. He also misses the fact that in societies where most people are illiterate a letter addressed to a group of people will be heard and not read. In addition, many other texts are written to a known audience. This was explicitly the case with Luke's Gospel in relation to Theophilus (see 1:1-4) and also for the community to whom Luke first published the text and among whom he almost certainly lived. The Fourth Gospel was also almost certainly directed to a known group of people in the first instance, the "you" of John 20:31, even though the text no doubt achieved a wider circulation subsequently. Matthew ends his Gospel with an injunction from Jesus to the eleven disciples (those remaining after the defection of Judas) to go forth and make disciples of all nations, baptizing them in the name of the Father and the Son and the Holy Spirit and teaching them to observe all his commandments (Matt 28:19-20). It is difficult not to believe that Matthew's immediate audience would have understood that these words (and the whole Gospel which they conclude) were directed to them.

Ricoeur is clearly delighted with this alleged phenomenon of inscription producing the semantic autonomy of the text—describing it as a liberation from "the narrowness of the face-to-face situation." But what is wrong with writing which fulfills an important function in the maintenance of actual interpersonal relationships, especially in the inscription of a process where "one heart speaks to another"?[96] For many people this would redound to the honor of writing, but for Ricoeur it represents its bondage! For him writing facilitates a desirable flight from personal engagement. While I will not speculate on why he should hold such a view, it is clearly one that will strike many, if not most, observers as unattractive. Here again, therefore, Ricoeur discloses his propensity to attribute dehumanization, depersonalization, and desocialization to the process of writing, and to rejoice in that result.

According to Ricoeur, "a text is potentially addressed to whoever knows how to read," a text creates its own audience. In addition, "It is part of the meaning of a text to be open to an indefinite number of readers and, therefore, of interpretations."[97] Yet in response to this notion we need to make some careful distinctions. On the one hand, we might have a text directed to a particular person or group of people (for example, a letter or the constitution of a particular sporting club) that is, at some stage, read by people outside of the original intended audience. Just as a conversation may be overheard by people who were not meant to be party to it, so too a letter may be discovered and read by someone other than its addressee. Or people considering setting up their own club may read the constitution of another to see if it offers any helpful precedents. As Plato commented at one point in the Phaedrus, "once a thing is consigned to writing it circulates equally among those who understand its subject and those who have no business with it."[98] In such cases, the meaning for the original audience will come into interesting juxtaposition with the interests and interpretations of the subsequent readers. Yet the other readers and other interpretations are just accidental by-products of the fact of inscription, not integral to their meaning. In the case of texts such as these, it makes no sense to say that they create their own audience or that their meaning is open to an indefinite number of readers and interpretations, since in fact they were created for a specific audience. Any other meanings they acquire later are accidental by-products of their history. On the other hand, a literary work, a poem, play, or novel, will usually not be linked at its inception to a designated audience (except perhaps the very broadest one, the literate public in the country in which it appears) and Ricoeur's description may well apply to it. A medial case between these two extremes might be a text that an author aims at and tailors for a specific audience while yet open to the possibility that its message will have a significance for others who hear or read it, in other places or other times. In such a case, however, we should be alive to the problems of 20/20 hindsight and hence avoid being too liberal in attributing prophetic powers and universalizing intentions to such authors.

Soon after this Ricoeur reveals some of the remarkably implausible assumptions of his approach:

> Thanks to writing, man and only man has a world and not just a situation. This extension is one more example of the spiritual implications of the substitution of the material marks for the bodily support of oral discourse. In the same manner that the text frees its meaning from the tutelage of mental intention, it frees its reference from the limits of situational reference. For us, the world is the ensemble of references opened up by texts, or, at least for the moment, by descriptive texts.[99]

Who but a Western intellectual (who no doubt loves his books) could ever suggest that writing is necessary for and indeed constitutive of the world?[100] Where does this leave the members of illiterate cultures, or the numerous illiterate people in literate societies, past or present? The logic of Ricoeur's position demands they had and have only a "situation," not a "world." At the same time, Ricoeur revealingly relies on a highly suspect dualism to denigrate oral discourse (as "bodily") and valorize writing (as "spiritual"). The number of those subscribing to the view that a conversation is "bodily" and hence inferior, but that when it is inscribed in writing it becomes "spiritual" and hence superior (becomes indeed a constituent of the world that its oral original was not), cannot be large. An alternative possibility, raised by Paul, certainly deserves consideration: "For writing kills, but the Spirit gives life" (2 Cor 3:6).

A few pages on, having said that the transfer from hearing to reading is fundamentally linked to the transfer of the temporal properties of the voice to the spatial properties of the marks inscribed on the page, he states:

> This general spatialization of language is complete with the appearance of printing. The visualization of culture begins with the dispossession of the power of the voice in the proximity of mutual presence. Printed texts reach man in solitude, far from the ceremonies that gather the community. Abstract relations, telecommunications in the proper sense of the word, connect the scattered members of an invisible public.[101]

Again, all this is immensely revealing. First of all, it is indeed printing, and only printing, a comparatively recent invention, that makes possible Ricoeur's prioritization of writing. Second, the voice as the mediator of interpersonal presence loses its power and, in context, Ricoeur is happy with this result. Lastly, the earlier theme of the desocialization that accompanies writing is further expressed in the statement that "printed texts reach man in solitude," which is presumably the place and state in which Ricoeur prefers to encounter them (his study, no doubt), "far from the ceremonies that gather the community." Here, then, we have a theory apparently based on the principle "Don't bother me, I'm reading."

I will end this discussion with two more quotations from Ricoeur that will substantiate the point I am making. The following summarizes his position on what is "to be understood—and appropriated—in a text":

> Not the intention of the author . . . not the historical situation common to the author and his original readers; not the expectations or feelings of those original readers . . . What has to be appropriated is the meaning of the text itself, conceived in a dynamic way as the direction of thought opened up by the text. In other words, what has to be appropriated is nothing other than the power of disclosing a world that constitutes the reference of the text. In this way we are as far as possible from the Romanticist ideal of coinciding with a foreign psyche.[102]

While this view is susceptible to the criticisms leveled against the earlier parts of his argument, it is worthwhile noting once again the profound devaluation of interpersonal understanding involved in Ricoeur's hermeneutical theory. It is not surprising, moreover, that Ricoeur should find a soul mate in none other than Hans-Georg Gadamer: "In this sense, appropriation has nothing to do with any kind of person to person appeal. It is instead close to what Hans-Georg Gadamer calls a fusion of horizons (*Horizonverschmelzung*): the world horizon of the reader is fused with the world horizon of the writer. And the ideality of the text is the mediating link in this process of horizon fusing."[103] As we have argued in the preceding chapter, Gadamer's notion of the fusion of horizons entails a model of dialogue fixated on agreement as the point of dialogue, the hegemonic supplanting of the historical other and a disregard for the frequency with which those socialized in one culture can take steps to understand people socialized in another. It is no wonder, therefore, that a theory embodying such an imperfect and attenuated understanding of relationships between people across historical and cultural divides should attract Ricoeur, who regards the very notion of person-to-person relation as inimical to interpretation.

THE NATURE OF THE READING PROCESS

Our model of communication and study of historiography has one important result: it is absolutely inevitable that even when we are interested in the original meaning of a text to its author and the author's first audience, it will convey quite different meanings to later readers. In this chapter we have been arguing that the New Testament writings are not literary texts, although we are open to the idea that some of them (mainly, the Gospels, Acts, and the Apocalypse) do have some literary, especially narrative, features. Nevertheless, since our model of communication applies to all texts, literary and nonliterary, and since many of us will continue to read the New Testament, the reading process is worth considering.

Wolfgang Iser has offered an important explanation for what happens when we read. He discusses solely reading literary texts, but in fact his perspective relates to all texts of any complexity, literary (complex by definition) and nonliterary (especially ancient texts whose cultural context is quite alien from ours). Thus, following Roman Ingarden, Iser speaks of a literary work having two poles, the artistic and the aesthetic. The artistic refers to the text created by the author and the aesthetic to the realization accomplished by the reader. For a nonliterary text, using our model of communication, we might modify these to the "communicator" and "communicatee" dimensions. Iser claims that "a literary work cannot be completely identical with the text, or with the realization of the text, but in fact must lie halfway between the two" and that the "work is more than the text, for the text only takes on life when it is realized."[104]

Similarly, a communicator's message is inevitably modified by its receivers when they seek to understand it within their own social context and individual circumstances. If the message's receivers are removed from the communicator in space and time there will be a considerable indeterminacy in the text that requires some measure of interpretation. This equates to what in chapter 2 I described as "slippage" of meaning, which occurs in any communication, even a face-to-face one.

Iser notes that it "is the virtuality of a text that gives rise to its dynamic nature." As the reader uses the various perspectives offered by the text in order to relate its patterns to one another, this process results in the awakening of responses within the reader.[105] This view, made in relation to literary texts, is also relevant to some complex nonliterary texts from the past, especially those with literary characteristics, including parts of the New Testament.

Iser comments: "literary texts are full of unexpected twists and turns, and frustration of expectations."[106] Even in the simplest story there are bound to be omissions, through which it gains its dynamism. This leaves gaps in the text that the reader fills using his or her own imagination: "For this reason, one text is potentially capable of several different realizations, and no reading can ever exhaust the full potential, for each individual reader will fill in the gaps in his own way, thereby excluding the various other possibilities . . . By making his decision he implicitly acknowledges the inexhaustibility of the text." This means that the text is "infinitely richer than any of its individual realizations."[107]

But one can say much the same about many, especially complex, nonliterary texts. This includes texts from a social setting remote from ours that bear some literary characteristics. Using our model of communication, the message's receiver has to labor to fill in the text gaps brought about by an inability to understand cultural features or even personal details known to the author and first audience but unknown to later readers. In reading the New Testament for its original meaning, we have to struggle to situate its discourse within a cultural system very different from our own. It is inevitable that if later readers of the New Testament do not take great pains to substitute first-century CE Mediterranean values for their own, they will interpret it in the light of their own social and individual circumstances.[108]

CONCLUSION

This chapter's argument justifies maintaining authorial intention as an essential feature in New Testament interpretation. Within a framework explicitly concerned with the role of the New Testament texts in contemporary Christian life, identity, and reflection, they are best not regarded as "literary" works. Literary works are divorced from the mundane world of purpose and responsibility and transported off to the realm of mimetic play; the New Testament documents are practical messages intended to directly impact their audiences. They were written to bring their addressees to faith in Christ or to confirm them in that faith in the distinctive cultural context in which they were first published. I will elaborate this point more fully in chapter 7.

5

INTERPERSONAL UNDERSTANDING AND THE SPOKEN WORD IN SCHLEIERMACHER'S HERMENEUTICS

One of the big surprises I experienced writing the present volume was to discover how close my own ideas were to the hermeneutics of the great nineteenth-century theologian and philosopher Friedrich Schleiermacher (1768–1834). Schleiermacher was the first thinker to appreciate the universal character of the problem of interpretation and to recognize the need for a philosophically based theory of understanding. This approach also led him to regard biblical interpretation not as a unique, unparalleled form of interpretation, but as one species of a larger process of interpretation.[1] Many specialists in hermeneutics, for whom his views often serve to illustrate the road not to be taken, however, do not share my enthusiasm for Schleiermacher in this area. In the present chapter, I aim to demonstrate Schleiermacher's hermeneutics as an example of an admirable interpersonal and dialogical approach to textual interpretation that enriches this book's thesis. I also show that critical dismissal of Schleiermacher is evanescent and dissipates on close inspection.

THE CASE AGAINST SCHLEIERMACHER

If you mention to those familiar with the hermeneutical debate that you have become enthusiastic about Schleiermacher's hermeneutics, the standard reaction is a quizzical smile followed by a comment along the lines, "So you're returning to Romantic hermeneutics," or "What do you see in the psychologizing approach?" In hermeneutical circles, Schleiermacher is almost a comic figure. What is the case against him?

Hans-Georg Gadamer

Gadamer has made what is probably the most extensive case against Schleiermacher, in his essay, "The Questionableness of Romantic Hermeneutics and of Its Application to the Study of History," contained in his major text *Truth and Method*.[2] He begins by considering the prehistory of Romantic hermeneutics. Luther, and most of the Reformers after him, had favored a literal interpretation of the Bible and believed that Scripture was its own interpreter. This was tied to the dogmatic postulate that Scripture was a unity. During the eighteenth century, however, under the Enlightenment's influence, scholars such as Semler and Ernesti began to abandon the idea of scriptural unity and insisted on exploring the individual texts, in all their differences, using historical criticism. Since this meant there was no longer any difference between the interpretation of sacred or secular writings, the hermeneutics necessary involved historical research itself. The problem had become the broader one of the nature of understanding. This was Schleiermacher's particular interest, a theoretical foundation for any attempt to understand discourse. He was not just seeking to make sense of one particular tradition. For Schleiermacher, the effort to understand was necessary whenever there was a possibility of misunderstanding. According to Gadamer, "Schleiermacher's idea of a universal hermeneutics starts from this: that the experience of the alien and the possibility of misunderstanding is a universal one."[3] Schleiermacher's characteristic extension of the task to understanding significant conversation showed how much he differed from his Enlightenment predecessors and moved away from the advocacy of rational ideas. "In a new and universal sense, alienness is inextricably given with the individuality of the 'Thou.'"[4]

Yet Gadamer interprets Schleiermacher's extension of the role of hermeneutics to understanding all discourse, spoken or written, in a way that careful analysis and a close inspection of Schleiermacher's own words will show to be inadequate: "What is to be understood is now not only the exact words and their objective meaning, but also the individuality of the speaker, that is, the author. Schleiermacher holds that the author can only be understood by going back to the origin of the thought." A little after this he continues: "Thus beside grammatical interpretation he places psychological [technical] interpretation. This is his original interpretation." Although Gadamer is willing to concede that early on in his career things might have been different, he proposes that the psychological interpretation gradually came to dominate Schleiermacher's thought:

> Schleiermacher's particular contribution is psychological interpretation. It is ultimately a divinatory process, a placing of oneself within the mind of the author, an apprehension of the "inner origin" of the composition of a work, a recreation of the creative act. Thus understanding is a reproduction related to an original production, a knowing of what has been known . . .[5]

Worth noting here, for closer attention later, is the fact that Gadamer does not mention that "psychological" has a meaning for us in our post-Freud, post-Jung, and even post-Adler era that is entirely different from how Schleiermacher understood the term in the first half of the nineteenth century.

What does Gadamer find objectionable in Schleiermacher's position (as he understands it)? First, Schleiermacher does not find understanding a text written in a foreign language and in a past age fundamentally more problematical than any other kind of understanding. "Schleiermacher's problem is not historical obscurity, but the obscurity of the 'Thou.'"[6] Palmer, too, criticizes Schleiermacher on the basis that "Such a concentration on the psychological conditions of dialogue can lead to slurring over the historical element in interpretation and even the centrality of language for hermeneutics."[7] But here Gadamer and Palmer have fallen into error, not Schleiermacher. In chapter 2 we showed that communication between representatives of different cultures is an everyday reality in our world. For reasons set out in chapter 3, moreover, the notion that the past is ontologically remote from us in a way that phenomena in "the present" are not is unsustainable. Schleiermacher had a sounder approach to history than Gadamer or Palmer. It is Gadamer, not Schleiermacher, who fails to take the temporal gap between ourselves and the past with sufficient seriousness, in his notion of the fusion of horizons, whereby the historical other can never be known (or criticized) in his or her difference from us, because Gadamer thinks that all understanding involves agreement.[8]

Second, Gadamer is unhappy with Schleiermacher's assertion that the object of hermeneutics is to understand a writer better than he understood himself. This dictum seems to have originated with Kant, in his *Critique of Pure Reason.*[9] Gadamer finds problematic that Schleiermacher sees

> the act of understanding as the reconstructive completion of the production. This inevitably makes conscious many things of which the writer may be unconscious. It is obvious that here Schleiermacher is applying the aesthetics of genius to his universal hermeneutics. The mode of creation of the artistic genius is the model on which this theory of unconscious production and necessarily conscious reproduction is based.[10]

Although this view would indeed turn the interpreter into the writer, analyzing what Schleiermacher himself says falsifies this formulation.

Other Complaints

As the foundation for his critique of Schleiermacher, Paul Ricoeur offered the following, fairly accurate summary of his position:

> Hermeneutics as issuing from Schleiermacher and Dilthey tended to iden-
> tify interpretation with the category of "understanding," and to define
> understanding as the recognition of an author's intention from the point of
> view of the primitive addressees in the original situation of discourse. This
> priority given to the author's intention and to the original audience tended,
> in turn, to make dialogue the model of every situation of understanding,
> thereby imposing the framework of intersubjectivity on hermeneutics.
> Understanding a text, then, is only a particular case of the dialogical situa-
> tion in which someone responds to someone else.[11]

Ricoeur's perspective is that the fact of writing means that the author has been supplanted, that the text escapes from its original context, and represents a text-centered carping against "the narrowness of the face-to-face situation." Ultimately this leaves us with the solitary man (Ricoeur and similar critics) alone with his printed texts; naturally enough, he sees Schleiermacher's model of hermeneutics objectionable. But once one critically scrutinizes Ricoeur's view (see the preceding chapter), and points out the desocialization and dehumanization entailed in its hyperbolic enthusiasm for the printed word accessed by a reader in solitude, Schleiermacher emerges as a powerfully corrective and salutary vision of a far more appealing, and fundamentally human(e), hermeneutics.

Thomas Torrance suggested in 1962, during the course of a eulogistic introduction to some early writings of Karl Barth, that although the theology of Schleiermacher was Christocentric, "Jesus Christ fits rather badly into the system." He then sought to illustrate this problem from the point of view of Schleiermacher's hermeneutics. Torrance's substantive point was:

> Normally when one reads an author one understands what he says by look-
> ing *with* him *at* the "object" to which he points or which he describes, but
> early in the nineteenth century there grew up the tendency to study the
> text of an author in its correlation with the "subject" or the author himself
> rather than its correlation with the objective reality he intended, and so to
> read it as an expression of his individuality or genius.

It was, Torrance suggests, largely under Schleiermacher's influence (followed by Dilthey's) that theological interpretation made this "fundamental change in direction," even though it was essentially a by-product of the nineteenth-century Romantic movement as a whole, derived ultimately from the Renaissance.[12] We will see that Schleiermacher's interest in the author lies in the purchase an interpreter thereby obtained on the meaning of the discourse—even if he was rightly open to the genius that produced great works of art. Thus Torrance's view distorts Schleiermacher's position. It is clear that Torrance has been driven by a desire to promote a Barthian vision of reality (with its sharp division between divine and human levels of reality) against early-nineteenth-century figures who (rightly?) saw the situation as rather more complicated.

James Torrance has launched a different line of attack on Schleiermacher. He suggests that Schleiermacher's "preoccupation with the subjective reference of language and the accompanying view of faith" precludes "an adequate consideration of the 'objective' 'factual' reference of theological statements."[13] He further argues that Schleiermacher's approach becomes "so preoccupied with the self-understanding of the human subject, that it fails to yield any positive affirmations about the Being of God as He is in Himself."[14] Thiselton gives some credence to Torrance's view and suggests he has pinpointed "a recurring difficulty in the application of hermeneutics to theological texts." The danger, according to Thiselton, is that theology is reduced to anthropology.[15]

This objection carries little weight. Schleiermacher saw hermeneutics as a means of understanding the meaning of discourse (oral and written) at the time of its first appearance. He was concerned with what an author meant when he or she said or wrote something. How such utterances related to the objective realities of existence, whether their contents were (in some ontic sense) true or not, is another question altogether. Torrance and Thiselton are castigating Schleiermacher for failing to achieve some result that was never, as far as his hermeneutics were concerned, within the scope of the project. In chapter 11 I will consider how the historical determination of what the New Testament authors conveyed to their audiences when their works first appeared can be integrated with models of divine inspiration.

Defending Schleiermacher

To answer the case against Schleiermacher, it is necessary to pay closer attention to his actual writings in the context of his intellectual development than has often been done, given the widespread tendency to laugh him off as some benighted romantic laboring under the—for some reason—curious idea that interpersonal understanding could matter in hermeneutics. In the remaining five sections of this chapter I will: (a) set out an important, although neglected, feature of Schleiermacher's writings, namely, his interest in Platonic dialogue, before (b) outlining his writings on hermeneutics. I will then (c) assess what he really meant by an interpreter understanding the creator of a discourse, before (d) considering his insistence that hermeneutics embraced spoken as well as written conversation, which reveals his adherence to dialogue as the model for the entire enterprise. Having exposed the flaws in the criticism that has been leveled against his hermeneutics, I will then (e) conclude by setting out the positive role his ideas will play in this volume's thesis.

SCHLEIERMACHER AND DIALOGUE

We are best able to comprehend Schleiermacher's vision of hermeneutics by relating it to his interest in dialogue, both as a practical activity, namely, social conversation, and also in the literary form perfected by Plato.

Schleiermacher was an intensely sociable man with a wide circle of friends whom he frequently met and engaged in conversation. He also kept up a voluminous correspondence throughout his life. He was prepared to reveal himself candidly to others and he expected his friends to do the same.[16] The traits he found most attractive in Eleonore Grunow, the woman he courted for years—unsuccessfully—in the hope she would divorce her husband to whom she was unhappily married, were "her abundance of feelings and her unusual ability to communicate."[17] He was a lively conversationalist who missed nothing going on in a room around him.[18]

One of the presuppositions of this volume is that the warm and lively social intercourse practiced by Schleiermacher represents an admirable expression of our common humanity. That it has become so much less a feature of modern intellectual life, at least in the humanities, where the model is largely one of solitary research in library or study interspersed with occasional bouts of conversation in staff rooms or academic conferences, is a cause of deep regret. The intensity of personal interaction among the people of Schleiermacher's Germany in the late eighteenth and early nineteenth centuries was a feature of the face-to-face societies that had been the norm in southern and northern Europe right from ancient times. I noted in the introduction the well-documented view of William Graham that solitary reading habits only became universal in Europe with the widespread literacy of the nineteenth century. This appears to have happened just after Schleiermacher's time and he was fortunate enough to miss it. With the development of mass communication and telecommunications during the nineteenth and twentieth centuries, this feature of human experience has become greatly attenuated. But that is our loss. Yet intense personal interaction is still with us, still part of what it means to be human in Buber's I-You sense argued for in this volume. It deserves to be promoted rather than marginalized further.

This dimension to Schleiermacher's life and character was matched by his profound interest in the Platonic dialogues. In 1799 he set about translating them in cooperation with Friedrich von Schlegel and carried on the project alone after Schlegel left Germany in 1802.[19] Scholarship has been rather slow to appreciate Plato's significance for Schleiermacher. In 1942 Rudolf Odebrecht published a critical edition of Schleiermacher's *Dialektik* that, in a valuable introduction,[20] for the first time emphasized the significance for Schleiermacher of his analysis and translation of Plato's works and the dialogical form in which they were expressed. Because he published his book in World War II Germany, Odebrecht's insights failed to receive the prominence they deserved until Richard Niebuhr heavily relied upon them in a monograph entitled *Schleiermacher on Christ and Religion*, published in 1965.[21]

In his introductions to his translations of Plato's dialogues, Schleiermacher set out his understanding of the form.[22] Niebuhr has isolated three major features of his exposition that merit particular attention. The first is that the dialogue reflects Plato's own idea of how philosophical communication occurs and that in this literary form we have a basic and distinctive characteristic of Plato himself. Second, it is a mistake to identify Plato's own view with a particular member of the colloquy. "The dialogue is not a collection of discrete views; it is a living whole. It is a reproduction of thought in motion." The author is trying to reenact the thought processes by which a discovery was reached and arouse in the readers a similar process.[23] The third feature follows on from these: the unfinished appearance of the dialogues is not a defect in their construction but an essential feature of the form itself. In chapter 11 I will adopt Mikhail Bakhtin's views on the dialogical character of Dostoevsky's novels, which bear strong similarity to Niebuhr's exposition of Plato.

In the final weeks of 1805, when he was a professor at the university in Halle (which was closed in 1806 on Napoleon's order), Schleiermacher actually composed a work that was both in Platonic form and also concerned a conversation about Christmas among a fictitious group of relatives and friends in the Germany of his time. This was *Die Weihnachtsfeier: Ein Gespräch* ("Christmas Eve: A Dialogue"), which appeared in January 1806.[24] This text allowed him to valorize the process of conversation, which he himself valued so highly, and also to use a literary form that replicated that process.

It is no accident that Schleiermacher's first hermeneutical writings date, as we will soon see, from 1805, when his grappling with Plato had no doubt forced him to give close attention to the nature of interpretation. At this early stage in his conscious hermeneutical reflections (in the *Aphorisms*), we find him affording a central place in interpretation to the encounter between two human beings who reveal themselves to one another through the spoken word. This theme persisted in all of his hermeneutical writings down to some of the latest extant, the "Academy Addresses of 1829." His vision very closely resembles our model of interpersonal communion.

Some have opined that Schleiermacher was not totally committed to an ongoing discussion that remained open-ended and unresolved. Niebuhr has suggested that he does at times favor closure of the discussion and a resulting unity of view, a tendency he attributes to Spinoza's influence.[25] James Graby has criticized Niebuhr for emphasizing the dialogical dimension to Schleiermacher's thought to the neglect of other aspects, especially the extent to which in Schleiermacher's hermeneutical works he sometimes suggests the completion of an argument that would terminate the dialogue.[26] Yet Niebuhr and Graby exaggerate this dimension to his thought. It is beyond dispute that Schleiermacher saw in conversation the occasion in which two people disclosed themselves to one another. Like Buber and unlike Gadamer, Schleiermacher did not consider that the aim of conversation was to reach agreement. In each such encounter, Schleiermacher thought, the participants would grow in understanding, even if the process itself meant that they would learn even more of one another the next time. This was merely one side of the hermeneutical circle that, as we will see, he commented upon in the Aphorisms: "One must already know a man in order to understand what he says, and yet one first becomes acquainted with him by what he says."[27]

It is difficult to accept that Schleiermacher could ever have been of the view that one person had learned all that was possible to know of another, or that an interpreter could learn all there was to know of a text characterized by complexity and depth. This means that the conversation, the shuttling back and forth of language between two persons, provided the best model for the practice of interpretation. Yet the literary form of dialogue, although closest in nature to this process, was not the only form. Schleiermacher himself published works in different genres, as with his 1799 work *On Religion: Speeches to Its Cultured Despisers* and his treatise *Brief Outline on the Study of Theology* (first published in 1811), where he did argue for a particular point of view, rather than setting up a colloquy of different views. For this reason it would be quite wrong to suggest that the dialogical form was the only one he knew.

AN OVERVIEW OF SCHLEIERMACHER'S HERMENEUTICAL WRITINGS

Although Schleiermacher produced a number of handwritten documents on hermeneutics in the years 1805 to 1833 as the basis for the lectures he delivered on the subject throughout that period, he published nothing on the subject in his lifetime. After his death, however, his student and friend Friedrich Lücke brought out a volume from this corpus that was based on one of Schleiermacher's writings (the most developed, admittedly), the "Compendium of 1819," supplemented by student notes taken during the academic year 1832–33. This was the version relied upon by scholars, including Wilhelm Dilthey in his important 1896 Berlin lecture, published in 1900 (to which we will return below), until 1959 when Heinz Kimmerle published a careful edition of all of Schleiermacher's holograph materials.[28] An English translation of Kimmerle's work appeared in 1977.[29]

The corpus of Schleiermacher's handwritten writings on the subject (omitting a number of extant loose pages) consists of seven substantial extant documents. The first is a manuscript sixteen pages long and entitled by Schleiermacher "On Hermeneutics 1805 and 1809," usually referred to as the "Aphorisms 1805 and 1809," because of their form. These cover the period of his last lectures in Halle and then his early years at the newly founded University of Berlin.[30]

The second, which Schleiermacher entitled "Hermeneutics First Draft," is a manuscript of seventeen pages and apparently written around 1810–19.

The third is a four-page manuscript which Schleiermacher entitled "Application of Knowledge about the Author's Distinctiveness to Interpretation" (*Anwendung der Kenntnis der Eigenthümlichkeit des Schriftsellers auf die Interpretation*).[31]

Fourth is the so-called "Compendium of 1819," which Schleiermacher entitled "Hermeneutics." This document was the basis for Lücke's 1838 volume in the *Collected Works*, which contains Schleiermacher's marginal notes from 1828.

The fifth document is an eight-page manuscript probably dating from the period between 1820 and 1829 that Schleiermacher entitled "Second Part, on Technical Interpretation."

The sixth document consists of two addresses that Schleiermacher made to the Prussian Academy of Sciences on 13 August and 22 October 1829. These "Academy Addresses of 1829" constitute the only texts by Schleiermacher on hermeneutics in finished form. It is somewhat frustrating, therefore, that he chose to structure these addresses as a response to the writings of Wolf and Ast rather than allowing greater scope for the development of his own insights.

The seventh document comprises the marginal notes made by Schleiermacher for his last series of lectures on hermeneutics in 1832–33.[32]

The strength of the introduction to Kimmerle's 1959 edition is to draw attention to the fact that Schleiermacher's thought developed and thus of our need to look at the entire course of his reflection across nearly thirty years.

It is worth noting at the outset that throughout his writings on hermeneutics Schleiermacher distinguished between "grammatical" and "technical" aspects of interpretation. By "grammatical interpretation" he meant the formal and material elements of language. He also referred to this dimension as "objective." To grasp what he meant by "technical" we need realize its origin in the Greek *technē*, and as thus means "relating to a person's skill in a particular activity." For Schleiermacher, technical interpretation was the "subjective" dimension. It embraced the distinctiveness of the linguistic composition and was "chiefly concerned with the over-all coherence and with its relation to the universal laws for combining thoughts." He sometimes referred to the technical dimension as "psychological," but it would be a mistake to impute into this word twentieth- and twenty-first century meanings of "psychological."[33] Although Ricoeur has claimed that these two areas, grammatical and technical, are not so easily distinguished as Schleiermacher thought,[34] the broad distinction between the study of the linguistic (and, to an extent, social) context (= the "grammatical" element) and the particular way in which an individual author has composed his or her work within this context is plainly a real and useful one.

SCHLEIERMACHER ON UNDERSTANDING A DISCOURSE'S CREATOR

It is also possible to plot Schleiermacher's developing conception of the importance of understanding a discourse's creator, an area in which (as we have seen above) he has been heavily criticized, by tracing the history of his hermeneutical investigations.

In one of the "Aphorisms of 1805 and 1809" he wrote: "In interpretation it is essential that one be able to step out of one's own frame of mind into that of the author (*Eine Hauptsache beim Interpretiren ist dass man in Stande sein muss aus seiner eigenen Gesinnung herauszugehen in die des Schriftstellers*)."[35] This a fairly modest claim, saying little more than that an interpreter should try to see something in the same way the author did. That this is a very limited statement, which has nothing to do with penetrating the depths of the author's psyche (something which causes such consternation among most modern theoreticians of hermeneutics), is revealed by the illustration that Schleiermacher immediately supplies for it.[36]

More interesting, perhaps, is another of the aphorisms, which requires quoting in context:

> (1) Combining the objective and subjective so that the interpreter can put himself "inside" the author (*Combination des ob[jective]n und sub[jective]n dass man sich dadurch in den Schriftsteller "hinein" bildet*). (2) On understanding an author better than he understands himself (*Vom den Schriftsteller besser verstehen als er selbst*). (a) increasing that understanding, (b) correcting that understanding . . .[37]

The quotation marks around *hinein* ("inside") in the first proposition, which are original, indicate that Schleiermacher did not really think an interpreter could put himself inside the author in the sense of obtaining access to his innermost thoughts. That he does not sanction such a notion is also apparent from the fact that the interpreter must combine objective factors (Schleiermacher's "grammatical" dimension) as well as subjective ones (the "technical" features in the original Greek sense, meaning the skills of a particular author). Francis Watson has rightly noticed the importance that Schleiermacher accords to the grammatical dimension of interpretation, which has nothing to do with the author's personality.[38] This quite nonpsychological approach (in our modern sense of "psychological") establishes the context for understanding the second proposition (understanding the author better than he understood himself), which must be understood in the same way. This is not to be taken too literally, but as a touch of interpreter's bravado in relation to just how much one can learn from the combination of the "objective/grammatical" features and the "subjective/technical" ones. Certainly, Schleiermacher is interested in understanding the author's message, but he does not propose intimate knowledge of the author's thought processes as part of this task.

In light of this analysis (which paints a very different picture of Schleiermacher's position than current theoreticians do), it comes as no surprise that he states in another of these early aphorisms: "The interpreter must try to become the immediate reader of a text (*Man muss suchen der unmittelbare Leser zu werden*) in order to understand its allusions, its atmosphere, and its special field of images."[39] This is another way of saying that the interpreter must pay close attention to objective and subjective features.

Important statements on this subject appear in the "First Draft of 1809–1810." In his analysis of this task, Schleiermacher notes that "It proceeds from two entirely different points: understanding by reference to the language and understanding by reference to the one who speaks. Because of this double-character of understanding, interpretation is an art. *Neither can be completed by itself* [emphasis added]."[40] When he adds, "One must understand as well as and better than the author,"[41] it is indisputable that he still has in mind this twofold understanding with its objective and subjective features, not some inward voyage through someone else's psyche.

Schleiermacher's title for the next document, "Application of Knowledge about the Author's Distinctiveness to Interpretation," seems to offer promising material for the critics who accuse him of "psychologizing." In the first sentence, however, it appears that he has not forgotten the importance of the grammatical dimension: "By a knowledge of the individuality of an author, grammatical interpretation can be brought to a level that it could not reach on its own." He announces his goal as being "to reproduce the subjective bases for the combination of particular elements of a text in order to grasp the train of thought."[42] On a number of occasions in this text, it is true, Schleiermacher refers to understanding the author as a relevant factor in interpretation. He speaks of "the totality of his personality" (*die Totalität s[eine]r Persönlichkeit*) and raises the possibility of knowing the whole personality of an author (*die ganze Persönlichkeit*). Yet we must not overestimate the extent to which knowledge of an author's personality can assist in interpretation, nor, indeed, what Schleiermacher means by "personality." The thrust of this document is how to discover the train of thought in a work, which means being able to distinguish the major ideas from the secondary ones. He repeatedly mentions the "grammatical/objective" aspects of the task as he delves into the "technical/subjective" ones.

In one particularly revealing statement, Schleiermacher says: "Even if the author's personality is known in its entirety, the secondary ideas can never be discovered at the beginning merely from the author's principle of selection and method. The author himself did not have them in mind at that time; rather, they were aroused in him in the course of his work."[43] This suggests both that Schleiermacher was alive to the possibility that knowledge of an author might not help explain certain ideas and that "personality" seems to mean little more than an author's "principle of selection and method." It is a word that relates not so much to the author's psychological character as to the characteristic way he or she works. When Schleiermacher refers to the personality of an author, he means little more than his or her "taste" (*der Geschmack*), "peculiar viewpoint" (*die Eigenthümliche Ansicht*), and even "style of writing" (*die Schreibart*). The significance of an author's style is revealed in Schleiermacher's emphasis on the capacity to reproduce an author's style as a sure sign that the work has been understood. There is no sign in this document that Schleiermacher envisages having any access to an author other than by analyzing his discourse. We will see in a later document that Schleiermacher makes this point expressly. His mention of the New Testament authors Matthew, Mark, John, Paul, and Peter toward the end of this document, however, confirms that this was already his view.

A balance between understanding the author and understanding the overall linguistic context in which he operated also appears in the "Compendium of 1819." Here Schleiermacher divided the art of interpretation into aspects using two pairs of opposites: the historical or prophetic (also called "divinatory") and objective or subjective aspects. This gave him four possible ways to describe any statement:

(a) Objective-historical, referring to the statement in its relationship to the language as a whole;
(b) Objective-prophetic, referring to the way the statement will stimulate future developments in the language;
(c) Subjective-historical, how the statement, as a fact in the person's mind, has emerged; and
(d) Subjective-prophetic, meaning how the thoughts contained in the statement will exercise further influence on and in the author.[44]

Schleiermacher formulates the overall task of interpretation as being "To understand the text at first as well as and then even better than the author (*die Rede zuerst eben so gut und dann besser zu verstehen als ihr Urheber*)."[45] This focus on understanding the text (not, as earlier, the author) represents little more than the widespread modern view that a critic can often understand a work better than its author or that authors make poor interpreters of their own works. (These insights argue against the charge made against Schleiermacher, for example, by Klyne Snodgrass, that he has a "psychologizing" approach as revealed in his "Romanticist ideas of getting into the mind of an author so that the interpreter knows the author's mind better than he himself or she herself.")[46] Schleiermacher then added, "*Since we have no direct knowledge of what was in the author's mind* [emphasis added], we must try to become aware of many things of which he himself may have been unconscious, except in so far as he reflects upon his own work and becomes his own reader (*Denn weil wir keine unmittelbare Kenntniss dessen haben, was in ihm ist, so müssen wir vieles zum Bew[usstein] zu bringen suchen was ihm unbewusst bleiben kann ausser sofern er selbst reflectirend sein eigener Leser wird*)."[47]

This develops the position expressed in the Aphorisms, where Schleiermacher thought that the interpreter could step inside the author.

Now he disavows *direct knowledge* (*unmittelbare Kenntniss*) of what was in the author's mind, but still aims for knowledge, presumably by indirect means, even knowledge of which the author was unconscious. He is now looking more at what one can deduce the author must have known and he consolidates his earlier position that the interpreter should aim to become the original reader of the text, by focusing on the very first reader of the text—the author himself. Schleiermacher considers that before the art of hermeneutics can be practiced "the interpreter must put himself both objectively and subjectively in the position of the author."[48] This means knowing both the author's language (objective side) and the inner and outer aspects of his life. While the latter is clearly a tall order (although one that brings out well the personal dimension to Schleiermacher's hermeneutics), he considered that one could learn of an author's character and circumstances from his writings. At this point Schleiermacher explicitly formulates one aspect of the hermeneutic circle mentioned above: "Complete knowledge always involves an apparent circle, that each part can be understood only out of the whole to which it belongs and vice versa." In addition:

> To put oneself in the position of an author always means to follow through with this relationship between the whole and the parts. Thus it follows, first, that the more we learn about an author, the better equipped we are for interpretation, but, second, that a text can never be understood right away. On the contrary, every reading puts us in a better position to understand because it increases our knowledge. Only in the case of insignificant texts are we satisfied with what we understand on first reading.[49]

Although much of the "Compendium of 1819" after this discussion is taken up with grammatical interpretation,[50] toward the end of this text Schleiermacher returns briefly to technical interpretation. After noting that both "technical and grammatical interpretation begin with a general overview of a text designed to grasp its unity and the major features of its composition,"[51] he again focuses on the centrality of understanding the work in relation to the author: "But in technical interpretation the unity of the work, its theme, is viewed as the dynamic feature impelling the author, and the basic features of the composition are viewed as his distinctive nature, revealing itself in that movement."[52] Here we see the close association Schleiermacher draws between understanding the nature of a word and the character of its author. A little further on he notes that "Technical interpretation attempts to identify what has moved the author to communicate."[53] Only technical interpretation can grasp "how the work is a necessary undertaking of the author, since a sense for this necessity emerges only if the genesis of the text is never lost from view."[54] Schleiermacher does not, however, suggest that an author can be understood in a manner divorced from his or her linguistic and literary context; on the contrary, he is adamant that an interpreter must delve into how "the author received his subject matter and the language." This means "learning about the state of a given genre when the author began to write" and "knowing about related literature current in that era as well as earlier models of style."[55] He rather disparages the use of authors' biographical sketches, since they usually fail to include the issue of literary models.

From the moment when it begins, technical interpretation aiming at the integrated understanding of a text in relation to its writer embraces two inseparable components: the divinatory and the comparative. It is necessary to pay careful attention to what Schleiermacher actually says here, since, as Jeanrond notes,[56] his use of the word "divination" has been a point of enormous misunderstanding. The common understanding of this word as a secret or mysterious feeling of or entry into the world of the speaker or author does not do justice to Schleiermacher's position. Here are some crucial statements relating to it: "By leading the interpreter to transform himself, so to speak, into the author, the divinatory method seeks to gain an immediate comprehension of the author as an individual. The comparative method proceeds by subsuming the author under a general type. It then tries to find his distinctive traits by comparing him with the others of the same general type."[57] Divination, therefore, refers to gaining an insight into the author as an individual. Yet soon after Schleiermacher this unambiguously situates the divinatory aspect of interpretation in the context of interpersonal understanding: "The divinatory is based on the assumption that each person is not only a unique individual in his own right, but that he has a receptivity to the uniqueness of every other person."[58] There is nothing mysterious or secret here, since Schleiermacher simply has in mind the innate capacity (of sensitivity, no doubt) one human being has to understand another. Since we have already observed Schleiermacher's adherence to the hermeneutical circle, he could not have envisaged that an interpreter's attempt to understand another human being or someone's textual production would ever reach closure. For this reason Jeanrond is justified in arguing that divination entailed the "necessarily courageous risk taken by an interpreter who approaches a text" even though he knows that no approach will ever exhaust its individuality,[59] except that the point applies as much to someone seeking to understand a person as a text.

Early in the "Second Part, on Technical Interpretation," there is a valuable reminder that although Schleiermacher wanted to know the author, there was only very limited scope for deriving such knowledge apart from the discourse in question: "Technical interpretation: not possible without grammatical interpretation. For how shall I know a person except from his discourse, specifically, from this text before me?"[60] This manuscript contains frequent references to discerning the individuality of the author as it is reflected in the nature and style of the author's work.

In the "Academy Addresses of 1829," Schleiermacher also refined his earlier views on the comparative and divinatory aspects of the interpretative process. Both methods were essential and interpretation required a constant shifting from one method to the other. Speaking of interpretation in general, he wrote:

> [T]he finest fruit of all esthetic criticism of artistic works is a heightened understanding of the intimate operations of poets and other artists of language by means of grasping the entire process of composition, from its conception up to final execution. Indeed, if there is any truth to the dictum that the height of understanding is to understand an author better than he understood himself, this must be it.

While understanding "an author better than he understood himself" certainly needed the comparative method, to reveal how the author's work is similar to or different from that of others (which is further confirmation that by understanding an author "better than himself" Schleiermacher does not intend some impossible direct access to his or her thinking processes), the divinatory method was also essential:

> For whenever we come upon a gifted author (*genialer Autor*) who has for the first time in the history of the language expressed a given phrase or combination of terms, what do we want to do? In such instances only a divinatory method enables us rightly to reconstruct the creative act that begins with the generation of thoughts which captivate the author and to understand how the requirement of the moment could draw upon the living treasure of words in the author's mind in order to produce just this way of putting it and no other.[61]

At one point in the second "Academy Address of 1829" Schleiermacher explains how the comparative and divinatory approaches are both necessary in the interpretation of important literary works, even though he reveals a realistic appreciation of the difficulties involved in relation to divination.[62] When we look at works from classical literature, we often have virtually no knowledge of the life and existence of the authors that can help us to interpret their works, for example, the plays of Sophocles and Euripides. In these instances, although the comparative method looks far more promising than the divinatory, he insists on the continuing role of divination. It is an enriching experience to try to understand an author, always granted that "a knowledge of a given person as such is not the aim of this side of our task, but a means of enabling us to master the author's activities and so of leading us to an objective consideration of his way of thinking."[63]

A number of features in Schleiermacher's last extant writings on hermeneutics, the "Marginal Notes of 1832–33," deserve mention. He now uses new terminology in place of "grammatical" and "technical" (or "psychological"): "linguistic" and "personal." These are more appropriate terms, especially the latter, given that interpersonal understanding was the central feature of this area of interpretation. Neither of these two tasks is of greater importance since "Both require a linguistic talent and knowledge of human nature."[64] He clearly states the historical dimensions of interpretation, beginning with "the goal of hermeneutics is to understand the texts as their original readers understood them." The interpreter must "establish the same relationship between himself and the original author as existed between the author and his original audience." This means, "the interpreter must be familiar with the whole sphere of life and the relationships between author and audience."[65]

At one point Schleiermacher distinguishes between the technical and psychological dimensions of interpretation, which he had previously tended to use interchangeably in contrast to the grammatical (or linguistic) aspect of the task. Psychological interpretation "focuses more upon how thoughts emerged from the totality of the author's life." It "seeks to understand the creative ideas, including those fundamental thoughts which gave rise to the entire train of thought and the secondary thoughts." Technical interpretation, on the other hand, "focuses more upon how a set of thoughts arose from a particular thought or intention"; it "seeks to understand the meditation and composition."[66]

THE SPOKEN WORD IN SCHLEIERMACHER'S HERMENEUTICS

The Significance of the Issue

Contemporary views on hermeneutics treat it as a subject wholly related to the interpretation of *texts*. Not surprisingly, this view appears in discussions of the person widely and rightly perceived to have founded modern hermeneutics—Friedrich Schleiermacher. Modern commentators regularly portray his theory as one related to the interpretation of texts. Anthony Thiselton, for example, in his major 1980 work on New Testament hermeneutics, *The Two Horizons*, concentrates solely on Schleiermacher's view on how to interpret a *text*.[67] Similarly, Werner Jeanrond, in his fine 1991 text on theological hermeneutics, at one point acknowledges that Schleiermacher was concerned with all aspects of understanding, whether of statements spoken or written,[68] but thereafter discusses his theory mainly in relation to texts. This accords with Jeanrond's general definition of hermeneutics as being solely related to the interpretation of texts or works of art.[69]

We shall soon observe, however, that throughout the twenty-five years or so that he wrote on the subject of hermeneutics, Schleiermacher insisted again and again that this was a theory of understanding that necessarily applied to *spoken* as well as written discourse, given its context in interpersonal understanding through dialogue. Although past writers have occasionally commented on this feature of Schleiermacher's hermeneutics, they have attracted little attention. Thus, both Rudolf Odebrecht's and Richard Niebuhr's analyses of this point pass unnoticed both by Thiselton and Jeanrond.[70]

Why does the neglect of this element of Schleiermacher's hermeneutics matter? Apart from the general desirability of an accurate understanding of his hermeneutical theory, the question has a direct relevance to the very lively debate about authorial intention and reader response, currently agitating scholars, that we considered in chapter 4. There is a pronounced difference of opinion between those who think that the author of a biblical text intentionally inscribed a message that interpreters must analyze, and those who advocate that interpreters *create* meaning when they read texts rather than discovering it and that the interpreter has no obligation to discern the original author's message. Underlying each position is a specific model of communication. Those who presuppose communication as an interpersonal process and activity interpret biblical texts in light of the author's original intention. Reader response interpreters take their cues from Derrida, Ricoeur, and similar theorists who rely upon semiotic theory.[71]

Since he was the founder of modern hermeneutics, it is obviously of great interest to determine where Schleiermacher stands in relation to this debate. The current attitude to Schleiermacher, relating him mainly to the understanding of texts, might lead one to expect that he would be found on the semiotic side. In fact, an examination of this writings on hermeneutics shows that he is aligned firmly with the former view of the nature of communication and that he continually emphasizes the process model, which highlights interpersonal dimensions of communication.

Perhaps, to engage in some tentative sociology, the exclusive focus of hermeneutics on texts is to be explained by the fact that those who advocate such a view spend much of their lives on their own seeking to make sense of texts that they are reading, even though that is not all they do. The centrality of conversation in Schleiermacher's life, in the context of late-eighteenth- and early-nineteenth-century Germany, gave him a very different set of priorities.

Part of the aim of this chapter is to reconsider Schleiermacher's reflections on hermeneutics with the aim of retrieving from them important issues relating to interpersonal understanding and the spoken word that have been largely forgotten in modern discussion of his work, with the result that he is wrongly thought to legitimate the current obsession with textuality.

Tracking the Spoken Word through Schleiermacher's Hermeneutical Writings

A number of the "Aphorisms of 1805 and 1809" bear on this issue. A revealing starting point is the "hermeneutical circle."[72] One aspect of this concept is the need to interpret the whole of a discourse in relation to the parts and the parts in relation to the whole. Yet contemporary commentators most frequently refer to the dynamic process that occurs when a person *reads a text*. The reader approaches the text with a certain understanding that is challenged by its contents, thus prompting him or her to reread it with a new understanding, and so the circle (or spiral?) goes on. Thiselton characterizes the hermeneutical circle as the way in which the center of gravity in interpretation "moves back and forth between the two poles of the interpreter and the *text* [emphasis added]."[73] Jeanrond, who also restricts the discussion to texts, traces the idea back to Schleiermacher and from him to Dilthey, Bultmann, and Ricoeur.

It is very striking, therefore, that in his earliest writings concerning the hermeneutical circle, in one of "Aphorisms of 1805 and 1809," Schleiermacher is not talking about texts at all! He is working instead with a model of *understanding between two persons* that is effected *through speech*: "One must already know a man in order to understand what he says, and yet one first becomes acquainted with him by what he says."[74] The fundamental issue that Schleiermacher addresses is that of understanding human language. He regards knowledge of a person as a helpful aid in understanding what he or she says; but his primary hermeneutical concern is to understand the discourse. In addition, this aphorism raises the question of whether all understanding requires some pre-understanding. On this issue Thiselton quotes John Macquarrie: "We could never enter into any understanding of it [a text] unless there were at least some minimum ground between ourselves and text."[75] Perhaps so, but

Schleiermacher's school for learning about the need for pre-understanding is not the asocial experience of the solitary individual reading a text, but the encounter between two human beings who wish to make themselves understood to one another through the spoken word.

Schleiermacher's interest in the interpretation of oral discourse surfaces in several other aphorisms: "One cannot understand a spoken statement without knowing both its most general and its most personal and particular value." And: "If every act of speech were a living reconstruction, there would be no need for hermeneutics, but only for art criticism."[76] Or again: "Every child comes to understand the meanings of words only through hermeneutics."[77]

The next relevant document is the "Compendium of 1819," where the fundamental status of spoken discourse for interpretation appears very early. Having stated that "the art of speaking and the art of understanding stand in relation to each other," he elaborates as follows:

> Speaking is the medium for the communality of thought, and for this reason rhetoric and hermeneutics belong together and are related to dialectics.
>
> 1. Indeed, a person thinks by means of speaking. Thinking matures by means of internal speech, and to that extent speaking is only developed thought. But whenever the speaker finds it necessary to fix what he has thought, there arises the art of speaking, that is, the transformation of original internal speaking, and interpretation becomes necessary.
> 2. Hermeneutics and rhetoric are intimately related in that every act of understanding is the reverse side of an act of speaking, and one must grasp the thinking that underlies a given statement.[78]

Noteworthy here is that Schleiermacher does not circumscribe speaking and understanding in the manner that Gadamer has done, with his untenable limitation that "true conversation" should be aimed at agreement. Instead, Schleiermacher fixes on what he calls "communality of thought" (*die Gemeinschaftlichkeit des Denkens*), the condition in which participants in a conversation have their minds focused on the same ideas, where the speaker's message is understood by the listener, whether they agree about those ideas or not.

Schleiermacher then continues with a section that explains certain conditions that affect every "act of speaking."[79] Immediately thereafter he refers at times to spoken statements and at times to texts.[80] The distinction between spoken and written discourse appears explicitly when he discusses whether the "inspiration of the Holy Spirit" means that the Scriptures must be interpreted in a way peculiar to themselves. He denies that this question can be answered by any dogmatic decision about inspiration, since such a decision itself depends on interpretation, and then continues: "We must not make a distinction between what the apostles spoke and what they wrote, for the church had to be built on their speeches."[81] This statement recognizes the important truth, a pervasive theme in this volume, that the foundations of the Christ-movement lay with oral proclamation and not written texts. I will return to this issue in chapters 6 and 7.

Schleiermacher comes closest to theorizing about the difference between spoken and written discourse when he is discussing "artful" and "artless" interpretation, the former occurring on occasions when the art of interpretation is employed and the latter on occasions when it is not. He begins with the general statement that the distinction between the two types rests "not on the difference between what is familiar to us and what is unfamiliar, or between what is spoken and what is written. Rather, it is based on the fact that we want to understand with precision some things and not others."[82] His thoughts on spoken and written discourse require the closest consideration:

> Nor do written texts alone call for the art of interpretation. Were that true, the art would be necessary only because of the difference between written and spoken words, that is, because of the loss of the living voice and the absence of supplementary personal impressions. But the latter must themselves be interpreted, and that interpretation is never certain. To be sure, the living voice facilitates understanding, and a writer must take this fact into consideration. Were he to do so, then, on the assumption that the art of interpretation is not necessary for oral statements, the art would not be necessary for his written text. But that is simply not the case. Therefore, even if an author did not consider the effects of the living voice, the necessity for the art of interpretation is not based on the difference between oral and written statements.

Thus he is able to reiterate his point—that the difference between artful and artless interpretation is that we wish to understand some things with precision but not others.

From this passage we learn quite a lot concerning Schleiermacher's views on this matter. First, he states that oral and written statements both need interpretation. Second, the fact that the former are conveyed by the living voice accompanied by facial expressions and the speaker's gestures does not constitute any fundamental difference between the two types since these expressions and gestures themselves stand in need of interpretation. Third, even aside from the effects of the living voice, the difference between oral and written statements has no impact on the need for both to be interpreted. In a footnote to this passage he appends the revealing statement: "That the art is necessary more for spoken than written language, because as the speech is spoken one cannot remember the various rules which are to be used."[83]

In the "Academy Addresses of 1829" the emphasis on interpretation embracing spoken discourse found in Schleiermacher's earlier writings re-appears. He disagrees strongly with the opposite view of Wolf and Ast.[84] For Schleiermacher, interpretation "refers to understanding all foreign or strange speech"[85] and this certainly includes oral and written discourse. He expands upon this later: "wherever one encounters something strange in the way thoughts are being expressed in speech, one is faced with a task which can be solved only with the help of a theory, presupposing of course some common point (*etwas gemeinsames*) between the speaker and the one who is to under-stand."[86] Note that here Schleiermacher does not require that the speaker and listener agree; he merely requires that both share some point of understand-ing. Immediately after this, Schleiermacher criticizes Wolf for stating that "he is interested only in understanding authors, as though the same problems do not arise in conversation and direct speech."[87] Later he adds a fundamentally important comment:

> Indeed, I must reiterate that hermeneutics is not to be limited to written texts. I often make use of hermeneutics in personal conversation when, discontented with the ordinary level of understanding, I wish to explore how my friend has moved from one thought to another or try to trace out the views, judgments, and aspirations which led him to speak about a given subject in just this way and no other. No doubt everyone has such experiences, and I think they make it clear that the task for which we seek a theory is not limited to what is fixed in writing but arises whenever we have to understand a thought or series of thoughts expressed in words.[88]

Again, Schleiermacher is interested in understanding what is said, not necessarily in agreeing with it. This is not to say that agreement could not occur, merely that it is not essential to the process.

A little later he continues this theme in a way worthy of note:

> Indeed, I readily acknowledge that I consider the practice of hermeneutics occurring in immediate communication in one's native language very essen-tial for our cultured life, apart from all philological or theological studies. Who could move in the company of exceptionally gifted persons without

endeavoring to hear "between" their words, just as we read between the lines of original and tightly written books? Who does not try in a meaningful conversation, which may in certain respects be an important act, to lift out its main points, to try to grasp its internal coherence, to pursue all its subtle intimations further? . . . Should the way we observe and interpret experienced, worldly-wise and politically shrewd persons really differ from the procedure we use with books? Should it be so different that it would depend on entirely different principles and be incapable of a comparably developed and orderly presentation? That I do not believe. On the contrary, I see two different applications of the same art.[89]

Soon after this Schleiermacher eloquently sets out the superiority of what might justly be called interpersonal communion over the model of an individual alone with a book:

I would strongly recommend diligence in interpreting significant conversations. The immediate presence of the speaker, the living expression that proclaims that his whole being is involved, the way the thoughts in a conversation develop from our shared life, such factors stimulate us far more than some solitary observation of an isolated text to understand a series of thoughts as a moment of life which is breaking forth, as one moment set in the context of many others. And this dimension of understanding is often slighted, in fact, almost completely neglected, in interpreting authors.[90]

Schleiermacher concluded his first address of 1829 with an argument that the way in which a young child acquired the capacity to think and speak was simply a reflection of the creative and perceptive capacity (that he called "divinatory") that interpreters employed.[91]

The second address of 1829 (delivered on 29 October) is devoted mainly to determining the unity of a discourse. It begins with his acceptance of Ast's view that the totality of a work could be understood from the parts and the parts can be understood only from the whole. I have noted above that this is the second main aspect of the hermeneutical circle (the first comprising the shuttling back and forth between interpreter and what is interpreted).

In a notable section of this address, Schleiermacher reveals his continuing interest in oral as well as written discourse. He inquires how one can obtain a sense of a work's unity when it lacks the modern aids of a preface or a list of contents that were not available for ancient readers. Such interpretative aids are still not available when we seek to interpret an oral address or have a work read to us (something that still happened in some circles in the Germany of his day): "In the case of speeches which are not available to us in written form and so can be heard only once, our provisional grasp of the whole cannot extend beyond what we can gather from our general knowledge of the genre and from our acquaintance with the speaker and his habits, unless the speaker himself gives us an overview of what he is going to say." But even when a provisional grasp of the whole is not possible, a person is still able to grasp the whole from the parts. Such an understanding will be incomplete unless one remembers the parts and can situate them in respect of the whole. If the listener is successful in this, "the difference between oral and written statements disappears, because in dealing with the former our memory supplies all of the information that the written form alone seemed to insure." At this point he illustrates this assimilation of the interpretation of oral and written statements by referring to Plato's *Phaedrus*: "Thus, as Plato said long ago, we need to write only to make up for defects in our memory, a vicious circle, since writing arises from the corruption of the memory and further corrupts the memory (276d and 277c–278b)."[92] For Schleiermacher, the effect of writing was merely to store a statement in a permanently memorable form. On this view there is no magic in a text or in textuality itself. Indeed, they represent a lamentable deterioration in the primary linguistic pattern of gifted speaker and attentive listener.

Although in the "Marginal Notes of 1832 and 1833" Schleiermacher does not expatiate upon the fact that hermeneutics embraced spoken as well as written discourse (as he had in the "Academy Addresses of 1829"), he does on one occasion use the phenomenon of conversation to illustrate a particular point and this indicates that he had not changed his mind on this subject.[93]

Given the importance of the spoken word for Schleiermacher, it will be worthwhile at this stage to consider how hermeneutics after him came to be so tied to interpreting texts. Since the prime culprit here seems to be Wilhelm Dilthey, I will consider his influence in this area.

Wilhelm Dilthey, Schleiermacher, and the Interpretation of Texts

The prime culprit for the prevailing misinterpretation of Schleiermacher as being concerned predominantly with interpreting texts appears to be the philosopher Wilhelm Dilthey (1833–1911), whose interest in Schleiermacher's hermeneutics is the main reason, somewhat ironically, for their eventual influence.

Dilthey faced a situation in the mid- to late nineteenth century in which the confidence and optimism shown by the natural sciences in their positivist methodology had caused something of a loss of nerve among humanities scholars. He distinguished the role of the sciences to *explain* natural phenomena from that of the humanities, with the latter seeking instead to *understand* human life and its various forms of expression. For Dilthey, such understanding required a critical foundational theory. He regarded hermeneutics as that theory, in particular the version propounded by Friedrich Schleiermacher.[94] This view is central to Dilthey's essay "The Development of Hermeneutics" (*Die Entstehung der Hermeneutik*), an essay based on a lecture delivered at the Prussian Academy of Science in 1896 and first published in 1900 that has shaped the views of many since.[95]

Dilthey begins his explanation of hermeneutics (at first without reference to Schleiermacher) promisingly enough by highlighting the role of philology and history as being to allow us to understand *unique* phenomena in the past. This characteristic differentiated human studies from the physical sciences. The former were, moreover, superior to the latter because their subject was "not merely an appearance given to the senses, a mere reflection in the mind of some outer reality, but *inner reality directly experienced in all its complexity*" [Dilthey's emphasis]. This consideration necessarily raised the related questions of individuality and interpersonal relations, since "that inner experience of my own states can never, by itself, make me aware of my own individuality. Only by comparing myself to others and becoming conscious of how I differ from them can I experience my own individuality." Yet the only way to gain insight into the inner life of others is "through the impact of their gestures, sounds and acts on our senses. We have to reconstruct the inner source of the signs which strike our senses." Dilthey notes that this process of reconstructing the distinct individuality of another, of recognizing a mental state from a sense-given sign by which it is expressed, is called "understanding."[96] All of this is virtually identical with the views of Schleiermacher for whom, as noted above, while it was necessary to get to know a speaker/author better than he knew himself, there was no direct access to his thinking processes. His further explanation of understanding in relation to listening to a speaker's words goes further down the psychological route than Schleiermacher would have gone. "In other cases," Dilthey notes, "we strain to get inside a speaker through every facial expression or word."[97]

It is at this point, however, that the wheels really begin to fall off Dilthey's argument, for he immediately goes on to say: "But even the most strenuous attention can only give rise to a systematic process with a controllable degree of objectivity if the expression has been given permanent form so that we can repeatedly return to it. *Such systematic understanding of recorded expressions we call exegesis or interpretation* [Dilthey's emphasis]." A little later he adds: "The art of understanding therefore centres on *the interpretation of written records of human existence* [Dilthey's emphasis]." Similarly, hermeneutics is "the methodology of *the interpretation of written records* [Dilthey's emphasis]." As we have already seen, in the "Academy Addresses of 1829" Schleiermacher took Wolf and Ast to task precisely for refusing to accept that hermeneutics applied to spoken as well as to written discourse.

It is clear that Dilthey has let scientific method, with its model of repeatable experiments in controlled conditions, supplant the deep and humane insight of Schleiermacher that there was no fundamental difference between interpreting oral and written discourse, since both existed in the living context of interpersonal understanding. While Dilthey professed to accept this model, by excluding the spoken word from hermeneutics he severed the hermeneutical process from the experience, aptly described by Schleiermacher, of the "immediate presence of the speaker, the living expression that proclaims that his whole being is involved, the way the thoughts in a conversation develop from our shared life." According to Schleiermacher, these are the factors that "stimulate us far more than some solitary observation of an isolated text to understand a series of thoughts as a moment of life which is breaking forth, as one moment set in the context of many others."[98] While—as a matter of fact—most hermeneutics limit the interpretative process to written texts, there is the strongest imaginable temptation to forget the real person who produced the text and to address it as an artifact floating free of its genesis in the dynamic of interpersonal understanding and dialogue, in the style of Paul Ricoeur. The semiotic theory of communication, discussed in chapter 2, with its embodiment in the solitary reader engaged in the intense scrutiny of a particular text, stands in a direct line of descent from Dilthey's unfortunate deviation from the interpersonal model pioneered by Schleiermacher.

When Dilthey discussed Schleiermacher's own views, he proposed that Schleiermacher "could only analyze understanding which is a reshaping or reconstruction on the basis of its relationship to the process of *literary creation* [emphasis added]." Yet this grossly misrepresented Schleiermacher, given that he insisted throughout his career that his theory of hermeneutics encompassed human understanding in both spoken and written forms. Similarly, when Dilthey claimed that Schleiermacher "recognized the imaginative consideration of the creative process through which a vital *literary work* [emphasis added] originates as the basis for appreciating the process by which we understand the whole of a work from its written signs and from this the purpose and mentality of its author,"[99] his limiting interpretation solely to a literary work was blatant prevarication on Dilthey's part.

The curiosity of all this is that Dilthey even recognized the importance of the Platonic dialogue at this time. Speaking of Friedrich Schlegel's translations of Plato (in a manner equally apposite for Schleiermacher), he wrote: "Here philosophy is still alive, rooted in conversation; its literary presentation is only an aid to memory. So it must be dialogue, and so stylized in form that it forces us to recreate the living context of thought."[100] Shortly after, he added: "All interpretation of literary works is merely the methodical development of the process of understanding, which extends over the whole of life and relates to any kind of speech or writing. The analysis of understanding is, therefore, the basis for making the interpretation systematic." This is entirely in accord with Schleiermacher's views, as expressed both above and in his general introduction to his translation of Plato's dialogues.[101]

Yet Dilthey continues in blank defiance of Schleiermacher's position (presumably under the influence of the natural sciences, as noted above) by immediately adding: "But this can only be done in the analysis of literary productions."[102] This view, with its insidious elimination of interpersonal dialogue from hermeneutics, gave an early stimulus to concentration upon the spoken word that would culminate eventually in a model of communication in which a text's author became essentially irrelevant to a single reader constructing meaning from the signs inscribed on its pages. Whereas Dilthey developed Schleiermacher's ideas in a manner cognate with them "in his notion of hermeneutics as the recovery of the I in the Thou through a transposition by the interpreter of his own self into the other and a reliving of his experience in himself,"[103] his insistence on texts as the only subject of hermeneutics ran the risk of downgrading the interpersonal context which was the foundation for such an understanding. In short, Dilthey's approach was the beginning of a movement toward the disappearance of the interpersonal and dialogical dimension to hermeneutics so central to Schleiermacher's vision of the process.

One of the routes by which Dilthey's unfortunate insistence on texts as the sole interest of interpretation became commonplace among biblical critics was his impact on Rudolf Bultmann. For Bultmann accepted Dilthey's definition of hermeneutics as the "technique of understanding expressions of life set in written form."[104] With Bultmann, as with Dilthey, we find a curiously and unfortunately linked recognition that Schleiermacher is concerned with hermeneutics as a project of interpersonal understanding and a failure to see that such insights are gravely imperiled when interpretation is limited to texts. Thus, the same Bultmann who accurately says, in discussing Schleiermacher, "The work must rather be understood as the life-moment of a particular man. To the comprehension of the 'external form' must be joined that of the 'internal form,' which is, he would say, the subject not of an objective, but of a subjective, 'intuitive' interpretation . . ."[105] can also misrepresent him by stating that his interpretation is "orientated to the interpretation of philosophical and literary texts,"[106] when Schleiermacher opposed limiting hermeneutics to written texts throughout the thirty years he lectured and wrote on this subject.

CONCLUSION: SCHLEIERMACHER AND HERMENEUTICS AS INTERPERSONAL COMMUNION

Thomas Torrance well summarizes the core of Schleiermacher's hermeneutics that I have identified in this chapter: "The great presupposition with which the interpreter must go to work, according to Schleiermacher, is that he is concerned with speech or language, with what is spoken and heard in acts of communication between subject and subject. That must not be forgotten even when it is a written text that is understood."[107] Yet, in the long development of hermeneutics since Schleiermacher, it is precisely this insight that has been forgotten, especially in semiotic approaches to interpretation.

Werner Jeanrond, for example, notes at one point in his monograph *Theological Hermeneutics* that "Some hermeneuts liken the interaction between reader and text to the conversation between two persons." While this statement neatly encapsulates Schleiermacher's position, it stands out in Jeanrond's text by virtue of the sentiment's rarity. Moreover, Jeanrond immediately rejects it as a model for hermeneutics:

> Yet this image does not capture the full nature of reading. Reading is not a conversation between two equal partners who possess equal ability of acting and reacting. Rather the text is a somewhat weaker partner which, for instance, is unable to defend itself against violations of its integrity by ideological readers. At best the text is empowered by a reader to unfold its meaning during the act of reading.[108]

The automatic assumption that hermeneutics is about reading is very revealing. For Schleiermacher, in contrast, hermeneutics was about understanding all discourse, spoken and written, as dialogical interaction between persons to foster communication and understanding. The inscription of some discourse on paper, which necessitates reading in order to access the communication, does not affect the fundamental realities of the situation.

Yet it is true that texts are at the mercy of their reader. This is especially so in approaches such as reader-response theory, where the interpretative aim is to *deny* the extent to which every text is the product of a human person and deserves to be interpreted accordingly. But this phenomenon is not some inescapable rule of the game of interpretation, as Jeanrond implies, but a lamentable dereliction from Schleiermacher's vision of hermeneutics that must be resisted at every turn. Although it is self-evident that the author of a text from the past will not be able to prevent modern distortion of his message, to read such texts historically within a framework of interpersonal communion, to treat the "You" who authored them as a real human person, necessitates doing all that we possibly can to hear that voice sounding forth to the full extent of its ancient otherness, yes, its strangeness from us. We do justice to Schleiermacher's hermeneutics when we bear in mind that every complex text is the product of a perceptive person and that understanding that text is not simply construing squiggles on a page. Rather, it is remembering the author's very particular context and construing the text as an attempt at interpersonal understanding. Attentive listening lies at the heart of genuine dialogue and Schleiermacher above all wanted those who encountered biblical texts to be good listeners.

Finally, it is worth reiterating Schleiermacher's commitment to the processes of historical inquiry that alone allow us to listen attentively to texts written two thousand years ago. "[O]nly historical interpretation," he wrote, "can do justice to the rootedness of the New Testament authors in their time and place."[109] A little later he made an eloquent plea for the particularity of the original audiences of New Testament texts, a subject to which we will return in chapters 6 and 7:

> But for this reason we must not suppose that their writings were addressed to all of Christendom, for in fact each text was addressed to specific people, and their writings could not be properly understood in the future unless these first readers could have understood them. But these first readers would have looked for what was specifically related to their own situations, and from this material they had to derive the whole truth of Christianity. Our interpretation must take this fact into account, and we must assume that even if the authors had been merely passive tools of the Holy Spirit, the Holy Spirit could have spoken through them only as they themselves would have spoken.[110]

Let us now consider the realities of interpersonal communication in the first-generation Christ-movement's oral context in the bustling Greco-Roman port city of Corinth.

6

FACE-TO-FACE COMMUNION BETWEEN NEW TESTAMENT CHRIST-FOLLOWERS

1 CORINTHIANS 10–14 AS A TEST CASE

The time has now come to analyze some New Testament texts in the light of the theology of interpersonal communion set out above. Our aim is to consider first-century CE data that can be understood as expressing this underlying theological reality. We will concentrate on the oldest extant New Testament writings—the letters of Paul, especially 1 Corinthians, which prove to be a decidedly rich source on interpersonal communion.

GROUP ORIENTATION AND THE SPOKEN WORD IN THE FIRST-CENTURY MEDITERRANEAN WORLD

The recent shift from individualistic to relational theological construals of the human person is apt in considering first-century Mediterranean culture. Numerous writers have applied recent anthropological insights about the Mediterranean to biblical texts, beginning with Bruce Malina in 1981.[1] They have noted the extent to which ancient Mediterranean societies were group-orientated, not individualistic. This is not to say that that individuality was not evident in this setting. It is to say that the pronounced *individualism* of modern North Atlantic cultures was not a feature of the ancient Mediterranean world.[2]

The various ancient Mediterranean cultures were also marked by the power and pervasiveness of the spoken word. While writing was known, and appeared everywhere as public inscriptions incised on stone, only a small percentage of the population, mainly the elite and the scribes who served them, was literate. William V. Harris has marshaled evidence for low literacy rates in the Greco-Roman world at this time.[3] Moreover, although it has been suggested that literacy among Israelites may have been higher because of synagogal reading practices, Catherine Hezser has recently presented a compelling case for very low levels of literacy in Roman Palestine.[4] Orality was dominant across the region. The power of the spoken word was evident in popular assemblies and law courts, so much so that the techniques of rhetoric were developed to assist the participants in preparing and delivering speeches. Traveling philosophers, orators, and performers declaimed publicly in the cities on a wide range of subjects. In synagogues throughout the diaspora, Judeans spent much of each Sabbath listening to readings from their sacred writing as interpreted by priests or elders who were present.[5] The power of the spoken word was also felt in its dark side, namely, the use of gossip and slander to damage reputations, destroy competitors, and win personal contests. The (usually unnoticed yet remarkable) prevalence of gossip and slander in the New Testament, and their various social functions among nonliterate people, has recently been the subject of an important essay by Richard Rohrbaugh.[6]

The omnipresence of the written word with which we are familiar—reflected in the contemporary scholarly obsession with textuality—only became possible with the invention of the printing press in the fifteenth century. This must not blind us to the very different realities of social life in a world where orality prevailed. In an age of textuality, the phenomenon of the solitary reader alone with a text—a fitting icon for an individualistic society—is universal; societies characterized by orality, however, embody the dialogical reality of the spoken word where every speaker requires a listener and every listener a speaker.

Paul's cultural milieu thus represents an environment where Franz Rosenzweig's advocacy of speech and dialogue as fundamental to the relational nature of the human person is confirmed with notable strength. Among the peoples of the ancient Mediterranean, the affairs of life were conducted orally in a manner unknown to us in the modern world, for whom getting to the heart of so many problems entails close attention to voluminous quantities of written material. Ancient orality not only subsisted in the lively processes of interpersonal dialogue, but also flourished in the context of one speaker addressing an audience. The frequency of such events, in judicial, political, military, or occasional settings, was the driving force for the centrality of rhetoric in the educational process. The trouble taken by a speaker to ensure the persuasiveness of his discourse was predicated upon the existence of listeners thoroughly trained through long experience in weighing the merits of what was being said and in responding with approbation or dissent. Speakers needed to pay the closest attention to the effect their words were having on the audience and were ready and able to modulate their message if necessary. This feature in particular closely conforms to Rosenzweig's understanding of the dynamic nature of interpersonal dialogue and the priority of the spoken over the written word.

PAUL'S PROBLEM IN CORINTH

While this is the broad context from within which Paul wrote his letters, Paul's letters contain much information about relational issues because he often needed to combat tendencies toward divisiveness or even factionalism. This was the case not only with congregations he had founded (Corinth, Galatia, and Philippi), but also with the groups of Christ-followers in Rome, a city he had never visited prior to writing (his longest extant letter) to them in the late 50s of the first century CE.[7] In letter after letter, Paul strove to remind his addressees of their unity in Christ through baptism and which they should continue to develop rather than endanger. Interpersonal relations, expressed both in the dynamics of speaking and listening, and also in the practice of the common meal, prove central to his vision of what it means to be a person within the new dispensation inaugurated by Christ. Although his statements in this area were stimulated by his need to counter pressures threatening to destroy congregational unity, and each of them reflects particular contextual problems, they yet contain a substantial positive expression of his views on interpersonal communion in Christ.

The main passages containing Pauline views on this subject occur in 1 Corinthians 10–14. As Margaret Mitchell has demonstrated, Paul's dominant purpose in writing 1 Corinthians was to persuade the Christ-followers of Corinth to become unified.[8] He announces this concern in general terms at the start of the body of the letter (1 Cor 1:10-16). Thereafter, most of the problems Paul addresses are either represent variations on this theme of division and factionalism or, if not, can only be solved by the unity the Corinthian believers should manifest in Christ.

We noted above that Rosenzweig identified three stages in the process leading to communion between persons. The first was that of speaking and listening, the second that of the common meal, and the third that of the perfect communion represented by the ultimate experience of common silence. My argument will follow this order. (This means that we will first discuss the spoken word in 1 Corinthians 12–14 before discussing common meals in 1 Corinthians 10–11.) Although Rosenzweig's third stage of communion between persons, common silence, is not a phenomenon likely to leave many traces in our sources, I will return to it briefly at the end of this chapter.

1 CORINTHIANS 12–14

The focus of 1 Corinthians 12–14 is "matters of the Spirit" (*ta pneumatika*; 12:1). It is highly probable that this discussion was prompted by the Corinthians' concerns about glossolalia, "speaking in tongues," in view of Paul's extensive attempt in 1 Corinthians 14 to depreciate the importance of glossolalia in relation to intelligible verbal messages. For Paul and his audience, glossolalia did not mean being inspired by the Spirit to speak in foreign languages they did not know ("xenoglossy"), but rather signified nonarticulate sounds, perhaps a kind of tuneful ululation.[9] It is likely that those members of the Christ-movement in Corinth who did produce glossolalia magnified their status at the expense of those who did not. This was an unsurprising consequence of glossolalia being interpreted as the result of possession by God and as identical with the language spoken by the angels. This attitude gave glossolalia an undeserved priority over other gifts of the Spirit characterizing the movement, as well as producing a damaging division among the members. Thus we have disunity instigated by a pathological use of the spoken word. Instead of building communion, the (inarticulate) spoken word is threatening to sunder Christ-followers from one another. The ability of language either to build or to destroy community, especially in contrast with the totally positive function of *agapē* (the love that should typify the Christ-movement), is a pervasive theme throughout 1 Corinthians 12–14. Therefore this section of the letter offers fruitful data for analysis within the theological framework of interpersonal communion.

Communion through Language between God and Christ-Believers: 1 Cor 12:1-11

The prominence of oral discourse in the passage begins very early. After announcing the subject of "matters of the Spirit" (12:1), Paul continues in 12:2 with a sentence that is somewhat difficult to construe and is also an anacoluthon (that is, it lacks a grammatical connection with the preceding verse): "You know that when you were heathen (*ethnē*) you were carried away to voiceless idols, however you would be led."[10]

Commentators have struggled to identify the reason for the inclusion of v. 2 at all at this point.[11] One popular solution is that Paul alludes to former experience of ecstatic speech among his addressees when they were attached to idolatrous cults. He then contrasts that with their current enjoyment of superior phenomena in the Christ-movement. This view, advocated by Fee, for example,[12] should be rejected. It assumes that urban Greek and Roman idol worshipers were widely acquainted with speech under the influence of divine possession, a view for which there is no evidence. As Christopher Forbes has shown,[13] it is very difficult to find any parallels for the early Christ-movement's glossolalia elsewhere in the Greco-Roman world of this period. In addition, Paul would have been a most incompetent communicator if he assumed his addressees would understand he was referring to *spoken* phenomena in idolatrous worship when his only description of the objects of such worship was "voiceless idols" (*ta eidōla ta aphōna*; 1 Cor 12:2).

It is possible from Paul's reference to their being "carried away" and "led" that he has in mind that the Corinthians had previously experienced some form of "possession" or altered states of consciousness in idolatrous worship that were not associated with glossolalic speech.[14] But these expressions could just as easily refer to their having formerly been dominated by demons, the actors in the pagan cult (see 1 Cor 8:1-6; 10:20).[15]

The most probable reason for v. 2's inclusion is that Paul is seeking to contrast the idolatrous practices of Greco-Roman worship with the very different realities of the Christ-movement. The former was directed to voiceless statues and did not involve speech in an altered state of consciousness, while the Holy Spirit's presence among the latter ensured a diversity of oral phenomena. This meant turning existing Israelite categorization of idolatry as voiceless[16] in an entirely new direction. This is not a "minimal" explanation, as Fee suggests, by contrast with his postulation of their previously having experienced inspired utterances in pagan settings.[17] Rather, it rests plausibly on Paul's concern to differentiate life in the Spirit for members of the Christ-movement from the Greco-Roman idolatry he described earlier (in chapter 10 most notably). Only now Paul relates life in the Spirit to exciting manifestations of God's presence, especially in forms of discourse (including a form of divine possession unique to the Christ-movement), in contrast to the mute lifelessness of pagan idolatry.

In 1 Cor 12:3 Paul inaugurates his discussion of speech in the Christ-movement with a pair of contrasting statements: "No one speaking in the Spirit says, 'Jesus is cursed,' and no one is able to say, 'Jesus is Lord,' unless in the Holy Spirit." Here he stresses the articulation of the spoken word as a response to the presence or the absence of the Spirit. Paul installs appropriate language as fundamental to the right relationship between a person and God at the very outset of the discussion.

Much ink has been spilled unnecessarily on proposing actual settings in which someone might have said "Jesus is cursed," usually preferring a context in Greco-Roman cult over meetings of the Christ-movement. But there is no need to presume that Paul is referring to an actual practice anywhere. "'Jesus is accursed,'" as Conzelmann notes, "is an *ad hoc* construction on Paul's part to form an antithesis to κύριος Ἰησοῦς."[18] Paul's interest does not lie in actual expressions of the curse (which is really just a hypothetical utterance), nor indeed with the literal truth of the second statement, since anyone at all could say "Jesus is Lord," whether in the Spirit or not. Rather, these two statements represent emphatic and contrasting ways in which Paul can relate the presence of the Spirit of God to the recognition of Christ's lordship in spoken form. Their purpose is to assert continuity between God and the human beings who employ the spoken word to acknowledge Christ as Lord. They make possible a unified interpretation of the being of God and of that part of the created order represented by the language-using human beings who comprise the Christ-movement. As noted above, this is very close to the way in which Alan Torrance has formulated John Zizioulas's unique contribution of his understanding of the communion between persons and God. In addition, however, Paul's postulation of a hypothetical cursing of Jesus does remind his readers of the possibility that language can negate faith and fracture community as well as build community. He presses that message with some urgency in 1 Corinthians 12–14.

The relational character of the process expressed here is quite striking. By imparting his Spirit into certain human beings, God ensures that they recognize and verbally acknowledge that Jesus is Lord. Just as important is the precise modality in which God is present to these people in God's Spirit. They are actually *in* that Spirit, that *Pneuma*. Paul conceives of the Spirit as a zone of divine being and activity in which certain human beings subsist. Immediately after this, he will make plain to his audience that the Spirit produces dramatic human responses so stamped with their origin as to be called *pneumatika* (1 Cor 12:1).

The oral dimension is critical to these opening assertions in v. 3. Paul is not interested in private and silent assent, but in spoken discourse, presumably produced before an audience as a public assertion of the heart of the new faith. That the words in question, "Jesus is Lord," are intelligible, rather than nonintelligible, glossolalia is central to Paul's meaning in a situation where the latter was elevated above its proper station. Rosenzweig's notion of language as the "organon of revelation" applies quite closely to what Paul is communicating here.

Verses 4-5 comprise three finely balanced statements that integrate an assertion of a diversity of gifts (summary form) with an insistence on the unity of the divine source from which they derive:

> There are varieties of gifts, but the same Spirit;
> There are varieties of ministries, but the same Lord;
> There are varieties of workings, but the same God
> who works all things in all people.

The first point to note here is the similarity to what Zizioulas has referred to as the *ekstasis* of being that characterizes any person, human or divine. By this he means that generous openness of being, that movement toward communion that transcends the boundaries of the self. For Paul, God is not an entity locked up in the remote and lofty fastnesses of his own being. Instead, God is a person who expresses his being by active and varied involvement with the human persons of his creation, an involvement realized and manifested in the presence of his Spirit. Second, we note the remarkably proto-trinitarian character of Paul's triadic description of the divine origin of these gifts in these verses. On the reasonable assumption that by "God" in v. 5 Paul means "God the Father" (as at 1 Cor 8:6), we find here a differentiation of activity as between the Spirit, (Christ the) Lord, and the Father. C. K. Barrett rightly notes here that the "Trinitarian formula is the more impressive because it seems to be artless and unconscious."[19] Although Paul is propounding a reasonably sophisticated account of the interaction of the triune God with human beings (that aspect of the Trinity now known as the "economic"), there is nothing here of the "immanent" dimensions of the Trinity, and nor would it be reasonable to demand that from Paul at this early stage in the history of the Christ-movement. That Paul had simply not thought about this issue seems more probable than that he had (and consequently had hit upon a view similar to Catherine LaCugna's close connection of the immanent and economic elements of God's trinitarian nature; see chapter 2).

In vv. 7-11 the focus changes from the God who is the source of gifts to a more detailed account of how each member of the movement is given "a manifestation of the Spirit for the common good" (*pros to sympheron*; v. 7). Even here, however, the passage ends with the statement that "the one and the same Spirit works all these things, distributing to each one individually as he wills" (v. 11). Paul insists on the unity of God in spite of the diversity of gifts lavished on the Corinthians.

Paul lists nine manifestations of the Spirit:

1. A word of wisdom;
2. A word of knowledge;
3. Faith;
4. Gifts of healing;
5. The working of miracles;
6. Prophecy;
7. The ability to distinguish between spirits;
8. Various kinds of tongues; and
9. The interpretation of tongues.

Of these the majority (1, 2, 6, 8, and 9) necessarily involve spoken discourse. But each of the other four also seems to have an oral dimension. For whatever else faith entails (possibly the particular faith that moves mountains, mentioned in 1 Cor 13:2), it is presumably always encapsulated in the affirmation "Jesus is Lord" (see v. 3). Gifts of healing and the working of miracles probably require the use of words of power.[20] Distinguishing between spirits presumably involves some statement about the character of the spirit in question. All of these modes of speech are intelligible, except for glossolalia (the "various kinds of tongues"), which is no doubt mentioned near the end of the list as a reflection of Paul's overall strategy of reducing its importance among the Corinthian believers in Christ.

From this it is clear that the spoken word, which Paul here interprets as a fruit of the Spirit's activity, played a central role in the life of the city's Christ-movement. The distribution of the gifts sets up a communion between God and those who have faith in Christ. Nor can one fail to notice that in each of these manifestations of speech (except, one suspects, for glossolalia, and that suspicion is confirmed later) one Christ-follower reaches out to one or more members of the group: to enlighten, to inform, to heal, to prophesy, to discern between spirits, to express a glossolalic utterance requiring someone to interpret it, or to offer such an interpretation. Here speech is the embodiment of an "ekstatic" outpouring of one person beyond the boundaries of self in the direction of another. We might adapt Rosenzweig to suggest that "a Christ-follower becomes a Christ-follower when he or she speaks," or that "language makes faith."

Yet it is equally clear that these ministries vary widely in their capacity to build communion among the community members themselves. In each case they become effective when *one* person reaches out to others; that is, in all of them *an individual is the agent, not the group itself*. In addition, although often the person concerned will engage with the whole group (as with many occasions when messages of wisdom or knowledge are delivered or a prophecy spoken), at other times perhaps only one other person is in view, as when someone is healed, or the nature of a spirit discerned. In these latter cases, where the relationship is person-to-person ("dyadic"), not person-to-group, the activity will not necessarily benefit the whole group. We have already noted that a problem with Zizioulas's theological model of communion between persons is that it fails to address the fact that any group is distinct from the members that comprise it. To build communion within a group it is necessary to take into account the special social factors at work among members of the whole group and not just the relationships between individual members. Furthermore, in a culture, such as that of the first-century Mediterranean region, when one's gift to another required reciprocity to preserve the recipient's honor,[21] exercising any of these ministries possessed great potential to be locked into a purely dyadic relationship. In other words, the possibility inherent in separate individuals bearing different gifts is that the community will dissolve into a set of individual relationships or transactions. Worse still is the possibility that a gift like glossolalia will actually be corrupted through its use to promote the status of one person at the expense of others who do not possess this gift.

Accordingly, these ministries—all of them characterized by, or encompassing, the spoken word—do not inevitably lead to the unification of the community. While that will often be the case (as when a person preaches to or prophesies before all the members), these gifts do not by their nature necessarily produce unity. It is a tribute to Paul's insight into how groups operate, no doubt developed through long and often difficult experience, that he is very much alive to this problem and to its ramifications in Corinth. This is evident both in his insistence on the unified divine source of the multiplicity of gifts in 1 Cor 12:4-7 and 11 and in his explicitly mentioning in 1 Cor 12:7 that the manifestation of the Spirit is given to each "for the common good." Even in the setting of a meeting of a congregation, Paul is aware that these gifts have a variable impact on community formation; as he says later: "The person who speaks in a tongue builds up himself, whereas the person who prophesies builds up the community" (1 Cor 14:4). For this reason, it is to be expected that after his discussion of the communion between God and Christ-believers in vv. 1-11, he will move to relations among the Christ-followers themselves (1 Cor 12:12-31).

Communion through Language among Christ-Followers: 1 Cor 12:12-31

This section comprises an introductory statement (vv. 12-13), an exposition of this via an extended metaphor of a human body (vv. 14-26), and then an application of this discussion to the character and status of ministries within the body of Christ (vv. 27-31). Verse 14 begins the metaphor of the body; it does not, as some critics interpret it,[22] conclude vv. 12-13. The main point of 1 Cor 12:12-31 is to emphasize the need for unity among the membership in spite of the variety of ministries represented among them. The problem, as Paul perceives it, is that the existence of a variety of manifestations of the Spirit, with some (notably glossolalia) being valued more highly than others, is causing, or is likely to cause, divisions among the members. It is most surprising to find some commentators (such as Fee and possibly Conzelmann) torturing the text to have it produce the opposite view: that they need to be mindful of the differentiation of ministries among them in spite of their unity. Unfortunately for Paul, he was rarely lucky enough to be writing to a group of Christ-followers where unity could be taken for granted and he needed to insist on its diversity!

This does not, however, mean that he downgrades the status of the individuals within the movement. A central element of the model of Zizioulas's interpersonal communion is that each individual making up the whole is a hypostasis, a free and concrete person. True communion is not possible other than among persons who maintain the integrity of their own selfhoods throughout the process. As we have already noted, LaCugna insists: "*Koinōnia* does not swallow up the individual, nor obscure his or her uniqueness and unique contribution, nor take away individual freedom by assimilating it to the collective will."[23]

That Paul's interest is the need for unity emerges in the opening statement and in the body imagery. He announces this theme of unity in the first verse in this section:

> For just as the body is one and has many organs,
> and all the organs of the body, though many, are one body,
> so also is Christ. (V. 12)

This issue flows naturally from the discussion in 1 Cor 12:1-11, which itself was probably prompted by conditions among the movement in Corinth. He has just expatiated upon the diversity of gifts of the Spirit that, in spite of their single divine source and intention to promote the common good, plainly held the potential for disunity. He now squarely faces this problem by helping his audience understand how diversity might find unity—in the image of the body, which he identifies with Christ. He immediately reveals the reason for this assertion, by reminding his audience that one Spirit has incorporated the admittedly diverse human beings who comprise the movement into a unity in Christ through baptism:

> For in one Spirit we were all baptized into the one body,
> whether Judeans or Greeks, slaves or free,
> and we were all given to drink the one Spirit. (V. 13)[24]

Here we see the twofold dynamic characteristic of baptism among early Christ-followers: first baptism, immersion in water, and second the first outpouring of the charismatic gifts of the Spirit upon the person concerned, for that is what "to drink the one Spirit" means here. That this was the customary process is seen in the incident involving Cornelius and his relatives and close friends in Acts 10:44-48. When they begin to manifest the Spirit, including by glossolalia, *before baptism*, Peter is concerned to regularize the situation by having them baptized immediately! Whether Judean or Greek, slave or free, all members of the Christ-movement have received the Spirit and continue to be bearers of it. Just as Paul had previously insisted in vv. 4-6 that behind the diversity of phenomena was a single divine source, so now he maintains that the recipients of these spiritual gifts form a unity among themselves. That unity is the body of Christ into which they were incorporated by the Spirit-charged experience of baptism. Here we find Paul intent on underlining the group's social dimension, its character transcending the individuals who comprise it, by reference to the body of Christ and its metaphor of the human body.

Earlier in the letter Paul had introduced body imagery when he asked his addressees, "Do you not know that your bodies are members of Christ?" (1 Cor 6:15) as an argument aimed at encouraging them to keep away from prostitutes. Now he uses the body metaphor for a different purpose, as a way pleading for unity based on the interdependence of all its organs. Margaret Mitchell has usefully investigated the Greco-Roman parallels to this image. The most famous of these concerns the resolution of a secession by a considerable number of plebeians from Rome. The people still in the city sent out to them one Menenius Agrippa. He told them a fable concerning a body in which the hands, mouth, and teeth decided to stop providing food for the stomach (which seemed to be passive and useless). When the whole body became seriously weakened, the rebellious organs came to their senses. Thus Menenius Agrippa managed to persuade the plebeians to return to Rome and harmony among the citizens was restored.[25] Mitchell has shown that the Greeks and Romans used the image "to demonstrate the interrelatedness of all members in one body politic in order to urge concord and end factionalism." She has also argued that Paul's version of the image exactly correlates with these Greco-Roman counterparts both in its details and in its application.[26]

The accuracy of Mitchell's position is confirmed by briefly considering Paul's use of this image. His introductory statement, "For the body is not one organ but many" (v. 14), paves the way for a discussion about each organ of the body needing the others and its inability to function on its own (vv. 15-17). The arrangement of the body's organs is a result of God's action (v. 18). After stating that the body is a unity comprising many parts (vv. 19-20), Paul then more closely applies the metaphor to the situation in Corinth. The eye cannot tell the hand it has no need of it, nor the head say that to the feet (v. 21). Now Paul makes a lengthy statement that the parts of the body that seem to be the weakest and most dishonorable are actually indispensable and clothed with honor (vv. 22-24). It is highly probable that behind these assurances lies a situation in Corinth where some members were parading their roles as more important and honorable than those of other members. Finally, Paul explicitly summarizes the point of the metaphor:

> But God has so composed the body . . . in order that there may be no division in the body, but that the organs should have the same care for one another. If one organ suffers, all the organs suffer together; if one organ is honored, all the organs rejoice together. (Vv. 25-26)

Faced with fissiparous tendencies in Corinth stemming from some believers exaggerating the importance of their role as if the others did not matter, Paul asserts the mutual interdependence of the parts, in effect, the necessity of concord, of unity. Although they are certainly each separate persons, their lives and status are inextricably linked within the community: "You are the body of Christ and individually members of it" (v. 27).

Having established these general principles, Paul is now able to relate the metaphor directly to the issue that has prompted it: divisiveness produced by the differentiation of ministries in the movement in Corinth. Just as God has arranged the organs of the body (v. 18), so he has also arranged the members in the community (*en tē ekklēsia*) into ministries, in an explicitly hierarchical arrangement:

1. apostles
2. prophets
3. teachers
4. miracles
5. gifts of healing
6. helpful acts
7. acts of guidance
8. kinds of tongues (V. 28)

It is worth noting, anticipating the discussion below, that the first three ministries mentioned (the only ones expressly enumerated in the text) are characterized by rational discourse. This is clearly the case with apostles (although, like Paul, they no doubt manifested other gifts) and with teachers. One pervasive feature of prophetic activity was to make intelligible statements in the first person singular where God was taken to be the actual speaker.[27]

Following immediately upon the heels of this list, Paul attempts to ensure that his addressees do not forget his metaphor about the human body.

Parallel to his view that a body cannot consist of one organ (no matter how valuable the organ may be), but rather contains a variety of different, mutually interdependent organs, he now adds:

> Are all apostles?
> Are all prophets?
> Are all teachers?
> Do all work miracles?
> Do all have gifts of healing?
> Do all speak in tongues?
> Do all interpret?
> Be ambitious for the greater gifts. (V. 29-31)

The point of the concluding exhortation in v. 31 is that the Corinthians should put a greater stock on the higher gifts that (as we know from v. 28) are ministries using intelligible discourse, rather than the exciting, yet unintelligible gift of glossolalia that they apparently valued too highly.

We have noticed above that the gifts of the Spirit Paul has been discussing, all involving spoken discourse, are not specifically focused upon building a unified community—even if some of them do just that. But now, rather unexpectedly, Paul relativizes the importance of all of the gifts in relation to the most important and fundamental aspect of life in Christ, namely, *agapē*, the love that should characterize the movement. This love is the subject of 1 Corinthians 13, which he begins with the final statement in v. 31: "And I am showing you a still more excellent way."

Love Is Greater Than the Gifts of the Spirit: 1 Corinthians 13

We know from elsewhere in his correspondence that Paul viewed *agapē* as produced by the Spirit. In Gal 5:22 it is listed as the first fruit of the Spirit. In Rom 5:5 God's *agapē* is poured into our hearts through the Holy Spirit. Yet here Paul is clearly differentiating *agapē* from the spiritual gifts, the *pneumatika* he begins to discuss at 1 Cor 12:1. At 1 Cor 14:1 he will even say: "Pursue love [*agapē*], and zealously seek the spiritual gifts [*ta pneumatika*] especially in order that you may prophesy." Paul regards *agapē* (described in 1 Cor 12:31 as a "way," *hodos*) and *ta pneumatika* as quite different. Whereas the *pneumatika* consist of particular activities (all with a spoken dimension), *agapē*, as its manifestation in a human person and not as a divine gift, is a disposition—a settled and stable capacity, tendency, or propensity possessed by a person. A disposition itself narrates no incidents in a person's life but is satisfied by narrated incidents.[28] Moreover, it is reasonable to regard *agapē* as a "virtue," that is, a disposition that makes its possessor morally virtuous and contributes to his or her growth. Paul's emphasis on *agapē* indicates that he regarded it as central to the Christ-movement's identity.[29]

But for Paul *agapē* is not only different from the *pneumatika*, it is superior to them. One reason for this is that *agapē* unambiguously and unarguably produces group unity in a way that "gifts of the Spirit" do not. Paul intimated this view earlier in the letter when he said, "Knowledge puff ups [*physioi*], but love builds up [*oikodomei*]" (8:1). In other words, *agapē* promotes *oikodomē*, a key term in the letter that expresses Paul's vision of a community characterized by unity and not division (the word appears several times in 1 Corinthians 14). Greco-Roman writers used the language of *homonoia/concordia* to describe the internal condition of a family or city at peace with itself.[30]

Some critics, such as Barrett and Conzelmann,[31] have regarded 1 Corinthians 13 as an originally separate composition that Paul inserts at this point in his argument rather artificially linking it to 1 Corinthians 12 and 14. Yet, while it may be unpalatable to some that Paul is diminishing the status of the gifts of the Spirit (particularly ones involving the ministry of the word), it is impossible to ignore the lengths to which he goes to do just this by his integrating this encomium on *agapē* into his whole argument. Especially notable is that chapter 13's I-voice, prominent throughout the passage, begins by stigmatizing four of the spiritual gifts that are mentioned in chapter 12 as useless without *agapē*: speaking in tongues, prophecy, knowledge, and faith (1 Cor 13:1-2). Later he mentions that love never fails but that prophecy, tongues, and knowledge will disappear (1 Cor 13:8). While it is true that he mainly targets speaking in tongues, which is why he dealt with it first (in 1 Cor 12:1), even prophecy, knowledge, and faith are less important than love.

It is possible that although most of 1 Corinthians 13 has been formulated for the purpose of making the gifts of the Spirit (especially glossolalia) subservient to *agapē*, some material in the chapter may reflect Paul's customary proclamation about love. This is probably the case with vv. 4-7 where Paul's statements about *agapē* are comparable to his more substantive teaching in Rom 12:9-21.[32] Upon examination, vv. 4-7, representing the chapter's only section that tells us what *agapē* means in practice, reveal themselves as ideally suited to the production of personal intercommunion within the group. In essence, they advocate putting other persons ahead of oneself. We are so used to this type of exhortation in Christian contexts that we miss the powerfully radical impact such a message had in its original context. There people were honor-bound to protect the ramparts of self against any invasion, from an insult on the one hand to a physical assault on the other, where any such assault was bitterly resented, where one plotted vengeance against one's enemies and railed at their successes, and where it was acceptable to speak haughtily and disdainfully to those who were not relatives or friends. The advice in vv. 4-7 represents a Pauline version of what Zizioulas calls openness or *ekstasis* of being, that movement toward communion with others that leads to transcending the boundaries of the "self."

The Superiority of Intelligible Discourse: 1 Corinthians 14

The first verse of 1 Corinthians 14 marks a transition from the treatment of *agapē* in the preceding chapter. Having established in 1 Corinthians 13 that love takes precedence over the *pneumatika*, Paul now repeats the importance of *agapē* but then returns to the *pneumatika*, especially emphasizing prophecy: "Pursue love, and zealously seek the spiritual gifts, especially that you might prophesy." Although the spiritual gifts are not as fundamental as love in community maintenance, they are still important and Paul considers them at some length.

The dominant theme of chapter 14 is that intelligible utterance, especially prophecy, is more useful for building up the community than the nonintelligible utterance that is glossolalia. The person who speaks in tongues speaks not to human beings but to God; no one understands him, since he is speaking mysteries in the Spirit; he builds up (*oikodomei*) only himself. On the other hand, the one who prophesies speaks to other persons, "building [them] up" (*oikodomē*), produces encouragement and consolation, and builds up the community (*ekklēsian oikodomei*; vv. 2-4). Glossolalia can only build up the community if it is interpreted (v. 5).

Paul is adamant that intelligibility is essential if language is to serve a positive role within the community. Even his glossolalia could not help them unless he provides revelation, knowledge, prophecy, or teaching, all of which imply comprehensible discourse (vv. 6-8). So also with them; their discourse (*logos*) has to be intelligible or they will not be understood (v. 9). They will be as unintelligible to one another as two people speaking two different human languages (vv. 10-11). Granted they desire the spiritual gifts, their goal should be to abound in those that cause a building up (*oikodomē*) of the community (*ekklēsia*; v. 12), those gifts in which they use their mind (*nous*), and not the gifts in which their minds are "fruitless" (v. 14). Five words of this type are preferable to tens of thousands in tongues (v. 19). They must be mature in their rational intelligence (v. 20). By recourse to a non-Septuagintal version of Isa 28:11-12 ("'By foreign tongues and by the lips of others I will speak to this people, yet even so they will not listen to me,' says the Lord"), Paul argues that tongues are a sign for those who do not believe, not for those who do. By this he means that nonbelievers will not be won over by glossolalia; they will think that the congregation's members that practice it are mad (v. 23). Prophecy, on the other hand, is a sign for believers and not nonbelievers. This means that if nonbelievers enter a congregation where prophecy is being practiced, they will be persuaded of the truth of the message and will worship God for the reason that God is truly among them (vv. 24-25).

In the next section (vv. 26-33), Paul drives home this message. His concern is that spiritual gifts ensure that every gathering ("Whenever you come together"), when each of them produces a psalm, or teaching, or an apocalypse, glossolalia, or its interpretation, becomes an occasion for *oikodomē* (v. 26). He is all too aware that not every gathering will necessarily produce this result. His statement at v. 33, that God is not a God of *akatastasia* but of peace, raises an alternate possibility. Instead of peace, the meeting will be characterized by *akatastasia*, a word especially frequent in references to political upheaval and civic strife meaning "instability," "confusion," "factionalism," or "anarchy."[33] Part of Paul's recipe for the congregation being built up and at peace is that only a small number speak, one at a time, with the rest keeping silent. And glossolalia should not even be uttered if there is no one to interpret its meaning (vv. 27-31). At the end of chapter 14, however, while repeating his injunction to desire prophecy (see 1 Cor 14:1), he directs that glossolalia should not be banned (v. 40).

COMMUNION THROUGH COMMON MEALS IN 1 CORINTHIANS 10–11

Having considered 1 Corinthians 12-14 as it bears upon speaking and listening, the first stage of Rosenzweig's three-stage process leading to interpersonal communion, we now pass to his second stage, the common meal, by looking briefly at 1 Corinthians 10–11.

In Barrett's view: "This threefold ministry of the word [in 12: 28] is, according to Paul, the primary Christian ministry. By it the church is founded, and built up. Other activities, such as baptism (1.17) can occupy only a secondary place."[34] Here Barrett treats "other activities"—specifically baptism, but we could easily add the Lord's Supper—as included in a single category that also contains the ministry of the word but are inferior to it. Yet this view merely reflects a theological prejudgment that prioritizes proclamation of the word; this is an unsustainable exegesis of Paul's meaning. The ministry of the word and rituals such as baptism and the Lord's Supper are each of different natures and are strictly speaking incommensurable. Yet we can gauge their respective contributions to establishing the kind of communion between members that should characterize the Christ-movement. By this criterion, we cannot relegate baptism and eucharist to a subsidiary rank. In Paul's view, no amount of preaching the word can actually effect a person's incorporation into the body of Christ; that is the function of baptism alone (1 Cor 12:13). Similarly, Paul speaks of the one loaf and one cup (of the Lord's Supper) as embodying the community's oneness in a manner not matched in his statements concerning the ministry of the word. We must remember, moreover, that Paul himself relativizes the value of the gifts listed in 1 Cor 12:28-30 by showing the Corinthians, in 1 Corinthians 13, an even better route—that of *agapē*.

TRUE AND FALSE COMMUNION IN 1 CORINTHIANS 10–11

In 1 Corinthians 10 Paul is concerned with the question of idolatry and idol food. The two were closely linked because in the ancient Mediterranean world the worship of gods was preeminently effected through the sacrificial slaying of animals, followed by the consumption of the meat by those taking part. Sacrifice, as Walter Burkert, an eminent authority on Greek religion, observes, was "ritualized slaughter followed by a meat meal."[35] This meant that a major source of meat in Greco-Roman cities was meat from animals that had been sacrificed to the various gods worshipped in each city. In Jerusalem, also, the Judeans who took part in some forms of sacrifice to God ate the meat of the victim (as Paul will mention in v. 18), even though in that type known as the *olah*, the burnt offering, all of the victim was burned on the altar. Burkert notes that, although it is difficult to understand how the Greek form of sacrifice, where the gods' share of the victim consisted only of the smoke from burned fat rising to heaven, affected the gods concerned, what it meant for the people involved "is always quite clear: community, *koinonia*."[36] "What sacrifice is pleasing to the gods without the fellow banqueters?" wrote Dio Chrysostom.[37] Burkert explains as follows: "Membership of the community is marked by the washing of hands, the encirclement (sc. of those involved around the altar) and the communal throwing (sc. of barley groats onto the altar); an even closer bond is forged through the tasting of the *splanchna*." In short, "The order of life, a social order, is constituted in the sacrifice through irrevocable acts; religion and everyday existence interpenetrate so completely that every community, every order must be founded through a sacrifice."[38] The role of communal sacrifice in maintaining and legitimating civic identity in the Greco-Roman cities of the East no doubt meant that Christ-followers who withdrew from this practice ran the risk of being labeled a-theist.[39] Derek

Newton has recently argued in some detail that the meals associated with the Greco-Roman cults in Corinth with which Paul was concerned did embrace social and religious elements.[40] Although there is a lively recent discussion concerning the occasions for, and precise character of, the consumption of idol meat in Corinth and Paul's response to this phenomenon,[41] the general explanation of its significance just offered will suffice for the purposes of the present discussion.

Paul's instruction on idolatry makes good sense in this context. He takes up the question by recourse to an exemplum from Israel's past reinterpreted in a daring way. He recalls how the Israelites, after their escape from Egypt and in spite of God's help in the form of spiritual (*pneumatikon*) food and drink, displeased him and were overthrown in the wilderness (1 Cor 10:1-5). Paul does not mention the reason for this divine punishment, the Israelites' idolatry in the wilderness (including worship of the golden calf); presumably he can rely on their knowledge of this from familiarity with the contents of Exodus 32 (as confirmed by the quotation of Exod 32:6 in v. 7) and Deut 32:15-33. To bring the fate of the wilderness generation more closely to bear on his audience, Paul engages in what is usually referred to as "typological interpretation" but which can be interpreted with more relevance here as Paul's colonization of the tradition of Israel in order to generate a new collective memory for the Christ-followers of Corinth. By passing through the sea, they were "baptized into Moses" (similar to the baptism into Christ of his addressees), the spiritual food and drink foreshadows the ingredients of the Lord's Supper, while the rock that followed them was Christ. *Paul's highlighting baptism and food and drink confirms their importance in his argument.* Yet in spite of these benefits, the Israelites of old still fell into idolatry and were punished. Paul is determined to dissuade his Corinthians from the same mistake and takes great pains to drive home the lesson that they should shun *eidōlatria*, the worship of idols (1 Cor 10:6-14).

At this point Paul moves from criticism of idolatry to a positive statement concerning the common meal of the Christ-followers, the Lord's Supper (*kuriakon deipnon*) to which he will return in chapter 11:

> The cup of blessing which we bless, is it not communion [*koinōnia*] with the blood of Christ? The bread which we break, is it not communion [*koinōnia*] with the body of Christ? Because the bread which we break is one, we, although many, are one body, for we all share in the one bread. (1 Cor 10:16-17)

For Paul, this meal is analogous to Israelite sacrifice, since those who eat the sacrifices are people-in-communion-with[42] (*koinōnoi*) the altar (v. 20). He follows this with his most pressing concern: while there may be no substance to idols (here meaning the cult objects) or idol food, what their worshippers offer they offer to demons and not to God, and he does not want them to be people-in-communion-with (*koinōnoi*) demons. This brings him back to the Lord's Supper:

> You are not able to drink the cup of the Lord and the cup of demons, you
> are not able to participate in the table of the Lord and the table of demons.
> Shall we provoke the Lord to jealousy [*parazēloumen*]? Are we stronger than
> he? (1 Cor 10:21-22)

Here Paul is bringing out the theological foundation for his opposing idolatry, but his use of the highly significant word *parazēloumen* (which appears in the Septuagintal version of Deut 32:21) reveals the extent to which it is firmly laid on Mediterranean culture. By this word Paul indicates that God will be "angrily protective of and concerned for his honor" if the Corinthian Christ-followers participate in the table of demons, just as God was in relation to the Israelites in Deut 32:21.[43] It is not possible to have communion with demons and God will take such behavior as a serious affront and will punish those who engage in it.

In this case, therefore, Paul underlines the seriousness of engaging in communion with the Lord and with demons. Sanction is threatened of a kind which is not in view in relation to pathologies in the oral phenomena discussed in 1 Corinthians 12 and 14. All this suggests the importance attached to the eucharist in how Paul understood the character and identity of the Christ-movement. A similar attitude surfaces when, in 1 Corinthians 11, he moves to another issue related to the Lord's Supper—misconduct that actually affects the way it is conducted.

The precise nature of the problem in relation to the Lord's Supper in 1 Cor 11:17-34 has been the subject of immense discussion which it is not possible to canvas within the compass of this volume. At a general level, as is apparent from 1 Cor 11:18, the problem is factionalism, which we have already noted is an issue for Paul throughout this letter. The doubt surrounds the cause and nature of the divisions. Suffice it to say that the most influential, although contested, contribution on the subject has been the suggestion of Gerd Theissen that the context for the disturbances surrounding the eucharistic meal was the existence of differentials of wealth and status among the members of the congregation that manifested themselves in meals of varying quantity and quality being replicated in the meetings of the Christ-movement where they were entirely inappropriate.[44]

This part of the letter includes a precious passage containing the earliest evidence of the words uttered by Jesus over the bread and wine at the Last Supper and their significance (1 Cor 11:23-26). Yet this passage really establishes the warrant for a solemn warning Paul immediately proceeds to enunciate:

> So whoever should eat the bread or drink the cup of the Lord unworthily, will be guilty of profaning the body and blood of the Lord. Let a person examine himself and so eat of the bread and drink of the cup. For he who eats and drinks without discerning the body eats and drinks judgment on himself. This is why many of you are weak and ill and some have died. (1 Cor 11:27-30)

As Gerd Theissen has noted, here "Eschatological punishments correspond to violation of the norm."[45] Here again, therefore, we see that the Lord's Supper is so foundational for the communion between Christ-followers and Christ that distortions of it can bring catastrophic consequences on the heads of the perpetrators.

CONCLUSION: APPLICATION OF THE THEOLOGY OF PERSONS IN COMMUNION TO 1 CORINTHIANS 10–14

We must now draw the threads of the preceding discussion to a focused conclusion. The fullest expression of the communion existing between Christ-followers and Christ is found in the reality of their forming one body. First, they become part of this body with baptism. Since baptism is the mechanism by which members are incorporated into the body of Christ, that means it has a more foundational function in the establishment of communion than the ministries of the word can have. Baptism establishes Christ-believers in a form of unity which the ministries of the word either enhance or imperil, but do not themselves produce. Second, the communion between Christ-followers in the body of Christ is powerfully enacted in the Lord's Supper, with its shared loaf and shared cup, which is so theologically charged that to partake of it unworthily can lead to sickness and death. Paul uses the language of *koinōnia* in 1 Corinthians only in relation to the common meal (1 Cor 10:14-22). Third, Paul insists that love is greater than any of the ministries of the word (1 Corinthians 13).

Nevertheless, in spite of these considerations, the spoken word has an important role in establishing communion. The face-to-face reality it represents forms the foundation for other kinds of interpersonal communication and communion based on discourse that continues among Christians to this day. Paul's community in Corinth (and presumably other places as well) was the site of a flourishing range of spoken phenomena. In the meetings the members gave vent to prophecy, teaching, apocalypses, psalms, and glossolalia and its interpretation. Either in meetings (the principal focus of 1 Corinthians 12 and 14) or in other contexts, the spoken word also played a role in healings, miracles, discerning spirits, and in assistance and guidance. In each instance, the use of language was central to the life and identity of the person in Christ. In all cases (except for uninterpreted glossolalia), spoken discourse was the means by which one Christ-follower could reach out to others in an "ekstatic" movement—a movement beyond the boundaries of the self in the direction of an interrelationship that is recognizably akin to the communion we have discussed above. Paul's expressions for the best (and it is a good best) that might be achieved are *oikodomē* and peace, which are forms of communion within the terms of the socio-theological model that I have set out in chapter 2 in that they pertain to optimal modes of interpersonal relationships within the group.

But even these realities were not inevitable. The individual nature of the gifts threatened to create divisions that had always to be controlled. That is why Paul stresses the unity of the divine source of the *pneumatika*, emphasizes the body of Christ into which they have been baptized (using the human body as a metaphor) as the context of their use, notes that they must be exercised for the common good, prioritizes those uttering intelligible language over glossolalia (especially when it is uninterpreted), and warns of *akatastasia* as the consequence if they are not employed appropriately. Yet Paul's attitude to the spiritual gifts, even glossolalia, is positive. They do, properly applied, have the potential to build community and to promote peace, both being indices of communion. It is therefore necessary to consider more closely the nature of the processes involved. Foundational for our reflection is that all of these ministries involve the spoken word, even if some do so more than others. We are dealing with oral phenomena. For Rosenzweig, speech, *not writing*, was humanity's morning gift from the creator. Both he and Buber placed the spoken word ahead of writing. This spoken word was probably attractive to them because it involves at least two people in one another's presence; it generates a two-way dynamic, a relation between persons not present with a solitary person reading a text.

How do we pay sufficiently serious attention to this pervasive orality within which our New Testament texts (and "scripts" might be a more appropriate way to capture the fact of their original delivery in oral performance) were first written and read aloud to groups of Christ-followers scattered around the Mediterranean? For an example of the route not to take, we need go no farther than the notion of textuality, or its equally suspect offspring intertextuality.[46] To become absorbed with the textual dimension of biblical works is not merely to mistake the medium for the message but to make a realistic understanding of that message all the more difficult by insufficient attention to the actual social context of its genesis. To valorize textuality in the interpretation of the New Testament documents is to interpret these ancient works in a manner that has only been possible since the invention of printing and which is indelibly stamped with the mark of its modern origins.

Within the Pauline communities, the spoken word was delivered in a variety of configurations. The most basic pattern, the one that Paul preferred, was where one person said something using intelligible discourse and the rest of the group listened. Prophecy was the mode of such discourse favored by Paul. It was the highest of the spiritual gifts, because God was regarded as being present speaking through mouth of his human agent (see 1 Cor 14:24-25). Other modes of intelligible discourse included teaching and revelations.

Yet we should not imagine these occasions as the speaker making static declamations to the group. Also, the audience may have well used active listening. We have cited Rosenzweig above to the effect that those who listen are able to convey their views of agreement or disagreement to the speaker through their facial expressions, but we should also recognize the possibility that the listeners made critical interjections and comments. Philo claims that Judeans, in their Sabbath-day synagogue meetings, kept silence, "except when it is customary to say any words of good omen, by way of assent to what is being read." Thus he agrees that there was audience reaction (even to a reading from Scripture) but limits it to shows of agreement. This seems a rather implausible attempt to disguise the liveliness of Sabbath meetings and the extent of the congregants' interjections. Even more so, at these Sabbath meetings, there would have been an even greater level of reaction to the priests' and elders' interpretations of Torah.[47] There is every reason to suppose that in the Christ-movement's more informal meetings—informal in the sense that they lacked the fixed hierarchy of officials known to us from the synagogues[48]—there would have been an even greater degree of discussion and disagreement. This means that whoever was offering the prophecy or the teaching would have needed to be sensitive to the shifting currents of opinion among the members and have been able to modulate the message accordingly, thus exhibiting a sensitivity to the audience that also formed an important goal of ancient rhetorical training. The result of all this is that even where, perhaps most commonly, there was one speaker addressing the other

Christ-followers, the dynamic of the exchange may have been closer to a dialogue than a monologue.

There is one further issue that we must not overlook in considering the Christ-movement's oral communications. When Paul proceeds to "a still more excellent way" (1 Cor 12:31) with the discussion of *agapē* in 1 Corinthians 13, he is careful not to divorce the nature of love from his exposition of the spiritual gifts. His point is that although love is distinct from and superior to phenomena such as prophecy and glossolalia, it should nevertheless accompany them. When he says, using an "I"-voice that represents the members as a whole, "If I speak in the tongues of human beings and of angels, but have not love, I am a become noisy gong or a clanging cymbal" (1 Cor 13:1), he inevitably implies that the use of intelligible or unintelligible discourse in the meeting should be done so only by someone who possesses *agapē*. The expression of the spoken word must be conditioned by the presence of love in the speaker; otherwise it will be as meaningless as the loud clanging of metal vessels. Those who prophesy or teach, or deliver an apocalypse, must be patient and kind, not jealous or boastful, arrogant, or unseemly in their behavior; they must not be self-seeking, nor easily angered, nor brood on suffered wrongs, nor delight in evil, but rejoice in the truth (1 Cor 13:4-6).

We end, fittingly, with the reality of silence. Rosenzweig regarded silence as central to communion. "In eternity," he wrote, "the spoken word fades away into the silence of perfect togetherness for union occurs in silence only; the word unites, but those who are united fall silent."[49] Common speech and shared meals unite but the ultimate experience of communion is silence. Silence of this kind exists as the horizon of our expectations, as the goal achieved only in eternity but to which our current efforts to build communion are directed.

I have now constructed a theological model of interpersonal communion and applied it to 1 Corinthians 10–14. But what happened when the early Christ-movement began communicating through writing? This is the subject of the next chapter.

7

NEW TESTAMENT CHRIST-FOLLOWERS AND THE EFFECTS OF WRITING

In the preceding chapter we sought to delineate various aspects of the inter-personal communion that characterized the face-to-face experience of the first generation of Christ-followers. Yet what has this to do with Christians today? However important the spoken word was in creating communion among the followers of Christ in the first and even second generations after his death and resurrection, modern Christians cannot escape the fact that a profound distance separates us from that primordial interpersonal experience. The distance between us and them is constituted primarily by two factors. First, we are separated from these first Christ-followers chronologically by two millennia and geographically, most of us at least, by thousands of miles. There is a great cultural chasm between them and us. Were we to be magically transported, with fluency in first-century Greek, back in time to one of their meetings,[1] we would still have trouble understanding their conversations by being unfamiliar with their sociocultural context. Even if we did comprehend their statements, we would not like much of what we heard—their acceptance of the institution of slavery, for example. Comprehending the messages communicated by the "cultural scripts" of the New Testament therefore requires not only historical research, but also sensitivity to a culture very different from our own.

Second, the vigorous dialogue between leaders (such as apostles, evangelists, teachers, and prophets) and the members of the movement that characterized this initial stage remains for us only as the written word. Of the vast amount of oral proclamation, prophecy, teaching, and consolation that filled the meetings of the first Christ-followers, all that remains to us are the admittedly magnificent reverberations inscribed in the New Testament documents.

Yet it is part of the thesis of this book that whenever we read or listen to the New Testament within a Christian framework (as opposed to studying it like any other ancient text) we should take seriously the personal dimension of the orality that gave it birth. We need to stand in the shoes of those who first encountered the dialogical communications that it records. We have already seen in chapter 2 that communication between people of different cultures is possible and there is a thriving pedagogic industry that equips people to communicate in this way. In chapter 3 I argued that it also possible to know people *from the past* in a way that respects their alterity within this broad framework of intercultural communication.

In this chapter, I aim to address just this issue separating us from our first ancestors in faith—the fact that all that remains of them are the written documents of the New Testament. This discussion must encompass the movement from spoken to written word reflected in the New Testament itself and in the Christ-movement's subsequent development in the following centuries. We must also relate our contemporary appropriation of these texts to our arguments about authorial intention advanced in chapter 4.

ALLEVIATING PERSONAL SEPARATION THROUGH LETTERS IN THE NEW TESTAMENT

Maintaining Personal Connections When Separated

Even in that early period, there were times when communication in person was impossible because of geographic separation. To judge from Paul's practice, the earliest proclaimers of the gospel were determined to keep alive the sense of personal connection even when distance rendered face-to-face communication and communion impossible.

It is worth noting the pains Paul takes in his letters to remind his addressees of the strength of the personal ties connecting them in spite of being far apart. From the movement's very beginnings the followers of Christ brought other Christ-believers to mind and prayed for them even though great distances separated them from one another. Paul was continually thinking about the members of the communities he had established around the eastern Mediterranean and praying for them. "We give thanks to God always for you all," he says in 1 Thess 1:2, "as we unceasingly bring you into remembrance in our prayers, remembering your work of faith, your labor of love and the endurance of your hope in our Lord Jesus Christ before our God and Father." In 2 Cor 13:9 he says to his addressees, "We pray for your improvement." Writing to the Philippians he asserts: "I thank God in all my remembrance of you, always in every prayer of mine on behalf of all of you, making my prayer with joy in respect of our communion (*koinōnia*) in the Gospel from the first day until now" (Phil 1:3-5). He prays that the love of the Philippians may abound more and more (Phil 1:9). Paul also bore in mind Christ-followers in congregations he had not founded, such as those in Rome. He told the Romans that he mentioned them without ceasing in his prayers, asking that he might somehow succeed in coming to them (Rom 1:9-10).

He also regularly invokes God's blessing on those to whom he writes (1 Thess 5:28; 1 Cor 1:3; 16:23; Gal 6:18; Philemon 3, 25). The blessing at the end of 2 Corinthians is particularly ample and also prototrinitarian: "May the grace of our Lord Jesus Christ and the love of God and communion [*koinōnia*] of the Holy Spirit be with you" (2 Cor 13:14).

On occasion, moreover, he asked them to pray for him. In 1 Thess 5:25 he says simply, "Brothers, pray for us." He is far more specific in Rom 15:30-31 (where it is relevant to note that he is writing from as far away as Corinth, Rom 16:1, 23): "I beseech you, brothers, through our Lord Jesus Christ and through the love of the Spirit, to compete alongside me [*synagōnisasthai moi*] in your prayers on my behalf to God that I may be delivered from the unbelievers in Judea and that my ministry for Jerusalem may be acceptable to the holy ones."

We can relate this body of material to our model of interpersonal communion set out in chapter 2. Paul seeks both to maintain a relationship with distant congregations of Christ-followers and even to inaugurate a relationship with the congregations he has not established, such as those in Rome. He does so with a passionate intensity. He is ceaselessly bringing them into recollection, reminding himself, in effect, that they are "Thous" to his "I." At the same time, his relationship with them exists in the larger framework of God's care for him and for them. For this reason, he can ask God to bless them generally or in some specific way, thus indicating his belief in the powers of intercessory prayer. Equally, he can ask them to pray to God on his behalf. The sense of relationship he has with his audiences even extends to his envisaging that the Christ-follower in far-off Rome can join together with him in a contest (even though he is in Corinth) to pray to God on his behalf, so that his mission to Jerusalem will be successful (Rom 15:30-31). It is noticeable that in Rom 15:30 he mentions the three persons who comprise the divine economy: God, Jesus Christ, and the Holy Spirit. The fatherhood of God, although not mentioned here, is mentioned elsewhere in the letter (Rom 6:4; 8:15; 15:6). The prototrinitarian shape of Paul's thought in Rom 15:30-31 as he urges the Romans to act in solidarity with him is closely consonant with the trinitarian dimension to our model of socio-theological communion set out in chapter 2.

Letters in the Early Stages of the Christ-Movement

The evidence for the maintenance or even establishment of personal relationships across distance among first-generation Christ-followers all comes from Paul's letters. That communities of Christ-followers were scattered around the Mediterranean littoral meant that written communication, usually by letter, became absolutely essential. Much research has been conducted in the last few decades on letter writing among members of the early Christ-movement.[2]

In the New Testament, letter writing is seen most typically when a leader of the movement is concerned for one or more congregations in a particular area. Perhaps because they are falling away from their initial commitment or are facing persecution, the leader writes a letter to them to give directions, offer advice, or express sympathy. At times the sender named in the letter will be the actual author. This is the case with the seven epistles of Paul universally accepted as genuine (Romans, 1 and 2 Corinthians, Galatians, Philippians, 1 Thessalonians, and Philemon). Perhaps this is the case also with 2 and 3 John, which specify "the elder" as their author. On other occasions, a person wishing to communicate with some section of the Christ-movement produces a pseudonymous letter attributed to some great figure of the recent past, especially Paul (Ephesians, Colossians, 2 Thessalonians, 1 and 2 Timothy, and Titus), James, Peter, and Jude. A minority of New Testament critics think that some or all of the authors mentioned in the last group were the actual authors. Yet even if the majority scholarly view is correct and these are pseudonymous documents, a real human presence lies behind each of them and the fact that the author has chosen to cloak his or her identity behind a great figure like Paul does not mean we should adopt a condemnatory attitude toward him or her. Pseudonymity is a common feature in the Bible. It is also very common in the Pseudepigrapha. D. G. Meade has plausibly argued that it occurred when it was felt necessary to make traditions capable of application to new situations. Thus pseudonymity represents an assertion of authoritative tradition, not literary origins.[3] It stands as vivid testimony to the importance of attaching a particular message to an important figure from the recent past of the movement.

While the writer's absence must have negatively affected the character of the communion, the extent to which letter writers sought to transcend such difficulties was quite remarkable. Taken together, these twenty-one writings in letter form (including Hebrews) comprise about 35 percent of the text of the New Testament in its original Greek. The remaining 65 percent is taken up with the four Gospels, the Acts of the Apostles, and the Apocalypse.

But there were many more letters that have not survived. Paul's Corinthian correspondence refers to a number of letters between him and the Corinthian Christ-movement that have disappeared (see 1 Cor 5:9; 2 Cor 2:3 and 7:8 [probably referring to the same letter]; 10:10), unless parts of some of them have found their way into 1 or 2 Corinthians. In addition, in 1 Cor 7:1 Paul refers to a letter that the Corinthians had written to him.

THE TRANSITION FROM THE SPOKEN TO THE WRITTEN WORD

The transition from oral communications to writing prompts a series of questions. What was the effect of the spoken word being inscribed on a codex or scroll in a world where the vast majority of people were illiterate? What difference did it make to the lives of those concerned? Does this mean that the early oral stage of the Christ-movement, of face-to-face interpersonal relationship and communion, is lost to us irrevocably and forever?

The Importance of a Residually Oral Culture

In 1989 William Harris argued for low literacy rates in the Greco-Roman world. Catherine Hezser has recently suggested that his figure of 10-15 percent for fourth century BCE Greece probably applies to the Roman period as well. Hezser herself argues, in her monograph *Jewish Literacy in Roman Palestine*, that despite the common view that literacy rates were higher among Judeans because they used written texts in prayer and worship, in fact their literacy rate must have been lower than elsewhere, especially because of the high percentage of the population living in rural areas in Palestine. The rate was possibly as low as 3 percent.[4] Harry Gamble has recently estimated that literacy levels among Christ-followers were probably similar to those in the population at large—about 10–15 percent.[5] In 1983 Werner Kelber published an important monograph affirming the essentially oral character of the first-century Mediterranean world and looking at the startling transformations that occurred when oral traditions were set down in written form (as in the Gospels, for example).[6] He has continued to pursue this theme in his later writings.[7]

In addition, in an article published in 1990, Paul Achtemeier urged biblical critics to take far more seriously the New Testament's oral character. Following Walter Ong, he described this culture as one of "high residual orality." This meant one that was characterized by "habits of thought and expression . . . derived from the dominance of the oral as a medium in a given culture,"[8] that nevertheless used written literature to communicate. Achtemeier then astutely observed: "Such a predominantly oral environment presented a situation almost totally different from that within which we currently operate, even though they had written documents as do we. The apparent similarity has led modern scholars to overlook almost entirely how such an oral overlay would affect the way communication was carried on by means of written media."[9] We need to be continually alert to this residually oral context in assessing the character of communications among various groups of Christ-followers in the first century CE.

Letter Writing As a Mode of Minimal Change

It is worth bearing in mind that the first stage of the use of writing, namely, apostles like Paul dispatching letters to congregations he had founded, was one of *minimal change*. These congregations were used to his presence with them: teaching, prophesying, encouraging and consoling, chastising, speaking in tongues. Yet Robert Funk has pointed out that there were actually three ways in which an apostle like Paul could be present to his congregations: personally, through an envoy (like Timothy in 1 Thessalonians 3), or through a letter. From the earliest records we have of people writing letters to one another in Greek, the notion was common that these letters provided a form of the sender's presence (*parousia*) among the recipients, that letters served as a substitute for personal presence.[10] This idea was occasionally expressed by the formula "absent in body but present through the letter," a variant of which Paul himself employs in 1 Corinthians in his statement "absent in body but present in spirit" (5:3). Particularly interesting is the parallel Paul himself draws between his personal presence and his letters in 2 Cor 10:9-11: "I would not seem to be frightening you with letters. For they say, 'His letters are weighty and strong, but his bodily presence is weak, and his speech of no account.' Let such people understand that what we say by letter when absent, we do when present" (RSV). Sometimes Paul formally demanded a letter he had written be read to all the Christ-followers in a certain area (1 Thess 5:27). This demand brings home quite powerfully some of this culture's dimensions where the vast majority of people were illiterate. We must imagine a scene where a group of largely illiterate Christ-followers gather to hear Paul's letter read out to them. We must assume that this was how they had access to all the documents that now form the New Testament canon, including the Gospels, Acts, and the Apocalypse. They were read aloud in the Christ-movement's communal gatherings.

In his letters to them, Paul continued to communicate using most of the methods mentioned in 1 Corinthians 12–14. Only now, instead of his physical presence, someone read his letters aloud to convey his messages to his audiences. His own words were spoken, but now through voice of another person. A close analogy of this arrangement was familiar to the members in the phenomenon of prophecy where a human being acted as a spokesperson (literally, a *prophētēs*) on behalf of God. In such a case, the congregation would recognize that God was truly present among them (1 Cor 14:25). While Paul was not God, we should not underestimate the extent to which Christ-followers, familiar with prophecy and hearing another person read his message to them out loud, would have felt his presence among them.

We suggest that a similar identification with the presence of a distant authority figure exists in all of Paul's letters and those letters of authentic authorial attribution. Whether there are any other New Testament letters within this latter category is disputed, although there are some who maintain that the author of the Letter of James was James, the brother of the Lord, and that Peter himself wrote 1 Peter.[11]

Without deciding which New Testament letters are pseudonymous, we may envisage two main possibilities for their origins. In the first case, the document began life as a letter. Some early communities of Christ-followers accepted such letters without necessarily accepting their supposed authorship. First Peter seems to have been a document of this sort. If the recipients of such a letter believed the sender was still alive, the dynamics of his or her presence would have been very similar to the dynamics of a community who had received a letter by Paul. The second type of pseudonymity consists of cases in which a document in letter form was never sent as such to a particular community or person. Such a "letter" was written later than the supposed author's lifetime. The real author sought to capitalize on the alleged author's authority over the supposed addressees in order to make a point to some group or groups of Christ-followers, who may or may not have been the supposed addressees. For example, assume someone in Ephesus in the 90s CE composed a letter allegedly by Paul to the Smyrnaens with the aim of saying something actually of relevance to the Ephesians (or an even wider group of Christ-followers). In such a case, we are moving away from a real sense of apostolic presence. The recipients who heard such a letter believed that the real Paul's message to the Smyrnaens had relevance to their life of faith. Yet even here we would still have an actual author of the text, seeking to make a communicative point, even if not the author apparent from the document.

Narrative Writings in the New Testament

Documents that take a narrative form, such as the Gospels and the Acts of the Apostles, probably only came into existence after the first generation of Christ-followers. In light of the styles of discourse Paul mentions in 1 Corinthians 12–14, their most obvious categorization is that of teaching (*didachē*). The book of Revelation would be classed as a (very extended) apocalypse (such as Paul also mentions). We are handicapped in gauging the impact of such documents when they first appeared by a total lack of any direct evidence as to the circumstances of their promulgation. In spite of this, we are able to hypothesize to a small degree. In a predominately illiterate culture, the members of the Christ-movement must have first encountered these documents when they heard them read aloud at their meetings. It is probable that on their very first recitation the audience knew the identity of their composers. The creation of the Gospels, beginning with Mark, may have been in response to failing memories, or to present a particular slant on the early events for particular audiences. Only the author of Revelation seems to have thought he was writing something like Scripture (see Rev 22:18-19).

Yet even a written text, such as the Gospels, Acts, or Revelation, remained an oral and an interpersonal phenomenon. Revelation 1:3 shows this pattern unmistakably: "Blessed is he who reads aloud the words of the prophecy, and blessed are those who hear, and who keep what is written therein; for the time is near" (RSV).[12] The illiterate members of the Christ-movement could only access these writings aurally, while even the possibly literate, richer members probably had slaves read the letters to them, in line with Greco-Roman custom.[13]

One popular recent view is to see the four Gospels as each having been written for a particular community, to legitimate, that is, to explain and justify to its members, a view of the Christian message that made particular local, contextual sense. This was a key insight of redaction criticism, beginning in the late 1940s with Günther Bornkamm's essay on the stilling of the storm in Matthew and continuing with Marxsen's work on Mark and Conzelmann's on Luke.[14] The view that the Gospels were directed to particular communities, a view held by the present writer and Gerd Theissen,[15] among others, is probably still the dominant one. Richard Bauckham and others have recently launched an important and continuing debate with the proposal that the Gospels were written for all Christians.[16] Although it has run into criticism, this view deserves close attention.[17] One problem with Bauckham's view is in explaining the differences between the Gospels. One option is simply to postulate individual differences in how the authors interpreted the meaning of the Christian proclamation. But it is possible that this represents the ethnocentric imposition of modern individualist views on ancient group-oriented culture. To imagine that there was a generalized "Christian" audience when the Gospels were written and to whom they were directed probably underestimates the degree of intergroup dissension in the early Christian world. If a Gospel was intended to be read beyond the author's own group (his target audience), maybe the gospel writer hoped that it would "colonize" other groups whose gospels the author thought were deficient. Luke makes something very like this suggestion in the prologue to his Gospel (Luke 1:1-4). Perhaps one community would alter gospels from other communities to accord with their local views. This latter factor probably explains why Matthew and Luke altered Mark.

Yet we do not have to reach a decided view on this contested subject here. On the former view (that each Gospel was written for a particular community, or an ensemble of communities having a similar composition and context), the community would certainly have known the author of a document written to and for them directly. Even on the second scenario, espoused by Bauckham, the gospel most likely had its *first* airing in the author's local community, even if he had written it with all Christ-followers in mind and the gospel was then widely distributed. When documents such as Gospels, Acts, and the book of Revelation were first recited in meetings, we may reasonably postulate the same sense of intercommunion and authorial presence that we noted with a letter by Paul. The authors of these texts and their audiences would have established the same personal communion with each other as that possible through the spoken word.

The works of the New Testament seem to have carried an author's name from the earliest times (even if these names were educated guesses). Martin Hengel, for example, has argued this position for the Gospels.[18] This urge to attach a name to the various writings testifies to the early communities' strong sense of the person, that is, the author, behind them and the desire not to lose sight of the author's presence. Margaret Mitchell has recently mounted a powerful case for the early Christ-movement's having clung to the notion that behind each of the Gospels lay the "actions of an individuated perhaps variously motivated human person."[19] This is seen most clearly in the early traditions that associated "each gospel with a major Mediterranean locale: Mark with Rome (and/or Alexandria), Matthew with Judea, Luke with Achaia, John with Ephesus (and/or Patmos)."[20] As the centuries wore on, the Gospels had prologues attached to them. This indicates that the author and the historical occasion of each Gospel was considered an important piece of information that readers or listeners should hear before encountering the text. For each evangelist: "A full biographical curriculum (influenced by ancient encomiastic traditions) for each would emerge, which included their homeland, the language, place in which they wrote and, often, the specific occasion that moved them to do so which involved a particular audience and need that had been addressed."[21]

These circumstances of the writing and first promulgation of most of the various documents that comprise the New Testament—circumstances embedded in the exigencies of an oral culture and its concomitant interpersonal dialogue—justify us in attempting to categorize them in a way which valorizes their original context. Clearly, "text" is not very appropriate, although it is almost universally applied to these documents, in view of its association with publication practices and the development of post-Gutenberg methods of literary criticism. A word that does not suffer from these disadvantages is "script." As the word used in relation to an oral performance (such as a film or play), "script" underlines the fact that we are dealing with a document which at its first appearance was not an item in itself, to be perused in silence by a solitary reader. Rather, its significance is in its embodiment in a performance involving the living voices of and the interpersonal relationship between an audience and a lector (possibly the author). As Paul says in 1 Thess 5:27: "I adjure you by the Lord that this letter be read out [*anagnōsthēnai*] to all the brothers." To introduce a neologism, "scriptality" seems to capture the essence of this process at the time of first performance of the New Testament writings in a way that "textuality" most certainly does not.

Continuing the Oral Tradition

For the early Christ-movement "Scripture" (*graphē*) meant the various writings of what we now call the Old Testament (see Rom 1:2 and 2 Tim 3:16). Initially, proclamation about the life, death, and resurrection of Jesus circulated in oral form. As late as 120–140 CE, Papias could still say he preferred these oral communications to the written message of books, such as Matthew and Mark (cited in Eusebius, *Ecclesiastical History* 3.39.4). As James Barr has noted, the "idea of a Christian faith governed by Christian written holy scriptures was not an essential part of the foundation plan of Christianity."[22] The living witness of Jesus Christ was carried on first by the apostles and then by prophets and teachers. Even in the middle of the second century, Irenaeus could write that if there was a difficulty about the meaning of the faith, the appropriate course would be to consult the most ancient churches with which the apostles had dialogue and learn from them the answer to the problem (*Against Heresies* 3.4.1). He does not say we check Scripture.

But once we have the New Testament documents in existence, largely by the end of the first century, the question becomes: Why were they preserved?

Initially, this was most certainly *not* because of their status as *texts*. There are many references in early Christian literature to the recollection of the words of Jesus. There are frequent quotations of Jesus's words in the second century, but they are significant because they are his words, not because they are scriptural.[23] One sign of this phenomenon, as John Barton has noted, is that there is a tendency to distinguish between the words of Jesus and the story of his life, death, and resurrection. "The authority of these words is certainly not that of the books in which they are recorded, but inheres in the words themselves because of who it was who uttered them."[24]

The fact that the writings were regarded as the *very* words of the apostles was also regarded as especially significant. In *2 Clement* 14:2 (ca. 120–140 CE) it is said that the books (*ta biblia*) and the apostles (*hoi apostoloi*) declare that the church belongs not to the present, but has existed from the beginning. Here "books" almost certainly refers to the Old Testament and the apostles to the New Testament tradition in both oral and written form. Justin Martyr (150–160) refers to the Gospels as the "memoirs of the apostles" (*apomnēmoneumata tōn apostolōn, Trypho* 100.1).[25] Irenaeus (170–180) is very revealing: "the Lord testifies, as the apostles confess, and the prophets announce" (*Against the Heresies* 3.17.4). All this suggests that in the second century the story of Jesus was seen as essentially independent of any literary embodiment of it; that is why the four Gospels are entitled "the Gospel according to X," not "X's Gospel." This attitude is also starkly revealed in the action taken by Tatian (150–160) to create a harmony of the four Gospels and other gospel traditions (the *Diatessaron*), an enterprise that showed he had little regard for their individual integrity.[26]

Evidence such as this leads Barton to, accurately, conclude that although we tend to treat the Gospels as works of literary art, this was not a common perception in the ancient church, where they were seen "not as great 'texts,' but as the raw materials for an essentially oral presentation of the 'things concerning Jesus.'"[27]

The Transition from "Scripts" to "Texts"

In time, from the late second century onwards, the New Testament "scripts" did come to be treated as "text," as *graphē*. We need to explain this. The answer seems to lie in the process of the gradual "canonization" of certain New Testament writings. This was the evolving understanding that some of the large number of Christian scripts were to be included within a circumscribed, authoritative group and some were to be excluded. We will consider certain aspects of this process in chapter 11. Suffice it to say for the present, however, that by the end of the second century, where previously the early Christians had seen these documents as significant in containing proof for the voice of Jesus and the apostles, now they were coming to be seen as authoritative in themselves.[28] This was the process of textualization or inscripturation.

And yet that the New Testament "scripts" acquired the status of texts does not mean that they have lost their connection with their original authors. Nor does it mean that we should abandon oral methods of accessing their inscribed messages. In this chapter's final section, I will consider three issues: first, the connection between the role of the author (outlined in chapters 4 and 5 above) and the textuality of New Testament writings; second, an analogy from the Muslim world on keeping written Scripture alive orally; and, third, the views of Martin Buber and Franz Rosenzweig on the need to recognize and preserve the oral dimension of Scripture.

THE AUTHOR AND AUTHORIAL INTENTION IN THE NEW TESTAMENT

My analysis in chapter 4 requires that I now state (at least in this work aimed at bringing the New Testament, historically interpreted, into creative interactive with contemporary Christian life, reflection, and identity) that it is unhelpful to treat its twenty-seven constituent documents as literary productions. This is not to deny that outside such an interpretative framework they may be construed as literature (in a comparative literature program, for example) or that some or some parts of them are subject to literary analysis (such as narrative-critical studies of Mark), but rather, that to speak of them as literary is an unhelpful distraction in an interpretation directed to maintaining these documents' importance in the relation with human beings to God inaugurated in the life, death, and resurrection of his Son. Thus, Rhoads and Michie's admittedly fine study of Mark as narrative has been criticized "because they do not speak of God in connection with the historical figure of Jesus Christ."[29]

There are a number of ways of illustrating this claim. Beginning with W. K. Wimsatt and Monroe Beardsley's classical attack on the "intentional fallacy," it is relevant that their disapproval of authorial intention as a guide to meaning was meant for poems only, a literary creation that they considered "should not mean but be." They reinforced this all-important limitation to their view in their statement: "In this respect poetry differs from practical messages, which are successful if and only if we correctly infer the intention."[30] The New Testament documents are "practical messages" of this sort. By this I mean that they are functional communications formulated with the intention of assisting those who hear or read them to take or avoid some view, disposition, or action in relation to the world beyond the substance of the message, which will be to their advantage. They were all composed to encourage their addressees to take full benefit of the new mode of being human in relation to God, now and in the future, made possible by Christ. John 20:31 probably expresses this most clearly: "these things are written that you may believe that Jesus is the Christ, the Son of God, and that believing you may have life in his name." Yet this is also the implied intention of all these writings.

Further assistance in characterizing the New Testament as nonliterary is available from Hans-Georg Gadamer's theory of art (which includes literary art), even though in chapter 4 we had occasion to doubt his explanation's ontological dimensions. He rightly fixes on the elements of play, and the representation central to play, in artistic composition. It is possible to retain this feature of his thought without attaching it (in a manner that would have astonished Plato) to Being itself. There is a "characteristic lightness and sense of relief which we find in the attitude of play." The fulfillment of the task in play does not point to any "purposive context" but occurs in its own "closed world of play," to which outsiders may at times have access, as in the performance of "play" on stage. Literary works of art are explicable in the same way. When we read a poem or novel, "all those purposive relations which determine active and caring existence have not simply disappeared, but in a curious way acquire a different quality."[31] While we read, we are temporarily withdrawn from the mundane realities of purpose and responsibility in a way typical of all play. If we are interpreting the New Testament so as to bring its resources to bear on our individual situation in relation to God, other human beings, and the rest of creation in the present, it is clear that its twenty-seven texts do not have the qualities Gadamer so helpfully attributes to literary texts. These texts are concerned with matters of the greatest moment. There is very little sign in them of "lightness" or "a sense of relief"; they are too serious for that. They do not withdraw us from the everyday demands of purpose and responsibility, but make us directly confront such demands. These texts do not dissolve, or even transmute, the purposive relations that "determine active and caring existence," but rather bring those relations to the very forefront of our concern.

We are able to develop this perspective with respect to Wolfgang Iser's insight that literary texts "do not correspond to any objective reality outside themselves."[32] For Christians, however, turning to the New Testament in faith for the Gospel they will find there, its texts are important precisely in that they do point to objective reality beyond their pages. They clearly have an expository and didactic purpose that would constitute a blemish, if not a fatal flaw, were it to be found in a novel or other literary work. Readers of novels do not wish to be taken by the author and pushed down the road of accepting the author's particular views about the world. Christians reading or listening to the New Testament in faith, on the other hand, find such persuasive purposes impossible to avoid. This is the case not just with respect to Paul's letters, where his rhetorical techniques undoubtedly connect with ancient strategies of persuasion, but also in the narrative texts that have the purpose of pushing their audiences to views concerning the identity and role of Jesus Christ and their involvement with him.

A similar conclusion can be reached by means of speech act theory. The authors of the New Testament works were trying to "do things with words," to cite J. L. Austin's primary notion,[33] in a very strong sense. In the perspective of this theory, as set out in chapter 4, nonliterary texts are predominantly performative, illocutionary, and perlocutionary in character, while literary texts are predominantly nonperformative and locutionary in character. The New Testament documents are best analyzed as performative, illocutionary, and perlocutionary in nature. The utterances they contain are notably illocutionary and perlocutionary (in an actual sense, not in the mimetic sense that Richard Ohmann rightly attributes to literary works). By what their authors wrote they were seeking their audiences to hold or to acquire faith in Jesus Christ. Among the groups of Christ-followers scattered around the Mediterranean, this was a convention of the writings that they sent to one another. The communications in their writings are capable of analysis in a number of John Searle's categories: "assertives," which commit the speaker to the truth of what is said; "directives," where the speaker attempts to get his or her audience to do something; "commissives," which commit the speaker to some future course of action; and "expressives," "which express a psychological state in relation to a state of affairs."

These reflections on the nonliterary nature of the New Testament writings lead us to the role of their authors. In chapter 4 I suggested that Roland Barthes's hyperbolic assertions, clearly stamped with their structuralist pedigree, concerning the death of the author and the disconnection between the authorial voice and its origins once writing has occurred, applied, if at all, only to fiction. Barthes himself no doubt meant that his writings would be taken seriously and that some effort would be made to understand them as he intended, not simply cast into as many kaleidoscopes of meaning as he had readers. Why should we think the New Testament authors were any different?

Paul Ricoeur has posed a more serious challenge to the role of authorial intention. Central to Ricoeur's thesis that the author is supplanted in any act of reading is that wherever an "I" voice is inscribed in a text the reader replaces this voice with his or her own. This is a theory of reading as reader colonization. In chapter 4, I argued that this notion did not work with the genre where it seemed to have the most promise, a lyric poem, since no reader ever displaces the remarkable personal presence that crafted the poem on the basis of the insights in the poem. In almost every letter, including those in the New Testament, the sense of connection between the writer and his or her addressees will be a major part of its meaning. But in any other practical or persuasive writing, it will be equally difficult to ignore the author. This applies to the Gospels and to the Acts of the Apostles as much as it applies to Paul's letters.

Even less convincing is Ricoeur's remarkable idea that the "human fact disappears" in any act of writing, in other words, that the human, authorial dimension of a discourse is not conveyed by its *contents*. In chapter 4, I contested this view and suggested that in fact writing can enhance the human dimension. The truth is that writing is not a technology for the dehumanization and hence depersonalization of discourse. We have seen earlier in this chapter that in the first generations of the Christ-movement letter writing was seen as a means to maintain personal presence across distance. Letter writing enables groups and individuals to maintain existing person-to-person relations and even to inaugurate new ties, as when Paul writes his letter to the Christ-followers of Rome, a city he has not yet visited. We have far less to go on with the narrative documents in the New Testament but some of them clearly show the author's desire to connect with their addressees (Mark 13:14; Matt 24:15; Luke 1:1-4; John 21:31; Acts 1:1; Rev 22:18-19). Writing fosters interpersonal relations and Ricoeur's proposal that it represents the disappearance of the human is entirely inapposite for the New Testament.

While a text will certainly have different meanings in contexts beyond those of its first audience, this does not mean that it escapes the horizon of its author. Historical analysis will always reveal, though imperfectly, that horizon sufficiently enough for the text to convey meaning. Even in the case of communication by the actual living voice between two speakers in one another's presence, communication is never perfect and there is always some slippage of meaning. Each speaker will not say quite what he or she intended and his or her message will, to some extent, be misunderstood. That is simply one aspect of being human; it is no reason to rule out of court the possibility of understanding a textual communication from the past. For some types of writing in the New Testament, Paul's letters, for example, the pressure points of their original destination are everywhere present, even though scholars disagree about the exact nature of these contexts. The original contexts and original communicative function of nonepistolary forms, such as the Gospels, are susceptible to the processes of historical understanding.

Ricoeur (driven by the untenable assumption, so natural to a modern intellectual, that only through writing do we have a "world" rather than a situation and by the equally untenable dualistic metaphor of writing as "spiritual" and oral discourse as "bodily")[34] makes the proposal that writing "liberates" from the "narrowness" of the face-to-face second person address of spoken discourse by "universalizing" its audience. This plainly fails in the case of all the New Testament writings that are letters. Yet, as we have seen earlier in this chapter, we must not forget the residually oral environment in which these works were produced and the fact that they would have been accessed aurally. The primacy of spoken discourse persisted well into the second century CE. Historical analysis that highlights the function of these writings, including the Gospels, to be communicated orally to groups of Christ-followers does justice to the face-to-face context in which they originally appeared and continued to be expressed for some two centuries.

The New Testament documents came into existence as expressions of intense interpersonal communications in a largely oral culture. There is no reason why we should let the modern scholarly valorization of printed texts and the subsequent rise of solitary reading, which have occurred only since the fifteenth-century invention of printing, deflect us from using historical approaches to continue to read the New Testament documents as originally oral productions.

On the other hand, there can be no doubt that a text from the past will contain a measure of "virtuality," meaning that anyone who reads or even hears it in the present will need to work assiduously to fill the interpretative gaps caused by the cultural distance between the contemporary world and its time and place of origin. Those who wish to determine (as far as it is possible) the original sense of the New Testament writings need above all to replace the cultural scenarios, derived from their upbringing and socialization in some modern culture, with those appropriate to the ancient world of the first-century Mediterranean.

We have seen in chapter 5 that Friedrich Schleiermacher was of the view that "only historical interpretation can do justice to the rootedness of the New Testament authors in their time and place."[35] His whole theory of interpretation, rooted in the practice of spoken dialogue and dedicated to discerning what an author meant from the shape of his or her argument and style, offers us a fine model for what is needed. For in Schleiermacher we have a method of New Testament interpretation that both fixes upon authorial intention and is also alive to the fact that in reading these ancient texts there will be indeterminacies caused by their cultural difference from us. These can only addressed by a deliberate effort to substitute first-century CE Mediterranean social scenarios for the modern ones we would automatically bring to the task.

A NON-CHRISTIAN MODEL FOR THE ORAL RECEPTION OF WRITTEN TEXTS

In the preceding section, I made a case for concentrating upon the interpersonal character and original mode of promulgation of the New Testament texts as critical for their interpretation. Yet this is not an entirely novel proposal. There already exists—in Islam, for example—models for maintaining such dimensions in a community that has long possessed written scriptures. William Graham demonstrated the significance of this pattern in his work *Beyond the Written Word*.[36] In Islamic societies there is an all-pervasive written text, the Qur'an, yet most of the encounters of ordinary people with that text occur orally: in mosques, classrooms, on the radio, in the workplace, and so on.[37] The printed text "exists as a support to the orally transmitted and recited text, not as a determinant of it."[38] In this respect, the Islamic world has resisted pressures toward silent reading that began in Europe with Gutenberg's fifteenth-century invention of the printing press and eventually triumphed with the widespread literacy achieved in the nineteenth century.[39]

Graham reasonably insists that neglect of the oral dimension of Scripture, such as has occurred in the Christian West, not only leads to excessive concentration on the documentary text, but also leads to a loss of the functional aspect of Scripture: "The relationship to the spoken word of the text is inherently dynamic and personal in a way that the relationship to the printed word alone is not, or is only rarely and with difficulty, at least in the present day."[40] The oral dimension of Scripture is the one most intimately bound up in the major personal and communal roles of Scripture in religious life, "especially those that move not only in the intellectual or ideational realm, but also in that of the senses—as, for example, in ritual or devotional use."[41]

Although not cited by Graham, Martin Buber and Franz Rosenzweig expressed similar views on centrality of the spoken element in Scripture in the 1920s. Since these views connect closely with the model of socio-theological communion expressed in chapter 2, I conclude with them.

BUBER, ROSENZWEIG, AND THE CONTINUING IMPORTANCE OF SCRIPTURE'S ORAL DIMENSION

In the 1920s Martin Buber and Franz Rosenzweig recognized that in translating the Bible they shared a profound concern in going behind the *writtenness* of the biblical word and in returning to its *spokenness*, a spokenness that was both original to these documents and made anew every time one of them was read aloud. Although their views on the matter were, therefore, directed to translation more than to interpretation, what they had to say about the spokenness of the Bible has just as much application to interpretation and is worth considering in some detail.

We will begin with Buber: "'Spoken' means: spoken in a specific situation. The biblical word cannot be separated from the situations of its spokenness; otherwise it loses its concreteness, its physicality." He illustrates this general principle with a number of illustrations, the first of which is as follows: "A command is not a maxim but an address—spoken to the people, heard always by the generations as having been spoken to that original generation, but never to be lifted out of time. If it becomes a maxim, if it is moved from the second person to the third, from the obligatory relation of hearing to the optional relation of interested reading, its flesh and blood are gone." Buber was absorbed with the "I-Thou" relation; here it is transposed to the plural "Ego-Vos" ("I-You [plural]"), yet still embedded in the actuality of words once spoken in a context of obligatory listening and, while capable of being repeated to later generations, never to be sundered from the concrete occasion of their first expression.

A similar tension between the primacy of the original setting of the spoken word and its repeatability once inscribed as a text affects prophecy: "A prophecy is a speech of a man speaking under commission to a human group at a particular moment, in a particular situation; its effects depend on the decision that the group will take in response to it at this moment—or not take. Precisely in the held breath of this vastly decisive moment lies the secret of the eternal validity of the prophetic word." The same applies to other modes of biblical utterance:

> The biblical stories are only to a small extent mere transcribed chronicles; in most of them we hear still the voices of their story-tellers, exhorting, compelling, exemplifying, warning. Many psalms exhibit the character of liturgical poetry, some the character of litany; but the fundamental tone is that of the lived immediacy of cries of need and jubilations of thanks—the speech of personal speakers, who precisely when and because they mean

the "I" of the genuine person can as choral leaders of the community speak of the fate and salvation of that community in their song.

Having considered these examples, Buber returns to statements of general principle: "This concreteness, born of the situation and fitted to it, must be retained for the biblical text; the text must be taught not as pieces of literature, but rather as parts of a vast, multivocal conversation, arising from the first cause of the creating and revealing word, and issuing back into that first cause again in the form of prayer." Finally, Buber offers advice on historiography appropriate for engaging with this conversation, with the stress falling not on the prehistory of a document, but on what today we would call its sociolinguistic connection with its original context, the primary interest of social-scientific interpretation:

> That is why it is not so important when, or where, or in what circumstances this or that text arose; historians, even those who constitute and interpret history, are confined to the realm of the mediated, and restricted to the means that realm offers. The important thing is to learn from the text itself the things concerning its particular situational rootedness that it and it alone can tell.[42]

Rosenzweig set out his views on the matter in his essay entitled "Scripture and Word," written late in 1925. The following, arguing for an approach to biblical documents as "scripts" or "scores" similar to that proposed above, gives a flavor of his position:

> Every word is a spoken word. The book originally served the word, whether declaimed, sung, or spoken; it sometimes still serves it today, as in theatrically living drama or opera. Opera people talk of the score and theater people talk of the script as something technical, instrumental, provisional; once, that was how people characterized the rank and condition of books generally, vis-à-vis the spoken word. But technique has a dangerous power over those who wield it; all unintentionally the means becomes an end, the provisional becomes the permanent, the technical becomes a magic spell. The book no longer serves the word. It becomes the word's ruler and hindrance; it becomes Holy Scripture.[43]

While we now possess a New Testament that has become Holy Scripture, the purpose of this book is to argue for a method of interpreting its constituent documents historically and theologically that insists upon taking the interpersonal dimension seriously. The ultimate aim is to fix upon the (necessarily intercultural) communion that occurs between our ancestors in faith who left us these works and ourselves when we read or listen to them in a context of Christian faith. The time has now come to examine ways in which we may give substance to such communion between the living and the dead.

COMMUNION WITH
THE SAINTS

ORIGINS AND DEVELOPMENT

In this volume I am attempting to construct a historical interpretation of the New Testament aimed at enriching contemporary Christian life and identity within a framework of personal interrelationships, indeed personal intercommunion. I must now validate the claims made in chapter 2 concerning the possibility of intercultural communion between contemporary Christians and those Christians who composed the twenty-seven New Testament documents. It is essential to my argument that this is possible in some meaningful sense and this task will occupy the next three chapters.

Yet does this enterprise not fly in the face of the extreme difficulty that the authors of the twenty-seven writings of the New Testament and the Christ-followers for whom they composed these works are long dead? How can relationship or communion subsist between the living and the dead? The time has come to address this question, for unless a satisfactory answer can be given to it, the thesis I am advancing must fail.

My initial response to this dilemma is to observe that, as a matter of empirical fact, Christians have always considered that those of their number who died in Christ were in some sense still present. This sense of the presence of the dead has taken many forms, among others, from the modest one of the dead living on in the memory of their survivors, to the notion that they "slept" in Christ until they were resurrected on the last day, to the idea that their souls survived death in heaven (or some lesser state) and would be reunited with their bodies at the resurrection at the parousia.

It will soon become apparent that there are, in fact, a number of ways to model this type of communion, ranging from a minimal model which fixes on respect for an author as an author even if he or she is dead (which may be so minimal as not to warrant the designation "communion") to a fully fledged theology of the communion of saints that is predicated upon the living presence of these authors with God (and with us) in the period preceding

191

the parousia and the resurrection of the righteous. By setting out a number of such models, I hope to address the wide variety of Christian views concerning the postmortem status of those who have died in Christ, a topic on which there is a particularly lively debate at present.

In considering all of these models, we will need to bear in mind that because of the great cultural distance between the early Christ-followers and us, every form of communion must be intercultural. This means that we must critically assess their messages, but also that we must expect to be enriched by the different worldviews and life experiences that lie behind and are embodied in those messages.

In the present chapter I will, briefly, consider the historical development of the notion of communion between living and dead Christ-followers in the New Testament period and in the first few centuries.[1] We will see that central to the development of this idea was a belief in some form of postmortem existence distinct from belief in the general resurrection on the last day. There is a strong current of Christian thought today that is opposed to such a view and understands resurrection to be the only form of ultimate vindication. This position is especially well represented in a recent collection of essays about human nature and in N. T. Wright's monumental exposition of the meaning of the resurrection in the ancient world, Israelite tradition, and early Christianity.[2]

On the other hand, the history of the idea of communion between living and dead Christians is closely integrated with belief in a postmortem existence in the period before resurrection. Therefore, this subject will figure prominently in my discussion. To the extent that Wright and those who hold similar views deny or minimize the importance of this belief, they must be challenged. A belief in communion between living and dead Christians embedded in belief in an afterlife and some form of communication between these two realms has been a feature of Christian identity since the second century CE at the latest. Such a belief still figures in the beliefs of Roman Catholics, members of the autocephalous Orthodox churches, and even among some members of Protestant and Reformed traditions (some Anglicans especially). It is also a belief that I will seek in chapter 10—very gently, given that many committed Christians do not accept it—to make a case for.

THE ORIGIN AND MEANING OF THE PHRASE "COMMUNION OF SAINTS"

The communion of saints is one of the least explored dimensions of Christian theology, as Elizabeth Johnson has shown. It was not the subject of any systematic treatises in the early centuries, nor in the medieval period, and there have been few attempts to explicate the idea in Protestant, Orthodox, or Catholic theology. Reformation battles were largely restricted to the role of named saints as intercessors, not to the notion generally. This may be why the Council of Trent considered the matter only on the last two days of its eighteen-year deliberations. Thus, when the Second Vatican Council briefly discussed the communion of saints in chapter 7 of its *Dogmatic Constitution on the Church, Lumen Gentium*, this was the first time a pope or council had treated the subject in a sustained way.[3] Dietrich Bonhoeffer's doctoral thesis and first book was called *Communio Sanctorum* but his interest was in the living "saints."[4]

We will begin by considering the meaning of the expression "communion of saints" in the early church. "Communion of saints" is a translation of the Latin *sanctorum communio*. J. N. D. Kelly has argued that this is a Latin version of the Greek expression *koinōnia tōn hagiōn* that originated in the East and had the sense of "participation in the blessings (or 'good things,' neuter plural) of salvation," especially as experienced in the eucharist. From there, he argues, the phrase moved to the West, where the translated form *communio sanctorum* came to signify the communion of saintly persons, a spiritual interchange between Christians living and dead, as seen first in Nicetas of Remesiana's fifth-century commentary on the Apostles' Creed.[5] More recently, Robert Wilken has argued instead that the "provenance of the phrase is seems to be in the Latin West and this suggests that it is to be understood within a Latin, not a Greek context."[6] The origins of the phrase are irrelevant to our current purpose.

The expression makes its earliest appearance in the minutes of a regional council convened at Nîmes, Gaul, in 394 CE. Around the same time it had found its way into the Apostles Creed: "I believe in the Holy Spirit, the holy Catholic Church, the communion of saints [*sanctorum communionem*], the forgiveness of sins, the resurrection of the flesh, and life everlasting. Amen." The Apostles' Creed is a later version of an earlier Roman creed and is similar to other creeds, yet none of these contain the words "communion of saints." These words were a late insertion into the Apostles' Creed and are first attested there in the commentary on this creed by Nicetas of Remesiana at the end of the fourth century CE. For Nicetas, the "communion of saints" meant having fellowship or communion with the saints. For Nicetas, the "saints" included the patriarchs Abraham, Isaac, and Jacob, the prophets, the apostles, the martyrs, and the "other just who were and are and will be," together with the angels. As Wilken notes, the vital point was that the saints included deceased Christians so the "communion of saints" designated the close bond that exists between the church of the present and those who have gone before.[7] The high point of such a belief was expressed in the practice of asking those who had died in Christ, especially martyrs like Peter and Paul (killed in Rome during the emperor Nero's reign), to pray to God on their behalf. In Latin this was expressed by use of the word *petite*, as in the famous late-third-century graffito in the catacomb under the church of San Sebastiano in Rome in which the remains of Peter and Paul were then thought to be resting: "Peter and Paul pray [*petite*] for Victor."[8] How did such a belief develop? Clearly, a belief in communion between living and dead Christians, even that the latter were able to pray for the former, was only possible with a conviction that they were in some meaningful sense still alive. In spite of N. T. Wright's recent arguments to the contrary,[9] it is quite clear that such a belief existed alongside confidence in the vindication that would eventually come with resurrection at the last day. When and how did this view arise? We will begin with the various Israelite conceptions of what happened after death.

THE OLD TESTAMENT AND INTERTESTAMENTAL LITERATURE: BELIEF IN AN INTERMEDIATE STATE

Richard Bauckham has suggested that most Israelites in the Second Temple period retained the old Israelite idea that the dead existed as "shades" (*repa'im*) in the underworld of Sheol, a place of darkness and life from which no one returned. This was not a belief in the survival of a spiritual part of the body (which came into Greek thought after Plato, where the soul was thought to enjoy a kind of "natural" immortality by its very nature),[10] for the "shades" were "shadowy, ghostly versions of living, bodily persons who could hardly be said to be alive. They were the dead, in a silent, dark, joyless—indeed, deathly—existence, who were cut off from God, the source of all life."[11]

Yet this may understate somewhat the extent to which the dead were thought to have some form of existence. John W. Cooper has proposed that those in Sheol maintained a somewhat shadowy and insubstantial but nevertheless real existence. Here persons are separable from their bodies and can continue to exist without them. This is a form of dualism quite distinct from that of Plato or Descartes.[12] In support of Cooper, the vivid incident of the necromancer of Endor conjuring the dead Samuel to prophesy what would happen to Saul indicates that there was something that continued to exist even in death. The necromancer describes Samuel as an *elohim*, a supernatural being (1 Sam 28:13), admittedly one resentful that his rest has been disturbed (1 Sam 28:15). The only text in the Old Testament that refers unequivocally to a desirable existence after death is Dan 12:2-3: "Of those who lie sleeping in the dust of the earth many will awake, some to everlasting life, some to shame and everlasting disgrace. The learned will shine as brightly as the vault of heaven, and those who have instructed many in virtue, as bright as stars for all eternity" (Jerusalem Bible). This promise is reaffirmed in Dan 12:13. There are other passages in the Old Testament that possibly evince a belief in (desirable) life after death, but their meaning is disputed.[13]

Bauckham agrees that in the postbiblical period, belief in life after death "came to be the general belief of Judaism." Apart from the Sadducees, most Judeans believed in a desirable immortality for the righteous and punishment for the wicked.[14] The primary form in which it was envisaged that this immortality would take was the resurrection of the body. This belief was stimulated by (though not necessarily original to) Antiochus IV Epiphanes' terrible persecution of Judeans during the years 167–164 BCE. The Maccabean literature mentions that those who were put to death during this period would be vindicated through resurrection (2 Macc 7:9, 11, 22-23, 28-29; 12:43-45).[15]

Yet in the intertestamental period, there also developed different understandings of what would happen after death. Bauckham has noted that one of these views conceived of the human person as a body and a soul or spirit that were separated at death, with the body being laid in a tomb while the soul or spirit went to the "chambers of the souls." At resurrection the two would be reunited. Bauckham says this is closer to the Greek view (in that it seems more "dualistic" than the older Israelite "holistic" view), but it differs decisively from Greek conceptions in that "the souls in Sheol are the souls of *the dead* who return to *life* only when soul and body are reunited. Both components of human nature die. Eternal life requires both together to live again."[16] Later Bauckham makes the important point that (as distinct from Greek ideas in an immortal soul being part of the natural human condition) in Israelite thought any postmortem state was a consequence of a divine gift.[17]

The above example of Samuel's *elohim* conjured up to speak to Saul indicates that there may not be so sharp a distinction between older Israelite "holism" and the newer intertestamental view as Bauckham proposes. Bauckham also goes too far in saying that these separated souls are "dead." The oldest reference to souls being separated from bodies after death and lodging in "chambers" is probably to be found in *1 Enoch* 22.[18] Here we find reference to "the spirits of the souls of the dead," and "the spirits of the children of the people who were dead," whose voices were actually reaching into heaven (*1 Enoch* 22:4-6). One of these spirits is Abel's which continues to speak against Cain. How can it be said these souls are dead?

But there were other ways of understanding the postmortem state. Some Judeans had a purely spiritual vision of human existence with the body crumbling to dust while the soul receives eternal life or ascends to God with the bones remaining in the earth.[19] Although Collins considers 1 *Enoch* 22 (which seems clearly indebted to Babylonian and Greek sources) as "exceptional in Jewish sources and has little influence on subsequent tradition,"[20] we will see that the picture of Abel finds a clear echo in Hebrews 11.

THE NEW TESTAMENT

The New Testament, while certainly not containing an explicit and fully elaborated theology of communion between living and dead Christ-followers as developed in later centuries, possesses much material in some of its twenty-seven writings that make such ideas seem a rather natural development. Since this evidence is infrequently considered *and* to dispel any suggestions that the central insight of the theology of the communion with the saints represents a radical departure from the views of the New Testament writers, we will here review some of the data. In assessing this material, it is necessary to recognize the diversity of the twenty-seven canonical writings. We will be alert to the particular ideas about interpersonal communion in whatever document(s) we find them. On the other hand, we will take little notice of any author's failure to mention a particular idea. Thus, in a canonical context, the probability that Paul did not subscribe to the idea of an intermediate state between death and resurrection, as N. T. Wright has recently argued,[21] carries little weight if such a belief is present elsewhere in the corpus, as in Hebrews 10–12, for example. Our bias will be toward the positive statements of each canonical voice, and not to build arguments from the silence of other authors on such issues.

Death and Interpersonal Communion in Paul

If, as we have seen in chapter 7, spatial distance is no obstacle to communion between living Christ-followers and living Christ-followers with God, what difference does death make? The relationship of one Christ-follower to others during life, on Paul's view, is to always remember them, to think about them constantly, to hope for a solution to their problems, to thank God for them, to pray to God to bless them generally, to help them in particular ways, and even to ask others to pray to God on one's own behalf (1 Thess 5:25). We have already seen in chapter 7 how from the very beginnings of the Christ-movement the followers of Christ prayed for one another. Thus Paul was continually praying for the members of the communities he had established around the eastern Mediterranean (1 Cor 1:3; Phil 1:3-4, 9; 1 Thess 1:2-3). On occasion he asked them to pray for him. All of this occurs within "the fellowship [*koinōnia*] of the Holy Spirit." Does death end all this love and concern? Could the earliest advocates of a faith that offered triumph over death, paradigmatically in the resurrection of Jesus Christ, ever imagine that the strong ties among fellow believers and with God disappeared forever with death?

Strong evidence that they did not entertain such a thought is in 1 Thessalonians, the earliest extant document in the New Testament. Although Paul was very happy with his Thessalonian converts, they lacked hope. Timothy had brought Paul good news of their faith and love but not, revealingly, of their hope (1 Thess 3:6).[22] Hope had failed them in one particular area. They were grieving for those of their number who had died, before the second coming of Jesus. Hence Paul writes to them: "We do not wish you to be uninformed, brothers, concerning those who are asleep, lest you grieve as the others who have no hope. For if we believe that Jesus died and rose again, so then will God, for Jesus's sake, lead with him those who have fallen asleep" (1 Thess 4:13-14). Next he tells them, "by a word of the Lord," that is, on the highest authority, that "we who are alive, who survive until the coming of the Lord will not precede those who have fallen asleep" (v. 15). Then follows a famous passage, one replete with the first century's mythological language: "Because the Lord himself—with a cry of command, with an archangel's voice and with a blast on the trumpet of God—will descend from heaven and the dead in Christ [*hoi nekroi en Christō*] will rise first, and next we, the living ones who survive, shall be caught up together with them in the clouds to meet the Lord in the air, and so we will always be with the Lord" (vv. 16-17). He concludes by saying, "Comfort [*parakaleite*] one another with these words" (v. 18).

In his important recent monograph on Jesus's resurrection, N. T. Wright devotes five pages to 1 Thess 4:13—5:11, yet only one paragraph to how this passage functions "within Paul's larger picture." He is more concerned, perhaps not surprisingly given his thesis, to press the passage for what it reveals about resurrection and to argue that it shows Paul did not believe in an intermediate state for Christ-followers between death and resurrection. Wright notes that this part of 1 Thessalonians is

> as close as we come in early Christian literature to the theme much beloved of preachers at funerals, namely the promise of reunion beyond the grave with Christians already dead. Nothing is said, one way or the other, about such a reunion taking place before the resurrection itself; but the pastoral logic of the passage insists that an eventual reunion is what the creator God has in mind, and will accomplish at the time of Jesus' return.[23]

Let us focus a little more on what Wright (somewhat disparagingly?) concedes to be the "pastoral logic" of the passage, an expression I understand as encapsulating the precise reason that Paul composed these words, as opposed to information Wright dislodges from them to serve his own very different argumentative purpose.

In 1 Thessalonians Paul proposes three qualities as characterizing the identity of Christ-followers: faith (*pistis*), love (*agapē*) and hope (*elpis*). This triad, which he himself may have coined,[24] receives prominent notice in 1 Thess 1:3 and 5:8. As already mentioned, the Thessalonians lacked hope. Thus, they were shaky in one of the three pillars of the movement's identity. In 1 Thess 4:9-18 we learn of the main reasons for their lack of hope and Paul's response to them. First, they are grieving (*lupein*), like others in their society, for friends or relatives who have died. Second, the Thessalonians are particularly concerned that certain deceased persons will not experience the second coming of the Lord, which shows that, in life, they were Christ-believers too. We should not miss the magnitude of what is at stake here. *The love the Thessalonians felt for their relatives and friends who had died in Christ was stronger than death.* Though they had died, the Thessalonians grieved for them, which meant not only that they were themselves suffering the pains of separation, but that they were also distressed that those who had died would miss out on the glorious events of the Lord's return.

Paul fully understands the depth of their anguish. He does not try to tell them that their love is misdirected, but rather offers the promise that it will have a happy ending, not the tragic one they currently expect. Apparently (at least at this point in his career) considering that Jesus will return fairly soon, Paul assures them that when that occurs the dead in Christ will first be raised and that "we, the living ones who survive, shall be caught up together with them [*hama syn autois*] in the clouds to meet the Lord in the air" (v. 17). So there will be a reunion between living and once-dead Christ-followers and they will all be with the Lord as well. Stripped of its first-century mythological language, Paul is communicating to his addressees an understanding of final salvation that fixes upon interpersonal presence and communion between Christ-followers and Christ. The communion they enjoyed in life will be restored after death. At the same time, we must not forget that Paul has devised this narrative as a way to strengthen their wavering hope. He is proposing imagery of a final reunion beyond death as central to the identity of those who believe in Christ. There is very good reason, accordingly, for this being a "theme much beloved of preachers at funerals," Christian ones anyway.

Other data in the Pauline correspondence indicate that Paul himself considered that the community of believers transcended the living and the dead; alternatively, such data could have fostered such a belief in others. The clearest example is in Rom. 14:7-8: "None of us lives for himself, and none of us dies for himself. If we live, we live for the Lord, and if we die, we die for the Lord. Therefore whether we live or whether we die, we are the Lord's." A similar sentiment occurs in Phil 1:23. There is no sign in the authentic Pauline letters, however, of a prayer for the dead. The closest one comes to such prayer is 2 Tim 1:18. Here "Paul" prays for (the apparently dead) Onesiphorus: "may the Lord grant him to find mercy from the Lord on that Day." While not by Paul, this text indicates that such a prayer was not regarded as inappropriate in Pauline circles after his death.

In conclusion, Wright is correct to argue that *Paul* does not propose a significant intermediate state for Christ-followers who have died that precedes the resurrection other than the "sleep" of death. Nevertheless, we must be careful here not to entirely eliminate the significance of this "sleep," since, as Cullmann has suggested, it "refers to the *condition* of the dead before the Parousia," perhaps as in Rev 6:10, "'How long, Oh Lord?' cry the martyrs who are sleeping under the altar."[25] Nor does Paul deny the possibility of different models for understanding the state of the dead; he leaves the question open. These considerations and Paul's strong sense of communion between the living and the dead in Christ provided a fertile environment for different and powerful notions of postmortem vindication to develop, as indeed, against Wright, they did. Strong evidence that at least one part of the New Testament does entertain belief in a postmortem existence distinguishable from resurrection comes from Hebrews.

Communion between the Saints in Hebrews

COMMUNION BETWEEN ANCESTRAL AND CONTEMPORARY CHRIST-FOLLOWERS

The account of Israelite ancestors' faith in Hebrews 11 culminates with: "Therefore, since we are surrounded by so great a cloud of witnesses, let us also lay aside every weight, and sin which clings so closely, and let us run with perseverance the race that is set before us" (Heb 12:1). What is the nature of the presence of the witnesses? According to Craig Koester, "Hebrews does not develop a theory of the afterlife in this section."[26] Yet while it is reasonable to suggest that there is no such *theory* in the text, if by "theory" we mean a systematically assembled body of thought, the author nevertheless does subscribe to a belief in postmortem existence separate from resurrection. Moreover, in Heb 12:1 the author envisages a scene in which the faithful from the past support and applaud the faithful in the present. In other words, there is a form of communion between them. Yet, even more, he envisages this communion being perpetuated in a heavenly state.

To appreciate the author's message, we must consider the immediately preceding passage that sets the context for it, Heb 10:19-39. Here the author initially urges his audience to hold fast to their faith without wavering (10:19-25) and then warns them against sinning now that they have received knowledge of the truth (10:26-31). Then he reminds them of the former days, after their conversion, when they endured various sufferings, yet showed compassion to prisoners and even accepted the plundering of their property with joy, knowing that they had a better and abiding possession (10:32-34). They must not throw away their confidence, with its great reward, but must endure, doing the will of God and receiving what is promised (10:35-36). For in a little while the coming one will arrive; the righteous one will live by faith or will come to grief if he shrinks back (10:37-38). This section concludes with the following summary (10:39): "But we are not of those for shrinking back to destruction, but of faith for the preservation of the soul." The critical question here is the meaning of "the preservation of the soul" (*eis peripoiēsin psychēs*). Koester notes that it often meant "saving one's life from death" (as at Ezek 13:18, 19) but that it "ultimately means life beyond death." He adds that "Hebrews speaks interchangeably of preserving one's soul (10:39) and having one's spirit made complete in the heavenly Jerusalem (12:23)."[27] It is, indeed, highly probable, as we will see, that there is an equivalence between the preservation of the soul in 10:39 and the condition of entering the heavenly Jerusalem and joining its inhabitants as depicted in 12:22-24.

In Heb 11:1-2 the author continues immediately with the theme of faith, as to it being the assurance of things hoped for and the conviction of things not seen, and illustrates this with the examples of the "elders" (*presbyteroi*). Since in these respects he is clearly highlighting them as examples of people not "for shrinking back to destruction" (10:39a), it is likely that the author intended (and his audience understood) that the second half of Heb 10:39 also applied to the elders of Heb 11:2, that they were "of faith for the preservation of the soul." This would mean that the author and his audience expected the elders to share the type of vindication for which they themselves were hoping, which would eventually be found in the city of the living God, the heavenly (*epouranios*) Jerusalem in Heb 12:22-24.

Unambiguous confirmation of this view is found in the text. We begin with the comment made about Abraham and the patriarchs at 11:13: "These died in accordance with faith, not having received the things promised, but having seen them and greeted them from afar, and having acknowledged that

they were strangers and resident aliens on the earth." The necessary implication here, that they were actually seeking a heavenly homeland, is confirmed
at length in the next three verses, especially in v. 16: "Now[28] they desire a better one [a homeland], that is, a heavenly one [*epouranios*]. Therefore God is not
ashamed to be called their God, for he prepared a city for them."

At the end of Hebrews 11, in vv. 39-40, the author makes the following
point about these figures from the past that closely parallels what he had said
in v. 13: "And all these, though attested by faith, did not receive what was
promised, since God had foreseen something better for us, in order that apart
from us they should not be made perfect." Clearly, the thrust of the argument demands that, although they did not receive the things promised in the
past, they should now have done so. Admittedly, the time for their perfecting
could only arrive with the perfecting of the Christ-followers addressed by
the author, which became possible with Christ's death and exaltation. The
figures from the past could not achieve perfection "apart from us" (meaning
up until the time of the author and his contemporaries in the Christ-movement), since the enabler of that perfection had not yet accomplished his mission. But Christ has now done precisely this.

The reasonable supposition that the elders have finally been perfected
is given firm foundation in the vignette of the heavenly Jerusalem in Heb
12:22-24. The author mentions the following as present in this city: (a) the
living God, a judge who is God of all; (b) myriads of angels; (c) the assembly
of the firstborn who are enrolled in heaven (*ekklēsia prōtotokōn apogegrammenōn en
ouranois*); (d) the spirits of the righteous (*pneumata dikaiōn*) who have been made
perfect; and (e) Jesus, the mediator of the new covenant. Who are those mentioned in (c) and (d)? That the assembly of the firstborn is enrolled in heaven
suggests that they are human beings, rather than a parallel expression to the
angels (v. 22).[29] Although some are reluctant to precisely identify this group,[30]
the reference after this to "the spirits of the righteous who have been made
perfect" seems to require some manner of differentiating between these two
subgroups in the heavenly city.

First, we already know from Heb 11:16 that the elders from the past
were destined at some future point to reach the heavenly city that God had
prepared for them, so it is necessary that they must be found somewhere
among its inhabitants mentioned in Heb 12:22-24. Second, Heb 11:40 provides further help, in its assertion that God had foreseen something "better for us" and that the figures from the past were not to be made perfect
"apart from us." By these statements the author differentiates between the
elders of Hebrews 11 (figures from the past) and his contemporary Christ-
followers who have been the direct beneficiaries of Christ's saving acts in

the present time. Only when these have been perfected will the elders be able to achieve perfection.

It is difficult, admittedly, to determine which of these two groups is indicated by which group designation in 12:23. Providing support for the elders from the past being "the assembly of the first-born that are enrolled in heaven" is that elsewhere in Hebrews "first-born" does refer to chronological anteriority (1:6; 11:28). But this is probably not the better view. It seems more likely that "first-born" is metaphorical and refers to present-day Christ-followers. In Heb 11:40 not only are they accorded priority over the elders but the same verse indicates that the elders would achieve perfection (as a consequence of Christ's coming and sacrifice and the resulting possibility for perfection). Their designation as "having been made perfect" in 12:23 means they have indeed now attained this state. They had to wait, or, more precisely, their *spirits* had to wait, for these events before they could receive what had been promised and be perfected themselves. Although the word "righteous" (*dikaios*) generally refers to those who belong to the new dispensation (10:28), this word and its paronym "righteousness" (*dikaiosunē*) refer three times to the elders (Heb 11:4, 7, 33). Nothing ultimately turns on this issue, however. The author differentiates the two groups and depicts them together with God, Jesus, and the angels in the heavenly city.

Thus, the heavenly Jerusalem in Heb 12:22-24 is depicted in the very early stages of the new dispensation that has commenced with God's intervention in the world through his Son. This accords with the fact that the author of Hebrews envisages an ongoing period of existence before the end, which he describes as both a "day" drawing near (10:25) and a judgment (10:27, 30-31).

This interpretation depends upon those mentioned in Hebrews 11 having some form of existence after their earthly life until Christ comes again. We must imagine their spirits (*pneumata*) existing in a form of afterlife but only being perfected with the coming of Christ and the perfection of those of faith from his own time. Although this view entails that there is some difference between the firstborn who are enrolled in heaven and the spirits of the righteous who have been made perfect, it is inappropriate to push this too far. They really form two subgroups of the larger gathering in heaven, with their commonality far outweighing their differences. They are both in the heavenly city and in the presence of the living God, Jesus, and the angels. Both groups have received what was promised to them and have attained perfection.

The continuing existence of these figures from the past in the heavenly city, foreshadowed in 11:16 and confirmed in 12:23, takes on a graphic, visual form in 12:1: "Therefore, since we have such great a cloud of witnesses surrounding us, laying aside every weight and sin which clings so closely, let us run with endurance the contest that is set before us . . ." The "witnesses" (*martyres*) mentioned here are the Old Testament characters of Hebrews 11, those who have been attested (*martyrēthentes*; 11:2, 4, 5, 39) by God. Their current status in the heavenly city, admittedly something only clarified later in the text (12:23), necessitates that we take their existence in a literal and not metaphorical sense. That is, although they are made to play a role in the race metaphor, as spectators of the efforts of Christ-followers contemporary with the author of Hebrews, this does not militate against their being actually present to these Christ-followers.

These images of communion between the living and the dead in Heb 12:1 and between various groups of the dead in Heb 12:23 almost certainly form the foundation for later descriptions of communion between the saints that encompassed Old Testament figures and those from the time after Christ. We have already seen that in Nicetas of Remesiana's commentary on the Apostles' Creed the "saints" included the patriarchs Abraham, Isaac, and Jacob, the prophets, the apostles, the martyrs, and the "others just who were and are and will be," together with the angels.

The Role of the Resurrection

The author also exhibits some interest in the resurrection of the body, which we will survey briefly before considering how the author related this to the final judgment. Hebrews remarkably attributes to Abraham the belief that God could raise people from the dead (11:19). Also noteworthy is the statement that "Women received their dead by resurrection, while others were tortured, having refused release, in order that they might obtain a better resurrection" (11:35). The first resurrection mentioned here presumably refers to cases where children who had died were brought back to life, such as 1 Kgs 17:17-24 and 2 Kgs 4:18-37. The second resurrection mentioned in Heb 11:35 is that which occurs after death and burial and results in everlasting life for the resurrected body, such as that to which the martyrs of the Maccabean period looked forward (2 Macc 7:9, 11, 14, 23, 29).

The audience of Hebrews had themselves been taught to believe in the resurrection of the dead. In Heb 6:1-2 the author refers to the instruction his addressees have received that he summarizes as "a foundation of repentance from dead works and of faith toward God, with instruction about baptisms, the laying on of hands, the resurrection of the dead, and eternal judgment." This passage assists in determining how resurrection fits in with the teaching concerning the coming judgment. These features listed in 6:1-2 seem to be in chronological order and suggest that resurrection of the dead precedes final judgment. While Heb 9:27 states that "it is appointed for human beings to die once and for all, and after this [comes] judgment," there is no justification for Koester to argue that this verse "seems to assume that a person is judged immediately after death."[31] Hebrews quite clearly looks to one judgment that will occur on the "day" and will involve a fire that consumes the opponents (10:25-27), not a plethora of judgments that occur after every person dies.

In commenting upon Heb 12:23, Koester expresses the view, derived from David Peterson, that "Hebrews provides no clarity about a person's state between death and final judgment."[32] Yet this is a surprising failure to appreciate what we find in Heb 12:22-24, as we have just seen. While it is certainly true that Hebrews does not offer a carefully articulated view of the state of a person in faith between his or her death and the final judgment, it is possible to piece together, from these scattered references in the text, a fairly cohesive picture that the author of Hebrews and (one presumes) his audience had of the future. Thus, there will be a period of time between the actions of Christ and the resurrection of the dead and the judgment of God. During this period heaven will hold God, Jesus, the angels, (the spirits of) those who had died with faith in God through the death and exaltation of Jesus, and the spirits of the righteous who had died before the coming of Jesus (such as those mentioned in Hebrews 11). The phrase "the spirits of those who had died with faith in God as a result of Christ's actions" appropriately describes their existence prior to the resurrection and the judgment. In this respect they parallel the righteous from the period before the new covenant whose spirits (*pneumata*) have now been perfected.

The conclusions that we have reached so far about Hebrews 10–12 are confirmed by the presentation of some of the individual figures mentioned in Hebrews 11. To keep the discussion within manageable limits, I consider only three of them: Abel, Enoch, and Noah.

ABEL, ENOCH, NOAH, AND THE AFTERLIFE

How are we to understand the remarkable statement in Heb 11:4 about Abel that "by it [faith] although he died, he still speaks [*apothanōn eti lalei*]"? According to Koester, "Hebrews assumes that Abel was still dead; there is no speculation about his current heavenly existence (cf. *Life of Adam and Eve* 40)."[33] He refers to *Life of Adam and Eve* 40 since at that point in the work (and, indeed, throughout the text) there is no interest shown in the postmortem existence of Abel. It is elementary, however, that the failure of a single work like this to mention such a feature cannot constitute evidence against the author of Hebrews having accepted it—even if there were no other extant Israelite texts (as we will see there were) that exhibit great interest in Abel's activities in heaven. To make matters worse, Koester contradicts his view that "Hebrews assumes that Abel was still dead" by saying, far more plausibly, "Hebrews takes the cry of Abel's blood to show that he lives on, despite his death" and that the comment that Abel is still speaking "emphasizes that death is not the end of his story."[34]

Attridge offers a fuller and more persuasive, yet still incomplete, discussion of Abel's status in Heb 11:4.[35] He interprets Abel's continuing to speak, though dead, in the light of Heb 10:39 (itself closely related to the typically unannounced reference to Hab 2:3-4 in 10:39): "But we are not of those for shrinking back to destruction, but of faith for the preservation of the soul [eis peripoiēsin psychēs]." According to Attridge, Heb 11:4 exemplifies the principle of Hab 2:3-4 in that "[b]eyond death this righteous man still exercises a living function." It is possible that the Genesis account of Cain and Abel was the original stimulus for this notion in the imagination of the Hebrews author or his Israelite predecessors. In Gen 4:10, after Cain has murdered Abel, God lambastes him: "The voice of your brother's blood is crying out to me from the ground." In Heb 12:24, after all, the author refers to Jesus's sprinkled blood that "speaks better than Abel." There may have been additional Abel traditions in the collective memory of Israel that the author of Hebrews drew upon.[36]

There was, indeed, a rich tradition about Abel's activity after his death. Such activity happened in advance of any ultimate resurrection and is further evidence of the variety of Israelite beliefs in this area during the Second Temple period. At one point, as helpfully noted by Attridge,[37] Philo offers a fairly restrained interpretation of the statement in Gen 4:10 that the Abel's blood cried to God out of the ground: "he who appears to be dead is alive, inasmuch as he is found to be a suppliant of God and to utter a voice."[38] Nothing is said here of any activity in heaven.

Yet both Koester and Attridge overlook two important passages from Israelite texts that preserve other traditions about Abel. In *1 Enoch* 22, first, the angel Rufael shows Enoch a mountain with four corners designed so that "the spirits of the souls of the dead should assemble into them" until the day of their judgment. Enoch asks Rufael to which spirit belongs the voice that is reaching (into heaven) and making suit. Rufael answers: "This is the spirit which had left Abel, whom Cain, his brother had killed; it [continues to] sue him until all of [Cain's] seed is exterminated from the face of the earth."[39] This tradition is a development beyond Genesis 4 in its express reference to Abel's soul and its reference to all the souls waiting for the final judgment. In this text Abel's blood can cry to God out of the ground because of a belief in a postmortem disembodied soul.

Second, there is a section in the *Testament of Abraham* that describes how Abraham, while Michael was showing him around heaven, came upon a human being. This person was like a son of God, sat upon a throne, was judging and sentencing the souls, and had an angel on his right recording righteous deeds and an angel on his left recording sins. This human being was Abel, whom God had appointed to judge all creation, both righteous and sinners, until the parousia, when the twelve tribes of Israel would take over this role.[40]

These two passages are closely aligned with what is stated of Abel in Heb 11:4. Their relevance is not so much as possible literary sources alluded to by the author, but as Judean oral tradition preserved in the collective memory of the people. We have Abel enjoying a postmortem and disembodied existence in the afterlife,[41] continuing to speak (either against Cain or in judgment over other deceased humans), and associated with righteousness. Although he is not explicitly described as righteous in either of these passages, it is reasonable to assume that righteousness was attributed to him, given that he was charged with judging the righteous and the sinful.

The notable combination in Heb 11:4 of an assertion that Abel is righteous and that "although he died, he still speaks" strongly suggests that the author is reminding his audience of these particular features of the composite Israelite memory of Abel. From this perspective, against Koester, the current existence of Abel in the afterlife is assumed. In Abel, accordingly, we find a precise example of "the preservation of the soul" that results from faith, as announced in Heb 10:39.

In his mention of *Enoch*, the author offers a particular view on something that the reference to Enoch in Gen 5:24 had left mysteriously open, namely, the meaning of his being "taken" by God. He interprets this to mean that Enoch did not see death. This is significant, since there were a variety of views abroad as to what "being taken" meant in Enoch's case. Some ancient sources suggested that he was taken by death.[42] More common, however, was the view that Enoch had been assumed into heaven without dying.[43] Hebrews emphatically aligns itself with this latter tradition. In doing so, it provides another example of "the preservation of the soul" (*peripoiēsis psychēs*) that results from faith (Heb 10:39). It is also possible that the author was attracted to the Enoch story by the circumstance that, just as with Abel, there were Israelite memories of Enoch also having been a judge in heaven.[44]

Although Hebrews expressly asserts the continuing postmortem existence of Abel and Enoch, it also implies in Heb 11:7 that *Noah* enjoyed this state: "he became an heir of the righteousness that comes by faith." Properly interpreting "he became an heir" is the key to realizing this.

An "heir" is someone with a present *entitlement* (either under a will or by the operation of law) *to receive property in the future* on (or at some stipulated time after) the death of the testator or property owner. In Greek this concept was expressed by a semantic field that includes *klēronomos* ("heir"), *klēronomia* ("inheritance"), and *klēronomeō* ("inherit" or, far less commonly, "to be an heir"). In the Septuagint, the verb almost always means "to inherit something," with whatever is inherited in the genitive or accusative case.[45]

The notion of heirship—of an entitlement to something which one will receive in the future after someone's death—is a significant motif in Hebrews. The word *klēronomos* appears three times in the text (1:2; 6:17; 11:7), while *klēronomia* occurs twice (9:15; 11:8) and *klēronomeō* on four occasions (1:4, 14; 6:12; 12:17). It is not difficult to see why heirship proved such a congenial concept to the author. A feature of his communicative strategy is to emphasize the need to endure what may well be present difficult experiences in view of the great prospects in the future. Thus he stresses the need for endurance (10:32, 36; 12:1, 2, 3, 7) and patience (6:12, 15) as appropriate attitudes to the current situation, as well as confidence (3:6; 4:16; 10:19) and hope (3:6; 6:11, 18; 7:19; 10:23; 11:1) in relation to the rewards that are the subject of promises (6:12, 13, 15, 17; 7:6; 8:6; 9:15; 10:23, 36; 11:9, 11, 13, 17, 33, 39; 12:26). The notion of heirship, of a present entitlement to a future benefit, is closely cognate to this pattern of meaning. It also provided the author an analogy from a well-known institution in his culture to express his point with great precision. For this reason, translations (such as those of the RSV at Heb 1:4, 14) which remove any reference to the basic meaning of heirship, by using words such as "obtain," do readers of the text a serious disservice.

This context indicates how the original audience of Hebrews would have understood Noah as someone who became an heir of the righteousness that comes from faith (Heb 11:7). Although Noah was remembered in some reaches of Israelite tradition as righteous (most notably Gen 6:9 and 7:1), we must remember that the author here refers not to the generalized righteousness that marked Israelite covenant identity, but the righteousness *that comes by faith*. It is of critical importance that the text does *not* say that Noah *inherited* such righteousness (as Attridge wrongly states),[46] for this would indicate that he had come into possession of it. This was impossible since righteousness by faith would only appear in the world millennia after Noah's death, as a result of the death and exaltation of Jesus. Rather, Noah "became an heir" of righteousness by faith, meaning that he gained an entitlement to righteousness by faith at some future time on or after someone's death, in this case, that of Jesus.

This conclusion leads inexorably to the following questions: How could Noah, long dead after all,[47] have been able to become an heir to the righteousness that comes by faith? And did he (in the view of the composer and first recipients of Hebrews) actually do so? We have already seen that the author of Hebrews emphasizes the continuing existence of Abel and Enoch beyond their earthly lifetimes, in Abel's case in spite of death and in Enoch's by direct assumption into heaven. While Genesis contained no such idea about Noah, nor does the idea seem to occur in other Israelite traditions, it is highly likely that the author of Hebrews and his audience assumed some form of postmortem existence for Noah as well.

COMMUNION WITH THE SAINTS
IN EARLY CHRISTIANITY

Late-First- and Second-Century Developments

In Christian writers from the late first and second centuries, it is common to find beliefs both in a temporary disembodied existence after death and in a final resurrection. This is similar to the picture in Hebrews 10–12. Irenaeus, writing ca. 175–185 CE, drew a parallel with Jesus, who between his death and resurrection descended into Hades (1 Pet 3:19), asserting that since no servant is above his master: "The souls go to an invisible place designated for them by God, and sojourn there until the resurrection . . . Afterwards, receiving their bodies and rising again perfectly, that is with their bodies, just as the Lord himself rose, they will so come to the sight of God."[48] Tertullian took a similar view, in the period 190–220 CE. He believed that all souls would remain in the underworld until the day of the Lord came, when the earth would be destroyed, with the just having the consolation of the resurrection that was to come and the sinful experiencing a foretaste of their future condemnation.[49]

Yet from a very early date we find that a rather happier fate was in store for martyrs. It was believed that they were admitted immediately to the joys of heaven. We find this pattern as early as the mid-90s of the first century CE, the probable date of a letter known as *1 Clement*.[50] The author speaks of Peter and Paul having gone to a "place of glory" and "a holy place," respectively, and states that the martyrs had received "a noble reward" and had obtained the gift of "life in immortality."[51] These expressions seem to refer to a temporary existence in some form of "heaven."[52] In addition, however, *1 Clement* strongly affirms the resurrection.[53] At one point in the text the author expressly links a period of waiting in the "chambers" (as in *1 Enoch* 22) followed apparently by resurrection.[54]

Both Irenaeus and Tertullian believed that the martyrs were in a special position, of gaining entry to some heavenly state on their death, even though resurrection also awaited them.[55] Polycarp, writing about 110 CE, expressed a similar view, stating that the martyrs "ran not in vain, but in faith and justice, and that they are in their due place in the presence of the Lord, with whom also they suffered."[56] Some included the apostles among the ranks of the privileged in heaven. Thus Hermas, writing probably in the mid-second century CE, states that the apostles and teachers, after they died in the power and faith of the Son of God, preached to the departed saints of the Old Testament, who were brought to life and came to know the name of the Son of God. Hermas depicts the martyrs, the Old Testament figures, and the apostles as being in heaven.[57]

Christian devotion to the apostles and martyrs, most notably Peter and Paul, exists from an early date in Rome. There is archaeological and literary evidence for a monument to Peter on the Vatican Hill from as early as the mid-second-century CE.[58] Many graffiti were found when Peter's grave was excavated on the Vatican, most of them from the time of Constantine onward. One reads: "Peter, pray for the holy Christian people buried near your body."[59] This reveals the characteristic pattern of belief. First, Peter is believed to be alive and capable of receiving requests of this type. Second, Peter himself is not capable of providing any benefits; he is simply being asked to pray (to God) on behalf of certain persons (in this case deceased persons), just as you could ask a fellow Christian in this life to pray for you. Third, it was thought valuable for Peter's remains to be close to the remains of those for whom he was being asked to intercede.

About a century later, we find a well-developed devotion to Peter and Paul at the catacomb near the Via Appia that was believed to contain their remains, now located under the church of San Sebastiano. These date from about 260 CE to the time of Constantine. One possibility is that the remains of Peter and Paul were brought there from their respective resting places on the Vatican Hill and beside the Via Ostiensis during the time of the Valerianic persecution in 258 CE.[60] Excavations carried out in 1915 revealed a large number of graffiti containing requests directed to the two saints jointly.[61] Typical invocations included "Peter and Paul keep X in mind" and "Peter and Paul make petition [to God] on behalf of Victor." These graffiti attest a belief similar to that seen above: the saints (described in one graffito as "holy martyrs") were alive and could pray to God on behalf of a person, just as they could in their former earthly existence.

Two Models of Sainthood

Central to Elizabeth Johnson's 1998 book *Friends of God and Prophets* is the delineation of two approaches to the communion of saints. The first to develop, in the age of the martyrs that we have just considered, was that of a companionship of friends in Christ. "The living were partners, companions, co-disciples with those who had given their lives, one witnessing to the other, both carried along by the saving grace poured out in Christ." This view emerges very clearly in one of Augustine's sermons on the feast of Perpetua and Felicity: "We rejoice for them, they pray for us . . . Yet do we all serve the one Lord, follow the same teacher, accompany the same leader" (*Sermon* 280.4, 6).[62] Augustine encourages his readers to pay attention to what the martyrs set before us, to believe this, and to embody it in our lives, for this is the truest way to celebrate and venerate their memory.[63] Johnson summarizes this idea: "The communion of saints in the companionship model forges intergenerational bonds across time that sustain faith in strange new times and places. Surrounded by a cloud of witnesses, we cherish in very different circumstances what they cared enough to live and die for."[64] Johnson finds a New Testament parallel to this approach in the roll call of ancestral friends of God in Hebrews 11 which "flows into exhortation to the community currently alive on earth to find courage and heart for the journey" in Hebrews 12.[65]

The second approach to the communion of saints, according to Johnson, began to develop late in the third century and reached its peak in the late fifth, roughly matching the rise of a new church order having imperial support from the time of Constantine onwards. Now the Christian imagination began to cast the saints in the role of sponsors, or rather patrons, who could plead one's cause before God and even dispense favors in their own right. This development paralleled the increased power and trappings of office of bishops after the Edict of Milan in 313 CE. These features are very visible in the case of Ambrose, himself from an aristocratic family, who was bishop of Milan from 374 to 397 CE.[66] Bishops actively sought control of the remains of martyrs and saints, thereby gaining power over the faithful who came to pray near them. Thus, as Peter Brown has argued, the martyr became a heavenly *patronus* and also the invisible concomitant of the patronage exercised on earth by the bishop.[67] The notion of living and dead Christians being "friends and comrades in the egalitarian experience of grace receded in favor of living persons being needy petitioners vis-à-vis powerful heavenly intercessors."[68] The patron-client paradigm became the dominant feature of medieval devotion to the saints and led to the various well-known abuses that became a central target of criticism from the Reformers,[69] even though elements of the first approach to the communion of saints survived.

FROM THE REFORMATION TO VATICAN II

The Reformers opposed invoking the saints or seeking favors from them, especially as this lessened the trust Christians placed in Jesus Christ, who they feared otherwise became merely a dreaded judge only approached through others. But the Augsburg Confession, written by Philip Melanchthon in 1530, while rejecting invocation of the saints, did say: "It is also taught amongst us that the saints should be kept in remembrance so that our faith may be strengthened when we see what grace they received and how they were sustained by faith. Moreover, their good works are to be an example to for us . . ."[70] In Lutheran circles the communion of saints continued in this mode. Even among Calvinists, where there was a much stricter attitude to images of the saints than among Lutherans, there was no outright denial of the communion of saints. Thus, the second Helvetic Confession, while rejecting invocation, said:

> At the same time, we do not despise the saints or think basely of them. For we acknowledge them to be living members of Christ and friends of God who have gloriously overcome the flesh and the world. Hence we love them as brothers, and also honor them; yet not with any kind of worship but by an honorable opinion of them and just praise of them. We also imitate them.[71]

The Second Vatican Council considered the communion of saints in chapter 7 of *Lumen Gentium*. While retaining a belief in the possibility of spiritual interchange between living and dead Christians, it did so in a fashion that was strongly Christocentric, that reflected the radically reformed ecclesiology advocated by the Council, and that restored "the friends of God" approach to the heart of its teaching in this area. Johnson comments:

> The teaching of Vatican II restores the companionship model to the forefront of theology, and does so with a zest that results from a deep shift in its theology of the church. Specifically, the profound connection that *Lumen Gentium* forges between the people of God, called to be holy and those faithful friends of God already in glory articulates the biblical and early martyrs' pattern in a new idiom. Far from being isolated patrons, saints in heaven are enfolded into the whole people of God as companions in Christ who are the beginning of the great harvest . . . Remembering them strengthens hope as the community forges ahead in the struggle of history; joining with their praise of God enriches our own worship.[72]

Having considered the origins and development of the attitudes of living to dead Christians, especially their intercommunion, we will now discuss various models for such communion. It is important to emphasize that although a high theology of spiritual interchange (see chapter 10 below) is largely restricted to Roman Catholics, Orthodox Christians, and certain Anglicans, even in the Lutheran and Calvinist traditions it is accepted that living Christians should remember, love, and imitate the saints. This outlook can easily be integrated with a model for communion based on memory, which we will consider in the next chapter.

9

COMMUNION WITH
THE SAINTS

MODELING THE NATURALISTIC
POSSIBILITIES

In the preceding chapter, I considered the origins and development of the concept "the communion of saints" to understand the extent to which we and the authors of the New Testament writings are situated within a framework of intercultural and socio-theological communication and communion. We must now consider a number of models that could provide an intelligible foundation for such communion in this chapter and the following one. In this chapter, I will address "naturalistic" possibilities, those that do not require some form of postmortem existence; these latter possibilities I will address in the next chapter.

RESPECT FOR DECEASED AUTHORS:
A FORM OF COMMUNION?

The simplest form of the relationship we have with New Testament authors is that we possess writings they composed. We will leave aside for the moment any other point of connection. Is this enough for communion between these ancient authors and us? Does the model of socio-theological communion set out in chapter 2 apply here? The question of the relationship that exists between certain authors and us can hardly fail to take seriously the circumstance that those authors are dead. According to Robert Morgan and John Barton, this makes a big difference to how we receive texts. These critics argue that although "in the case of a conversation or personal communication we are bound to the author's intention because the author is alive and has some moral right to be understood as intended,"[1] all this changes with the death of the author, when the "balance of power and moral rights" shifts to the interpreters: "Texts, like dead men and women, have no rights, no aims, no interests. They can be used in whatever way readers or interpreters choose . . .

it is the interests or aims of the interpreters that are decisive, not the claims of the text as such. Any suggestion that a text has rights is a deception concealing someone else's interests."[2] Since this is an argument which really applies to the interpretation of any historical text, my initial reply is drawn from the historicist theory of Cox and Reynolds: "The notion of Otherness is essential to historicism, for the historical imagination exists only when one can conceive of a time, a place, a people, a culture different from ours, only when the past becomes something other than a mirror image of our concerns and interests."[3] In other words, historical interpretation involves a respect for the other that has ethical dimensions. To use the distinction outlined by E. D. Hirsch (see discussion on authorial intention in chapter 4), Cox and Reynolds are in effect adopting an "allocratic" mode of interpretation, that is, one in which the voice of the other (*allos*) prevails (*kratei*), rather than an autocratic one, where the reader disregards the other and produces his or her own (*autos*) meaning from the text. Hirsch asserts that unless there is "a powerful overriding value in disregarding an author's intention, we who interpret as a vocation should not disregard it."[4]

But is an allocratic mode of interpretation appropriate when the author is dead? G. K. Chesterton said something about tradition in his 1909 work *Orthodoxy* that is worth repeating here: "Tradition may be defined as an extension of the franchise. Tradition means giving votes to the most obscure of all our classes, our ancestors. It is the democracy of the dead. Tradition refuses to submit to the small and arrogant oligarchy of those who merely happen to be walking about."[5] Yet more must be said than this, for the particular problem besetting the view of Morgan and Barton is that it seems to assume that moral discourse relating to the dead is exhausted by the language of rights. But while our deceased relatives and friends have no rights, who would deny that we have a duty, at the level of common humanity, to honor their memory?[6] We do so in diverse ways, from keeping portraits of them on our walls, to visiting their graves, to dedicating books to their memory, and so on. We honor them for what they were in themselves and also for the way in which they touched our lives and shaped our identity. There seems no reason why this type of obligation should not also extend to authors, now deceased, who have had a lasting impact on us.

It seems, therefore, that our model of socio-theological communion is applicable to deceased authors. On the other hand, if we have no connection with them other than possessing what they had written, then the group dimension of intercommunion, the importance of which was mentioned in chapter 2, would be lacking. Since we are connected to the New Testament authors in that both we and these authors belong, in a certain sense, to the same faith-commitment group, we now consider the more ample models of communion available in such a context. The first model is to construe these authors as our "ancestors in faith." The other models will be considered under the expression "the communion of saints" in the strictest sense, even though it embraces a number of distinct types of communion. I have used the expression "ancestors in faith" a number of times earlier in this volume as a general designation for the New Testament authors and the time has now come to explore in more detail the meaning of this expression.

ANCESTORS IN FAITH

It appears from recent scientific research that human beings are genetically disposed to respect their ancestors. In 2001 Bryan Sykes, Professor of Human Genetics at Oxford, published a book called *The Seven Daughters of Eve*. In it he showed how investigation into mitochondrial DNA since the mid-1980s has produced remarkable findings about the course of human evolution. It now seems that all human beings descend from a human population in Africa about one hundred thousand years ago and that virtually all Europeans can trace their ancestry back to one of seven women who lived between forty-five thousand and ten thousand years ago. Some of his own research has revealed striking similarities in the DNA between people living in parts of Europe today and the DNA extracted from skeletons thousands of years old discovered in various parts of the European continent. In some cases, the discovery of such links has triggered in the modern descendants feelings of concern and regard for their distant ancestors. Most striking, perhaps, is the instance of an Irish woman living in Bournemouth, England. Sykes discovered that she had the same DNA sequence as the five-thousand-year-old "Iceman" found in the Italian Alps in 1991 and therefore both descended from one of the seven women ancestral to all modern Europeans. When the woman learned of this, she began to have serious concerns about the way scientists were treating his corpse. "She had started to think of him as a real person and as a relative—which is exactly what he was."[7]

Many cultures have highly developed practices to show respect to their ancestors and to acknowledge the interconnection between the living and the dead. China offers the clearest example, where some clans have been known to honor named ancestors extending back sixteen generations.[8] In China, houses are not regarded so much as "places to house the individual members in comfort and ease as they are signs of unity and social prestige for the family as a whole—the dead, the living and the generations to come."[9]

Ancestors also play a vital role in African society. T. Tshibangu, in summarizing the essential elements of African religion, describes it as including a belief in a supreme creator and a belief in two worlds: the visible world of the living and the invisible world of the spirits of the dead (the ancestors). These worlds are always closely interacting, with the ancestors serving to guarantee the integrity and vitality of the community. All this produces an intensely felt sense of solidarity between members of a community.[10] Similarly, Harry Sawyer observes that Africans see themselves "as part of a cultic community—a community which is incomplete without the supernatural world. The worship of the ancestors, the attitude to birth and death, sin, sickness, forgiveness and health all converge on the central role of the community."[11] Ancestor commemoration has also figured prominently in both Jewish and Japanese folk religion since the earliest times.[12]

What, then, of the people who were involved in the communicative process leading to the New Testament? Some of these are the named authors of texts, Paul especially. There are the real yet unknown authors, such as the evangelists "Matthew," "Mark," and "Luke." There are people named in the texts, like Phoebe (Rom 16:1) and Chloe (1 Cor 1:11). There are also the unnamed yet just as real persons, such as the members of Paul's congregations in Thessalonika and Galatia, some from the very first generation of the Christ-movement. There are a large number of such "ancestors," sending and receiving the messages a part only of which survive in the New Testament.

It is accurate and helpful to describe all of these people as our "ancestors in faith." For they are among the earliest people who heard the words of Jesus. They heard the word about him as the Messiah, proclaimed in the years shortly after this death and resurrection, and responded to it, adopting new ways of being human in the world in relation to God. They began and passed on a lineage of faith and an identity that have survived and flourished and come down to us today. It was they who first responded to the message of salvation announced by Jesus and embodied it in distinctive modes of thought, feeling, and behavior that have provided a paradigm for subsequent followers of Jesus across nearly seventy generations, despite the very different cultural contexts of these later generations. The documents of the New Testament are an incomplete though precious repository of the messages passing between our primordial ancestors in the church. Perhaps to put it better, these documents are a hard-copy version of the living voices of Paul and all the rest—proclaimed, heard, and acted upon.

I propose that the moral obligation we feel toward the memory of our own recent dead also exists to honor the memory of our ancestors in faith who first accepted and lived in consequence of the Gospel of Christ. We especially remember the actual persons who composed the letters and other writings that now comprise the New Testament and the actual persons to whom they were first directed. In short, we remember all those individuals and communities who formed part of the communicative process that resulted in today's New Testament. Furthermore, we can expand this group to include the other real persons referred to in these writings who did not actively send or receive them. These people from an admittedly distant past were nevertheless both significant in themselves and because they also inaugurated and transmitted to us Christian modes of belief and being in the world.

So far I have been considering the "communion of saints" purely at the level of human obligation. What are the theological dimensions of the status of these ancestors in faith? This question brings us to the practices of memory as a way to construe the communion between Christians living and dead (here, especially, the New Testament authors).

COLLECTIVE MEMORY, SOCIAL IDENTITY, AND COMMUNION WITH THE SAINTS

Memory and History

To be mindful of those who wrote the various documents of the New Testament inevitably involves memory. At the heart of any concept of the communion of saints must lie practices of anamnesis, of calling into memory and memorialization, of enacting memories so recalled. The dead in Christ, including the New Testament authors, are persons known to us in memory, however else we might encounter them.

Yet it is through history that these memories are summoned forth, a point made eloquently by Nils Dahl in his inaugural lecture delivered at the University of Oslo in 1946: "The historical enterprise makes sense only on the presupposition that there is something in the past that deserves to be preserved in memory or to be rescued from oblivion. Historical research must always take into consideration that persons or past events have produced such an impression that the memory of them has been perpetuated."[13]

Historical research is the means by which we keep these memories alive to the fullest extent, including their painful and subversive features, for otherwise we risk succumbing to nostalgia or anesthesia.[14] In addition, history attuned to the realities of the lives of our ancestors in faith inevitably highlights their cultural distance from us, the fact that they are not mirror images of ourselves. One of the finest achievements of feminist biblical criticism, beginning with

Elisabeth Schüssler Fiorenza's *In Memory of Her*, has been developing practices of memory using historical techniques to recover the memories of women who have been nearly or entirely forgotten.[15]

Two important passages in the New Testament that expressly refer to the memorialization of the saints, both concerning women, deserve notice. The most pertinent is the Magnificat in Luke 1:46-55. In this passage, steeped in Old Testament piety (most obviously Hannah's song in 1 Sam 2:1-10), Mary enunciates an old but central, subversive theme in the life and religion of Israel: the Lord is a holy God who brings down the mighty from their thrones and exalts the lowly; or, to use liberation theology's catchphrase, he is a God who has "a preferential option for the poor." Most relevant to our purposes is when Mary says, "For behold, henceforth all generations will call me blessed" (Luke 1:48b; RSV). Luke has either created, or at least agrees with, a sentiment that both indicates an extended future for the Christ-followers as a movement and looks forward to the memorialization of Mary. Somewhat similar is Jesus's remark concerning the woman who anoints him at Bethany: "And truly, I say to you, wherever the gospel is preached in the whole world, what she has done will be told in memory of her" (Mark 14:9; par. Matt 26:13). Feminist criticism rightly laments the fact that this woman is anonymous— although in time she came to be assimilated to Mary Magdalen. Nevertheless, the anamnetic instincts of the text are clear.

To explore further the anamnetic dimensions of communion it is necessary at this point to introduce two theoretical resources. The first consists of the ideas concerning collective memory formulated by the French sociologist Maurice Halbwachs (1877–1945) and the second is the social identity theory developed by Henri Tajfel in the University of Bristol, England, in the 1970s and early 1980s.

Theorizing Collective Memory

As demonstrated by Gerdien Jonker in a succinct summary of theories of memory,[16] Maurice Halbwachs's work represents a new development in theories of memory, current since the time of Aristotle and Augustine, that held that to remember was an act by an *individual* of retrieving images that were stored in within his or her self.[17] Under the influence of his teacher in sociology—none other than the great Émile Durkheim (1858–1917)—Halbwachs articulated a new approach to memory that first appeared in 1925 in his *Les cadres sociaux de la mémoire*.[18] Further thoughts he had on the subject appeared in the posthumous 1950 work *La mémoire collective*, which has given the name to his perspective.[19] Halbwachs regarded memory as the production of human beings living together in society: "[I]t is in society that people normally acquire their memories. It is also in society that they recall, recognize and localize their memories."[20] His thesis was that memory is socially determined; it is a collective and social phenomenon. Collective memory is the means by which a group associates and identifies with its own past.

Prior to his exposure to Durkheim, Halbwachs had worked with the individualistic philosopher Henri Bergson (1859–1941). Perhaps because of this, Halbwachs was able to resist some of the more extreme reaches of Durkheimian social determinism. Bergson's influence may explain why Halbwachs interested himself in groups within society, rather than just with the larger reality of society itself.[21] Lewis Coser notes that almost everywhere that Durkheim speaks of "Society" with a capital S, Halbwachs speaks of "groups"—that is, a more cautious usage.[22] Collective memory relates to groups, not society at large. Halbwachs was also sensitive to the role of individuals: "While the collective memory endures and draws strength from its base in a coherent body of people, it is individuals as group members who remember."[23]

Halbwachs observed that we have two broad types of memories. First, there are memories that consist of remembrances of one's own personal experiences. These he called "autobiographical," "individual," or "internal" memory. Second, there are memories derived from membership in particular groups, meaning an individual's memory of events or persons known to him or her not through personal experience but from the memory of others, written records, or commemorations, including events before that individual was born. Such a memory "remains a borrowed memory, not my own."[24] These he called "social" or "external" memory.[25] There is obvious truth in this; I have vivid memories of time I spent with my maternal grandparents, but I also, as an Australian, remember the Gallipoli campaign in the First World War that ended long before I was born. Yet Halbwachs insisted that it was wrong to overemphasize the distinction between autobiographical and historical memories, for in fact they interpenetrated one another. The reality of that interpenetration is "collective memory" that represents the zone of interaction between individual and personal remembrances and reference points from the memories of others or from historical records.[26]

Halbwachs had a particular interest in the way a group reconstructed its memories in the present. While some theorists, such as Barry Schwartz,[27] have argued that he advanced too far in this direction, thus jeopardizing the continuity between a group and its past, he was right to insist upon the ability of groups to reconstruct the past, typically by the invention of tradition or capturing traditions generated by other groups. More problematic was Halbwachs's neglect, as Paul Connerton has shown, of the way collective memories are handed on, communicated, from one generation to another. Connerton correctly maintains that "to study the social formation of memory is to study those acts of transfer that make remembering in common possible."[28]

Halbwachs's interest in the vibrant process whereby a group maintains a living connection with its past to satisfy the demands of the ever-changing present meant that he took issue with certain features of modern historiography. Halbwachs envisaged a sharp division between history and collective memory, with the former beginning where the latter ceased. History helped to prevent forgetting. Collective memory was the spontaneous product of a group, while history was scientific and "objective." Collective memory was an unbroken tradition localized in the life of a community that bore directly on the present. History, on the other hand, was universal in scope, seeking to map all events that occurred in a particular epoch and postulating a view of time that gave equal weight to the past and the present.[29] Yosef Yerushalmi adopted Halbwachs's dichotomy between collective memory and history in his work *Zakhor: Jewish History and Jewish Memory,* in which he argued that there was no place for historiography in the Jewish collective memory since this would entail a rupture with the Jewish past.[30]

To this we might add that while human beings seem driven to compose narratives of the past as a way of retaining significant memory, it is necessary to distinguish collective memory from the activity of historical reconstruction. The latter involves systematic and dispassionate investigation into human activities in the past from the traces that have been left behind, whether there is a living memory of those activities or not.[31] So how can collective memory and history be reconciled?

In answer to this question Jonker has helpfully observed that neither Halbwachs nor Yerushalmi was opposed to history per se. Halbwachs did not reject history in favor of the absolute claims of a living tradition but rather "pointed to the essential difference between 'remembering' and 'history' in respect of their association with and claim to the past." Halbwachs and Yerushalmi took up a position against the claim to authority of historiography that recognizes only one form of time, that of universal chronology. Halbwachs was concerned with one particular segment of the past (not with all of past time) and with particular groups, not with the entire history of any particular period.

This would suggest that historiography that played to the life and tradition of a particular group would not have been beyond the pale for Halbwachs. Indeed, Yerushalmi urges something very like this: a historiography that is aware of its origins in a particular group practiced by historians who are advocates for the group, asserting the claims of its distinctiveness and character.[32] Jonker usefully assesses the dynamics of such and approach as follows:

> The difference between "collective memory" and "history," seen by Halbwachs as meaningful . . . enables a distinction to be made between a past which is "of itself" present in society and a past which must first be "dug up." Delving for new images can be a subversive act, intended to attack the self-image of a society, or on the contrary it can be a fundamental one, by which the society is tied to its supposed "origins."[33]

If we now apply this perspective in relation to contemporary Christianity, we are able to propose that a historical investigation of the origins of Christianity has a vital role to play in the formation and re-formation of its collective memory. Historiography serving the needs of this group digs into its earliest period, thus unearthing a body of material that might subvert or confirm current memories but will certainly not be indifferent to them.

Yet we must not forget the personal dimension to the thesis argued in this volume. To introduce this dimension into our evolving theoretical framework, we must link these ideas on collective memory with perspectives on group identity.[34]

The Integration of Social Identity and Collective Memory

James Fentress and Chris Wickham helpfully observe that "When we remember, we represent ourselves to ourselves and to those around us. To the extent that our 'nature'—that which we truly are—can be revealed in articulation, we are what we remember." This induces them to suggest that "a study of the way we remember—the way we present ourselves in our memories, the way we define our personal and collective identities through our memories, the way we order and structure our ideas in our memories, and the way we transmit these memories to others—is a study of the way we are."[35]

The close connection between memory and identity, pointed to by Fentress and Wickham, especially in view of Halbwachs's emphasis on collective memories being situated in groups, prompts us to use Henri Tajfel's social identity theory as a body of ideas helpful for augmenting the collective memory model.[36] Tajfel, who died in 1982, defined "social identity" as that element of an individual's identity that derives from belonging to a particular group. It encompassed three distinct dimensions: first, a cognitive dimension (the sheer fact of belonging to a group like this); second, an emotional dimension (how it feels to belong); and third, an evaluative dimension (how members rate their groups in relation to others). Since the members of one group often tell themselves who they are in contrast with out-groups to which they do not belong, intergroup phenomena play a prominent role in social identity theory.[37]

The initial phase of social identity research tended to analyze groups at one particular point in a group's existence and thus neglected historical or diachronic issues. More recently, however, social identity theorists, such as Susan Condor and Marco Cinnirella, have begun investigating group identity as it endures over time. It would be difficult, if not impossible, to possess a personal identity if one lacked the competency for relating individual experiences across time. Condor envisages social life as a trajectory through time rather than a static set of positions. She understands social agents as taking up identities, practices, and ideas and passing them on to others.[38] Cinnirella's concern lies in developing the theory of social identity in order that it might be brought to bear on past social identities and address the means by which groups reconstitute past, present, and future to create meaningful "stories" in relation to the group and its members.[39] He has introduced the very useful idea of "possible selves," which are beliefs held by individuals (= "personal selves") or groups (= "social selves") as to what they were like in the past and what they may become in the future. Cinnirella points out that a group that is oriented to the past will bring forward historical or imagined figures from the past as prototypes of group identity. These figures will in turn influence the possible social selves the group creates for the membership. By this means the group reactivates existing collective memories or invents new ones to tell itself who it is in the present.

Collective Memory, Social Identity, and the Communion of Saints

What role does this theory have in relation to the manner in which Christians encounter those who have died in Christ? Two answers are possible. The first is a historical answer that describes how a sense of connection with those who had died in Christ developed in the past (especially in the first few centuries). The second answer—more germane to this volume—bears upon retaining the saints in our memory as the means of constructing contemporary Christian identities. I will deal briefly with the first, before spending more time on the second.

Collective Memory, the Saints, and the Ancient Church

In the early centuries of Christianity there would have been some, perhaps many, Christ-followers who knew personally and were perhaps even related to fellow believers who had been martyred. These deceased fellow believers were thought to have gone to their eternal reward, from where they could receive invocations to pray to God on behalf of the living. In such cases, the living Christians would have had an "autobiographical" or "individual" remembrance of those who had so unequivocally died in Christ. On other occasions, Christians would remember martyrdoms that had occurred before they were born through hearing and recalling stories about these martyrdoms. These latter instances exemplify the processes of "collective" or "historical" memory. Yet, as Halbwachs has observed, the two types interpenetrate one another. A collective memory of past martyrdoms would shape the understanding of how Christians reacted to those occurring in their own experience, while the martyrdom of their family, friends, and acquaintance would affect their remembrance and understanding of earlier or distant deaths. There is no doubt, for example, that the account of the martyrdom of Polycarp in Smyrna about 155 CE had an enormous impact on Christian consciousness throughout the Roman Empire.[40] Narratives such as this had a major impact on the development of Christian identity. When Christians asked themselves who they were, part of the answer was that they were a people who would gladly endure agonizing and dishonorable deaths rather than deny their Lord.

Social identity theory allows us to see more precisely how these processes worked. The martyrs were heroic prototypes of Christian identity. They provided a stock of "possible selves" allowing Christians after them to come to terms with their often terrible experience and not forsake their identity. By activating memories of martyrdoms in the past, they were able to make sense of what was happening to them in the present and also keep alive the hope of the glories in store for them if they were faithful unto death.

A highly revealing insight into the place of memory in Christianity in the fourth and fifth centuries comes from Georgia Frank's elegant study of the practices of pilgrims to the Holy Land and Egypt during this period.[41] An important priority for these pilgrims was to visit the monks, who were regarded as living saints and who had settled in their thousands throughout these lands. The pilgrims perceived the saints they visited as living monuments (with the Latin *monumentum* meaning something written or produced for the sake of memory).[42] The monks were thought to "bear the legacy of the biblical past while living in the present."[43] The desert in which they lived was recast "as a biblical land where Paradise was restored and gospel miracles could find their full realization."[44] Commenting on the practice of these pilgrims, Frank comments: "One seeks out holy people to encounter faces from a biblical time, to look the past in the eye."[45]

At the same time, as far as deceased saints were concerned, there was more than memory involved. Early Christians, in Rome, for example, had a vivid sense that the martyrs were alive in some form of heaven and were capable of being invoked. This process was thought to be more efficacious if the petitioners could place themselves as close as possible to the particular martyr's physical remains. This factor explains the graffiti to Peter on the Vatican and to Peter and Paul in the catacomb off the Via Appia, now lying under the church of San Sebastiano. By the practice of invocation, living Christians thought that they enjoyed a personal interaction with the saints whose memories they treasured. Halbwachs himself had fully appreciated the importance of physical space in the formation of collective memory. "Thus every collective memory unfolds within a spatial framework,"[46] or, expressed more fully:

> [R]eligions are rooted in the land, not merely because men and groups must live on land but because the community of believers distributes its richest ideas and images throughout space. There are the holy places and other spots that evoke religious remembrances, as well as the profane sites inhabited by enemies of God, which may even be cursed and where eyes and ears must be closed.[47]

For the Christians of the first few centuries the holy places were preeminently the graves of the martyrs, while the amphitheaters where they were killed could be classed as the profane sites of God's enemies.

COLLECTIVE MEMORY, THE SAINTS, AND CONTEMPORARY CHRISTIANITY

Among contemporary Christians, *individual* or *autobiographical* memories of saints will be initiated by people known to us personally, who are or were exemplary figures of faith. Most of us are fortunate enough to know or to have known people like this (see my recollections of a relative of mine in the next chapter). More typically, perhaps, we will be sustained by *collective* memories of outstanding figures who either have appeal to a wide cross section of Christians, Dietrich Bonhoeffer, Oscar Romero, or Mother Teresa of Calcutta, for example, or who are mainly known within the confines of a particular denomination or other group. It is within the church at large or within our parish church or other small Christian group that we recall, recognize, and localize the memories of such saints. Christian groups endorse and perpetuate their memory as a way of telling the members who they are, of reinforcing their identity. As times change, group leaders will emphasize certain aspects of the lives of the saints deemed more relevant to present circumstances. In some cases, saints will pass out of fashion, to be replaced by new ones or old ones whose time has come. Every group is, to an extent, engaged in the reconstruction of its shared past to serve the needs of the present. Its leaders are social agents with a firm grasp on group identities, practices, and ideas who also have the capacity to pass them on to others. In addition, our personal experience of holy people will influence how we respond to the memories of saints put forward by our group. Conversely, we will also inevitably remember these holy people in the light of our understanding of the great saints.

I have noted above that one of the weaknesses in Halbwachs's theory is that he underestimates the continuity between the past and the present. He was so taken by the power of memory to be activated in the present that he tended to see history as "a series of snapshots taken at various times and expressing various perspectives."[48] If the past is completely alien, there is little scope for the processes of collective memory. Our link with the past is a balance of persistence and change, continuity and newness.[49]

The socio-theological model of communion set out in chapter 2 readily accommodates itself to such a perspective. The holy Christian men and women who have died in Christ will very often be culturally distant from us. Yet we hold in common with them a set of practices, beliefs, ideas, and aspirations centered on faith in Jesus Christ. Although their social setting was often very different from ours, we are able to see them as prototypes of Christian identity and as providing us with a stock of "possible selves." From what they have been in the past, we gain a sense of what we can be, now or in the future. This view is close to that expressed in the Augsburg Confession: "the saints should be kept in remembrance so that our faith may be strengthened when we see what grace they received and how they were sustained by faith."

That their experience differed from ours is actually vital to this process. For we can gain a *fresh* sense of how we may be our Christian selves in the world by considering the differences between us and those who have gone before us. Such an appreciation provokes the shock that produces fresh insights and behavioral patterns. This is one reason why historical investigation is so important. It allows us to understand the saints to the full extent of their individual and social particularity. Such knowledge provides an invaluable resource for the continuous appropriation and reworking of their memories that occur within every Christian group.

How do we apply this discussion to the subject of this volume? Paul, the most prominent known exemplar of those who composed the various writings of the New Testament, suffered grievously for his faith, probably even to martyrdom in Rome. Certainly, he was remembered later in Christian tradition as a martyr. This dimension of his life does not make him as important for us as does the fact that he has left a collection of letters, most of which contain communications going right to the heart of the Christ-movement. The same can be said for the largely anonymous band of Christ-followers that composed the other works in the corpus. When we remember them, we are latching onto the personal dimension of texts such as the four Gospels; these are people we know only to the extent that they composed one of these works. We remember them as the creators of these texts. This is how they are present to us in memory.

Lastly, we must include the significance of the historical task we undertake in studying what these authors' communications meant to their original audiences. Historiography can be reconciled with notions of collective memory, as noted above, if the focus rests on researching a particular group's traditions. Historians, committed to retrieving the meanings and experiences in a group's earliest writings that form its collective memory, can study the group's traditions, sometimes confirming the memory, sometimes subverting it. Consequently, such historians enrich that memory with the freshness that comes from studying the primary sources in their full alterity and strangeness. None of this dispenses us from exercising critical judgment toward the views of the authors or redactors who first inscribed the group's memories. Sometimes we will not like what we find. But that is the inevitable concomitant of closely studying the actual messages that the New Testament authors of writings sought to communicate. While these authors enliven our present identity, their words come to us not as binding decrees but as revelations of the lives in Christ possible when the faith was formed and shaped by the distinctive cultures in which it emerged.

The result of our inquiry is that we do have a viable dialogue and communion between the New Testament authors, historically investigated, and contemporary Christians through the medium of memory.

INVOCATION OF SAINTS
SYMBOLICALLY UNDERSTOOD

In the next chapter, we will consider the highest reaches of a theology of the communion of saints, including the practice of invoking them. Although, as we have seen in the preceding chapter, the Second Vatican Council defined the nature of the communion of saints in a theocentric and Christocentric fashion sensitive to Protestant difficulties with this belief, there remains a powerful objection to this practice. This objection is the sheer nature of our postmodern condition in which belief in the closeness of the dead has greatly receded, where we do not place much credence in communication with the dead, and where many believe this is a mystery where silence is the best option.[50] As one response to this situation, Elizabeth Johnson has made an interesting proposal for reconfiguring the belief in the saints symbolically so as to accord it a continuing role.

Given the New Testament practice of calling on people to pray for one another, Johnson suggests that if we understand the relationship between the living and the dead in Christ along the lines of what she calls her "companionship" model, "then saints in heaven are not situated *between* believers and Christ in a hierarchy of patronage, but are *with* their companions on earth in one community of grace. Then calling on a saint in heaven to 'pray for us' is one particular, limited, concrete expression of this solidarity in the Spirit, through the ages and across various modes of human existence."[51] As to the postmodern spiritual agnosticism toward communicating with the dead, she states: "read as symbolic rather than literal address, calling the other by name with a request for prayer is a concrete act by which we join our lives with the prayer of all who have gone before us in common yearning for God . . . [the] invocation of any saint, in Rahner's luminous words, 'is always the invocation of *all* saints, i.e., an act by which we take refuge in faith in the all-enfolding community of all the redeemed.'"[52] This finely expressed theological position is probably enough for the present. This model provides substance to the notion of communication and communion between the Christians living and dead, including that between the New Testament authors and ourselves. It should be noted, however, that there are still millions of Christians in various denominations, principally Roman Catholic (including Karl Rahner) and Orthodox Christians, who do accept interaction with the saints and the invocation of particular saints as literal, not just symbolical acts.

CONCLUSION

I suggest that the various proposals outlined in this chapter, whether taken individually or as a whole, provide sufficient basis for asserting that communication and communion between contemporary Christians and the Christ-followers of the first generation or so of the Christ-movement are a viable setting for historically interpreting the New Testament. In the next chapter, I further argue that the firmest basis for this position is in integrative dualist notions that see some element of the human person surviving death for a period prior to resurrection. Readers who find such ideas unpalatable may at this stage skip directly to chapter 11, on the nature of the canon. For although my preference is for a dualist account of our human nature in Christ and under God, the perspectives put forward in this chapter are sufficient for arguing that New Testament interpretation is an exercise in the interpersonal understanding for which I am arguing in this volume. Nevertheless, for those who are open to the possibilities of a dualist position, let us now proceed to the argument.

COMMUNION WITH THE SAINTS IN THE FULLEST SENSE

In the preceding chapter, I modeled a number of ways in which to understand "communion with saints" so as to support this volume's central argument: in reading the New Testament historically, we engage in intercultural communication with the authors of its writings in a manner that can enrich contemporary Christian experience, identity, and reflection on what it means to be in Christ under God. In the present chapter, I consider the remaining model, the one indeed that makes the greatest demands on our faith. This is the proposal that (1) the New Testament authors are alive with God and, in an important sense, with us in the period preceding the parousia and the resurrection of the just, and that (2) in reading their works we engage in not just ethical, symbolic, or anamnetic communion, but in actual communion with them.

Readers who are uncomfortable with this form of communion with "saints" may skip the present chapter and proceed to the next. By setting out in the previous chapters alternative models of how we could be in intercultural communication and communion with our ancestors in faith, I have sought to cater to those unwilling to take the high theological road upon which I will now embark. Nevertheless, many Christians do still believe that those who have died in Christ still live and may even be invoked. Therefore it is important to include such beliefs in the current discussion. And perhaps even those who do not hold this belief may be interested in the arguments for such a position, especially given the powerful, including Christian, challenges being mounted against it.

DEATH IN MODERN CULTURE

Since we are talking about people who have died, it is difficult not to experience a measure of awkwardness and discomfort. Modern culture emits remarkably contradictory messages concerning death.[1] On the one hand, experience of actual death and of dead people is increasingly rare in Western societies. There is a pervasive tendency for the old and the sick to die in hospitals and to be removed directly to the morgue or mortuary and then the cemetery. This practice has deprived the relatives of the awesome experience of having a deceased relative's body in the bedroom at home for a period prior to burial, where they could experience their loved relative in the final hours of his or her mortality and make their farewells. On the other hand, films and television expose us so routinely to cinematic representations of violent death that we have become largely inured to the phenomenon. This leads to the "materialistic trivialisation of death," where death serves as a thrilling spectacle to alleviate the boredom of life.[2] At the same time, death becomes something "we can switch off when we do not like its presence."[3]

Paralleling our alienation from the naturalness and reality of death has been a growing lack of interest in what, if anything, lies beyond it. While lip service is paid to traditional beliefs in "the immortality of the soul" and "the resurrection of the body," especially in liturgical contexts, such views are often affirmed more as statements of group identity than from a lively belief in their ontological truth. Nothing, it is true, should distract us from the finality of death, from the severing of relationships it represents, or from its unknowability that cannot be removed by any mythology;[4] as Karl Rahner stressed, "With death the one history of the human being ceases once and for all."[5] Yet while death is the ultimate experience that we all face, it also poses the question of whether the end of our earthly existence is also the end of our relationship with God, or whether there is more to come. Christians hope for the latter alternative. As Jeanrond notes, faced with death Christians can realistically "hope that our death is two things at once, namely the radical discontinuity of our life and a new opening, an opening to the consummation of a new relationship with God that has begun already in our life."[6] This suggests a way forward. If there is a "beyond" to death, it must in some way represent a continuation of a person's nature and his or her place within the creative and redemptive energies of God that have begun in this life. It is not inappropriate to consider in nonmythological terms the nature of the vindication that awaits those who die in Christ, as long as this involves modest extrapolations from our present nature as human persons blessed with the experience of Father, Son, and Spirit.

Such reflection in no way shelters us from the reality of death. We still face the inevitability of death that will come we know not when. Extremes of pain, discomfort, and indignity may still precede it. What it entails is still beyond our experience. We must still die alone. In death we must still be separated from friends and loved ones. Death will still extinguish our hopes and aims for the future on this earth. Perhaps, finally, there is that niggling doubt that death does mean our utter annihilation.[7] These factors encapsulate the immensity of death whatever our vision of ultimate vindication. They are the necessary presuppositions for reflecting upon a new relationship in Christ that may open up in death.

THE DECLINING SENSE OF CONNECTION WITH THE DEAD

One aspect of the diminishing interest in modern times in whatever lies beyond death that is of central concern here is the attenuation of the sense of connection with the dead, even within Christian denominations, such as the Roman Catholic, where such a sense was once very strong indeed. In 1971 Karl Rahner, ever alert to the impact of contemporary experience upon belief, eloquently described this decline:

> Most contemporary Christians have already ceased to have any sense of being actively in communication with their own dead, the members of their families and the relations whom they have lost. Though there are exceptions to this the general attitude is that they have departed and vanished from this life . . . It is not that we contest the fact that they are, in principle, living on in the presence of the God of the living, but so far as we are concerned they are not alive. They have been, so to say, completely and totally removed from our sphere of existence. Do we really believe that the city dweller still feels any need to visit the graves of his departed on Sunday after Mass as does the countryman?[8]

This loss of a sense of communication with our own dead relatives and friends clearly has implications for how we relate to the Christian dead of the past. As Rahner commented: "But if a man thinks even of his own 'nearest and dearest' as disappearing at death into that darkness which surrounds the meagre light of our existence with its silent infinitude how can he then find it in himself to take up an attitude of veneration towards other dead persons during his life merely on the grounds that they were holier?"[9] Although Rahner himself moved beyond such an attitude to offer a very ample theology of the communion of saints that included the idea of invocation (as we will see later), Elizabeth Johnson has noted the problem but advocated a very different response to it—silence:

[M]odern/postmodern Christian reflection, intensely aware of the unknown character of what lies beyond death and cognizant that there can be no direct communication between the living and the dead, sees the practice of invocation as spiritually deficient in yet another way. With a kind of naive imagination this practice seems to assume a relationship with a host of invisible persons who are cognizant of what people on earth are doing and saying; but this is precisely what we are unable to know. Silence is the more respectful stance.[10]

There is a major problem with Johnson's view. In spite of the belief among Christians from as early as the second century CE to the present (almost all Christians prior to the Reformation and a large number since) that those who died in Christ were still alive and that it was possible to ask them to pray to God on one's behalf, she has no interest in examining the theological nature and foundation of such a belief, but simply asserts that it is now out of date. Whatever one thinks of the traditional belief in the communion of saints, there is no doubt that it is based upon a particular understanding of the ultimate destiny of those who believe in Christ. This is an issue which certainly should be considered, and it seems unhelpful simply to advocate retreat into silence.

A PERSONAL VIEW

All of us bring to the issue of death and what, if anything, we imagine lies beyond it personal experiences which inevitably shape our attitudes. Since I am no different, it will be useful if I recount certain recent events in my own family that have had a considerable impact on my reflections. What I am about to describe will offer some illustration of what a high theology of communion of saints might entail.

On 12 March 2002, a sixteen-year-old nephew of mine, Anthony Stephen Esler, died suddenly in his family's swimming pool in Sydney, Australia. Anthony had suffered from a serious heart problem from his infancy, having his first heart operation when he was seven weeks old, with a fifty-fifty chance of survival. Although he had had further major surgery to replace a valve in his heart in November 2001 and seemed to be making a good recovery, his heart had stopped while he was taking his regular evening swim. The next day I flew out from the UK to Sydney for the funeral.

Anthony had been a young man of remarkable character and deep Christian faith. He was very active in the youth activities that were part of the ecumenical charismatic group in which his family was heavily involved. I had barely sat down with my brother Steve and sister-in-law Karen at their kitchen table after my flight from London when a man, whom they did not know, knocked at the door to express his condolences. He wanted to tell us about some acts of kindness Anthony had shown him recently when he had been experiencing racial discrimination. In spite of his condition, which made him tire easily, Anthony had loved sport, cricket especially, in which he was a highly effective wicketkeeper. He had been a member of the local suburban brass band, which had toured Europe in the northern summer of 2001, shortly before his operation. He was also full of humor and good-natured mischief. Anthony's requiem mass and funeral constituted the most powerful spiritual experience I have had. As we stood around the grave in the strong sunshine of an Australian autumn, his mother sang over her son's body a song in the Spirit that had first come to her when Anthony, aged two, was in the hospital with his heart condition and facing death. Now, she explained, she gave her son back to the Lord who had left him with them for sixteen wonderful years.

With the permission of Anthony's parents, I will relate a sequel to these events. In June 2002 Steve and Karen attended an art show at a school in Sydney. Karen felt particularly drawn to a painting of a streetscape of the German town of Rothenburg, a place they had never visited. They decided that if the painting was unsold at the end of the evening they would purchase it themselves. They did purchase the painting, and the next morning Steve was awakened by the sound of Karen crying in another room and rushed out to see what was the matter. He found her in the living room. She had decided that she would try to contact the families in Europe with whom Anthony had been billeted during the brass-band trip in the summer of 2001. He had told them he was facing a heart operation, which was why he needed to go to bed very early, and Karen had thought she would try to contact them with the sad news of his death. To this end she had got out the large number of photos he had taken in Europe that neither she nor Steve had looked at before. One of the photos had turned out to be of the same streetscape in Rothenburg, taken a few yards from where the artist must have set up her easel.

Clearly, these events are susceptible of a variety of explanations. On one view—whether one is an atheist or a theist—they are explicable simply as a remarkable coincidence. Second, if one held a theist view *and* thought God had been active in these events, they might seem to reflect God's message to Anthony's parents that all was well with their son. Third, however, one might hold a theist view and consider that Anthony, in some way alive in

Christ, was aware of his parents, and, empowered by the infinite mercy of God, had reached out to offer reassurance of his continuing love for them. Perhaps there are other possibilities. Whatever be the true explanation, onto-logically speaking, there is no doubt that as early as the second century CE Christians have been construing such phenomena in terms of the third pos-sibility. Moreover, such phenomena have tended to cluster around deceased Christians who were widely believed to have been touched by God in some unusual way. How might sense be made of such a belief? [11]

Considering what type of postmortem existence a person who dies in Christ may have turns upon the nature of his or her present life in rela-tionship with God through Christ. To consider what we may expect after death—always aware that we are really doing little more than making a few modest gestures in the direction of that mystery—we must begin with what we are now. What is a person? There are a variety of rival answers to this question. One of them—the purely materialist construal of the human person which says that at death the body decays and nothing abides—leaves no role for the dead except in the memories of the living. While that is by no means a negligible status, as we have seen in the preceding chapter, clearly a more ample historical reading of New Testament texts is possible if the dead in Christ are, in some manner, alive, as Christians have long believed they were. I have already argued in chapter 2 that human personhood is constituted by existence in relationship or communion with others. The question for consideration here is a more fundamental one, namely, the ontological foundations of the human person. In particular, we must pro-pose some concept of the person that allows us to make sense of the (pos-sible) interchange or intercommunion between Christians living and dead in the fullest meaning.

MODELS OF THE HUMAN PERSON

At the risk of oversimplifying, there are at present four major accounts of the nature of the person in Western cultures. [12] The first is "reductive or eliminative materialism." On this view, a person is a physical organism and nothing more. Emotional, moral, and religious experiences are reducible to the laws of the physical sciences, and if they have not yet been explained by science, one day they will be. Adherents of this view necessarily consider that death is the end of life and individual human existence, and that there is no afterlife. This account is often accompanied by a belief that God does not exist, but some reductive materialists are theists.

The second is "radical dualism." This view, principally identified with Plato and Descartes, holds that each person consists of a body and a soul (or mind) separate from the body. The person is mainly identified with the soul, which can survive death by virtue of its own nature. Whether this account actually exists or is just a straw man set up by proponents of the other views to push their own claims is a question worth asking.

The third is "nonreductive physicalism/materialism." Here the person is seen as a complex physical organism, in relation to both society and God, that gives rise to "higher" human capacities, such as morality and spirituality. On this view, since nothing survives of the body after death, hopes for an afterlife focus on a belief in the resurrection of the person.

The fourth account is "integrative dualism." The person is a composite of separable "parts," but is to be identified with the whole, which usually functions as a unity. One of the parts might survive death, but hopes for vindication often depend on the resurrection of the whole person.

The readers of this volume will probably find themselves favoring one of these four notions as representing the most plausible understanding of the human person. Adherents of the second, third, and fourth notions will almost certainly be theists, as are some who espouse reductive materialism. Given this range of views, we need to examine each position and see how it relates to the possibility that the dead in Christ are, in some sense, alive and how we might be in communion with them. Although I will argue that radical or holistic dualism allows for the most ample theology of the communion of saints, some versions of this belief are available on the other positions and must also be discussed.

Both the third model of the person (where it is accompanied by a belief in resurrection) and the fourth accept that God has immortality in store for human beings. Before proceeding further, it is worth considering why God would wish us to be immortal. Patrick Sherry's answer to this question is worthy of mention:

> Putting the matter negatively we might ask why a loving God would create people *not* to be immortal? For if death is the end of them, then their "immortal longings," particularly their desire to continue to know God and to be with Him, will be frustrated; and more importantly, their potentiality for transformation through God's grace into a likeness of Him will be unrealised. This is, of course, to see things from man's point of view. Nevertheless, the decisive consideration is God's love for us: one expects such a love to have a regard for people's aspirations and for their growth towards perfection . . .[13]

Reductive or Eliminative Materialism

The attractiveness of reductive or eliminative materialism is directly related to science's position as the dominant mode for interpreting reality in our current environment. This dominance has been fueled by the obvious success of science in offering satisfying explanations for many natural phenomena. This is nowhere more apparent than in Watson and Crick's 1953 discovery of the structure of DNA, the revolutionary step in understanding the biochemical basis for genetics that has recently culminated in determining the genome for a large number of organisms, from worms to human beings. Such success has encouraged, at least in the West, the widespread acceptance of materialist or naturalist interpretations of reality. On this view, nature (that is, the sum total of what is observable or inferred using scientific techniques) alone exists. Accordingly, there is no God. In addition, nature is uncreated and, in some modern cosmologies, eternal; nature is regular and uniform, meaning that there are no nonnatural events (such as miracles); and every event can be explained using the scientific method.[14]

The view that the reality examined by science is the only reality has propelled some scientists, like Richard Dawkins, to become crusading, or even "evangelical," atheists. Nevertheless, a survey reported in *Nature* in 1997 showed that some 35 percent of biological scientists are theist, compared with some 20 percent of physical scientists.[15]

Lurking behind the confidence (and, at times, arrogance) of much modern science is the dream of Auguste Comte (1798–1857), as expressed especially in *Cours de philosophie positive* (1830–42), that a rigorously empirical science would provide the "positive" knowledge necessary to displace the more primitive and mythological attempts deriving from religion and metaphysics and allow us at last to understand human nature and society.[16] Yet it has become increasingly obvious in recent decades that the status of modern science as a source of such hegemonic knowledge is open to serious challenge, principally because nonempirical assumptions frequently determine the development of a scientific theory. Matters of taste and judgments of elegance and economy play an important part in the development of science.[17] Science is a map of reality created by a community of researchers partly at least on the strength of epistemological, metaphysical, and even moral choices.[18]

In spite of the problems innate to scientific positivism, it has nevertheless found an appreciative reception in materialist philosophy, one of the strongest philosophical traditions at present. The work of the philosopher D. M. Armstrong starkly reflects this outlook: "it is the scientific vision of man, and not the philosophical or religious or artistic or moral vision of man, that is the best clue we have as to the nature of man."[19] Whatever one may think of the merits of a claim that finds the essence of human beings in the 99 percent of human genetic material that they share with the other primates, Charles Taliaferro correctly points out that there is nothing in science *as* science (and not as philosophy) that vindicates, or even could vindicate, a claim such as Armstrong's. The ultimate grounds for choosing this position are nonscientific; they are, in fact, philosophical.[20]

For many (like the present writer) for whom the evident inadequacies of scientific naturalism/materialism make it an unlikely candidate as the most persuasive construal of reality, the main alternative is "classical theism," the view "that there is an omniscient (all-knowing), omnipotent (all-powerful), good, purposive being who has created and conserves this cosmos."[21] While it is possible to make a strong philosophical case for the existence and attributes of such an entity, as seen in the writings of John Haldane and Charles Taliaferro,[22] it is not my intention to do so here. Rather, I accept in what follows that the existence of the world and our ability to have the knowledge of it that we do depends upon the existence of a creating, sustaining, and personal God. It is only on the basis of the existence of such a God that other consequent beliefs, such as a belief in the resurrection of the body and in (most cases) the immortality of the soul, can be entertained.[23]

Since I am not persuaded of the utility of "reductive or eliminative materialism" as a construal of reality, I am equally not persuaded of its claim that a person is a physical organism and nothing more. I will now pass on to the remaining accounts of the human person.

Radical Dualism

Radical dualism holds that the body and the mind/soul are different entities that are mysteriously locked together in life, while in death the mind/soul survives as a conscious entity.[24] On this view, the capacity of the mind/soul to survive death is inherent to its nature and does not depend on God. It should be noted that even though Descartes has been much maligned for this view, he did not in fact hold it. Descartes believed that it was by the grace of God, not by some property of the soul, that human beings do not pass out of existence at death.[25] In Western thought, the idea that mind/soul is imprisoned in the body during life and continues to live—or, more radically, is set free—after bodily death derives ultimately from Plato. This hypothesis was expressed largely in mythological terms. Its consequences for a mind/soul separated from its body remained largely unexplored until the philosopher H. H. Price gave the idea theoretical formulation in his essay "Survival and the Idea of 'Another World,'" initially published in 1953.[26] Price was not concerned with arguing for or against disembodied survival but solely with considering what it might be like it if occurred. He was open, however, to the view that postmortem existence had been proven empirically through psychic experiences. Nor was he interested in what role God might play in postmortem existence. His views are consonant with the capacity for disembodied existence being inherent to the mind/soul. He envisaged the next world as a kind of dreamworld, where we could still have experiences even though we were cut off from sensory stimuli (as when we dream). This would be world of mental images, fed by memories (which would survive death) and activated by desire.

Several philosophers, including Antony Flew, D. Z. Phillips, and Terence Penelhum, have argued that the concept of disembodied existence is incoherent or at least no such entity could be identified with a previously living human being.[27] A central feature of this position is the claim that whereas our memory of the past is essential to our sense of personal identity, a disembodied soul would have no sense of personal identity because, in the absence of its body, it has no way of distinguishing true and false memories.

But other philosophers, such as Richard Purtill and Paul Helm,[28] have more than adequately answered such an argument and have insisted that the notion of survival of death in disembodied form is intelligible and logically possible. Stephen Davis, supported by William Hasker, notes that those opposing the existence of souls on the memory criterion confuse talk about criteria for personal identity and talk about evidence for personal identity, a confusion of the ontological and the epistemological domains.[29]

There are clearly major problems with radical dualism. It is conducive to the view that the mind/soul is the essence of the person and a corresponding depreciation of the importance of our physical embodiment.[30] From a Christian perspective, moreover, forms of dualism that insist that the immaterial part of a person is his or her essence (the *real* you is your *soul*, *not* your body) are plainly at odds with the biblical position. The biblical authors do not speak of the soul as a person's essence that is temporarily housed or imprisoned in a body. In Scripture, human beings seem rather to be understood "as psycho-physical entities, as unities of body and soul."[31] The Christian idea is that the body is good as created by God and the whole complex, body and soul alike, needs to be saved. If we survive death it is because of God's action, not from something inherent in our nature.

On the other hand, the philosophical defenses of the intelligibility of disembodied survival can be used for theocentric notions of the soul's survival after death.

Nonreductive Physicalism

The carefully integrated set of essays *Whatever Happened to the Soul?* published in 1998 represents an important attempt to reconcile science and Christian faith regarding the nature of the human person.[32] The authors' primary aim is to build upon expanding knowledge in evolutionary biology, genetics, and neurology to argue for a monistic view. This view maintains that scientific statements about human beings are almost exactly the same nature as theological or religious statements about the spiritual nature of human beings. On this view, there is no spiritual essence or soul separable from the physical being examined by science.

This is plainly a "materialist" or "physicalist" interpretation, in the sense that the authors oppose the necessity of postulating a second metaphysical entity, the mind or soul, to account for human capacities and attributes. Nothing survives the death of the body (in the absence of resurrection of the body). Yet they assert that this position is "nonreductive" in the sense that they reject the position that a person is *nothing but* a body. The basis for this latter view is their claim that the human cognitive capacities (which in a dualist view are attributed to a mind or soul and in a reductive materialist one are nothing but chemical and physical processes) are "emergent properties." This means, according to Warren Brown's argument, that they result from a significant increase in a set of lower-level abilities but cannot be accounted for solely in terms of these abilities.[33] The "soul," on this approach, represents a person's "emergent property" for personal relatedness, not some separable entity. It is the capacity that enables higher forms of cognition dependent upon neurological systems but is not reducible to these systems.

Among the authors, Joel Green argues that there is biblical support for this position. He suggests that the biblical authors provide far less evidence for a dualist position than is usually thought and that ideas of an "escape from the body" or a "disembodied soul" fall outside the framework of New Testament thought. He maintains that New Testament authors insist on "soteriological wholism [*sic*]" and place a premium on one's relatedness to God and to others.[34]

On this understanding of human nature, the only form of future hope available to human beings is that God will grant them resurrection. According to Ray Anderson:

> Biblical revelation supports the belief that personal self-identity continues after death but that this is due solely to God's sovereign determination, not due to an immortal soul or mind residing in the human person. What is

at stake is not the belief that there is life after death but whether that life is due to something resident in human nature or whether it is due to God's power and Spirit.[35]

For Anderson, relying especially on his interpretation of Pauline statements about the postmortem state (1 Cor 15:42-54; 2 Cor 5:1-10), this expression of God's power will take the form of resurrection. It is through resurrection, something that Christ has already experienced, that "the mortal human person as a body/soul unity" achieves immortality. Thus, immortality is not endemic to human beings by their nature but is something granted by God. "Continuance of self-identity after death is, thus, entirely a product of the activity of a sovereign and omnipotent God."[36]

Although the argument of the essays in *Whatever Happened to the Soul?* is able and their tone equable, the authors' thesis ultimately fails to convince. The first problem is philosophical. Jaegwon Kim has shown that nonreductive materialism is not a stable position. The notion of emergent properties is really another variety of a phenomenon usually referred to as "supervenience," although "emergence" has a more scientific flavor. Supervenience is a way of saying that mental characteristics are in a certain sense dependent, or "supervenient," on physical characteristics but not reducible to them.[37] Kim has shown that supervenience requires two conditions to be simultaneously operative. First, the relation between mental and physical must be nonreductive (the mental must not be reducible to the physical) and, second, the relation must be one of dependence. The problem is that it has proved very difficult to find such a relation: "[I]f a relation is weak enough to be nonreductive, it tends to be too weak to serve as a dependence relation; conversely, when a relation is strong enough to give us dependence, it tends to be too strong—strong enough to imply reducibility."[38]

As a result of nonreductive materialism's inherent instability, its adherents tend to push this view either toward collapsing the distinction between mental or physical or toward an explicit form of dualism.[39] Not only have the proponents of nonreductive materialism not squarely faced their position's tendency to collapse into materialism on the one hand or dualism on the other, they have also neglected the force of arguments that can be put forward for dualism.

Dualism has certainly been attacked on the materialist basis that every aspect of the human person can be explained in terms of scientific, that is, physical, explanation. In addition to the contributors to *Whatever Happened to the Soul?*, a prominent example of such a position is Paul Churchland's eliminative materialism.[40] His thesis is that our commonsense notion of psychological phenomena ("folk psychology") represents a radically false theory that will eventually be replaced by completed neuroscience. William Hasker has convincingly demonstrated the flaws in such a theory, especially the extent to which it is self-refuting, in that it can only be asserted by recourse to mental phenomena *not capable* of replacement by scientific explanation.[41] In the various essays in *Whatever Happened to the Soul?*, the strong case for the existence of a mind or soul separable from the body, in spite of modern scientific research on human nature, has been essentially ignored. This represents a regrettable lapse into scientism, albeit a moderate form. Scientific materialism, whether it is reductive or nonreductive, does not provide an answer to the arguments for a separable mind posed by Swinburne and others.[42]

The second problem is that the biblical evidence for this position is, contrary to Green's arguments, weak. John Cooper has well surveyed this field in his *Body, Soul, and Life Everlasting: Biblical Anthropology and the Monism-Dualism Debate*. Cooper demonstrates the widespread existence of dualist thinking in biblical and intertestamental texts, but dualism of an integrative and not Platonic type. We have already considered some of this evidence in chapter 8 and particularly noted the strong evidence for a dualist concept of the person in Hebrews 10–12. While it is certain that resurrection is the primary form of vindication proclaimed in the New Testament,[43] there is also evidence for a separable soul and a disembodied existence in the period prior to the parousia. This is still the best explanation for Jesus's words to the thief on the cross at Luke 23:43: "Truly, I say to you, today you will be with me in Paradise." N. T. Wright, on the other hand, in the course of his eight-hundred-page text *The Resurrection of the Son of God,* devotes a mere footnote to Luke 23:43, saying, "It is similarly difficult to build much on the famous 23:43; 'Paradise' could well indicate a temporary resting place rather than a permanent destination."[44] This misses the point. There is no doubt of Luke's passionate conviction that Jesus had been raised and that the just would experience resurrection as well, or that resurrection represented the ultimate vindication. Luke 23:43 indicates that he *also* believed in a disembodied existence in paradise for the righteous prior to the resurrection. There is further direct evidence for a Lukan belief in a disembodied aspect of a human being at 24:36-37, 39: "As they were saying this Jesus himself stood among them. But they were startled and frightened, and thought they saw a ghost [*pneuma*] . . .Touch me and see; for a ghost does not have flesh and bones as you see that I have."

The third problem is that those advocating nonreductive materialism neglect the argument for the analogy that exists between the relationship of a separable mind to the body and the relationship between God and his creation. On the one hand, arguments against an immaterial feature of human persons apply with roughly equal force to the notion that there is some immaterial entity behind the universe and holding it in existence.[45] It seems inconsistent for nonreductive physicalists to advocate an immaterial God supporting creation and yet oppose an immaterial dimension to the human person. As John Macquarrie has noted, "If we have abandoned dualism when we are thinking of finite beings, does it make sense to retain it on the cosmic level in thinking of God and the world? It has no more plausibility there."[46]

Fourth, its proponents seem to assume that those who advocate a separable soul attribute to it an existence in virtue of its own nature and independent of divine activity, whereas in important versions of dualism the existence of the soul is just as much dependent on God's action as is the resurrection of the body, which is advocated by at least some of these authors. Thus, among the early church fathers the soul was not said to be of the essence of the person and was thought to survive death not because immortality was one of its inherent properties but because God caused it to survive.[47] As Irenaeus said, "Our survival forever comes from his [God's] greatness, not from our nature" (*Against Heresies* 5.3.2). Indeed, it is not clear who, perhaps apart from Plato, has ever opted for an immortality of the soul that was not the result of divine action. As noted above, Descartes did not. Accordingly, the notion of the natural immortality of the soul is a straw man. Why these nonreductive physicalists should be willing to embrace God's intervention to resurrect a human body but avoid the same possibility for the soul by irrelevantly attacking its "natural" immortality is very unclear.

Fifth, on the physicalist view, a person does not exist at all in the period between death and resurrection. If so, however, what sense can be made of the claim that a person who is resurrected by God at time Y is the same person as the one who died at previous time X? Many have suggested that two such people are not the same, or at least that we have no good reason to believe that they are.

The extent of the difficulties faced by those who wish to assert a physical resurrection of a person who has been dead for a period of time is starkly revealed in Peter van Inwagen's extraordinary proposal that when a person dies God immediately replaces his or her body with a simulacrum and takes the actual body away for resurrection.[48] William Hasker has given this view the cold reception it deserves by pointing out that a world where the corpses of the dead are not really their corpses and where God massively deceives us is simply too incredible to be accepted.[49]

John Hick's answer to the time gap between death and resurrection is that a resurrected person represents "the divine creation in another space of an exact psycho-physical replica of a deceased person."[50] For Hick, resurrected persons shall continue to exist as a consciousness and shall remember both having died and some at least of their "states of consciousness both before and after death." They "would be individually no more in doubt about their own identity than we are now, and would presumably be able to identify one another in the same kinds of ways and with a like degree of assurance as we do now."[51]

In answer to Hick's proposal comes the deflating certainty that a replica of a person is not and cannot be identical with that person. What comfort is it if *I* will not be raised, but an exact replica of me who *wrongly* thinks it is me?

Furthermore, there is a major biblical objection to this valiant attempt at preserving personal identity between mortal body and resurrection body. In the New Testament, resurrected persons are most certainly not psychophysical replicas of themselves before death. Christ was able to appear and disappear at will, passing through walls where necessary. Similarly, Hick's theory is contradicted by the clear words of Paul in 1 Corinthians 15:

> What is sown is perishable, what is raised is imperishable . . . It is sown a physical body, it is raised a spiritual body (*sōma pneumatikon*). If there is a physical body, there is also a spiritual body . . . flesh and blood cannot inherit the kingdom of God, nor does the perishable inherit the imperishable . . . we shall all be changed . . . For this perishable nature must put on the imperishable, and this mortal nature must put on immortality. (From vv. 42-53; RSV)

There will be some continuity (it is "we" who shall be changed) but also some difference.[52]

Another answer to the problem posed by the gap between death and resurrection is to argue that bodily resurrection occurs immediately after death. Karl Barth considered it to be New Testament teaching that the body's transformation (in resurrection) occurs for everyone immediately after the individual's death, as if the dead were no longer in time.[53] Somewhat similar approaches have been taken by G. Greshake and Murray Harris.[54] Nevertheless, as Oscar Cullmann has rightly insisted, according to the New Testament, the dead are still in time. Otherwise the problem identified in 1 Thess 4:13-18 would have no meaning.[55] The dead in Christ are still waiting; they are in time. Neither Luke 23:43 nor Luke 16:22 nor Phil 1:22 proves (as is often maintained) that the resurrection of the body takes place immediately after death. There is nothing in these texts about the resurrection of the body. "Instead, these different images picture the condition of those who die in Christ before the end—the interim state in which they, as well as the living, find themselves." They simply express a special proximity to Christ.[56]

Furthermore, the idea that a dead person has already risen is a view that seems counterintuitive in the extreme, given that it necessitates asserting that a person whose body we know now lies decomposing in the earth has actually been resurrected. This makes the actual body of the person irrelevant as far as resurrection is concerned. Joseph Ratzinger's critique seems well justified: "The thesis of resurrection in death dematerializes the resurrection. It entails that real matter has no part in the event of consummation."[57] One attempted answer to this problem involves the issue of time. Put crudely, it is suggested that although from our perspective there is a temporal gap between death and resurrection from God's perspective, from within eternity, there is no such gap. Here again Ratzinger offers a powerful riposte: "This theory reduces Christian hope to the level of the individual. If individual men and women *qua* individuals can, through death, enter upon the End, then history as such remains outside salvation and cannot receive its consummation."[58] It seems reasonable that temporality is a feature of resurrection worlds and resurrection bodies. This is reasonable, since it is, indeed, difficult to conceive of a resurrection body that could be timeless. It is hard to imagine how the notion of memory, an essential feature of personal identity, could possibly operate for a person transferred from a temporal to a timeless environment. The sense of the past would disappear and the entire experience of the person would appear to coalesce simultaneously into a timeless now. It is interesting to note that Thomas Aquinas understood the resurrection world in a notably material way (in his commentary on 1 Corinthians 15). This conclusion seems good, whatever position we take on the thorny question of the relationship of God to time. Although this issue is too complex for detailed discussion here, it will be useful to outline it to assist in the discussion to follow.[59]

Most Christian thinkers from Augustine to Aquinas held that God is *atemporal*; that is, God is outside time. Usually this means, first, that God does not exist at any time at all; he is beyond time altogether. Second, God does not experience temporal succession. Past and future do not exist for God and he experiences all events in the "eternal now." Occasionally it is suggested that the first of these applies but not the second: God does have temporal location but does not experience temporal succession. While this may have been a majority view among philosophers as recently as 1975, today most philosophers take a different view, arguing that although God is certainly eternal, this means that he is temporally *everlasting*, existing at all times and through all times. This means that he never began to exist and will never go out of existence but he does experience some events before others. A third option is to find neither of these atemporal or temporal alternatives satis-fying and to propose instead an intermediate position, such as that God is "omnitemporal," meaning that God is not in our time but experiences tem-poral succession in his being. On this view God's time is constituted purely by the succession of God's mental states, not by the physical time with which are aware, the sort of time measured by our physical apparatus.

These different views have consequences for how we perceive God's rela-tionship with his creation. A God who intervenes in history, by answering prayers, by sending prophets and a messiah, or by resurrecting the dead, is a God who acts at different times and thus seems to be temporal. On the other hand, it is possible that although the effects of God's actions are located suc-cessively in time, his acting is not. God could thus still be atemporal.[60]

How does this discussion affect the question of the resurrection of the body and the survival of the soul? If God is temporal, then temporality must also be the condition of postmortem disembodied souls; that is, they must exist in time. There must also be a period of time between a person's death and his or her resurrection. This result is consistent with the traditional Christian view that there would be a period of disembodied existence prior to final res-urrection. But it is not consistent with the physicalist notion that there are no souls and that a person is resurrected upon death. This view only works if the dead enter a zone of timelessness where death and final vindication occur simultaneously. We have already, however, noted a major problem with the idea that the dead enter a timeless state—that it would deny memory to those resurrected and thus a critical aspect of a sense of personal identity. But even if God is atemporal, as we have just seen, he could act in time and the creation and persons on whom he acts would be temporally located. The preferable view is that human beings are situated in time in their mortal and postmor-tem existence whether God is temporal, atemporal, or even omnitemporal.

For the reasons set out above, there seem formidable difficulties with the nonreductive materialist/physicalist account of the person. Nevertheless, for those who adhere to such a view in the form that resurrection occurs immediately after death, and many do, I argue that this scenario would pro-vide a foundation for a lively sense of communion between contemporary Christians and the New Testament authors. On this view they would be alive in Christ as already risen and in reading or listening to their communica-tions we would meaningfully and interculturally interact with them along the lines of the model set out in chapter 2.

David Brown, Van Mildert Professor of Divinity at the University of Durham and Canon of Durham Cathedral, has recently proposed an inter-esting variation of physicalist and nondualistic construals of the human person which we will now consider before addressing the integrative dualism account.

DAVID BROWN'S VERSION OF NONREDUCTIVE PHYSICALISM

With Brown we have the arresting phenomenon of someone whose instincts and best arguments favor a fairly traditional understanding of the communion of saints, but whose unfortunate rejection of any form of dualism pushes him toward a novel theory with little to recommend it.

Brown begins by noting that Christianity has thrown up two different ways of bringing the narrative it tells to an end. One speaks of "heaven as a present reality to which some go immediately on death; the other of a final resolution for all occurring at the end of history."[61] In the current period, he notes, much modern theology, especially among Protestants, emphatically rejects the former in favor of the latter. "With such a future hope there remains no further need for the image of heaven as already populated." This future hope is lodged entirely in resurrection and finds a recent defense in a lengthy monograph by N. T. Wright, recently appointed as Anglican bishop of Durham.[62]

Against this tendency, however, Brown very reasonably insists that "it is only belief in the postmortem survival of the 'saints' that allows the social character of Christian discipleship to be taken seriously, and indeed without it even to speak of Christ as risen becomes problematic." This view could fall happily from the lips of someone with a dualist belief in the human person, where some element of those who have died in Christ has a form of existence with him. Yet because Brown rejects any possibility of dualism, he needs to shape an argument for a heaven of saints as a present reality.

He begins by mentioning the strength of the recent insistence on human beings as unitary beings, allegedly a recovery of the biblical understanding, and not "a combination of two distinct entities, body and soul (dualism)." We have seen in chapter 8 that the biblical evidence for a dualistic understanding of the human person is much stronger than Brown suggests, especially in Hebrews 10–12. On Brown's alleged "biblical" view, human beings survive only in a kind of "sleep" or in the memory of God until Christ restores us to life at the end of history. He concedes, however, very reasonably in the circumstances, that a closer inspection of the New Testament, as well as later tradition, suggests a more complicated picture "with the two models running in tandem throughout."

Later Brown writes that "both scientific and philosophical considerations do point overwhelmingly towards the rejection of dualism."[63] Again, this view underestimates the powerful philosophical case that can be made against materialist views and in favor of some form of dualism.

His overall concern is encapsulated in the following: "What those who object to heaven as present reality fail to consider is the social dimension of human existence in general and the way in which not only its reality is threatened without a living community of saints, but even any meaningful notion of Christ's own humanity."[64] His approach to the problem consists of setting out evidence for this more variegated situation, proffering four arguments justifying the importance of heaven in later Christian tradition and then considering how current *nondualist* understandings of human beings still allow for the possibility of immediate postmortem survival.[65] I am happy to adopt his four arguments (all "premised on the assumption that the Church as the body of Christ entails mutual interdependence"),[66] even though I will argue below that an integrative form of dualism offers the best solution. Taken collectively, these arguments pose a direct challenge to the "resurrection only" case recently mounted by N. T. Wright.[67] His arguments may be summarized as follows:

First, countering the tendency of an indefinite delay until the end to reduce the effectiveness of Christ's resurrection, Brown observes that Christ was given an immediate role in the harrowing of hell tradition, which included the release of the dead from Hades, as told in the apocryphal *Gospel of Nicodemus*. Adam is among those led out of captivity. Christ's death and resurrection are seen to make an immediate impact on past history. "The new humanity's impact upon all of us is no less immediate than that of the old, and one social identity is replaced by another."[68]

Second, it is necessary to consider what is implied about "the nature of Christ's humanity if this is the only human nature presumed to exist in heaven until the consummation."[69] How could an ascended Christ live isolated from all other human beings who, like him, had experienced death? A person in isolation from everyone is not a person at all. This would deny the essentially social character of human beings into which Christ entered in his incarnation.

Third, there is the very idea of the communion of saints. Does it really make sense "to talk of a single body of Christ that bridges the divide of death unless there is at least some impact of the one on the other?"[70] A central problem is the question of whether the difficulties in our relations with others will remain forever unreconciled at death. Brown asks "Are the dead now irrelevant until the end of time? On this scenario Christ surely once more ceases to be the Lord of history. Jesus's resurrection proves incapable of providing good news of history's transformation except in the far distant future."[71] He insists, however, that any knowledge the dead have of the living must be mediated through God.[72]

Fourth, Brown suggests that it makes no sense to think of us rising at the end of time and immediately being capable of interrelationships with the other. To understand the others we would meet we need to live imaginatively through subsequent history and, if imaginatively, why not the real thing?[73] His point is that since we cannot change into a new identity immediately, why not imagine a gradual process of change, parallel with our own world?[74]

All of these arguments weigh against the antidualist argument. Brown accurately summarizes his dilemma by saying, "It is in fact much more difficult to comprehend how the gap between material (human) and immaterial (divine) is bridged, once we think of ourselves as essentially non-dualist psychosomatic unities, whose only hope is the resurrection of the body."[75]

But rather than being driven by this conclusion to reassess the foundations of his opposition to dualism, which seems to provide the obvious answer to these problems, Brown boldly invents a new proposal for how postmortem existence (in heaven) can make sense in the absence of a dualist belief in the soul. He uses the notion of parallel universes hypothesized in modern physics to envisage "heaven as alongside our world rather than totally above or beyond it, and so as purely 'spiritual' in a way that precludes humanity from ever entering its domain."[76]

Advancing the argument, Brown comes up with what seems to be the entirely novel notion of the "interim body" existing in something akin to a parallel universe that has only an analogous relation to our present existence. That Brown states he is not actually saying that heaven is a parallel universe, but only using the idea analogously, makes his proposal somewhat difficult to evaluate. Presumably, however, if it does not work at the level of science it would also not work as an analogy. Brown offers two arguments in support of his proposal.

First, he says that such a body would not undermine the final resurrection body. For the first resurrection body is incomplete in that it lacks communion or interaction with the full company of the saved (who will not all be there until the End) and also redeemed nature itself. This idea at least avoids the problem with the notion of resurrection at the time of death, pointed out by Ratzinger, that it dematerializes the resurrection, since our actual body plays no part in the process. Yet the difficulty with this refreshingly daring proposal is that at the end of time we then have a person with two bodies: one in a parallel universe, one in this universe. For Brown's theory to work, he needs some suggestion as to how the two bodies could be integrated into one person. He offers no such theory and the very notion is inconsistent with what physicists are saying about parallel universes, in that they do not intersect. Although he is using a scientific idea only analogously, it is most unhelpful if the analogy is inconsistent with the science.

Second, Brown opposes the idea that an interim resurrection body is "a total novelty." He does this by summoning certain data from the early church fathers suggesting a measure of materiality to the soul. Although such evidence does exist, the idea that a Christian who had died had already undergone resurrection is alien to the tradition. The texts to which he refers are simply developments of ways of understanding the soul in the time before the resurrection.

But we can surely agree with Brown's conclusion: "Take away the 'saints' in heaven, however that term is understood, and we end up with the incarnation as only a brief episode in the divine life, with even Christ's humanity not properly restored to him until the eschaton. Little wonder, therefore, that the Church sought to bridge the intervening period with images of Christ's continuing social existence."[77] Given the failure of this imaginative nondualist solution compared to the powerful case Brown has made in favor of postmortem existence for those who have died in Christ, as well as the problems with nonreductive materialism, I will proceed to what I regard as the most plausible position, that of integrative dualism.

Integrative Dualism

The chief alternative to such views, and one that has been continuously maintained among Christians since the second century CE and provides an explanation for the events surrounding my deceased nephew recounted earlier in this chapter, is that human beings comprise a material body and an immaterial soul. Although the soul is separable from the body, neither body nor soul on its own constitutes an entire human being. Stephen Davis accurately explains this approach as follows: "What this theory says, then, is that human beings are typically and normally psycho-physical beings, that the soul can exist for a time apart from the body and retain personal identity, but this disembodied existence is only temporary and constitutes a radically attenuated and incomplete form of human existence."[78] This belief has a number of advantages. First, it goes farther than the others in solving the problem of the existence of personal identity after death, even though it acknowledges a gap in human existence as a complete, unified person. Second, it seems to be in keeping with some biblical data in the Old Testament, intertestamental literature, and the New Testament that present a distinction between material bodies and immaterial souls. Examples include Hebrews 10–12 and Jesus's statement in Luke 23:43. It also fits with the idea that death is immediate gain, since one is immediately with the Lord (2 Cor 5:8; Phil 1:23).

Stephen Davis considers that the soul is conscious in the interim state, since it would be difficult to make sense of a disembodied entity being in the presence of God if the entity was not aware of him. Disembodied existence must be a minimal existence without a body, but the aspects that could remain are what we might call "mental" aspects of the human person. Davis, influenced by H. H. Price, suggests: "experiences, beliefs, wishes, knowledge, memory, inner (rather than bodily) feelings, thoughts, language (assuming memory of earthly existence)."[79] The presence of memory depends on the likelihood that those existing in a disembodied state are subject to time, whatever the relationship God himself has with time (as discussed above). Aquinas is plainly correct, however, to insist that true happiness is only possible when the soul is reunited to the body.[80]

Thomas Aquinas—whose understanding of the soul has been ably defended as philosophically viable by Elonore Stump[81]—considered the sort of knowledge that a soul could have out of its body after death at one point in his *Summa Theologiae*.[82] Initially, it is hard to see how it could know anything. When we are in the body we understand through sensory images. After death, the soul has no such images. Yet the soul still has some understanding when separated from its body, "in a way unnatural to it though natural to angels." What sort of understanding is this? Having excluded various possibilities, Aquinas concludes that there is only one possible source of knowledge—God himself. Such souls understand "by ideas deriving from God's mind, in the way angels understand." Whereas the soul needs a body to acquire knowledge of particular things (or, we might add) people, Aquinas explains that God has knowledge of the general *and* the particular. "Immaterial things," that is, souls, "share this knowledge through ideas which are likenesses of God." Yet then he proceeds in a way that seems to presuppose that these disembodied souls can have some memory of their previous existence: "But separated souls know in this way only the particular things to which they are already bound by some previous knowledge or affection or relationship or divine ordering: for what we receive we receive in ways appropriate to what we already are." Having asserted that the souls of the dead (meaning those who are not in heaven) are denied all converse with the living, he continues:

> As to the souls in heaven, Augustine thinks it unlikely that they know about us, since after his mother died she no longer visited and consoled him as she had before, and her happier state of life would surely not have made her less kind. But Gregory's opinion that those who see God know all that passes below seems more probable. But because they are perfectly attuned to God's will they remain content and do not intervene in our lives unless God plans it so.

For Aquinas, then, the souls with God have a sense of the past and, if God permits, may learn something of earthly events. These aspects of their consciousness probably require a sense of the passage of time. Thus, even though Aquinas considers God is atemporal, this does not mean the souls in heaven exist in atemporality, even if he has not expressed himself with great clarity on this particular issue.

In any event, Aquinas was undoubtedly of the view that the souls of the dead retained a sense of their previous connection with the living and could, through God's action, be aware of what continued to occur among them and, at God's behest, intervene in their lives. This position sits comfortably with strange phenomena that cluster around holy people who have died in Christ and indeed with the practice of asking the saints in heaven to intercede with God for those still on earth. This latter practice (as seen in graffiti of San Sebastiano mentioned in chapter 8, especially the famous example, "Peter and Paul pray for Victor") has been a feature of Christianity since the second century CE.

David Brown reaches a similar position—and one that denies that communion between the living and the dead represents a diminishment of Christ's role:

> Presumably, all such knowledge [that the dead have of the living] would need to be mediated through God, and so the indispensable role of Christ would remain intact. Likewise, in asking prayers of the saints it need not be supposed that they have any privileged access to our minds. That would make them more than human, and so destroy their shared identity with us. Rather, what is being sought is that God allows them to be made aware of what it is for which we pray, and how much of this is communicated and in what form would remain entirely in the divine discretion.[83]

This question of the invocation of the saints requires some further consideration before I set out my conclusions.

INVOCATION OF SAINTS IN AN ACTUAL SENSE

Karl Rahner's explication of the nature of the invocation of saints, expressed in a short but eloquent essay, "Why and How Can We Venerate the Saints?"[84] is worthy of close scrutiny, especially for his Christocentric understanding of this process. Having noted that even the "evangelical Christian" venerates the saints in a certain sense, "for he loves his dead, whom he believes to have gone home to the Redeemer," he continues as follows: "Now the further step of 'invocation' is at basis only the courage of that love which utters a 'thou' that extends beyond all death, and the courage to believe that no-one lives alone, but that the life of each individual in Christ had a value in God's eyes which makes it efficacious for all." This does not entail some notion of the agency of intermediaries, but rather this: "that every life lived in faith and love is of permanent value and significance for all, and that the redeemed man in the state of blessedness receives and lives this significance of his life." Hence, the invocation of one saint is always "the invocation of *all* the saints, i.e., an act by which we take refuge in faith in the all-enfolding community of all the redeemed."[85]

Yet Rahner is very alive to the operation of history and memory in relation to the practice of invoking the saints in a manner fully consonant with our presentation of history in this volume as "theologically charged."[86] For he sees anamnesis as central to Christian faith in general and to the theology of the communion of saints in particular. Articulating a key insight, Rahner notes that the act of Christian faith does not merely entail "a true and essential personal connection 'in Christ' with God," but it "is also and no less essentially an '*anamnesis*,' the recalling and rendering present of his history in the Eucharist and in the tradition of the Church." While the subject of faith "is the risen Lord as now living," Rahner continues, the act of faith "bears upon him precisely in so far as he once had a history of his own, a history which he has now left behind him as that which has passed away, and yet, insofar as he *has* his own history, still remains present and effective precisely as something which is no longer in process of development, but as something completed and existing in his 'eternity.'" This means that we connect with the risen Lord and the "historical Jesus" in one and the same act. This observation powerfully integrates "the historical Jesus" and the "Christ of faith" that, since the time of Martin Kähler,[87] have seemed to many to have been driven remorselessly apart. To make clear the basis of his understanding, Rahner expands on his understanding of time: "Eternity is not a further projection of history into another dimension of time, but the sheer reality of the history itself as accomplished and complete." So he concludes:

> And thus the connection with the glorified Lord is the *anamnesis* of the crucified and dead Lord not merely in the sense that we "know" that he whom we love "once" had this history, but in the sense that he is loved in the eternal and enduring reality of his *history*, and, precisely as the one who has lived through this history, is the mediator who brings us into the immediate presence of God.[88]

Nils Dahl had come to very similar conclusions in his 1946 Oslo inaugural: "These events were not recounted because of a detached historical interest; nevertheless, the stories [of the earthly Jesus] betray a concern to remember past events. In faith in the resurrected Lord, one calls to mind his mortal life, poor yet rich with hidden splendor. He was remembered in the certainty that he remained exactly what he had been then."[89]

We are able to apply all this to the saints, including those responsible for the writings of the New Testament, for they are justly classified as saints on the basis that they are among those "individual Christians whom we believe and hope have gone home to God, and whom we still love."[90] They exist in an eternity which is not another dimension of time or of history, but the accomplishment and fulfillment of history. When we encounter them in a process of anamnesis, recalling and rendering them present, either simply to honor or even to invoke them, we meet them as persons who have lived through their own history, in their own individual times and social contexts—a history now eternal and enduring, *never to be erased*. Yet all this occurs in a strictly Christocentric context. As Rahner puts it: "The 'saints'—in common with all who died in Christ—belong to Christ Jesus. They are part of his Body, are included in the *anamnesis* in which the Church becomes a further projection of the Body of Christ, and therein maintains herself as well as their history now become definitive and complete."[91]

CONCLUSION: NEW TESTAMENT INTERPRETATION AND COMMUNION WITH SAINTS

At the heart of this volume is the belief that when a contemporary Christian encounters the texts of the New Testament attuned to their meaning for their original first- or second-century audiences, that encounter is profoundly affected by the fact that these texts were written by (and, in many cases) to "saints," the faithful dead who are alive in Christ.

The twenty-seven documents in the corpus speak from a world profoundly different from our own cultural contexts, so that our encounter with their messages is necessarily intercultural. And yet, just as in modern cases of human cross-cultural communication, meaning gets through, imperfectly no doubt, but sufficient for the purposes of "Buberian" genuine dialogue—where the defining core is a full acceptance of the otherness of those with whom we dialogue, even in disagreement. Maintaining a critical attitude to what we hear during an intercultural engagement is in no way inimical to the authenticity of the encounter; indeed, it is an indispensable aspect of it.

In reading or listening to the messages of the New Testament writings historically interpreted, we come face-to-face with the actual experience of the first generations of those who built their life and identity around faith in Christ. We encounter them in the enduring realities of their particular histories that tell of the ways they responded to God's call in their specific, local, and historical circumstances. We may safely ignore the ghost of Lessing, with his "ugly, broad ditch" and his crippling message that historical details cannot lead to theological truth.[92] For people to learn from the experience of others, for people to have their identities shaped by exposure to the identities of others, is a universal feature of our common humanity. When the people from whom we would so learn are those closest to God's irruption into the world in the life, death, and resurrection of his Son, so that they represent the primordial pattern of the new life this made possible, all this applies even the more strongly. It is difficult to see how one can separate the historical from the theological in such communion.

Most of the time in this process, we will only listen. In chapter 2 we saw that listening has a vital role in any dialogue. Yet the nonreductive dualistic explanation of the human person I have argued for in this chapter, with its proposal of a continuing (even if admittedly attenuated) existence for those who have died in Christ before the resurrection at the end of time, suggests that perhaps quiescent silence is not the only posture we can adopt in these engagements. For we too can speak, uttering a "thou" to each of these authors "that extends beyond all death," confident that God in his mercy will bear our words to their destination. On Karl Rahner's Christ-centered account, we may even invoke them, if we have the courage to believe that no one lives alone, but that the life of every person in Christ has a value in God's eyes which makes it efficacious for all.

THE CANON AND
INTERPERSONAL COMMUNION

SETTING THE SCENE

The final substantial issue to be confronted in this volume is the circumstance that of all the writings that survive from the first and second centuries CE, there are only twenty-seven texts that comprise the New Testament. Further, this list, with the resolution of long-standing pressures for the inclusion and exclusion of texts that it represents, was settled by the late fourth century CE. With this phenomenon we come to the question of the "canon," the name given to this collection of texts, and "canonization," designating the process that led to the selection of such a closed list of texts as "canonical."

William Wrede, in his assertion of a form of New Testament theology entirely independent of dogmatic theology (that we considered in chapter 1), took the view that there was no good reason to restrict the texts subjected to examination to the canonical corpus. "Where the doctrine of inspiration has been discarded," he maintained, "it is impossible to maintain the dogmatic conception of the canon."[1] No writing in the New Testament came into existence with the predicate "canonical" attached to it. Such a description is merely the result of pronouncements by ecclesiastical authorities from the second to fourth centuries CE, often after extensive disagreement. To accept the idea of the canon means accepting the authority of the bishops and theologians of that period and why do that? It is really necessary to take into account all the early Christian writings, not just those in the New Testament but also the Apostolic Fathers. In reality, "the boundaries between the canonical books and the extra-canonical material closest to them fluctuate at every point."[2] Räisänen notes that one either confines oneself to the canonical New Testament writings (even if using other texts for the purposes of comparison and elucidation) and produces a New Testament theology, or pursues a Wrede-like history of early Christian religion with no limit on sources.[3]

Wrede's approach is not congenial to the thesis I am arguing in this volume. One answer to his insistence that we expand the circle of texts beyond the canon comes from Robert Morgan when he notes that the New Testament documents "are nevertheless generally the earliest specifically Christian tradition we possess, and their proximity to the contingent historical events which Christians consider fundamental has something to do with their special status."[4]

Yet, in a context where we are seeking to bring the results of historical criticism of the New Testament into fruitful conjunction with the ongoing life and belief of contemporary Christians, perhaps more persuasive is the case that can be made for according the canon a special significance from the sheer fact of its centrality in the continuous history of Christian liturgy and proclamation. This amounts to the "[d]efence of the canon by reference to the historical effects of what has in fact been done in the church."[5] For the consequences of a text being recognized as canonical were momentous. Not only did this represent the highest form of approbation by ecclesial authorities, but it had the very practical consequence that these were the writings from which the lectionary readings were chosen and then promulgated to the faithful in the liturgy through their being read and also expatiated upon in homilies. The canonical texts were also the prime source for Christian theology, with a qualitatively higher status than other texts that did not make it into the canon. Looked at pragmatically, this view entails that Christians are more likely to be open to the results of the historical investigation of texts that are close to their hearts as a consequence of such processes, the Gospels especially, than they are to whatever might be proposed in relation to *1 Clement*, the letters of Ignatius, or, to press the point, the *Shepherd of Hermas*.

Why do canon and canonization matter for this volume? We are interested in how New Testament texts, understood historically in terms of the meaning they conveyed to their original audiences, can enrich our Christian experience and identity today, especially as living voices in intercultural dialogue with us. The existence of the canon means that some 1,600 years ago the church selected some of these ancient voices and excluded others, thus limiting the voices with whom Christians would thereafter engage most fully. Writings such as the Gospels we refer to as Matthew, Mark, Luke, and John were included, as were a number of letters attributed to Paul, together with many other letters or documents in letter form, Hebrews, and the Apocalypse, to name most of them. On the other hand, all the texts we now refer to as the Apostolic Fathers were excluded, even though some of them (*1 Clement*, for example) are almost certainly older than some New Testament works, such as 2 Peter.

The primary issue for us is how to assess the relationship of the ecclesial act of canonization, completed in the late fourth century CE, an act that recognized the role and meaning of these texts in Christian life and thought at that time, to the original meaning of these texts for their original, first-century (in perhaps a few cases, second-century) audiences. Clearly, the logic of my argument entails maximizing this historical meaning, but at the same time it is not in my interest to downplay the character and effect of canonization. If one is intent on proffering an explanation for how these texts, understood historically, can affect contemporary Christian life, how is it possible to ignore the fact that for some 1,600 years these texts have been the officially approved primordial writings, the ecclesially sanctioned inscriptions of our earliest ancestors in faith?

This issue, or complex of issues, acquires its poignancy largely owing to Brevard Childs's major challenge, developed since the mid-1960s, posed to the significance of the original meanings of these texts in relationship to the meaning they maintained or secured by their canonization. In the last ten years Childs has won strong support from Francis Watson, whose position, however, is not identical with that of Childs. This particular reassertion of the primacy of the canon represents one dimension to the critique of the historical-critical method that has been mounted on a number of fronts in the last few decades. Although both Childs and Watson at times deny it, both tend to suppress the significance of the historical dimension of the New Testament writings. Thus, at one point Childs can write that efforts to tie the canonizing process to an acknowledgment of the historical particularities of the texts seem "unaware that the function of canonical shaping was often precisely to loosen the text from any given historical setting, and to transcend the original addressee."[6] I will leave aside here the very awkward question of how a human being could ever be "transcended" and note that elsewhere in the same work Childs speaks, less disturbingly but still questionably, of how the (canonical) New Testament frequently seems to transcend "its original historical context."[7] For Childs, this phenomenon, if it was something entailed in canonization (and I will argue below that it was not), was most definitely a good thing.

Similarly, in his 1994 work, Watson stated that it was "inherent in the genre of [biblical] canonical text to be transmitted in a form which has erased, to a greater or lesser extent, most of the particularities of its circumstances of origin." He went on to say that in a canonical perspective, for which he opts, "the erasure is to be seen as an intentional act rather than a regrettable accident, and *welcomed as such* [my emphasis] since it subordinates a merely historical curiosity about what was happening . . . to the ability of the text to function in quite different later circumstances."[8] There are clear echoes here of Gabler's aim in the 1780s to develop a biblical theology that would capture the timeless theological truths of the Bible, while ignoring aspects too closely tied to the first century. The notion that truth might be found precisely in those "particularities" of a text's "circumstances of origin" is equally foreign to Gabler and Watson. More recently, however, one senses from Watson less hostility to historical particularity. In 1997 he stated that the "endurance of classic or canonical texts such as the gospels does not erase the historical moment of their origin,"[9] although without mentioning that he had said essentially this only three years before. It is also unclear how far in practice this greater openness to the circumstances of the origin of the New Testament actually goes. In his important work, *Agape, Eros, Gender: Towards a Pauline Sexual Ethic* (2000), for example, Watson rejects the idea that interpretation should be controlled by a hypothetical "background" reconstructed by the interpreter working with the historical-critical method,[10] thus setting his face against a full investigation of the first-century, historical context of Paul's writings. Nevertheless, he does make (an admittedly attenuated) effort to situate his targeted Pauline text in relation to other biblical texts, some classical writings, and a note on ancient Greek and Roman male haircutting practices, but then only through the curious filter of a quotation from Calvin's commentary on 1 Corinthians.[11]

Childs has been rather severely criticized, by James Barr, for example, with Barr seeing canon as a formal, even accidental, occurrence.[12] Yet the commendable feature of the work of both Childs and Watson is the desire that the New Testament texts should come alive theologically, coupled with a deep concern that too much historical interpretation kills off theological interpretation. The challenge posed by the canonical approach, of which we will say more in a moment, is that it forces us to move beyond our focus, up to this point, on how each New Testament text can separately have an impact on Christian lives and identities in the present. In short, it impels us to consider the effect of the church's having chosen a corpus of twenty-seven texts as decisive for contemporary Christian lives and identities.

The problem is to find some way of accommodating the unity represented by the ecclesial definition of these texts as one canon (a process and result, I will suggest below, developed under the influence of the Holy Spirit) and the diversity exhibited by these texts in relation to one another. As we will see, the major weakness in Childs's project is his failure to provide an intellectual framework for holding these two aspects together. I will propose below that help is at hand in Russian literary theorist Mikhail Bakhtin's model of dialogicality. Like a Dostoevsky novel in which, argued Bakhtin, the

characters have an unparalleled freedom and autonomy vis-à-vis the author
and one another, where there is a combination but not a merger of consciousnesses, the individual voices brought together as the New Testament canon
have a large degree of autonomy yet derive a unity from the extent to which
they are inspired by the Holy Spirit and have been specially chosen as authoritative by the church, also under the influence of the Spirit. The canon brings
them into relationship with one another and sacralizes their association but
without extirpating the distinctiveness of their individual first- (and perhaps
second-) century voices.

In the remaining sections of this chapter, I will first provide a brief history of the canonization process, focusing on the criteria which ultimately
led to some early Christian writings being chosen as canonical and others
not. Second, I will critically review Brevard Childs's canonical proposal.
Third, I will analyze Childs's treatment of Romans. And fourth, I will outline
Bakhtin's ideas of dialogicality and outline how they can be fruitfully applied
to understanding the canon's character.

THE CHARACTER OF THE
CANONIZATION PROCESS

In a useful review of scholarship on the New Testament canon, John Barton
has shown that much scholarly disagreement on the subject derives from differences in how the word is understood. The two most popular options are
to regard "canonical" as virtually equivalent to "widely regarded as authoritative" or to reserve the term for those texts that have been officially approved
and included on an approved list after a long process of evaluation. To adopt
the former option pushes canon back into the first or second centuries CE,
while the latter produces a date in the late fourth century CE.[13] In his Thirty-
ninth Festal Letter (367 CE), Athanasius talks about the biblical writings that
have been put in the canon and lists the texts comprising the Old and New
Testaments. In the case of the New Testament, he lists the current twenty-
seven writings, but not in our order. Here we have by general consent the first
use of canon as a definitive list of biblical texts.[14]

It will be helpful to begin with the important distinction between
"Scripture" and "canon." The former refers to a body of literature that a community accepts in some way as authoritative for its existence, while the common meaning of "canon" is a well-defined list of scriptural texts. One needs
Scripture to have a canon. It took some hundreds of years for the books in
our New Testament to be accepted as canonical, at least in the second sense.

The church continued in spite of the fact that this issue had not been settled, indeed, in the first hundred years not even clearly formulated. We could have had, and did in fact have, a church without a canon. We could not have a canon without the church.

It is important to note that the history of the canon cannot begin with the word itself since this was only applied to the collection at the end of a long process. The word "canon" is first attested, admittedly in paronymic form, in the sense of an exclusive collection of biblical texts in the middle of the fourth century CE, from the records of the Council of Laodicea, which decreed that books which were not canonized (*akanonista biblia*) were not to be read in church. Only the canonical writings of the Old and New Testaments were allowed and these were then listed.[15] Yet this was really near the end-point in the process and in parts of the East this list was not entirely accepted. Nevertheless, Jerome did follow it in the Vulgate, even while pointing out reservations in some parts about Hebrews and Revelation. To determine what canonicity entailed, we have to look at the process that led up to this formulation. This is an area of enormous difficulty, yet one that still has important theological consequences.[16] For the purpose of my argument in this chapter, the critical issue is how the process of canonizing certain texts related to the particularities of their origins. In particular, were these particularities recognized or disregarded? We have already considered in chapter 7 the manner in which the early traditions of the Christ-movement moved over the course of some two centuries from oral to written form. For the purposes of this chapter, we must now briefly consider the processes by which some texts were taken into the New Testament canon and some were not.[17]

The Significance of the Gospels and Paul's Letters in the Second Century

Franz Stuhlhofer has advanced the discussion about the way that New Testament documents were regarded in the early church by more systematically analyzing how they were cited in other authors (the Apostolic Fathers, for example) than has previously been attempted. His results have consequences for the meaning of canonicity and we will return to that issue. For the moment, we are concerned more with what can be learned relevant to the argument of this volume by gauging the impact of the New Testament documents on other authors.[18] Stuhlhofer's approach represents a definite advance in that he does not merely seek to determine whether particular New Testament (or Old Testament) texts were cited, but how often they were cited. Most important, he also factors in statistics on how often they were cited in proportion to their size, since we would expect that longer texts would be cited more often than shorter ones. This procedure allows him to determine which books are cited much more than one would expect if all of them had been regarded as equally important (and due weight is given to their respective lengths), which are cited much less than one would expect, and which are scarcely cited at all.

From the period of the Apostolic Fathers (early second century CE onward), a clear pattern emerges. This is that Matthew, Mark, Luke, and John and the major Pauline epistles are cited much more frequently than one would have expected. The remaining texts of those that now comprise the New Testament (including the Acts of the Apostles) are cited far less frequently. In addition, the four Gospels and the major Pauline letters are quoted far more often than the Old Testament. This is in spite of the fact that usually the word "writing" (*graphē*) is used only of Old Testament texts. Barton comments, "All the indications are that the New Testament became almost instantly more important than the Old for the nascent Church."[19] This means that the gospels and Paul's epistles were accepted long before they acquired the aura of antiquity, no doubt on the basis of a conviction (in spite of the ambient culture's strong bias in favor of the old and the ancestral) that "a new an unprecedented era had arrived with Jesus and the apostolic Church."[20]

The Process of Canonization

According to an influential theory of the great German historian Adolf von Harnack (1851–1930), the codification of the New Testament Scriptures by the church as canon (which contributed to their textualization) was a response to the activities of the heretic Marcion in the middle of the second century (he died ca. 160 CE).[21] Marcion was influenced by gnostic beliefs to reject in toto Judaism and its Scriptures as reflecting a type of law-ridden religion completely alien to the love commandment of Christianity. He argued, in fact, that the God of the Old Testament was not the same as the unknown God of the Gospel and of Jesus. He rejected the Old Testament and adopted as his Scripture a version of the Gospel of Luke which had been shorn of all Old Testament references and a freely edited version of ten Pauline epistles, beginning with Galatians (his list does not contain 1 and 2 Timothy and Titus). Von Harnack argued that faced with this challenge the church had no alternative but to produce its own canon of Scripture.

Some recent scholars follow this view.[22] Others reject it. Gamble, for example, notes that Paul's letters had been collected well before Marcion and he did not stimulate their development.[23] We can also agree that the church may in due course have been forced to match the Jewish collection and, moreover, that there were several reasons at work. Nevertheless, it seems reasonable to argue that the efforts of Marcion may have added further impetus to the collection of the twenty-seven documents and contributed to their textualization (the recognition of their significance as texts).

Shortly after Marcion, and possibly in reaction to him, Irenaeus (ca. 180) proposed a four Gospel canon and had to argue creatively in favor of it (*Against the Heresies* 3.11.8-9). He was clearly proposing something novel—other gospels were still being used in the East. Irenaeus aimed to defend the Christian faith or "canon" (*regula fidei*) on which the church depended for its life, but in so doing he paved the way for the notion of the canon of Scripture. Marcion, therefore, probably did not create Christian Scripture, as Harnack suggested, but he certainly was a spur to its creation.

By the close of the second century, the prehistory of the New Testament came to an end and a period of consolidation began. There was felt to be more of a need to rule on what was and was not New Testament Scripture. Thus the bishop Serapion of Antioch about 200 CE at first allowed the congregation of Rhossus to use the *Gospel of Peter* but later, having convinced himself of its heretical nature, prohibited its use (Eusebius, *Ecclesiastical History* 6.12.2).

We have already seen that by the early second century the Gospels of Matthew, Mark, Luke, and John and the epistles of Paul were being cited far more frequently than the other documents that would eventually be canonized. What were some of the criteria that led to a text achieving this status? Here I will only mention two important criteria for establishing or solidifying the claim of a text to be canonized that linked the text to its origins.[24]

Probably the most important criterion of this type is that of apostolicity. Some of the documents were thought to have been written by apostles (for example, the Gospels of Matthew and John and Paul's letters). It was essential, as G. W. H. Lampe has argued, to the church in its defense against attack from gnostic Christians and other groups to be able to claim that its teaching stood in a direct line from Jesus, to the apostles, and thence to the leaders of the church.[25] But the position was complicated. Sometimes documents that did not have an apostolic claim got in, as with the Gospels of Mark and Luke, while others claiming to be apostolic did not get in, such as the *Epistle of Barnabas* and the *Gospel of Peter*. McDonald has noted that the criterion of apostolicity "is based upon the presumption that, since the apostles were close to Jesus historically, they must have a better knowledge of him and his ministry than others."[26] This clearly reveals the error in supposing that the process of canonizing erased reference to the circumstances of its origin; in fact, it acknowledged that origin as vital. Associated with apostolicity as a factor in eventual canonization was the assumed antiquity of the text. The author of the *Canon Muratori* argued against the acceptance of the *Shepherd of Hermas* as authoritative for the church on the grounds that it was not written in the apostolic age, but some time after it.[27] That the Gospels of Mark and Luke had been widely accepted by the early second century CE, even though they were not regarded as having been written by an apostle, must have cemented their claims for inclusion.

THE CANONICAL PROJECT OF BREVARD CHILDS

Brevard Childs has now been developing his canonical project for some forty years. It comprises a very substantial body of work and in many ways his ideas have shown clear signs of progression. On the other hand, he has occasionally reverted to an earlier view. This makes him hard to summarize and has given critics the opportunity to attack him for statements that may not represent his considered position.[28] In what follows I will briefly set out the major landmarks in his journey and comment on aspects of them germane to the argument of this chapter and, indeed, to the thesis of this volume.[29]

Childs inaugurated his approach in 1964 with an article entitled "Interpretation in Faith: The Theological Responsibility of an Old Testament Commentary."[30] This was a strong reaction to Krister Stendahl's 1962 article on contemporary biblical theology, which we have noted earlier in this volume has now acquired something of a classic status in its advocacy of a sharp separation between the historical investigation of biblical texts and their theological explanation, the "descriptive" and nondescriptive dimensions.[31] Childs countered with the suggestion that a commentary on an Old Testament text had a normative as well as a descriptive task. Yet Childs did not propose jettisoning the historical or descriptive aspect to the work, but rather relativized its importance in comparison with drawing theological insight from the text in question. He wanted the descriptive task to be informed by faith so that the descriptive and normative phases in the process were integrated. While Childs was motivated by the laudable aim of ensuring a greater role for the interpretation of Scripture in Christian theologizing, his proposal inevitably ran into the large problem of how faith and reason were related in this process, as Paul Noble has noted. The whole Enlightenment-inspired development of the historical-critical method from the seventeenth century onwards had represented an assertion of the claims of reason in understanding biblical writings over against those of faith.[32] Simply for Childs to assert that the two should now be integrated would not necessarily make it so: How could one read a biblical work in a way that was historically adequate and also aimed at situating it within a theological framework? How did one answer the charge that attending to the latter concern would inevitably distort the former?

Childs significantly developed this program with his 1970 *Biblical Theology in Crisis*. Here again he rejects Stendahl's disjunction between descriptive and normative approaches,[33] while reasserting the importance of faith for interpretation. The important new element is the proposal that the appropriate context in which to undertake theological interpretation is the canon.[34] Yet Childs also insists that it is necessary to retain the historical-critical method.[35] Problematic for his position, however, is his failure to indicate how the historical and canonical dimensions could be maintained simultaneously, a point well made by Paul Noble: "Yet how these very different approaches to meaning are to be reconciled is left in total obscurity—'original context' and 'canonical context' are simply juxtaposed, with both affirmed as indispensable."[36]

The difficulties Child found in reconciling these two contexts are revealed in his writings in the 1970s. Initially he began to exhibit a much more negative attitude to historical criticism. In *Exodus: A Commentary* (1974), we now find Childs beginning to insist that historical meaning should be subordinated to canonical meaning.[37] In a 1977 article he blames the historical method for making it difficult to move from the original meaning of a biblical text to a meaning for the present.[38] Yet with his important 1979 work, *Introduction to the Old Testament as Scripture*, he expresses a somewhat more benign view to history. Here he usefully acknowledges that the different purposes motivating critics to interpret biblical texts will inevitably influence the way they read them, with a historian using the evidence differently from someone reading them as sacred Scripture.[39] Childs concedes that historical criticism has led to important gains in understanding biblical texts, especially their difficult features, but opposes the antitheological bias he detects in much historical criticism as it is practiced.[40] He expressed similar views in two articles that appeared the year before this work.[41] Central to his point of view is that the canon of the Old Testament should not be regarded as "late extrinsic sanctioning of a corpus of writings," but was actually the culmination of an "interaction between a growing corpus of authoritative literature and the community which treasured it." Its formation involved "a lengthy series of decisions deeply affecting the shape of the material."[42] Taking this approach allowed him to integrate some historical research into the prehistory of a biblical text and its final canonical form. This is approval of historical-critical work, in a sense, but there are also worrying signs of his insouciance to the original context: "Even though the message of Second Isaiah was once addressed to real people in a particular historical situation, the canonical shape of the these chapters has drained them of their historical particularity and has subordinated their message to a new role within the canon."[43] Whereas clearly Childs has no problems with this "draining," from the perspective of the thesis argued in this volume, it would represent (if true) the lamentable obliteration of the personal presence and memory of the person responsible for what we call "Second Isaiah" and the first audience for the text.

The various tensions in Childs's position continued to reappear with his subsequent publications. In 1984 he published *The New Testament as Canon: An Introduction*. In this work he sought to offer a variation on the well-established genre of New Testament introductions that highlighted the question of canonicity. After four introductory chapters, he proceeds through the New Testament text by text. Above all he is proposing that what is needed is a new vision of the New Testament "which does justice not only to the demands of a thoroughly post-Enlightenment age, but also to the confessional stance of the Christian faith for which the sacred scriptures provide a true and faithful vehicle for understanding the will of God."[44] While he denies that the canonical approach involves fideism, "a form of uncontrolled subjectivity," and asserts that the canonical approach "combines both historical and theological analysis,"[45] it remains unclear how this can be achieved.[46]

In subsequent years Childs continued with his canonical project, publishing *Old Testament Theology in a Canonical Context* in 1985 and *Biblical Theology of the Old and New Testaments* in 1992. Central to the latter work is the nature of the relationship between the Old and the New Testaments. As Paul Noble has noted, Childs is preoccupied with wishing "to make a distinctively Christian reading of these pre-Christian writings, and yet still respect them as pre-Christian."[47] Yet this aspiration is really just another version of the quest to successfully integrate the historical and theological dimensions and it is precisely here that a solution continues to elude Childs.

I will conclude this discussion of Childs with an analysis of his views on Romans in *The New Testament as Canon: An Introduction*. This will illustrate his method and also reveal its weaknesses. It will also pave the way for a very different approach to a theological reading of Romans that involves the closest attention to its original setting which I will outline later in the next and final chapter of this volume.

CHILDS'S TREATMENT OF ROMANS

Childs first describes the modern critical debate on the epistle, which has been greatly concerned with its original setting. While appreciative of the insights that the historical-critical method has thus produced, he claims that "the basic hermeneutical issue of interpreting Romans, which is closely tied to its canonical function, has not been adequately faced."[48] Rather than moving from original context to contemporary theological relevance, he argues for the reverse of this process: "one begins by attempting to discern the canonical shape of the present text, and in the process seeks to determine the role that both the original and the subsequent elements play in the final form of this religious text."[49] But these "subsequent elements" turn out to be insignificant, since (following Harry Gamble's persuasive case for the original shape of the letter as we have it), he is compelled to agree that "there is no indication that the process of editing the letter for canonical collection altered substantially the original form of the letter."[50] The fact that subsequent Christian tradition chose not to meddle with Paul's own words and that they were taken into the canon as he composed them clearly has troubling consequences for Childs's whole position that he fails to acknowledge.

To give some substance to his approach to the letter that is arguably the most theologically significant work in the corpus, Childs falls back on what is a rather lame attempt to say that a canonical approach entails recognizing the "peculiar blend" of material from the concrete, historical context of Paul's ministry to the Christ-followers of Rome with "a theological message, grounded in Christology, which provides its own special dynamic of eschatological and universal transcendence." Here we are clearly back to Gabler's attempt to separate contingent historical details from universal theological truths. As with Gabler, the idea that Christian faith, experience, and identity might be enriched by dialoguing with the former type of material is nowhere to be seen. Childs sees no theological benefits to be derived from the contingent details of the original setting of Romans. This is revealed in his proceeding to summarize some, but by no means all, of the christological material in the letter. But his treatment is unbalanced and even inaccurate. He suggests that "the content of this letter is radically christological." Is it? He does not even mention the Holy Spirit, whom Paul mentions at important points in this letter (Rom 8:26-27; 9:1; 12:11; 15:13, 16, 19, 30; 14:17), and, although he does refer to God, he does not notice that God plays an extremely prominent role in the letter.[51] Lastly, Childs considers the question of righteousness in the letter.[52] He has little new to say here; the yield from his canonical approach boils down to little more than the assertion that since righteousness is grounded in Christology, this means that it retains its "full, eschatological, cosmic dimension," and that this is the basis for its being actualized in the ongoing life of the church.[53] Childs also overlooks one feature of Paul's message that one might think most certainly did have a continuing importance (especially for those of us convinced, with Wrede and Schweitzer, that righteousness was a reactive teaching developed by Paul only in response to the pressures of communities composed of Judeans and non-Judeans),[54] namely, *agapē*, the characteristic love of the Christ-movement (especially in Romans 12).

From this it is clear, moreover, that Childs has no interest from a theological viewpoint in the message that Paul was actually seeking to communicate to his Roman addressees. Childs wants to create a new message by snipping out a fragment here and a fragment there to create an idiosyncratic composite that accords with the christological views that are central to his own theology (in a way, it seems, that the Holy Spirit is not). In the end, then, the canonical approach as practiced by Childs involves his substituting Paul's own communication (a tight integration of particular circumstances and theological insight) with a new message composed of a few (but not all) of its theological dimensions. It is very difficult to see what, if anything, is gained by this process, even though we are speaking here of one of the richest theological texts in the New Testament canon. Putting the matter at its most brutal, why would we prefer Childs to Paul? The fact that the Christian tradition after Paul left his letter alone rather suggests that the Christians of this early period thought it more important to hear what he had to say than to alter, augment, or (like Childs) ransack his message in order to produce a new one of their own.

MIKHAIL BAKHTIN AND DIALOGICALITY

I will now make good my earlier claim that Mikhail Bakhtin's concept of dialogicality offers a framework for making sense of the ecclesial recognition of twenty-seven New Testament texts as canonical in a way that does not require derogating from their historical distinctiveness as first-century CE voices with whom we can engage interculturally. This approach also allows them a theological role sought by Childs but not attained because of the insoluble contradictions apparent in his position. In advancing my argument, I will rely upon Carol Newsom's essay that advocates a role for Bakhtin in mediating between the historical and theological dimensions of biblical, mainly Old Testament, texts (although without mentioning the canon or the question of the New Testament's historical distinctiveness that is the focus of this volume).[55]

Bakhtin distinguished between a monologic and a dialogic sense of truth.[56] Newsom helpfully and accurately summarizes Bakhtin's views on the monologic sense of truth under three headings.[57] First, the core of monologic truth is the "separate thought," that is, the thought that is separable from individual human speakers, meaning a proposition or what Bakhtin calls "no man's thought." Second, the monologic sense of truth expresses itself in a system where various propositions that comprise it are ordered into a unity. Third, a monologic sense of truth can be comprehended by a single consciousness and is capable of being spoken by a single voice. Newsom has well explained how the operation of these aspects of a monologic sense of truth has created problems for the understanding of the Bible, given its great diversity, and for the conversation between theology and biblical studies. Critical biblical scholarship was founded on the perception that the Bible was not monologic. The heterogeneity of the Bible, in both Old and New Testaments, made it difficult to interpret it as being spoken by a single voice. Theologians, on the other hand, tend to be committed to systems of thought that are powerfully monologic.[58]

Although Newsom does not refer to Childs or to his position on the canon in this article, it is clear that the theological truth that he insists is to be found by treating Scripture as canon is monologic. The core of this truth as he sees it is the affirmation of God's redemption in Jesus Christ. According to Childs, it was for this that the New Testament writings were preserved, "not because of interesting historical, religious, or sociological data."[59] In addition, in the light of this theological truth he also seeks to interpret the Old Testament. The difficulties he has in reconciling such a view with the heterogeneity of the biblical texts is readily explicable as a particular manifestation of the larger malaise so well exposed by Newsom. For Childs, the problem is rendered even more acute by his commendable disinterest in harmonizing the various biblical voices.[60]

So let us move on to an alternative vision of truth that closely accords with the emphasis on interpersonal communication central to this book. Mikhail Bakhtin developed his ideas on dialogical truth as a way of explaining what he found distinctive about the novels of Fyodor Dostoevsky. Bakhtin's central insight was that Dostoevsky allowed his characters an unparalleled freedom and autonomy in relation to him, their author:

> *A plurality of independent and unmerged voices and consciousnesses, a genuine polyphony of fully valid voices is in fact the chief characteristic of Dostoevsky's novels.* What unfolds in his works is not a multitude of characters and fates in a single objective world, illuminated by a single authorial consciousness; rather a *plurality of consciousnesses, with equal rights and each with its own world,* combine but are not merged in the unity of the event.[61]

His characters are *"not only objects of authorial discourse but also subjects of their own directly signifying discourse."*[62] This is why he described a Dostoevsky novel as polyphonic and considered that his work constituted a new novelistic genre.[63]

Newsom identifies four features of dialogic truth as portrayed by Bakhtin. First, in contrast to monologic truth, this mode "requires a plurality of con-sciousnesses . . . [that] in principle cannot be fitted within the bounds of a single consciousness."[64] Newsom observes that "dialogic truth exists at the point of intersection of several unmerged voices. The paradigm, of course, is that of the conversation."[65] Second, here each position (or, better, each voice) is not an abstract idea but comes embodied in a particular personality; here again, conversation is paradigmatic. Third, there is no drift toward the sys-tematic in dialogic truth; it is rather an event. A dialogic truth "requires the plurality of consciousnesses that can enter into relationship with it from a variety of noninterchangeable perspectives."[66] Fourth, dialogic truth is always open. As Bakhtin said, "Nothing conclusive has yet taken place in the world, the ultimate word of the world and about the world has not yet been spoken, the world is open and free, everything is still in the future and will always be in the future."[67]

Bakhtin's ideas on dialogicality have had a wider application than merely to Dostoevsky's novels. They have been widely used in literary studies and the social sciences, including in ethnography (where the problems of inter-cultural communication between persons assume critical importance).[68] "Dialogism is not only descriptive of certain kinds of literature," Newsom comments, "it is a prescriptive model for understanding persons and com-munities and for the conduct of discourse."[69]

It is self-evident that Bakhtin's ideas have an application to biblical texts. As Newsom notes, the Bible is not a monologic text. There is no single "author"—by which she means a human author—who controls and coor-dinates meaning across the whole collection of biblical texts. Yet this is not to say, she adds, that it is polyphonic in the same sense as, for example, *The Brothers Karamazov*, where we have a text that is "an intentional artistic repre-sentation of the dialogic nature of an idea."[70] Perhaps we could express her point here more directly by saying that the biblical writings, unlike the char-acters in a Dostoevsky novel, do not exist in what is obviously a single work by one author. The Bible is not that, she asserts, "unless one wants to claim that the Holy Spirit is the polyphonic author of the Bible in the same way that Dostoevsky is the polyphonic author of *Karamazov*."

Newsom herself obviously demurs from the idea that the Holy Spirit is such an author. Yet I argue that, in order to enrich contemporary Christian reflection and identity, interpreting the New Testament historically while also accepting the role of speaking of God's ongoing relationship with human beings and with the cosmos, the notion of Holy Spirit as "author" in the manner of Dostoevsky is a very appropriate concept. At this point we arrive at the question of Scripture's inspiration, a topic far too large for an extended treatment here. For present purposes, it will be enough to adopt the insights of Paul Achtemeier and Nicholas Wolterstorff.

Paul Achtemeier construes inspiration in terms of the Word of God uttered in relation to various historically contingent settings in the past yet still capable of speaking to us in our own situations. Achtemeier well brings out how the Holy Spirit was active in the composition of these writings in the past and yet continues to be active in them today and in the community of faith that proclaims their message today: "The Spirit which vivifies the community of faith is also the Spirit who has summoned forth the words of Scripture from various junctures within the life of that community, both before and after the historical event of Jesus of Nazareth."[71]

Wolterstorff has conceived an approach to inspiration that provides a more precise understanding of the process and that coheres closely with the dialogic character of the canon. He believes that Christian theologians have been too preoccupied with the idea of Scripture as revelation and have neglected the extent to which it is discourse. In trying to find some model of discourse that avoided the crudities of the divine dictation theory of inspiration, he saw the potential of the speech act theory of J. L. Austin (considered in chapter 4) and through it Wolterstorff proposes a creative way to envisage Scripture as "divine discourse." In essence, he argues that the utterances of the biblical authors are locutionary *speech actions that also function as illocutionary actions* by God.[72] This means that the biblical texts are cases of *double agency*, spoken both by their authors and by God.[73] As familiar examples of such a process, he cites the case of X speaking on behalf of Y as Y's deputy or where Y appropriates the discourse of X as his or her own. As Dan Stiver has rightly noted, this proposal "allows for the individuality of the authors and for it (sc. the Bible) to be divine discourse." Wolterstorff has drawn on "recognized human conventions to make a radical point, namely, that scripture is God's word in a literal sense that is nevertheless far from a dictation or inerrantist theory of inspiration."[74] It is also clear that Wolterstorff's proposal fits reasonably well with a dialogic model of canon based on Bakhtin's view on the independence of the characters in Dostoevsky's novels. The novelist is using what the characters say to comprise part of the artistic entity he is creating. He stands behind their utterances yet is differentiated from them. On the other hand, as we have seen in chapter 4 following an idea of Richard Ohmann, in a novel the illocutionary force is mimetic, *not* actual. The illocutionary force of God's discourse in the biblical texts *is* actual.

These insights bring us back to the canon and reinforce the utility of understanding it in terms of Bakhtin's model of dialogic truth. Dostoevsky's creation of virtually autonomous characters with combined but unmerged consciousnesses who continue to engage readers for generation after generation is closely consonant with the actions of the Holy Spirit. The Spirit has spoken in the past through a variety of writings that were gathered long ago into Old and New Testament canons and yet still press powerfully upon us in our very different cultural settings. It is also consonant with the idea that the locutionary speech acts of the biblical authors constitute the illocutionary discourse of God.

The usefulness of this analogy is not affected by the fact the most of the biblical "voices" (or texts) are not engaged in explicit dialogic interaction with one another, that they are, rather, gathered together side by side. For "juxtaposition itself can produce a kind of dialogism, Bakhtin uses the analogy of a painting in which the tone of a color is affected by the surrounding colors."[75] In addition, those who hear the various biblical "voices" or read their inscripted forms can also create a dialogue among them.[76]

On the other hand, we should not forget that in both Old and New Testaments we do, in fact, witness numerous examples of express dialogical interaction. In the Old Testament the most egregious example is the reworking of parts of Genesis and Numbers and large swaths of 1 and 2 Samuel and 1 and 2 Kings that is to be found in 1 and 2 Chronicles. In the New Testament, we have, most notably, the extensive engagement by Matthew and Luke with Mark and the use of the figure Paul and the Pauline corpus in later pseud-Pauline writings. Most remarkable is the extent to which 2 Thessalonians draws upon 1 Thessalonians and the close relationship between Ephesians and Colossians. Paul is drawn upon as the supposed author of 1 and 2 Timothy and Titus.

The final point in relation to the use of Bakhtinian dialogicality to explain canon is that it works not just for the biblical writings within themselves, but also for us in dialogue with them and those who produced them. The character of our intercultural communication and communion with our ancestors in faith who bequeathed us these works has been the prominent theme of this volume. To introduce the canon into the discussion both reminds us of the rich plurality of voices with whom this process is possible and compels us to attend to issues that flow from their unmerged but nevertheless combined coexistence. As Louise Lawrence has well observed, "For Bakhtin, *dialogism* indicates that language and meaning are never fixed in themselves but only work in situations of dialogue where meanings and understandings are contingent on other meanings and understandings." She cites Bakhtin's view that "discourse lives on the boundary between its own context and another alien context."[77]

CONCLUSION

During the course of this chapter I have sought to explain the significance of the canon within the interpersonal and dialogic model that I have been developing throughout this volume. I have urged (against Wrede) that the canon has an important role if we are interpreting the New Testament historically in way that will allow the results to be brought into contact with contemporary Christian experience. In response to suggestions by Childs and Watson, I have also argued that canonization did not erase interest in the origins of the New Testament texts. A critical appraisal of Childs's monologic understanding of canon paved the way for me to set out an entirely different model based on Mikhail Bakhtin's concept of dialogicality.

To illustrate what the style of interpretation I have been advocating in this volume means in practice and to provide a concrete example, I will offer an interpretation of one New Testament text. Since I have already considered, and found wanting, Brevard Childs's attempt to interpret Paul's letter to the Romans canonically and since this text has been the subject of most of my own exegetical activities for the last few years,[78] I will focus on it. This will occupy the next, and final, chapter.

12

HISTORY, HERMENEUTICS, AND COMMUNION

ROMANS

I began this book with the avowed aim of proposing a way of reading or listening to the New Testament that maximizes the impact that its twenty-seven distinct documents might have on contemporary Christian experience and identity. To demonstrate that this is not a purely theoretical exercise and to avoid the feeble claim that I leave demonstrating the utility of this approach to another day, it is my aim in this chapter to conclude my entire argument interpreting Paul's letter to the Romans as a test case.

To this end I will employ my recently published exegesis of Romans where my aim was the historical one of explaining the message Paul's letter would have communicated to his addressees in Rome, but where my theoretical framework—relating especially to issues of identity, ethnicity, and ethnic conflict—corresponds closely with major issues in our world today.[1] Indeed, it was my concern with how to respond to serious outbursts of ethnic violence and even genocide in the last decade—in Rwanda, Bosnia, Kosovo, Israel and Palestine, and Northern Ireland, for example—that fired my interest in trying this approach in historically investigating Romans. This is an issue, nevertheless, that finds ample data both in the letter itself and in its ancient Mediterranean context world. I began to conceptualize my current approach while working on my Romans monograph and gave a public lecture about this approach.[2] In the year after I completed that monograph, I was able to formally explicate my thoughts in this volume.

We should pause to consider how we might use biblical theology generally to lessen the incidence of interethnic hatred and violence in the world. We saw in chapter 1 that when Gabler inaugurated biblical theology in his address in 1787, he was looking for theological ideas that could be isolated from the Bible by historical investigation and then fed into the structured and philosophical procedures of systematic theology. This discipline represented one branch of the "knowledge" that constituted "religion," as opposed to the everyday "knowledge" of ordinary Christians who were not systematic theologians. In addressing ethnicity and ethnic conflict as the issue I will study in dialogue with Romans, I am obviously not enriching systematic theology, Gabler-style, with biblical data. Systematic theologians could pass their whole lives without giving any professional attention to this topic and many of them do just that, with Miroslav Volf in his 1996 monograph *Exclusion and Embrace: A Theological Exploration of Identity, Otherness, and Reconciliation* constituting a magnificent exception. To the extent that systematic theologians considered ethnic relations, they would probably regard them as part of ethics rather than as lying within their own field.

In 1994, Hutus in Rwanda killed approximately eight-hundred-thousand Tutsis, with machetes often their weapon of choice.[3] To follow Gabler's blueprint means excluding this tragedy from those with which the theological insights of the Bible, historically revealed, could be brought into conjunction. Without in any way denying the importance of systematic theology, the Rwanda genocide brings into sharp focus the bizarre nature of conceiving systematic theology as the only recipient of biblical insights. Rather, we need to return to the ordinary person's "religion" that Gabler excluded from the reach of biblical theology and restore it to its rightfully central place in applying biblical data to everyday life. For ordinary or everyday religion encompasses the whole range of what it means to be human under God—not just ideas, but also beliefs, values, aspirations, roles and practices (in day-to-day or liturgical settings), emotions, experience, and identity. Why should the historical analysis of the New Testament not be brought directly into contact with these factors? Why should relevant perspectives obtained in this way from the New Testament be corralled within the boundaries of systematic theology?

Since in the preceding chapter I defended the important role of the New Testament canon in a socio-theological interpretation, I should now relate my thoughts about the canon to my current discussion of Romans. My approach to the canon is dialogical in the Bakhtinian sense. I view the canon as an entity comprised of individual voices, each of which is allowed a remarkable degree of freedom and autonomy, while also accepting that it is inspired. The heterogeneity of the canonical documents necessarily entails that on occasions we will gain more by entering into intercultural communication with some of them than with others. We should expect that there will be times when some of these ancient voices seem more adapted to a particular modern situation than others. An important dimension of our selecting one New Testament text rather than another, and even our cautionary use of the text we have chosen, will be our continuing need to exercise critical discernment about what we are hearing or reading. This feature of our approach, which insists upon the ancient voice's alterity to us, is sadly lacking in Gadamer's widely (and regrettably) influential notion of the "fusion of horizons."

It is clear, for example, that if we hope to engage the New Testament witness in the contemporary problem of interethnic conflict, Paul's letter to the Galatians will be the wrong text to choose. For in this document, as I have argued elsewhere,[4] Paul's communicative strategy is to maintain the boundaries between the Galatian groups of Christ-followers and Judean and non-Judean outsiders. Faced with the threat that some of his non-Judean converts to faith in Christ would succumb to pressure to be circumcised and become Judeans, Paul does all he can to reduce the appeal that Judean ethnicity obviously has for some of his non-Judean addressees. To this end he makes highly artificial and provocative arguments that, for example, Judeans outside the Christ-movement are not the legitimate descendants of Abraham through Sarah, but are descended from Hagar, and that the Mosaic law is actually a yoke of slavery (Gal 3:15-18; 4:21-31).[5] All this produces a letter that is remarkably anti-Judean. It was no accident, therefore, that in Marcion's "Bible," which comprised a version of Luke's Gospel purged of Judean elements and a collection of letters by (or attributed to) Paul, Galatians came at the head of that collection.[6] Marcion recognized and thus sought to capitalize upon the anti-Judean character of Galatians. While Galatians might offer insights into the motivations for and patterns of anti-ethnic sentiments, it is unsuited and potentially dangerous for discussing means of reducing ethnic conflict. Therefore we must exercise our critical faculties and look elsewhere.

Romans represents a suitable text. Here Paul faced a situation in Rome very different from that in Galatia. In Rome the context was one characterized by tension and even conflict between Judean and Greek members of the Roman Christ-movement. There was also no pressure exerted on the Gentile Christ-followers to become Judeans. Consequently Paul adopted a very different communicative strategy. While he needed to address other issues, such as winning the Romans' support for his forthcoming visit to Jerusalem and his future mission to Spain, the issue of ethnic division figures far more prominently in the rhetoric of the letter.[7] The text of Romans contains extensive efforts by Paul to deal with this situation.

What does it mean to closely study what Paul was seeking to communicate to his original audience in Rome as an aid in addressing modern ethnic conflict? To answer this we must summon our model of socio-theological communion set out in chapter 2. The first step in the task of theological appropriation is to understand what Paul is saying in spite of the cultural distance between our worlds. While this is difficult, we have seen that it is not impossible and that modern researchers have studied the process of intercultural communication quite intensively for use in many practical situations today. Having crossed this hurdle, we can propose Paul as a "You" to our "I" within the framework of Martin Buber's position that genuine interpersonal relations are central to our shared humanity. Dialogue is the characteristic embodiment of such a relationship, a dialogue that can accept disagreement. The participants confirm one another even while disagreeing. We can be "I's" to Paul's "You" even while recognizing that we will at times be critical of what he says. In his *The Star of Redemption* (1921), Franz Rosenzweig usefully developed the I-You relationship by eschewing the atemporality that had characterized Buber's presentation. Instead he urged the temporal nature of speech between persons as central to the relationship. Such a relationship forms the basis for true interpersonal communion.

Certainly, interacting with Paul's thought on this basis accords with the recent movement among philosophers and theologians toward understanding the human person relationally and away from postulating human beings as little more than rational monads. We have seen the trajectory of this idea in the writings of John MacMurray, John Zizioulas, and Catherine LaCugna. The last two authors are alive to the close connections between such ideas and the trinitarian nature of God. LaCugna sums up much of this thought by stating: "Human beings are created in the image of the relational God and gradually are being perfected in that image (*theōsis*), making more and more real the communion of all creatures with one another."[8] In traditional theological categories, this approach is probably best seen as a form of ecclesiology. It is theological or, even "socio-theological," since God is central to the model. The distinctive feature of the approach is that the whole project of interpreting the New Testament historically (here Paul's letter to the Romans in particular) is set within a theologically and socially constructed framework of persons in communion. This is very different from separating the results of historical inquiry and handing them over to systematic theologians as a component in a larger ordered theological structure.

Christians who read Romans today, keeping the full particularity of its original meaning to the forefront so that Paul's words might speak to their own context and concerns, to help them know God's will in their own lives, are already engaging in a theological enterprise. There is no need for them to approach the text with some specific agenda derived from systematic theology. Nor do they need to hand their historical results over to systematicians to make theological use of them.

The fact that to know Paul we must undertake historical research into a figure long dead does not present an obstacle to our path. In chapter 3 I argued for the knowability of the past, in spite of recent skepticism about this enterprise. Knowable subjects from the past include Paul as the author of Romans, communicating in a particular historical context. In chapter 4 I took the next step of defending authorial intention as an interpretative key to nonliterary texts, such as Romans. This process does not necessitate a detailed knowledge of Paul's psyche and in chapter 5 I defended Schleiermacher against the charge that he advocated such psychological understanding. Schleiermacher's hermeneutics, in fact, provide a model for how one might read someone such as Paul. By fixing upon the oral nature of the publication of Romans (probably carried around the various communities of Christ-followers in Rome by Phoebe [Rom 16.1] and read to them, possibly by Phoebe herself)[9] and by attending to Paul's meaning within an overarching framework of interpersonal relations, we understand our interaction with the letter in a strongly dialogical manner.

Yet Paul is dead, long dead. While there might be scope for interpersonal communication and communion between the living, how can these dynamics function between the *living* and the *dead*? In what sense can we say that Paul is present sufficiently to make such communion a reality?

In chapter 8 I briefly traced some of the main lines in the developing idea that living Christians enjoyed communion with other Christians who had previously died in Christ. What can such a notion mean in our own period? In chapter 9 I set out a number of ways to answer this question from a naturalistic perspective that assumes that someone who has died is, irrevocably, dead. At the most elementary, yet still significant, level, respect for Paul as the author provides a firm enough foundation. As a dead person he has no rights. But the language of moral obligation is not totally comprised of rights-talk; the simple truth is that we have a duty to honor his memory as the author of Romans. The historical analysis of Paul's letter to the Christ-followers of Rome involves a respect for the other, its author, that has ethical dimensions.

A second way to conceive of Paul's presence to us is as our ancestor in faith. It appears that human beings are predisposed to respect their biological ancestors, a phenomenon present in many cultures. This orientation is carried across to our ancestor in the faith, Paul, who expressed himself with an intelligence, power, and conviction equaled only, and very differently, by the authors of the First and Fourth Gospels. He achieved this status by giving the Gospel of Jesus Christ a form, especially in his direction that converts to Christ need not become Judeans, that has become a permanent legacy for all subsequent Christians, including us. A large part of our identity as Christians owes its origins to Paul's interpretation of what the message that Jesus was the Christ really meant.

A third approach to understanding Paul as present with us when we read his words so as to give some real substance to the notion of communion between Paul and us is through memory. In remembering Paul, we activate a pattern of memorialization whose New Testament cognates include the reference in Luke's Gospel that all generations would call Mary blessed (Luke 1:48) and the statement by Jesus that the woman who anointed his feet would never be forgotten (Mark 14:9). Our memory of Paul forms part of the larger collective memory held by Christians. It is a memory that bears directly on the present life of the community by nourishing its identity. In remembering Paul, we also tie ourselves to the seventy or so generations of Christians before us who have remembered the dead in Christ. We honor Paul's memory by paying the closest possible attention to what he is saying in Romans, carefully reading or listening to his words within their original cultural context in order to comprehend their meaning to his immediate audience. By taking this route of memorialization, we will experience the shock of unexpected meanings that may be applicable to our own situations or which we must decide, exercising critical discernment, have little or no place among us today.

In chapter 10 we developed a model of the communion between saints that took up the traditional Christian belief that those who have died are alive in Christ. This approach offers the richest way of understanding Paul as present to us when we engage with his message in Romans. On one non-dualist Christian account of the human person, the promised resurrection occurs immediately upon death. On this view, for those who accept it, Paul would be alive as resurrected and this would plainly give substance to notion of communion with him when we read Romans. So too would David Brown's proposal of some existence after death analogous to life in a parallel universe. Yet we have seen that there are more difficulties with this view than with an integrative dualism, signs of which are to be found in the New Testament and which was widely adopted by Christians from the early second century CE onwards. This understanding postulates that some part of the human person survives death, no doubt existing with God in an attenuated form, until the resurrection on the last day. One aspect of such a belief is that the souls of the faithful dead would be granted by God some knowledge of what is occurring in this world and would be susceptible of invocation. Thus we could ask them to pray to God for us just as surely as if they were still alive, which reflects Paul's insistence that "neither death, nor life . . . will be able to separate us from the love of God in Christ Jesus our Lord" (Rom 8:38-39). This represents the fullest expression of communion between the living and the dead.

Therefore, in this or some other communion with Paul, we read or listen to Romans. How does what we discover bear upon our Christian life and identity now? We saw in chapter 11 how Brevard Childs illustrated his monologic position on the canon in relation to Romans by isolating from the text two main theological topics: Christology and righteousness. The theological yield, as Childs would have it, is to be obtained from this message by snipping out a fragment of Romans here and a fragment there to create an idiosyncratic composite that accords with his own theological views. He advocated no theological role for the particular details of the original Roman context in which Paul crafted his message. The approach I am suggesting, on the other hand, requires meticulous historical examination of Romans to see what Paul was actually communicating in a document embedded in the cultural realities of the Mediterranean world of the first century CE, *but within* a framework of interpersonal communication and communion.

If we were seeking to understand and respond to a particular modern outbreak of ethnic animosity, whether actual or merely potential, we would need to have the most accurate information possible about the nature of the ethnic groups in question. Above all, we would need to know how each defined its ethnicity and the history and character of the groups' interactions.

Similarly, since our particular concern is with ethnicity and ethnic conflict, we must penetrate the context of these issues in Paul's setting. Schleiermacher would have referred to this type of question as "grammatical." This involves considering the ethnic groups situated around the Mediterranean littoral, the cultural indicia they selected to define their ethnicity (including homeland, customs, and so on), and the presence of conflict between ethnic groups. This investigation would reveal bad feeling between Greeks and Judeans in various parts of the region, most notably the violent persecution of Judeans in Alexandria in 38 CE, only two decades before Paul wrote Romans.[10] We would then need to look in particular at the ethnic mix in Rome, especially the position and organization of the thousands of Judeans in the city, and how those phenomena had become integrated with Roman patterns of social relations, especially social stratification and honor-based hostility between groups, including those centered on houses.[11] These considerations would provide the setting within which to assess the character of what Paul has to say on ethnic relations.

By comparing and contrasting the context of the modern example with the context of Paul's message on ethnic conflict, we would be able to point to similarities and differences that would affect the degree to which his message applies today. This would allow us to proceed to the positive program that Paul sets out in the letter for reconciling tension and conflict between Judean and Greek members of the Christ-movement. This is the message, which we are hearing from Paul in the framework of dialogue and communion, that we would seek to relate to our own modern example of ethnic conflict. For we are seeking to interact, not with some collage of theological motifs ripped from their textual positions in the letter, as proposed by Childs, but with the very burden of Paul's own meaning.

We would find that Paul's guidance for the Roman Christ-followers meshes quite closely with one of the means that social scientists today advocate to end conflict between rivalrous or warring groups. This is to bring the two groups together into a new superordinate group, to establish for them a new common in-group identity. Paul follows this course by reminding his audience that they are now members of a new group, (to use modern coinage) the Christ-followers, and have a new identity, in Christ. This is an important theme in the letter. It finds notable expression in Paul's image of their all being members of the body of Christ (Rom 12:4-8). Yet Paul goes out of his way to connect this message with the monotheism of God: "Or is God the God of Judeans only? Is he not the God of non-Judeans also? Yes, also of non-Judeans, since God is one and he will make righteous the circumcised on account of their faith and the uncircumcised through their faith" (3:29-30).[12] The letter brings out time and again the role of Father, Son, and Spirit; it is prototrinitarian in emphasis, not christological as Childs suggests.

Modern theorists, who advocate the reconciliation of intergroup conflict by the formation of a common in-group identity route, have pointed out that this process will not succeed if it is accompanied by any effort to eliminate the constituent subgroups. Such efforts actually encourage the subgroups to assert their own identity to the detriment of the new common in-group.[13] Paul seems to have hit upon the same insight, perhaps because of his prior experience in Galatia, where his hard line against Judeans seems to have backfired, as shown by the failure of the Galatians to contribute to his collection for the poor among the Christ-movement in Jerusalem.[14] In Romans he does not advocate that Greeks or Judeans drop their ethnic affiliations (although that may have been a consequence of his message), but rather he carefully attends to each ethnic group at different places of the text. He does not demand the erasure of ethnic difference. His olive-tree metaphor in Romans 11, where Judean and non-Judean components, while forming one tree, remain distinct and even separable, provides proof of his attitude on this subject in the form of a provocative visual image.

Were contemporary Christians to seek to utilize precisely the same in-group identity approach as Paul, they would need to work with ethnic groups in conflict who happened to share a Christian faith. This is the case with the

Unionist and Nationalist communities in Northern Ireland and also with Croatians and Serbians in the former Yugoslavia. In other cases, for example, the Israelis and Palestinians, contemporary Christians would need to select a different superordinate in-group, perhaps one fixing upon the monotheism common to both groups. Yet we must not forget the very practical dimension to Paul's solution. One of the measures that he urges toward bringing rival groups together is that one group welcome the other (Rom 14:1; 15:7), presumably through meals in the houses of the former. This mechanism reminds us that the in-group need not be explicitly religious in character. During 2003 a group of Israelis and Palestinians set off in joint expedition to climb a mountain peak in Antarctica, with the intention that this shared experience and membership in a common venture would allow the participants to understand one another better and pave the way for wider efforts at peacemaking.

There is one particular feature of Paul's message to the Roman Christ-followers that is likely to speak to any modern occasion of ethnic animosity and violence. This is his elaborate treatment of *agapē*, the type of love that characterizes the Christ-movement, in four places earlier in the letter (Rom 5:5, 8; 8:35, 39) and crops up most noticeably in Rom 12:9-21.[15] Occurring just after his metaphor of the body of Christ, his account of *agapē* takes the form of thirty separate statements, arranged in paratactic style, that in the Greek original display such a concentration of mnemonic features (for example, rhyme, assonance, alliteration, and repetition of sounds and words) as to suggest that this is a precious fragment of his oral proclamation.[16] In this part of the text we actually hear Paul's voice using the very words that groups of Christ-followers around the Mediterranean must have heard when he preached. This brings us very close indeed to the spoken voice and the interpersonal nature of hermeneutics rightly valorized by Schleiermacher.

When one looks at the thirty exemplifications of *agapē* in Rom 12:9-21, it is clear that their significance goes well beyond what we would normally classify as "ethics." They really embrace major aspects of what it means to be followers of Christ, of the identity of those who belong to this movement. These include our relationships with God (prayer, service, and being filled with the Holy Spirit), general attitudes and dispositions (hating evil, being steadfast in affliction, and rejoicing in hope), and dispositions and practices directed toward others (brotherly love, giving way in precedence to others, thinking in harmony with one another, practicing hospitality, sharing the grief and joy of others). The final statement is a very general one, countercultural in this ancient social milieu (where taking vengeance on those who had wronged you was a matter of honor), but going to the heart of what it meant for Paul to be in Christ: "Do not be overcome by evil, but overcome evil with good" (12:21).

While with some features of Paul's thought we need to retain our critical faculties and possibly reject features of his message inappropriate for our time, it is difficult to read through the thirty embodiments of *agapē* in Rom 12:9-21 and not think that here we have a statement of something at the core of the identity of what it means to be a Christ-follower, whether then or in any other age. It is true that Paul relates his exposition of *agapē* very closely to the ethnic divisions he is seeking to resolve among the Roman Christ-followers. This is shown unambiguously in Rom 14:15 when he says, "If your brother [here most probably a Judean Christ-follower or at least one who lives in accordance with Mosaic precepts] is being injured on account of food [that is, the food eaten by another Christ-follower], you are no longer walking according to *agapē*." Nevertheless, in this aspect of Romans we clearly have a body of material that has something to say to any ethnic conflict wherever or whenever it might occur. By historically examining the letter, we are able to comprehend with a reasonable degree of accuracy the point Paul was trying to make.

Even while retaining our powers of critical discernment over him, we can see that in his teaching about our common identity with one another and with Father, Son, and Spirit, and also on *agapē*, his voice sounds forth to other times and other places. We do not need to feed this material into a systematic theology to apply it to our time and situation. For we are able to access it directly, as the ordinary and everyday people of God opening our minds and hearts to the words of Paul—author, our ancestor in faith, and living saint—so that, in spite of cultural and temporal distance, *cor ad cor loquitur*—heart speaks to heart.

NOTES

INTRODUCTION: THE NEW TESTAMENT AND CONTEMPORARY CHRISTIANITY

1. Räisänen 1990a:95–96.

2. Recent New Testament theologies include Jeremias 1971, Thüsing 1981–, Porsch 1982, Hübner 1990–95, Stuhlmacher 1997 and 1999, Caird 1994, Gnilka 1989 and 1994, and Strecker 1996.

3. Morgan 1996:207.

4. Ibid., 215.

5. Ibid., 217–29.

6. See Bauckham 1998b, 2002; and Esler 2003a:157–59.

7. Morgan 1996:206.

8. Ibid., 207.

9. Ibid., 230.

10. Ibid., 207.

11. Ibid., 231.

12. Ibid., 219 (emphasis added).

13. Ibid., 231; this phrase appearing shortly after the words "identity of Christianity" at the bottom of 230.

14. See Bar-Tal 1990; 1998:94.

15. See the discussion in Esler 2003c.

16. See Beauchamp 1982:153–54.

17. McLuhan 1962:250.

18. Graham 1987:40.

19. Ibid., 41.

20. Ibid., 29.

21. Ibid.

CHAPTER 1

1. Morgan 1973:22.

2. Ebeling 1963:82.

3. Boers 1979:16–19.

4. Ebeling 1963:82.

5. Ibid., 83.

6. Boers 1979:20.

7. Ibid., 20–21, discussing the *Pia Desideria* of Philipp Jacob Spener, published in 1675.

8. Ebeling 1963:84–85.

9. Ibid., 87, in discussion of Anton Friedrich Büsching's *Gedanken von der Beschaffenheit und dem Vorzug der biblisch-dogmatischen Theologie vor der alten und neuen scholastischen* (1758). On Zachariä see Kümmel 1978: 98.

10. See Locke's preface to *A Paraphrase and Notes on the Epistles of St. Paul: To the Galatians, I and 2 Corinthians, Romans, Ephesians*, published posthumously in 1705, in the 1987 edition by Arthur W. Wainwright. (I am indebted to Robert Morgan for this reference).

11. The book appeared in two volumes, the first in June 1835 and the second in November 1835 (although the second volume bore the date 1836); see Keck 1977: xxzi.

12. See the useful one volume Sigler Press 1994 edition of Eliot's translation.

13. Räisänen 1990a.

14. Gabler 1787; ET in Sandys-Wunsch and Eldredge 1980:134–44 (= the version cited here).

15. See Boers 1979:23–24 for some of his influences.

16. See the references to Semler in Sandys-Wunsch and Eldredge 1980:136.

17. See the references to Tittmann in ibid. (the difference between religion and theology).

18. See the references to Zachariä in ibid., 138 (on notions referring to the biblical times and those of universal application).

19. Ibid., 136.

20. Ibid., 137.

21. Ibid., 137–38.

22. Ibid., 138.

23. Ibid., 143.

24. See the comment in ibid., 157 and 157 n. 1. Boers continues to use the true/ pure dichotomy (1979:26), but Räisänen, at the urging of Robert Morgan rightly challenges its usefulness (1990a:157 n. 9).

25. Räisänen 1990a:5.

26. Boers 1979:27.

27. Ibid., 30.

28. Ebeling 1963:87–88.

29. Note the material in Sandys-Wunsch and Eldredge 1980:139–40 and the remarks of Räisänen 1990a:4.

30. See Kümmel 1978: 51–61.

31. Lessing 1957:53. Note that Stendahl, apparently responding to this view of Lessing, accurately interprets him to be saying "eternal truth cannot be derived from historical data" (1962:426).

32. For the influence of Leibniz and Spinoza on Lessing, see Chadwick 1957:30–31.

33. Lessing 1957:55.

34. Morgan 1986–87:168.

35. Kümmel 1978:120.

36. From Strauss's *Streitschriften*, No. 3, translated by Hodgson 1994:xxiii.

37. Hodgson usefully lists the modern works cited by Strauss (Strauss 1994:803–10).

38. Keck 1977:l–li.

39. Ibid., li, citing G. Müller.

40. Ibid., xxi.

41. Ibid., liv.

42. Hodgson 1994:xx.

43. Keck 1977:lii–liii.

44. Hodgson 1994:xxi, citing a letter from Strauss to Christian Märklin.

45. See Keck 1977:xxvi n. 47.

46. Räisänen 1990a:6.

47. Keck 1977:lviii.

48. Strauss 1994:780.

49. Hodgson 1977:xlv.

50. See Wrede 1973, which is Robert Morgan's translation of *Über Aufgabe und Methode der sogenannten neutestamentliche Theologie.*

51. Ibid., 84.

52. Ibid., 84–85 (emphasis original).

53. Ibid., 85 (emphasis original).

54. Ibid., 85–86.

55. Ibid., 94.

56. Ibid., 103–14.

57. Ibid., 116.

58. For the importance of acknowledging the reality of God in this context, see Morgan 1986–87:165.

59. Ibid., 29.

60. Ibid., 59.

61. For all of these quotations in relation to history allegedly being unable to serve the church, see Wrede 1973:73.

62. See Morgan 1973:12.

63. Ibid., 28.

64. From Schlatter's essay "The Theology of New Testament and Dogmatics," translated by Robert Morgan (1973:152 [117–66]).

65. Bultmann 1953 and 1955b, and 1971.

66. Bultmann 1955b:237–41 ("The Task and the Problems of New Testament Theology [The Relation between Theology and Proclamation]").

67. Ibid., 237 (emphasis original).

68. Ibid., 239.

69. Ibid., 240–41.

70. Räisänen 1990a:xi.

71. Stendahl 1962:420.

72. See Esler 2003a:197–98.

73. See ibid., 316–19.

74. Buber 1947:168.

75. Stendahl 1962.

76. Ibid., 418.

77. Ibid., 422.

78. Ibid., 419.

79. Ibid., 421.

80. Ibid., 422.

81. Ibid., 423.

82. Ibid., 431.

83. The word "normative" appears in the essay twice in relation to Jewish treatment of Scripture. Ollenburger actually devotes nine pages of his essay to a consideration of problems with "normative" and "normativity" from a philosophy of language point of view (1986:72–80) in spite of the fact that Stendahl does not use them in relation to what biblical texts mean in the 1962 article. Ollenburger can do this by focusing attention on a 1965 essay where Stendahl responds to Childs (1964). But the fact that Stendahl expressed his views in 1962 without such language indicates the misdirected nature of Ollenburger's critique.

84. Stendahl 1962:425.

85. Ibid., 428 (emphasis added).

86. Morgan with Barton 1988:179.

87. Räisänen 1990a:77.

88. Countryman 1988:4.

89. Räisänen 1990a:xv.

90. Ibid., xv–xvi.

91. Ibid., 120–21.

92. Ibid., 74–75.

93. Ibid., xviii.

94. Ibid., 105.

95. Watson's 2004 text, *Paul and the Hermeneutics of Faith*, appeared after the manuscript of this book had been sent to the publisher and I have not been able to interact with it here.

96. Watson 1994:15.

97. Bornkamm 1963.

98. See Theissen 2001.

99. Watson 2000:42, 45.

100. Ibid., 87–88.

101. Ibid., 131.

102. Ibid., 89.

103. Johnson 1998. These three dimensions do not represent the totality of the experience of the first Christ-followers, but each of them was central to it. For my own work in these areas, see Esler 1987:71–109 and 1998b:93–116 (table-fellowship), 1994:36–51 (glossolalia and other forms of Spirit-possession) and 2003a:202–17 (baptism).

CHAPTER 2

1. Stendahl 1962:428.

2. See Hogg and Abrams 1988 for a good application of this theory; for its application to Galatians and Romans, respectively, see Esler 1998b and 2003a.

3. Translations from Sirach here are from the Jerusalem Bible.

4. Werner Jeanrond has rightly insisted upon the absolute necessity for critical thinking in hermeneutical projects. Jeanrond 1994:114–18 and passim.

5. Friedman 1976.

6. Buber 1970:55. This translation predates gender-inclusive language.

7. Ronald Gregor Smith in Buber 1937:vi.

8. Buber 1970:55.

9. Ibid., 56.

10. Ibid., 80.

11. Ibid., 112.

12. Here cited in the English translation, "Dialogue," by Ronald Gregor Smith in Buber 1947:118-205.

13. Buber 1947:171.

14. Ibid., 168.

15. Ibid., 171.

16. "Dialogue" is here cited in the English translation by Ronald Gregor Smith in Buber 1947:1–39. "Distance and Relation" is cited here from its republication in Buber 1965:59–71.

17. Buber 1947:19.

18. Ibid., 19–21.

19. Ibid., 3–4, 19.

20. Buber 1970:57.

21. Ibid., 94.

22. Ibid., 98.

23. Buber 1947:31.

24. Ibid., 176.

25. Ibid., 175.

26. Buber 1965:69.

27. Gudykunst and Kim 2003:392.

28. Friedman 1986:xv.

29. Buber 1965:85.

30. Lenski and Lenski 1987.

31. This is not to overlook the very different latifundia style of farming that was quite common in Italy.

32. The phrase "culture shock" was devised by anthropologist K. Oberg in the 1950s (see Oberg 1960).

33. *Communicating with Strangers: An Approach to Intercultural Communication*, in its fourth edition in 2003, the first edition having appeared in 1984.

34. Esler 1998a:9–21.

35. See ibid., for a fuller version of the material in this paragraph. For an introduction to the study of communication, see Fiske 1990.

36. Krober and Kluckhohn 1952.

37. The phrase "software of the mind" is the subtitle to Hofstede 1991.

38. Gudykunst and Kim 2003:15–16.

39. Weber 1964:107–8.

40. Skeptics on this score can put their principles to the test next time they are crossing Turkey by bus by complimenting a peasant couple on the beauty of their baby child. In North America and northern Europe such a communication is likely to be well received. Expect a very different reaction in the Turkish bus. For a fuller discussion of this subject, see Esler 2005c.

41. Hofstede 1980; for a later and more succinct expression of his position, see Hofstede 1991.

42. Hofstede 1991:51.

43. See Triandis 1989, 1994; Triandis et al. 1993.

44. Mills and Clark 1982; their analysis is relied upon by Triandis 1989:62.

45. See Bayer 2001.

46. Gurr 1993:3.

47. I am grateful to Bruce Malina for alerting me (in a personal communication) to the usefulness of Gurr's notion of "communal groups" in relation to the early Christ-movement.

48. In this volume I use the word "Judean" instead of "Jew" or "Jewish" as the best means of doing justice to the ethnic identity of the *Ioudaioi* of the first century CE. For my reasons for taking this position, see Esler 2003a:62–74. I also use the expressions "Christ-follower" or "Christ-believer" of persons in the first century to avoid the anachronism entailed in referring to them as "Christians" (on which, see Esler 2003a:12–13.).

49. For an attempt to relate notions of communion to collectivism and individualism, see Kâgitçibasi 1994.

50. See Bond 1994, referring to Bond, Leung, and Wan 1982; and Bond and Forgas 1984.

51. Triandis 1994:42.

52. Triandis 1994:46. Note his amusing measure of the contrast between two national cultures: in the United States children are punished by being "grounded" (i. e. made to stay at home), whereas in Japan they are punished by being put out of the house (1994:49).

53. I wish to acknowledge my great debt to Professor Alan Torrance, of the University of St. Andrews, for his invaluable help in formulating my thoughts expressed in this section of this chapter. But he bears no responsibility for them.

54. Stendahl 1963.

55. Boethius, *De duabus naturis* PL 64:1343C.

56. Pannenberg 1985:236–7.

57. Torrance 2005:1.

58. See Gurevich 1995.

59. Taylor 1989.

60. Pannenberg 1985:179.

61. Ibid., 179–85.

62. Ibid., 180.

63. See the English translation by Smith in 1937 (which Buber himself praised) and the later translation, in 1970, by Kaufmann.

64. Rosenzweig 1971. The original German edition (*Stern der Erlösung*, begun while Rosenzweig was a soldier in World War I) appeared in 1921.

65. Ibid., 174.

66. Ibid., 110.

67. Buber 1994a:179.

68. Rosenzweig 1971:309.

69. Ibid., 309–10.

70. Ibid., 77.

71. Ibid., 308.

72. Ibid., 315–16.

73. Ibid., 322–23.

74. Ibid., 316.

75. Ibid., 219.

76. Ibid., 224.

77. Pannenberg 1985:182, commenting on Rosenzweig 1971:205.

78. Ibid.

79. MacMurray 1957.

80. MacMurray 1961:69.

81. Ibid., 164.

82. For these three quotations, see Zizioulas 1975:407–8.

83. Zizioulas 1975:408 n. 3. Also see Robinson 1981 (1936); and the development of much the same idea in Johnson 1961.

84. Zizioulas 1975:409.

85. Ibid., 410.

86. Zizioulas 1985:420.

87. Ibid.

88. Torrance 1996:194.

89. Ibid., 220.

90. Rahner, 1970:76, 106.

91. Note statements such as "The Father loves the Son . . ." (3:35); "For the Father loves the Son" (5:20); "The Father loves me" (10:17); "As the Father has loved me . . . " (15:9). The love of the Son for the Father is evident in the Fourth Gospel in the fact that the Son always does his will: "For I always do what pleases him" (8:29), "I honor my Father" (8:49). The mutuality of the Father and the Son finds powerful expression in the statement "the Father is in me and I am in the Father" (10:38). Translations are from the Jerusalem Bible.

92. Torrance 1996:276.

93. Torrance 1996:278.

94. Zizioulas 1985:16–17.

95. Ibid., 46.

96. Ibid., 17–18.

97. Torrance 1996:288.

98. Zizioulas 1985:60.

99. Ibid., 63–4.

100. For a good introduction to social identity theory, see Hogg and Abrams 1988.

101. Torrance 1996:302, citing Lewis 1987:351.

102. Lewis 1987:350.

103. Lewis 1987:345.

104. Zizioulas 1985:41–2.

105. Torrance 1996:290.

106. Torrance 1988:

107. Zizioulas 1985:17–18.

108. See Torrance 1985:293, for a criticism of Zizioulas on this point.

109. Torrance 1988:340.

110. LaCugna 1992:2.

111. Grenz 2001:55, 57.

112. See LaCugna 1992:267–78.

113. LaCugna 1992:305.

114. LaCugna 1992:292.

115. LaCugna 1992:299.

CHAPTER 3

1. Anderson 1983.

2. Evans 1997:76.

3. Thiselton 1980.

4. Vanhoozer 1998.

5. Schleiermacher 1958.

6. See Saussure 1971.

7. The quotations are cited by Evans 1997:94.

8. For the text of this lecture, see Derrida 1970 and 1981.

9. Derrida 1981:280.

10. Evans 1997:95; citing Derrida 1976, 1981, and 1983.

11. Derrida 1976:158 (cited by Vanhoozer 1998:63).

12. Vanhoozer 1998:63.

13. Evans 1997:112.

14. See the careful discussion in Vanhoozer 1998:59–67.

15. Evans 1997:95.

16. Stone 1991.

17. White 1973:xi-xii, 5-7.

18. Jenkins 1991:47; Ankersmit 1983.

19. Derrida LI, 123–24; cited in Searle 1994:638.

20. Evans 1997:104.

21. Searle 1994:637–38 (emphasis original).

22. Ibid., 639.

23. Evans 1997:106.

24. See Lipstadt 1993.

25. Evans 1997:124.

26. Friedländer 1992. In one of these essays Hayden White retreated from his earlier position about the equivalence of history and fiction to concede that the facts of the Holocaust did preclude certain types of representation (White 1992:39–40).

27. Evans 1997:185.

28. For discussion of the Paul de Man issue, see Hamacher, Hertz, and Keenan 1988 and 1989; Spitzer 1996; Lehman 1991.

29. *Le Soir*, 4 March 1941. For the details, see Lehman 1991:180–81.

30. See the useful discussion in Evans 1997:233–35.

31. Gadamer 1979:264.

32. Ibid., 263.

33. Thiselton 1980:306.

34. Gadamer 1979:267.

35. Ibid., 269.

36. Buber 1965:69.

37. I gratefully acknowledge a debt to my St. Andrews colleague, Professor Alan Torrance, for alerting me to the importance of Eph 4:15 in this context.

38. Gadamer 1979:270.

39. Ibid., 271.

40. Ibid., 73.

41. For the text and discussion, see Kirk and Raven 1971:193–94.

42. Gadamer 1979:267.

43. Stanford 1998:196

44. Gadamer 1979:273.

45. Stanford 1998:196.

46. Ibid., 199.

47. Ibid.

48. Hirsch 1967:40.

49. Ibid., 41.

50. Ibid., 43.

51. Ibid., 44.

52. Ibid., 256.

53. Stanford 1998:68; he cites Meiland 1965 and Goldstein 1976 as examples.

54. Augustine, *Confessions*, 11.15.

55. See Brannan, Esler, and Strindberg 2001 for a critique of the antipathy among international relations scholars for talking to those they categorize as "terrorists."

56. Thiselton 1980:306, citing Palmer 1969:177 (and cf. 183).

57. See Lundin 1999.

58. As one (very high-quality) example from a large field, see Gudykunst and Kim 2003 (= the fourth edition of this text, the first having appeared in 1984).

59. Betti 1962:19-22.

60. Ibid., 35.

61. Stanford 1998:176.

62. I have explained this process at some length in Esler 1998b:10–20. See Gudykunst and Kim 2003 and the copious literature they cite.

63. Max Weber 1964:107–8, cited by Stanford 1998:175.

64. Malina 2001.

65. Horden and Purcell 2000.

CHAPTER 4

1. For advocacy of the importance of literary approaches, although within a hermeneutical framework very different from mine, see Morgan with Barton 1988.

2. For Vanhoozer's programmatic defense of his use of the concept "literary knowledge," see 1998:23–24. And yet at one point he says: "As E. D. Hirsch Jr. points out, however, not all texts aim to be 'literary.' To focus on a text's formal features runs the risk of missing the main point. C. S. Lewis makes a similar observation: 'Those who talk of reading the Bible "as literature" sometimes mean, I think, reading it without attending to the main thing it is about; like reading Burke with no interest in politics, or reading the Aeneid with no interest in Rome.'" This latter citation is from Lewis 1958:2–3.

3. Räisänen 1990b:34; he had in mind Rhoads and Michie's excellent literary-critical treatment of Mark (1982).

4. Freadman and Miller 1992:198.

5. Hirsch 1967:210.

6. See Wimsatt and Beardsley 1946; Wimsatt 1954; and Molina 1976:1–13 (the version cited here).

7. Hirsch 1967:11–12.

8. Wimsatt and Beardsley 1946:1.

9. Bagwell 1986:2.

10. Wimsatt and Beardsley 1976:2.

11. See Hens-Piazza 2002.

12. See, for example, Eagleton 1983:67–71.

13. Hirsch 1967:240–41.

14. Note that Vanhoozer mentions the Wimsatt and Beardsley essay without noting that they expressly excluded "practical messages" (1998:82). On the other hand, the importance of this "practical messages" qualification has not escaped the attention of Snodgrass (2002:2 n. 5).

15. Molina 1976:2.

16. Gadamer 1979:91.

17. Ibid., 92.

18. Ibid., 96.

19. Ibid., 97.

20. Ibid., 92.

21. Ibid., 97.

22. Ibid., 98.

23. Palmer 1969:168.

24. Gadamer 1979:101.

25. Ibid., 102.

26. On this point, see the discussion in Palmer 1969:167–68.

27. For the extant texts of Parmenides and a helpful discussion, see Kirk and Raven 1971:263–85.

28. See Plato, *The Republic* 10.

29. Gadamer 1979:142.

30. Ibid., 143.

31. Ibid., 91.

32. Ibid., 143.

33. Iser 1974:276.

34. Ibid., 277.

35. Ibid., 278.

36. See Freadman and Miller 1992:218.

37. Austin 1962:5.

38. Ibid., 60.

39. Ibid., 62.

40. Ibid., 79.

41. Ibid., 98, 109, 151, 156.

42. Ibid., 85.

43. Ibid., 9.

44. Ibid., 22.

45. Ibid., 92 n. 2. Also cf. similar views on pp. 104–5.

46. Ibid., 94.

47. Ibid., 99–100.

48. Ibid., 100–101.

49. On occasion something will go wrong in the uttering or context of such statements, with the result that they will not have the intended effect. Thus a marriage celebrant may not be licensed as required by law, or a will may be invalid due to lack of proper attestation. Austin referred to cases where the performative statement miscarried as "infelicities" (ibid., 12–24).

50. Ibid., 11–17.

51. Ibid., 117–18.

52. So Fish 1980:107 and Briggs 2001:35.

53. Warnock 1973:70–71.

54. See, for example, Austin 1962:52.

55. See Searle 1968, 1969, 1975, and 1979.

56. Searle 1979:18.

57. Ibid., 12.

58. Ibid., 29.

59. See ibid., 12–20 for his taxonomy of performatives.

60. Ibid., 58–75.

61. Ibid., 58.

62. See Freadman and Miller 1992:219–23. For a critique of Searle's essay as illogical, see Rorty 1982.

63. Ohmann 1971:2.

64. Ibid., 13 (emphasis original).

65. Ibid., 14 (emphases original).

66. Ibid., 18.

67. Pratt 1977. For a summary and critique of Pratt's rather convoluted approach, see White 1988a:5–12.

68. White 1988b.

69. White 1988a:5.

70. Stock 1990:17.

71. Ibid., 21.

72. Ibid.

73. Barthes 1977:143.

74. Ibid., 146.

75. Ibid., 147.

76. Ibid., 148.

77. Freadman and Miller 1992:216–18.

78. Ricoeur 1976:1–23; note this a comparatively early work by Ricoeur.

79. See also Wolterstorff's critique of Ricoeur (Wolterstorff 1995:153–70). For a defense of Ricoeur against Wolterstorff, see Stiver 2001:131–36.

80. Saussure 1971 (first published in 1916); Ricoeur 1976:6–7.

81. Ricoeur 1976:9.

82. Ibid., 11.

83. Ibid., 12.

84. Ibid.

85. Ricoeur 1976:13.

86. Ibid.

87. Note Turner 2000:46–47, who recognizes that Ricoeur's point about texts becoming detached from their authors is least convincing with respect to letters.

88. Ricoeur 1976:23.

89. Vanhoozer specifically attributes to Schleiermacher the desire "to relive the mental life of the author so that interpreters might know the author better than the author knows himself or herself" (1998:230).

90. See Ricoeur 1976:25–44 (an essay entitled "Speaking and Writing").

91. Ricoeur 1976:26.

92. Ibid., 27.

93. Ibid., 29.

94. Ibid., 29-30.

95. Ibid., 31.

96. The phrase comes from Henry Cardinal Newman's pamphlet, "Cor ad Cor Loquitur."

97. Ricoeur 1976:31–32. The notion of the "open text" is discussed in a collection of essays bearing that title (Watson 1993).

98. Plato, *Phaedrus* 275e.

99. Ricoeur 1976:36. The logical conclusion of this proposition reveals its absurdity: all the preliterate peoples in human history (and, one must presume, the illiterate members of literate cultures) had and have only a "situation," not a "world."

100. See Ricoeur 1976:37.

101. Ricoeur 1976:42–43.

102. Ibid., 92.

103. Ibid., 93.

104. Iser 1974:274.

105. Ibid., 275.

106. Ibid., 279.

107. Ibid., 280.

108. Bruce Malina pioneered this approach using insights from Mediterranean cultural anthropology; Malina 2001 (first edition 1981).

CHAPTER 5

1. See Jeanrond (1994:44–50) for a succinct discussion of Schleiermacher's "philosophical hermeneutics" and the manner in which he subordinated biblical hermeneutics to his general hermeneutical principles.

2. See Gadamer 1979:153–234, esp. 162–73. Thiselton briefly discusses Gadamer's critique of Schleiermacher (1980:300–302).

3. Gadamer 1979:157.

4. Ibid., 158.

5. Gadamer 1974:164.

6. Ibid., 168.

7. Palmer 1969:96–97.

8. Thus Gadamer, in this section of the work (1979:158), observes, "Understanding is primarily agreement or harmony with another person."

9. Schleiermacher 1977a:242–43 n. 48.

10. Gadamer 1979:169.

11. Ricoeur 1976:22.

12. Torrance 1962:20; he notes that, when applied to the New Testament, this sort of approach meant that attention "was not so much upon Jesus Christ himself in his ontological reality as Son of God become man, or even as objective historical Figure, but upon the creative spirituality of the early Church which produced the interpretation of Jesus we have mediated to us through the New Testament."

13. J. Torrance 1968:272.

14. Ibid., 278.

15. Thiselton 1980:107.

16. Niebuhr 1965:73–74.

17. Redeker 1973:71.

18. See the memoir by his friend and colleague Henrich Steffens, cited by Niebuhr (1965:74–75).

19. Redeker 1973:68.

20. Odebrecht 1942:5–44. For an exposition of Odebrecht's thesis, see Krapf 1953.

21. See the comments on this work by Graby 1968:290–98.

22. See the English translation by Dobson (Schleiermacher 1836). Schleiermacher's *Platons Werke* was published in Berlin in 1804.

23. Niebuhr 1965:28.

24. For a critical edition of the German original, see Mulert 1908. There is an English translation by Hastie (1890).

25. Niebuhr 1965:90.

26. Ibid.; Graby 1968:296.

27. No. 99 in Kimmerle (Schleiermacher 1977a:56).

28. Schleiermacher 1959.

29. The translators were James Duke and Jack Forsman—Schleiermacher 1977a.

30. Schleiermacher was himself heavily involved in the foundation of the University of Berlin; see Redeker 1973:94–100.

31. This appears in the German original before the "Compendium of 1819" (Schleiermacher 1959:72–79), but after it in the English translation (Schleiermacher 1977a:153–59).

32. See the translation of Kimmerle's introduction containing this information in Schleiermacher 1977a:21–27.

33. See Schleiermacher 1977a:42, 69; and Kimmerle's summary, 34–35.

34. Ricoeur 1976:187–88.

35. No. 8 in Kimmerle (Schleiermacher 1977a:42); Schleiermacher 1959:32.

36. He says: "For example, against Morus, p. 18. Morus completely misinterprets the πᾶν [all] in Romans 14:23, where he could not remain fast to the strict moral idea but thought only about the result of the action."

37. No. 143 in Kimmerle (Schleiermacher 1977a:64); Schleiermacher 1959:50.

38. Watson 1997:171.

39. No. 12 in Kimmerle (Schleiermacher 1977a:43); Schleiermacher 1959:32.

40. Schleiermacher 1977a:68.

41. Ibid., 69.

42. Ibid., 153.

43. Ibid., 156.

44. Ibid., 112.

45. Ibid., 113; Schleiermacher 1959:87.

46. Snodgrass 2002:16.

47. Schleiermacher 1977a:112; Schleiermacher 1959:87–88. by Jeanrond has noted a similar point (1994:47).

48. Schleiermacher 1977a:113.

49. Ibid., 113.

50. Ibid., 117–47.

51. Ibid., 147.

52. Ibid., 147.

53. Ibid., 147.

54. Ibid., 148.

55. Ibid., 149.

56. Jeanrond 1994:47.

57. Schleiermacher 1977a:150.

58. Ibid., 150.

59. Jeanrond 1994:47.

60. Schleiermacher 1977a:161.

61. Ibid., 192.

62. Ibid., 205–8.

63. Ibid., 207.

64. Ibid., 215.

65. Ibid., 216.

66. Ibid., 223.

67. Thiselton 1980:5. Very revealing is his main treatment of Schleiermacher on "Every child arrives at the meaning of a word only through hermeneutics" (103), where the reference is not limited to text-based comprehension, Thiselton relates all this immediately to the question of "the interpreter and the text" (104).

68. Jeanrond 1994:45.

69. Ibid., 1.

70. See Odebrecht 1942 and Niebuhr 1965; their contributions were, however, noted by Graby 1968.

71. For a brief statement of this dispute, with useful bibliography, by a scholar opposed to reader-response approaches, see Snodgrass 2002:2–9.

72. This phenomenon has a number of dimensions; see Jeanrond 1990 and 1994:5–6.

73. Thiselton 1980:104.

74. No. 99 in Kimmerle (Schleiermacher 1977a:56).

75. Thiselton 1980:105.

76. Nos. 42 and 43 in Kimmerle (Schleiermacher 1977a:48).

77. No. 68 in Kimmerle (Schleiermacher 1977a:52).

78. Schleiermacher 1977a:97; Schleiermacher 1959:80.

79. Schleiermacher 1977a:97–99.

80. As to speech: "The art of interpretation is not equally interested in every act of speaking" (Schleiermacher 1977a:101); for references to texts, see ibid., 102, 103, 104–7.

81. Ibid., 107.

82. Ibid., 108.

83. Ibid., 109.

84. Ibid., 198.

85. Ibid., 175.

86. Ibid., 180–81; Schleiermacher 1959:129.

87. Schleiermacher 1977a:181.

88. Ibid., 181–82.

89. Ibid., 182.

90. Ibid., 183.

91. Ibid., 193–95.

92. Ibid., 200.

93. See ibid., 217.

94. See Thiselton 1980:235–36; Jeanrond 1994:51–52. For a succinct but informative introduction to Dilthey's life, thought, and impact, see Rickman 1976:1–25.

95. Rickman 1976:246.

96. Dilthey 1976:247–48.

97. Ibid., 248.

98. Schleiermacher 1977a:183.

99. Dilthey 1976:256.

100. Ibid., 257.

101. See Schleiermacher 1836.

102. Dilthey 1976:258.

103. T. Torrance 1968:261.

104. Bultmann 1955a:234.

105. Ibid., 237.

106. Ibid., 238.

107. T. Torrance 1968:258.

108. Jeanrond 1994:7.

109. Schleiermacher 1977a:104.

110. Ibid., 107.

Chapter 6

1. Malina 2001 (the first edition appeared in 1981). For a detailed contrast between Mediterranean persons and modern U.S. persons, see Malina 2001:76–78. Also see the various authors in Neyrey 1991, Rohrbaugh 1996, and Pilch 2001.

2. Charles Taylor has charted the development of the modern sense of self (Taylor 1989).

3. Harris 1989.

4. Hezser 2001.

5. See Philo's description of synagogue practices on the Sabbath in the first century CE in a fragment of his lost work *Hypothetica: Apology for the Judeans*, partially preserved in Eusebius (*Praeparatio evangelica* 8.5.11). This description includes the following passage: "[On the sabbath Moses] commanded all the people to assemble together in the same place, and sitting down with one another, to listen to the laws with order and reverence, in order that no one should be ignorant of anything that is contained in them; and, in fact, they do constantly assemble together, and they do sit one down with another, the multitude in general in silence, except when it is customary to say any words of good omen, by way of assent to what is being read. And then some priest who is present, or some one of the elders, reads the sacred laws to them, and interprets each of them separately till eventide; and then when separate they depart." The English translation is from Yonge 1993:744.

6. Rohrbaugh 2001.

7. For a detailed argument along these lines, see Esler 2003a.

8. Mitchell 1992. It is not necessary for our discussion to argue whether or not there were separate factions/parties in Corinth; Mitchell argues that there were such factions (1992); Munck (1959:135–67) and Fee (1987:47–51) argue against this position. Paul's message on the need for unity was applicable to either context.

9. For my argument supporting this view, see my essay "Glossolalia and the Admission of Gentiles into the Early Christian Community," in Esler 1994:37–51,

especially at 40–49. Also see much the same view by Fee (1987:598), especially his astute observation: "Moreover, his use of earthly languages as an *analogy* [Fee's emphasis] in 14:10-12 implies that it is not a known earthly language, since a thing is not usually identical with that to which it is analogous."

10. For some of the difficulties of translating this verse, see Fee 1987:576–77.

11. See ibid., 577.

12. Ibid., 577–82.

13. Forbes 1997.

14. Barrett 1971:278–79.

15. Conzelmann 1975:205.

16. See Ps 115:5 ("They have mouths, but they do not speak"); Hab 2:18-19; and 3 Macc 4:16.

17. Fee 1987:577.

18. Conzelmann 1975:204.

19. Barrett 1971:284.

20. See Theissen (1983:63–65) on miracle-working words.

21. See the remarks on this subject by Malina 2001:33–36.

22. So Fee 1987:600–607; and Conzelmann 1975:212.

23. LaCugna 1992:299.

24. Fee, remarkably, denies the verse refers to baptism (1987:603–6). For a very similar Pauline statement, where the reference to baptism is equally unmistakable, see Gal 3:27-28.

25. See Livy 2.32.12—33.1.

26. See Mitchell 1992:157–64 for her detailed treatment of the Greco-Roman versions, and 267–70 for a more detailed application to 1 Cor 12:14-26.

27. See Boring's excellent discussion (1982:128–31).

28. Ryle 1990:119–20.

29. For an analysis of Rom 12:1—15:13 that mentions the function of *agapē* in Rom 12:9-21, within the perspective of social identity theory and the virtues, see Esler 2003c.

30. See Mitchell (1992:165–71) for the relationship between ἀγάπη and ὁμόνοια/ *concordia*.

31. Barrett 1971:297, 299; Conzelmann 1975:217.

32. I have argued elsewhere that the intricate mnemonic features of Rom 12:9-21 mark it as a fragment of Paul's actual kerygma (Esler 2003a:316–30).

33. See Mitchell 1992:172–75.

34. Barrett 1971:295.

35. Burkert 1985:57.

36. Ibid., 58.

37. Dio Chrysostom, *Oration* 3.97; cited in ibid., 369.

38. Burkert 1985:58–59.

39. See Esler 2001b:1200.

40. Newton 1998:251–57.

41. On the question of idol-meat, see Gooch 1993, Newton 1998 and Cheung 1999.

42. I am adopting this somewhat ungainly translation of *koinōnia* to bring out the link with *koinōnoi* in vv. 16-17.

43. For my argument on Paul's use of *parazēloun* in Rom 10:19, 11:11, and 11:14, especially in relation to its use in Deut. 32:21, see Esler 2003a:288–93.

44. Theissen 1982.

45. Ibid., 166.

46. For the application of "intertextuality" (largely derived from modern literary critical theory) to Paul, see Hays 1989.

47. Philo, *Hypothetica: Apology for the Judeans*; see n. 5 above, citing a passage which mentions the presence of a priest and elders.

48. For the hierarchy of the synagogues in ancient Rome, see Williams 1994.

49. Rosenzweig 1971:308.

CHAPTER 7

1. This forms the scenario of Bruce Malina's imaginative venture in comparing and contrasting ancient Mediterranean and modern North Atlantic cultures (1993).

2. See Doty 1973, Stowers 1986, and J. White 1988.

3. Meade 1986.

4. Hezser 2001:496; this is a percentage proposed by another scholar with which she does not disagree.

5. Gamble 1995:5, 10.

6. Kelber 1983.

7. As an example, see Kelber 1987 and 1994.

8. Achtemeier 1990:27–28.

9. Ibid., 3.

10. See Funk 1967:264.

11. For James as the author of the letter bearing his name, see Bauckham 1999:11–25; for scholars who have argued that Peter was the author of 1 Peter, see those listed by Elliott 2000:118 n. 35, who include Cranfield, Van Unnik, Michaelis, Gundry, and Grudem.

12. Similarly Graham 1987:123.

13. It was, for example, a custom in Roman houses for an educated slave to entertain his owner and his owner's guests by reading aloud at table (see Cicero, *Epistulae ad Atticum* 1.12.4; Nepos *Atticus* 13.3 and 14.1).

14. Bornkamm 1963; Marxsen 1969; and Conzelmann 1961.

15. Esler 1987 and 1998a; Theissen 2001:7.

16. See Bauckham 1998b.

17. For critical responses to Bauckham's thesis, see Esler 1998a, Sim 2001, and Mitchell 2003.

18. Hengel 2000:50–56.

19. Mitchell 2003:7.

20. Ibid., 12.

21. Ibid., 20.

22. Barr 1983:12.

23. Von Campenhausen 1972:118–21.

24. Barton 1997:80.

25. For Justin's referring to the Gospels as the "memoirs of the apostles," see McDonald 1995:163.

26. On Tatian's *Diatessaron*, see the detailed treatment by Petersen 1994.

27. Barton 1997:86.

28. McDonald 1995:153–54.

29. Rhoads and Michie 1982; see Morgan with Barton 1988:233 for this critique.

30. Wimsatt and Beardsley 1974:2.

31. Gadamer 1979:91.

32. Iser 1974:276.

33. The phrase is taken from the title of Austin 1962.

34. Ricoeur 1976:36.

35. Schleiermacher 1977a:104.

36. Graham 1987.

37. Ibid., 96–109.

38. Ibid., 98.

39. Ibid., 39–48.

40. Ibid., 155.

41. Ibid.

42. These six quotations form a continuous passage in Buber and Rosenzweig 1994:173–74.

43. Rosenzweig 1994:40.

CHAPTER 8

1. A full historical treatment is impossible within the limits of this volume. For fuller surveys of this topic, see Benko 1964, Perham 1980, and Johnson 1998, and the literature they cite.

2. Brown, Murphy, and Maloney 1998; and Wright 2003. It is my intention to provide at least one model of intercommunion between us and New Testament authors acceptable to those who subscribe to such a view.

3. Johnson 1998:9–10.

4. See Bonhoeffer 1998.

5. Kelly 1972:388–97, followed by Johnson 1998:95. For an earlier defense of *sanctorum* as a neuter plural, see Benko 1964.

6. Wilken 2002:160.

7. See ibid., 159–61 for the contents of this paragraph.

8. See Ferrua and de Rossi 1971, no. 12989.

9. See Wright 2003.

10. Note the remark by Plato that "immortality is in us" (*Laws* 4.713E).

11. Bauckham 1998c:80.

12. This picture, notes Cooper, is compatible with "existential-functional holism," but not with ontological holism. Cooper opts for "holistic dualism," which, as William Hasker has noted (Hasker 1999:207), is remarkably similar to the integrative dualism of Charles Taliaferro (Taliaferro 1994).

13. Bauckham (1998c:81) cites as examples Isa 26:19; and Pss 49:15, 73:24.

14. Ibid., 81–82.

15. See the discussion by Wright 2003:150–53.

16. Bauckham 1998a:87–88.

17. Bauckham 1998a:90.

18. Collins 1997b:112.

19. Cooper 2000:91; see *1 Enoch* 104 and *Jubilees* 23 which envisage not a bodily resurrection but a resurrection of the spirit and its transformation into an angelic state (Collins 1997b:113).

20. Collins 1997b:113.

21. See Wright 2003:207–398.

22. On this aspect of the letter, see Esler 2001b:1206.

23. Wright 2003:213–19, at 217.

24. See Best 1972:67.

25. Cullmann 1965:39 n. 33.

26. Koester 2001:535 n. 435.

27. Ibid., 463.

28. There is little justification for the view of Attridge (1989:331) and Koester (2001:490) that the νῦν of v. 16 means "in fact," that it is a logical rather than a temporal adverb. The author is envisaging the position of those mentioned in v. 14 who are seeking a homeland; there is no difficulty with his saying in v. 16 "Now they desire a better one . . ."

29. Attridge 1989:375.

30. See Attridge (ibid.): "Further specification of this group, either as the faithful of the Old Testament or as earlier Christian apostles and martyrs, is unwarranted."

31. Koester 2001:306.

32. Ibid., 546, citing Peterson 1982:163–65.

33. Koester 2001:476.

34. Ibid., 481–82.

35. Attridge 1989:317.

36. For my disccussion of collective memory in relation to Hebrews 11, see Esler 2005b.

37. Attridge 1989:317.

38. Philo, *That the Worse Attacks the Better,* 70; ET in Yonge 1993:119.

39. *1 Enoch* 22:7; ET in Isaac 1983:24–25.

40. *Testament of Abraham* 12-13.

41. His disembodied state is explicit in *1 En* 22, since it is Abel's spirit that produces the voice, but must be implied in *T. Ab.* 12–13, from the fact that no mention is made of any bodily resurrection for Abel and he is attributed the same status as the souls he judges, in that he is a human being judging human beings (13:3).

42. *Targum Onqelos* on Gen 4:4; *Genesis Rabbah* 25.1.

43. See *1 Enoch* 12:2; *2 Enoch* 3:1-3; *Jubilees* 4:23.

44. Eisenbaum 1997b:151; See *Jubilees* 4:23

45. See Foerster 1966a:776.

46. Attridge 1989:320. Koester, similarly, errs in suggesting that Noah "received God's righteousness" (2001:483).

47. His death, at the age of 950 years, is mentioned in Gen 9:28.

48. Irenaeus, *Adversus omnes haereses* 5.31.1; cited in Perham 1980:2.

49. Tertullian, *De anima* 55.8; cited by Perham 1980:2

50. See Wright 2003:481–83.

51. *1 Clement* 5:4, 7

52. See Hill 1992:66–88.

53. *1 Clement* 24-25.

54. *1 Clement* 50:3-4. See Perham 1980:3, 8.

55. See Perham 1980:3, 8.

56. Polycarp, *Ad Philippians* 9.2; cited in Perham 1980:8.

57. *The Shepherd of Hermas, Vision 3.5*; cited by Perham 1980:10.

58. For the archaeological evidence, see Toynbee and Perkins 1956; and Guarducci 1984. For the literary evidence, see the letter of Dionysius, bishop of Corinth, sent to Rome in about 170 CE, cited in Eusebius, *Ecclesiastical History* 2.25.8, which refers to trophies to Peter and Paul on the Vatican and the Ostian Way.

59. Guarducci 1984:66–67.

60. See Toynbee and Perkins 1956:167–82.

61. See Ferrua 1991; and Toynbee and Perkins 1956:171–72.

62. Johnson 1998:80.

63. Ibid., 83.

64. Ibid., 85.

65. Ibid., 66.

66. See Davidson 2000.

67. Brown 1981:38.

68. Johnson 1998:91.

69. Ibid., 92.

70. Cited by Johnson 1998:109.

71. Cited in ibid., 111.

72. Ibid., 121.

Chapter 9

1. Morgan with Barton 1988:6.
2. Ibid., 7.
3. Cox and Reynolds 1993b:15
4. Hirsch 1976:90.
5. Chesterton 1909:83 (I am indebted to Professor Larry Hurtado of the University of Edinburgh for this reference).
6. See Esler 1998a:24.
7. Sykes 2001:8.
8. Hsu 1971:44.
9. Ibid., 37.
10. Tshibangu 1987:41–42.
11. Sawyer 1987:23–24.
12. See Wimberley and Savishinsky 1978.
13. Dahl 1976:11.
14. See Johnson 1998:65; Metz 1980; Morrill 2000.
15. Fiorenza 1983.
16. See Jonker 1995:1–31.
17. See Aristotle, *De memoria et reminiscentia*; and Augustine, *Confessions* 10.8.12; 10.11.18.
18. See Halbwachs 1992.
19. See Halbwachs 1980.
20. Halbwachs 1992:38.
21. Halbwachs 1980:33.
22. Coser 1992:22.
23. Halbwachs 1980:48.
24. Ibid., 51.
25. See ibid., 50–51; Coser 1992:23–24.
26. Halbwachs 1980:55–59.
27. Schwartz 1982.
28. Connerton 1989:39.
29. Halbwachs 1950:66; Jonker 1995:23–24.
30. Yerushalmi 1982; Jonker 1995:24.
31. Connerton 1989:13–16.
32. Yerushalmi 1982; Jonker 1995:26.
33. Jonker 1995:29.
34. For an exposition of collective memory and social identity in relation to Hebrews 11, see Esler 2005b.
35. Fentress and Wickham 1992:7.
36. Elsewhere I have integrated these two provinces of theory in relation to Abraham in Romans 4 (Esler 2003a:171–94) and the figures in Hebrews 11 (Esler 2005b).

37. Tajfel 1978; Hogg and Abrams 1988. See the discussion in Esler 1998b:40–57 (about Galatians); and 2003a:19–39 (about Romans).

38. Condor 1996.

39. Cinnirella 1998. For "possible selves," see Markus and Nurius 1986.

40. For an accessible English translation, see Staniforth 1968:155–64.

41. Frank 2000.

42. Ibid., 69.

43. Ibid., 75.

44. Ibid., 76.

45. Ibid., 101.

46. Halbwachs 1980:140.

47. Ibid., 139.

48. Coser 1992:26, commenting on Schwartz 1982.

49. Ibid.

50. Johnson 1998:131–32.

51. Ibid., 132.

52. Ibid., 135.

CHAPTER 10

1. See Ratzinger 1988:69–71 and Jeanrond 1995:47–50.

2. Ratzinger 1988:70, citing Josef Pieper (1968).

3. Jeanrond 1995:48.

4. See ibid., 52–53.

5. Rahner 1973:280; cited and translated by Jeanrond 1995:58.

6. Jeanrond 1995:63.

7. See Davis 1989b:viii for most of these aspects of death.

8. Rahner 1971:6–7.

9. Ibid., 7.

10. Johnson 1998:131–32.

11. The observations of Patrick Sherry on the saints and their importance are worth close attention (Sherry 1984).

12. I have adapted this outline from Murphy 1998a:24–25. I am omitting models of reincarnation that figure in Hindu and Buddhist versions of human nature for reasons of brevity.

13. Sherry 1984:82.

14. On these dimensions of naturalism, see Davis 1993:17–18.

15. Larson and Witham 1997.

16. See Peel 1985.

17. Polkinghorne 1986:10.

18. Crick 1976:137–43.

19. Armstrong 1980:193.

20. Taliaferro 1994:17.

21. Ibid., 13.

22. See Haldane's contributions in Smart and Haldane 2002; Haldane 2003; and Taliaffero 1994.

23. On this point, see Davis 1993:20–21.

24. Hick 1976:112.

25. Taliaferro 1994:17.

26. Price 1953; see Hick 1976:265.

27. See Flew 1967 and 1987; Phillips 1970; and Penelhum 1970.

28. See Purtill 1975; and Helm 1978.

29. Davis 1989c:137; Hasker 1999:208.

30. Davis 1993:113.

31. Davis 1993:86.

32. Brown, Murphy, and Malony 1998; the sub-title of the book is *Scientific and Theological Portraits of Human Nature*.

33. Brown 1998a.

34. Green 1998.

35. Anderson 1998:192.

36. So Brown (1998b:226), restating the position of Anderson 1998.

37. Kim 1994:250.

38. Ibid., 251.

39. Ibid., 257.

40. Churchland 1981.

41. Hasker 1999:1–26.

42. See Swinburne 1994 and 1996. Also see Yandell 1995.

43. See Wright 2003. But Wright underestimates the significance of the dualist picture of the human person in biblical and intertestamental texts (he has missed Cooper 2000) and their portrayal of the postmortem period before the End.

44. Wright 2003:438 n. 114.

45. Taliaferro 1994:4.

46. Macquarrie 1984:ix–x.

47. See Wolfson 1965:56–60 and 63–64.

48. See Inwagen 1988.

49. Hasker 1999:224.

50. Hick 1976:279.

51. Ibid., 285; Olding 1970.

52. See Davis 1993:114.

53. Karl Barth 1926 (*The Resurrection of the Dead*) and 1960 (*Church Dogmatics* III.2).

54. Greshake 1969; Harris 1983.

55. Cullmann 1965:38.

56. Ibid., 39.

57. Ratzinger 1988:267.

58. Ibid.

59. For an important recent discussion, see Ganssle 2002.

60. See Ganssle 2002:3–4, to whom I am indebted for this discussion. Another issue is the old conundrum of whether God can foreknow future free actions. If he is temporal it is not easy to see how he could foresee something that had not yet happened. If he is atemporal, he does not foreknow anything. His knowledge of any event has no temporal location; everything occurs in his present, even though from our perspective events have a temporal succession. The picture is a complicated one, however, and the postulation of atemporality as the way to secure God's foreknowledge of future free actions is not without its problems, even if it seems more attractive than the idea that God should be subject to a dimension of existence, time, that he himself has created.

61. Brown 2000:102.

62. Wright 2003.

63. Brown 2000:124.

64. Ibid., 110–11.

65. Ibid., 103–4.

66. Brown 2000:111.

67. Wright 2003.

68. Brown 2000:115.

69. Ibid.

70. Ibid., 117.

71. Ibid., 118.

72. Ibid., 119.

73. Ibid., 119–20.

74. Ibid., 121.

75. Ibid., 124.

76. Ibid., 125.

77. Ibid., 127.

78. Davis 1993:83.

79. Ibid., 90, citing Price 1953.

80. Thomas Aquinas, *Summa Contra Gentiles* 4.79.11.

81. Stump 1995.

82. Thomas Aquinas, *Summa Theologiae*, Prima Pars 89. I have used the translation of McDermott 1989:140–42. I also gratefully acknowledge help from Professor John Haldane of the University of St. Andrews in coming to grips with this aspect of Aquinas' thought, although he bears no responsibility for the views here expressed.

83. Brown 2000:119.

84. Rahner 1971.

85. Ibid., 23.

86. This is the fine phrase of Krister Stendahl (1962:428).

87. Kähler 1964.

88. Rahner 1971:15–16; emphases original.

89. Dahl 1976:28.

90. Rahner 1971:23.

91. Ibid., 21.

92. Lessing 1957:55.

CHAPTER 11

1. Wrede 1973:70.

2. Ibid., 71.

3. Räisänen 1990a:100–101.

4. Morgan 1973:65.

5. Ibid., 65.

6. Childs 1985:23.

7. Ibid., 52.

8. Watson 1994:40.

9. Watson 1997:49.

10. Watson 2000:42, 45.

11. Ibid., 87–88.

12. Barr 1983.

13. Barton 1997:1–14.

14. Ibid., 10.

15. See Kelly 1972.

16. For useful treatments, see McDonald 1995 and Barton 1990 and 1997.

17. See Gamble 1985:67–72 and McDonald 1995:228–49.

18. Stuhlhofer 1988; see summary and discussion in Barton 1997:14–24.

19. Barton 1997:64.

20. Ibid., 67.

21. On Marcion, see ibid., 35–62.

22. See von Campenhausen 1972.

23. Gamble 1992.

24. For a more in-depth discussion of this subject, see Gamble 1985; Metzger 1987; and McDonald 1985.

25. Lampe 1955:42.

26. McDonald 1995:232.

27. Ibid., 236.

28. On the other hand, to change one's mind does leave one open to attack. There is something to be said for seeing something clearly and correctly the first time and sticking to it!

29. I have been greatly helped by Paul Noble's fair-minded assessment of Childs (1995).

30. Childs 1964.

31. It is worth noting that in his 1962 article Stendahl did not use the word "normative" as the antithesis of "descriptive."

32. See Noble 1995:18.

33. Childs 1970:141–42.

34. Ibid., 102; on which, see Noble 1995:26.

35. Childs 1970:107–12.

36. Noble 1995:27.

37. Childs 1974:xv.

38. Childs 1977.

39. Childs 1979:76.

40. Ibid., 450–55.

41. Childs 1978a and 1978b.

42. Ibid., 67.

43. Ibid., 70.

44. Childs 1984:37.

45. Ibid., 37–38.

46. See Noble 1995:55–56.

47. Noble 1995:70.

48. Childs 1984:249.

49. Ibid., 250.

50. Ibid., 252.

51. Halvor Moxnes pointed this out in an important work published in 1980.

52. Childs 1984:255–57.

53. Ibid., 257.

54. For my views on this matter in relation to Galatians and Romans, bringing out the notion of righteousness as a way of referring to the privileged identity of a Christ-follower, see Esler 1998b:141–77 and 2003a:155–70.

55. Newsom 1996.

56. The primary sources here are the essay "Discourse in the Novel" in *The Dialogic Imagination: Four Essays* (Bakhtin 1981:259ff.) and the two essays "Dostoevsky's Polyphonic Novel and Its Treatment in Critical Literature" and "The Hero, and the Position of the Author with Regard to the Hero in Dostoevsky's Art" in *Problems of Dostoevsky's Poetics* (Bakhtin 1984:5–46 and 47–77).

57. See Newsom 1996:292.

58. Newsom 1996:292–93.

59. Childs 1984:43.

60. Note Noble's defense of Childs against the charge that he exhibits harmonizing tendencies.

61. Bakhtin 1984:6 (emphasis original).

62. Ibid., 7 (emphasis original).

63. Ibid.

64. Bakhtin 1981:81.

65. Newsom 1996:293–94.

66. Ibid., 294.

67. Bakhtin 1981:106.

68. See Lawrence 2003:52–56 on Bakhtin's influence.

69. Newsom 1996:293.

70. Ibid., 296–97.

71. Achtemeier 1999:159.

72. Wolterstorff 1995:37.

73. Ibid., 38.

74. Stiver 2001:127.

75. Newsom 1996:199, citing Bakhtin 1984:89–90.

76. Newsom 1996:299.

77. Lawrence 2003:54, citing Bakhtin 1981:95.

78. See Esler 2003a.

Chapter 12

1. See Esler 2003a.

2. This was in the Manson Memorial Lecture in the University of Manchester on 25 October 2001 (Esler 2001a), although I had been mulling over many of the ideas expressed here for many years beforehand.

3. Aguilar 1998:38–50.

4. See Esler 1998b.

5. For full details of this argument, see Esler 1998b:209–15.

6. Barton 1997:7.

7. For the detailed argument in support of these claims, see Esler 2003a.

8. LaCugna 1992:292.

9. For this proposal, see Esler 2003a:117–18.

10. See ibid., 40–76.

11. See ibid., 77–108.

12. For a fine treatment of God in Romans, see Moxnes 1980; see also Neyrey 2004:107–43.

13. For some of this theory, see Esler 2003a:29–33.

14. We know he asked the Galatians to contribute from 1 Cor 16:1; that they did not emerges from Rom 15:26.

15. Prior to this section of the letter, the verbal form *agapan*, "to love," appears at 8:28, 37; 9:13, 25.

16. For the details of this proposal, see Esler 2003a:316–19.

BIBLIOGRAPHY

Achtemeier, Paul J. (1990). "Omne Verbum Sonat: The New Testament and the Oral Environment of Late Western Antiquity." *JBL* 109:3–27.

——— (1999). *Inspiration and Authority: Nature and Function of Christian Scripture.* Peabody, Mass.: Hendrickson.

Aguilar, Mario (1998). *The Rwanda Genocide and the Call to Deepen Christianity in Africa.* Eldoret, Kenya: AMECEA Gaba.

Anderson, Benedict (1983). *Imagined Communities: Reflections on the Origin and Spread of Nationalism.* London: Verso.

Anderson, Ray S. (1998). "On Being Human: The Spiritual Saga of a Creaturely Soul." In Brown, Murphy, and Malony 1998:175–94.

Ankersmit, F. R. (1983). *Narrative Logic: A Semantic Analysis of the Historian's Language.* The Hague: Martinus, Nijhoff.

——— (1989). "Historiography and Post-Modernism." *History and Theory* 28:137–53.

——— (1994). *History and Tropology: The Rise and Fall of Metaphor.* Berkeley: Univ. of California Press.

Armstrong, D. M. (1980). "The Nature of Mind." In Block 1980:191–99.

Arnett, Ronald C. (1986). *Communication and Community: Implications of Martin Buber's Dialogue.* With a foreword by Maurice Friedman. Carbondale: Southern Illinois Univ. Press.

Attridge, Harold W. (1989). *The Epistle to the Hebrews: A Commentary on the Epistle to the Hebrews.* Hermeneia. Philadelphia: Fortress Press.

Aune, David E., ed. (1988). *Greco-Roman Literature and the New Testament.* SBL Sources for Biblical Study 21. Atlanta: Scholars.

Austin, J. L. (1962). *How to Do Things with Words.* Oxford: Clarendon.

Bagwell, J. Timothy (1986). *American Formalism and the Problem of Interpretation.* Houston, Tex.: Rice Univ. Press.

Bakhtin, Mikhail (1981). *The Dialogic Imagination: Four Essays.* Edited by M. Holquist. Translated by M. Holquist and C. Emerson. Austin: Univ. of Texas Press.

———— (1984). *Problems of Dostoevsky's Poetics.* Edited and Translated by Caryl Emerson. Introduction by Wayne C. Booth. Theory and History of Literature 8. Minneapolis: Univ. of Minnesota Press.

Barr, James (1983). *Holy Scripture: Canon, Authority, Criticism.* Oxford: Oxford Univ. Press.

Barrett, C. K. (1971). *A Commentary on the First Epistle to the Corinthians.* Second edition. Black's New Testament Commentaries. London: A. C. Black.

Bar-Tal, Daniel (1990). *Group Beliefs: A Conception for Analyzing Group Structure, Processes, and Behaviour.* New York: Springer.

———— (1998). "Group Beliefs as an Expression of Group Identity." In Stephen Worchel, J. Francisco Morales, Darío Páez, and Jean-Claude Deschamps, eds., *Social Identity: International Perspectives.* London: Sage, 93–113.

Barth, Karl (1933 [1926]). *The Resurrection of the Dead.* Translated by J. J. Stenning. London: Hodder and Stoughton.

———— (1936–68). *Church Dogmatics.* Edinburgh: T. & T. Clark.

Barthes, Roland (1970). *S/Z.* Paris: Seuil.

———— (1977). "The Death of the Author." In idem, *Image-Music-Text.* New York: Hill & Wang, 142–48.

Barton, John (1990). "Canon." In Coggins and Houlden 1990:101–5.

———— (1997). *Holy Writings, Sacred Text: The Canon in Early Christianity.* Louisville: Westminster John Knox.

Barton, John, and John Muddiman, eds. (2001). *The Oxford Bible Commentary.* Oxford: Oxford Univ. Press.

Bauckham, Richard J. (1998a). *God Crucified: Monotheism and Christology in the New Testament.* The Didsbury Lectures for 1996. Grand Rapids, Mich.: Eerdmans.

————, ed. (1998b). *The Gospels for All Christians: Rethinking the Gospel Audiences.* Grand Rapids, Mich.: Eerdmans.

———— (1998c). "Life, Death, and the Afterlife in Second Temple Judaism." In Longenecker 1998:80–95.

———— (1999). *James: Wisdom of James, Disciple of Jesus the Sage.* London: Routledge.

———— (2002). "Paul's Christology of Divine Identity." Paper delivered to the Pauline Epistles Section of the annual meeting of the Society of Biblical Literature in Toronto on 25 November 2002.

Baur, Ferdinand Christian (1973 [1864]). *Vorlesungen über neutestamentliche Theologie.* Darmstadt: Wissenschaftliche Buchgesellschaft.

Bayer, Richard (2001). "The Social Nature of the Human Person in Economic Personalism." *Markets and Morality* 4:304–10.

Beauchamp, Tom L. (1982). *Philosophical Ethics: An Introduction to Moral Philosophy.* New York: McGraw-Hill.

Benko, Stephen (1964). *The Meaning of* Sanctorum Communio. Studies in Historical Theology. Naperville, Ill.: A. R. Allenson.

Best, Ernest (1972). *A Commentary on the First and Second Epistles to the Thessalonians.* Black's New Testament Commentaries. London: Adam & Charles Black.

Betti, Emilio (1962). *Die Hermeneutik als allgemeine Methodik der Geisteswissenschaften.*
Philosophie und Geschichte series, Pamphlet nos. 78–79. Tübingen: Mohr/
Siebeck.

Block, Ned, ed. (1980). *Readings in Philosophy of Psychology.* Volume 1. Cambridge:
Harvard Univ. Press.

Boers, Hendrikus (1979). *What Is New Testament Theology?* Guides to Biblical Scholarship.
Philadelphia: Fortress Press.

Bond, M. H., and J. P. Forgas (1984). "Linking Person Perception to Behavior
Intention across Cultures: The Role of Cultural Collectivism." *Journal of
Cross-Cultural Psychology* 15:337–52.

Bond, M. H., K. Leung, and Wan K. C. (1982). "How Does Cultural Collectivism
Operate? The Impact of Task and Maintenance Contributions on Reward
Distribution?" *Journal of Cross-Cultural Psychology* 13:186–200.

Bond, Michael Harris (1994). "Into the Heart of Collectivism: A Personal and
Scientific Journey." In Kim et al. 1994:66–76.

Bonhoeffer, Dietrich (1998). *Sanctorum Communio: A Theological Study of the Sociology of the
Church.* Dietrich Bonhoeffer Works, Volume 1. Translated by Reinhard
Krauss and Nancy Lukens. Minneapolis: Fortress Press.

Boring, M. Eugene (1982). *Sayings of the Risen Jesus: Christian Prophecy in the Synoptic
Tradition.* Cambridge: Cambridge Univ. Press.

Bornkamm, Günther (1963 [1948]). "The Stilling of the Storm in Matthew." In
Günther Bornkamm, Gerhard Barth, and Heinz Joachim Held (1963),
Tradition and Interpretation in Matthew. London: SCM, 52–57. First published in
Wort und Dienst (1948), 49–54.

Brannan, David W., Philip F. Esler, and N. T. Strindberg (2001). "Talking to
'Terrorists': Towards an Independent Analytical Framework for the Study
of Violent Substate Activism." *Studies in Conflict and Terrorism* 24:3–24.

Briggs, Richard S. (2001). *Words in Action: Speech Act Theory and Biblical Interpretation.*
Edinburgh: T. & T. Clark.

Brown, David (2000). *Discipleship and Imagination: Christian Tradition and Truth.* Oxford:
Oxford Univ. Press.

Brown, Peter (1981). *The Cult of the Saints: Its Rise and Function in Latin Christianity.* Chicago:
Univ. of Chicago Press.

Brown, Warren S. (1998a). "Cognitive Contributions to the Soul." In Brown,
Murphy, and Malony 1998:99–124.

——— (1998b). "Conclusion: Reconciling Scientific and Biblical Portraits of Human
Nature." In Brown, Murphy, and Malony 1998:213–28.

Brown, Warren, Nancey Murphy, and H. Newton Malony, eds. (1998). *Whatever
Happened to the Soul?: Scientific and Theological Portraits of Human Nature.*
Minneapolis: Fortress Press.

Buber, Martin (1937). *I and Thou.* Translated by Ronald Gregor Smith. Edinburgh:
T. & T. Clark.

———— (1947). *Between Man and Man.* Translated by Ronald Gregor Smith. London: Kegan Paul.

———— (1965). *The Knowledge of Man.* Edited with an introductory essay by Maurice Friedman. Translated by Maurice Friedman and Ronald Gregor Smith. London: Allen & Unwin.

———— (1970). *I and Thou.* Translated by Walter Kaufmann (with a prologue and notes). Edinburgh: T. & T. Clark.

———— (1994a). "From the Beginnings of Our Bible Translation." In Buber and Rosenzweig 1994:176–83.

———— (1994b). "A Suggestion for Bible Courses." In Buber and Rosenzweig 1994:172–75.

Buber, Martin, and Franz Rosenzweig (1994). *Scripture and Translation.* Translated by Lawrence Rosenwald with Everett Fox. First published as *Die Schrift und ihre Verdeutschung* by Schocken Verlag (Berlin) in 1936. Bloomington: Indiana Univ. Press.

Bultmann, Rudolf (1953). *Theology of the New Testament.* Volume 1. Translated by Kendrick Grobel. London: SCM.

———— (1955a). *Essays Philosophical and Theological.* Translated by James C. G. Greig. London: SCM.

———— (1955b). *Theology of the New Testament.* Volume 2. Translated by Kendrick Grobel. London: SCM.

———— (1971). *The Gospel of John: A Commentary.* Translated by G. R. Beasley-Murray from the 1966 German edition. Philadelphia: Westminster.

Burkert, Walter (1985). *Greek Religion: Archaic and Classical.* Translated by John Raffan. Oxford: Basil Blackwell.

Caird, George B. (1994). *New Testament Theology.* Completed and edited by L. D. Hurst. Oxford: Clarendon.

Campenhausen, Hans von (1972). *The Formation of the Christian Bible.* Translated by J. A. Baker. Philadelphia: Fortress Press.

Chadwick, Henry (1957). "Introduction." In Lessing 1957:9–49.

Charlesworth, James H., ed. (1983). *The Old Testament Pseudepigrapha.* Volume 1. *Apocalyptic Literature and Testaments.* London: Darton, Longman & Todd.

————, ed. (1985). *The Old Testament Pseudepigrapha.* Volume 2. *Expansions of the "Old Testament" and Legends, Wisdom and Philosophical Literature, Prayers, Psalms and Odes, Fragments of Lost Judeo-Hellenistic Works .* London: Darton, Longman & Todd.

Chesterton, Gilbert K. (1909). *Orthodoxy.* London: John Lane.

Cheung, Alex T. (1999). *Idol Food in Corinth: Jewish Background and Pauline Legacy.* JSNT Supplement Series 176. Sheffield: Sheffield Academic.

Childs, Brevard S. (1964). "Interpretation in Faith: The Theological Responsibility of an Old Testament Commentary." *Interpretation* 18: 432–49.

———— (1970). *Biblical Theology in Crisis.* Philadelphia: Westminster.

———— (1974). *Exodus: A Commentary*. OTL. London: SCM.

———— (1977). "The Sensus Literalis of Scripture: An Ancient and a Modern Problem." In Donner 1977:80–93.

———— (1978a). "The Canonical Shape of the Prophetic Literature." *Int* 32:46–55.

———— (1978b). "The Exegetical Significance of Canon for the Study of the Old Testament." VTSup 29:66–80.

———— (1979). *Introduction to the Old Testament as Scripture*. London: SCM; Minneapolis: Fortress Press.

———— (1984). *New Testament as Canon: An Introduction*. London: SCM.

———— (1985). *Old Testament Theology in a Canonical Context*. London: SCM; Minneapolis: Fortress Press.

———— (1992). *Biblical Theology of the Old and New Testaments*. London: SCM; Minneapolis: Fortress Press.

Churchland, Paul (1981). "Eliminative Materialism and the Propositional Attitudes." *Journal of Philosophy* 78:67–90.

Cinnirella, Marco (1998). "Exploring Temporal Aspects of Social Identity: The Concept of Possible Social Identities." *European Journal of Social Psychology* 28:227–48.

Coggins, R. J., and J. L. Houlden, eds. (1990). *A Dictionary of Biblical Interpretation*. London: SCM.

Cole, Peter, and Jerry L. Morgan, eds. (1975). *Syntax and Semantics 3: Speech Acts*. New York: Academic Press.

Collins, John J. (1997a). *Apocalypticism in the Dead Sea Scrolls*. London: Routledge.

———— (1997b). "Resurrection and Eternal Life." In Collins 1997a:110–29.

Condor, Susan (1996). "Social Identity and Time." In Robinson 1996:285–315.

Connerton, Paul (1989). *How Societies Remember*. Themes in the Social Sciences. Cambridge: Cambridge Univ. Press.

Conzelmann, Luke (1961). *The Theology of St Luke*. Translated by Geoffrey Buswell. London: Faber & Faber.

———— (1975). *1 Corinthians: A Commentary on First Epistles to the Corinthians*. Translated by James W. Leitch. Bibliography and References by James W. Dunkly. Edited by George W. MacRae. Philadelphia: Fortress Press.

Cooper, John W. (2000). *Body, Soul, and Life Everlasting: Biblical Anthropology and the Monism-Dualism Debate*. Reprinting of 1989 edition with a new Preface (reviewing recent developments). Grand Rapids, Mich.: Eerdmans.

Coser, Lewis A. (1992). "Introduction." In Halbwachs 1992:1–34.

Countryman, L. William (1988). *Dirt, Greed, and Sex: Sexual Ethics in the New Testament and Their Implications for Today*. Philadelphia: Fortress Press.

Cox, J. N., and L. J. Reynolds (1993a). "The Historicist Enterprise." In Cox and Reynolds 1993b: 3–38.

————, eds. (1993b). *New Historical Literary Study: Essays on Reproducing Texts, Representing History*. Princeton: Princeton Univ. Press.

Crick, Malcolm R. (1976). *Explorations in Language and Meaning: Towards a Semantic Anthropolpogy*. London: Malaby Press.

Cullmann, Oscar (1965). "Immortality of the Soul or Resurrection of the Dead: The Witness of the New Testament." The Ingersoll Lecture for 1955. In Stendahl 1965a: 9–54.

Dahl, Nils Alstrup (1976). *Jesus in the Memory of the Early Church: Essays*. Minneapolis: Augsburg.

Davidson, Ivor (2000). "Ambrose." In Esler 2000:1175–1204.

Davies, W. D., and D. Daube, eds. (1956). *The Background of the New Testament and Its Eschatology*. Cambridge: Cambridge Univ. Press.

Davis, Stephen T., ed. (1989a). *Death and Afterlife*. London: Macmillan.

——— (1989b). "Introduction." In Davis 1989a:viii–xi.

——— (1989c). "The Resurrection of the Dead." In Davis 1989a:119–44.

——— (1993). *Risen Indeed: Making Sense of the Resurrection*. Grand Rapids, Mich.: Eerdmans.

Derrida, Jacques (1970). "Structure, Sign and Play in the Discourse of the Human Sciences." In Macksey and Donato 1970:247–65. Also in Derrida 1978.

——— (1976). *Of Grammatology*. Baltimore: Johns Hopkins Univ. Press.

——— (1978). *Writing and Difference*. Chicago: Univ. of Chicago Press.

——— (1981). *Positions*. London: Athlone.

——— (1983). *Dissemination*. Chicago: Univ. of Chicago Press.

Dienstbier, Richard A., ed. (1990). *Cross–Cultural Perspectives*. Lincoln: Univ. of Nebraska Press.

Dilthey, Wilhelm (1976). "The Development of Hermeneutics." In Rickman 1976:247–63.

Dimant, Devorah (1990). "Use and Interpretation of Mikra in the Apocrypha and Pseudepigrapha." In Mulder 1990:370–419.

Donnelly, John, ed. (1978). *Language, Metaphysics, and Death*. New York: Fordham Univ. Press.

Donner, Herbert, ed. (1977). *Beiträge zur Alttestamentlichen Theologie. Festschrift für Walther Zimmerli zum 70. Geburtstag*. Göttingen: Vandenhoeck & Ruprecht.

Doty, William G. (1973). *Letters in Primitive Christianity*. Philadelphia: Fortress Press.

Durkheim, Émile (1915). *The Elementary Forms of the Religious Life*. London: Allen & Unwin.

Eagleton, Terry (1983). *Literary Theory: An Introduction*. Oxford: Basil Blackwell.

Ebeling, Gerhard (1963). "The Meaning of 'Biblical Theology.'" In idem, *Word and Faith*. London: SCM, 79–97.

Edwards, Paul, ed. (1967). *The Encyclopedia of Philosophy* New York : Macmillan.

Eisenbaum, Pamela Michelle (1997a). "Heroes and History in Hebrews 11." In Evans and Sanders 1997:380–96.

——— (1997b). *The Jewish Heroes of Christian History: Hebrews 11 in Literary Context*. SBLDS 156. Atlanta: Scholars.

Elliott, John H. (2000). *1 Peter: A New Translation with Introduction and Commentary*. The Anchor Bible, 37B. New York: Doubleday.

Esler, Philip F. (1987). *Community and Gospel in Luke-Acts: The Social and Political Motivations of Lucan Theology*. SNTSMS 57. Cambridge: Cambridge Univ. Press.

——— (1994). *The First Christians in Their Social Worlds: Social-Scientific Approaches to New Testament Interpretation*. London: Routledge.

——— (1998a). "Community and Gospel in Early Christianity: A Response to Richard Bauckham's *Gospels for All Christians*." *SJT* 51:235–48.

——— (1998b). *Galatians*. New Testament Readings. London: Routledge.

———, ed. (2000). *The Early Christian World*. 2 volumes. London: Routledge.

——— (2001a). "Biblical Interpretation and the Communion of Saints: A Socio-Theological Rationale for Historical Criticism." The Manson Memorial Lecture at the Univ. of Manchester, 25 October 2001.

——— (2001b). "1 Thessalonians." In Barton and Muddiman 2001:1199–212.

——— (2003a). *Conflict and Identity in Romans: The Social Setting of Paul's Letter*. Minneapolis: Fortress Press.

——— (2003b). "Ezra-Nehemiah as a Narrative of (Re-Invented) Israelite Identity." *BibInt* 11:413–26.

——— (2003c). "Social Identity, Ethics and the Good Life: A New Approach to Romans12:1—15:13." *BTB* 33:51–63.

——— ed. (2005a). *Ancient Israel: The Old Testament in Its Social Context*. Minneapolis: Fortress Press.

——— (2005b). "Orality, Collective Memory and Hebrews 11: Outlining a New Investigative Framework." *Semeia* 151–71.

——— (2005c). "The Use of Social-Scientific Models in Biblical Interpretation and Contents Outline." In Esler (2005a).

Evans, Craig A., and James A. Sanders, eds. (1997). *Early Christian Interpretation of the Scriptures of Israel: Investigations and Proposals*. JSNTSup 146. Sheffield: Sheffield Academic.

Evans, Richard J. (1997). *In Defence of History*. London: Granta.

Fee, Gordon D. (1987). *The First Epistle to the Corinthians*. Grand Rapids, Mich.: Eerdmans.

Fentress, James, and Chris Wickham (1992). *Social Memory*. New Perspectives on the Past. Oxford: Blackwell.

Ferrua, Antonio, S. J. (1991). "Rileggendo i grafitti di S. Sebastiano." In idem, *Scritti Vari de Epigrafia e Antichità Cristiane*. Bari: Edipuglia, 297–314.

Ferrua, Antonio, S. J., and Iovanni Baptista de Rossi, eds. (1971). *Inscriptiones Christianae Urbis Romae Septimio Saeculo Antiquores*. Nova Series.Volume 5: *Coemeteria Reliqua Viae Appiae*. Vatican City: Pontificio Istituto di Archeologia Cristiana.

Fiorenza, Elisabeth Schüssler (1983). *In Memory of Her: A Feminist Theological Reconstruction*. New York: Crossroad.

Fish, Stanley (1980). *Is There a Text in This Class? The Authority of Interpretive Communities*. Cambridge: Harvard Univ. Press.

Fiske, John (1990). *Introduction to Communication Studies.* London: Routledge.

Flew, Antony (1967). "Immortality." In Edwards 1967.

—— (1987). *The Logic of Mortality.* Oxford: Basil Blackwell.

Foerster, Werner (1966a). "C. The Word Group κληρονόμος in the LXX." *TDNT* 3:776–79.

—— (1966b). "E. The Word Group (sc. κληρονόμος) in the New Testament." *TDNT* 3:781–85.

Forbes, Christopher (1997). *Prophecy and Inspired Speech in Early Christianity and Its Hellenistic Environment.* Peabody, Mass.: Hendrickson.

Frank, Georgia (2000). *The Memory of the Eyes: Pilgrims to Living Saints in Christian Late Antiquity.* Berkeley: Univ. of California Press.

Freadman, Richard, and Seumas Miller (1992). *Re-Thinking Theory: A Critique of Contemporary Literary Theory and an Alternative Account.* Cambridge: Cambridge Univ. Press.

Friedländer, Saul, ed. (1992). *Probing the Limits of Postmodernism: Nazism and the "Final Solution."* Cambridge: Harvard Univ. Press.

Friedman, Maurice (1976). *Martin Buber: The Life of Dialogue.* Chicago: Univ. of Chicago Press.

—— (1986). Foreword to Arnett 1986:vii–xix.

Funk, Robert W. (1967) "The Apostolic *Parousia*: Form and Significance." In W. R. Farmer, C. F. D. Moule, and R. R. Niebuhr, eds., *Christian History and Interpretation: Studies Presented to John Knox.* Cambridge: Cambridge Univ. Press, 249–68.

Gabler, Johan Philipp (1787). *De justo discrimine theologiae biblicae et dogmaticae regundisque recte utriusque finibus* (On the Proper Distinction between Biblical Theology and Dogmatic Theology and the Specific Objectives of Each). Translated by John Sandys-Wunsch and Laurence Eldredge. In Sandys-Wunsch and Eldredge 1980:134–44.

Gadamer, Hans-Georg (1979). *Truth and Method.* Second edition. Translation of the second edition (1965) of *Wahrheit und Methode* by William Glen-Doepel. London: Sheed and Ward.

Gamble, Harry M. (1985). *The New Testament Canon: Its Making and Meaning.* Guides to Biblical Scholarship. Philadelphia: Fortress.

—— (1992). "Canon: New Testament" *ABD* 1:952–61.

—— (1995). *Books and Readers in the Early Church: A History of Early Christian Texts.* New Haven and London: Yale Univ. Press.

Ganssle, Gregory E. (2002). "Introduction." In Ganssle and Woodruff 2002:3–18.

Ganssle, Gregory E., and David M. Woodruff, eds. (2002). *God and Time: Essays on the Divine Nature.* Oxford: Oxford Univ. Press.

Gnilka, Joachim (1989). *Neutestamentliche Theologie: Ein Überlick.* Würzburg: Echter.

—— (1994). *Theologie des Neuen Testaments.* Freiburg im Breisgau: Herder.

Goldstein, Leon J. (1976). *Historical Knowing.* Austin: Univ. of Texas Press.

Gooch, Peter D. (1993). *Dangerous Food: 1 Corinthians 8–10 in Its Context.* Studies in Judaism and Christianity 5. Waterloo, Ont.: Wilfred Laurier Univ. Press.

Graby, James K. (1968). "Reflections on the History of the Interpretation of Schleiermacher." *SJT* 21:283–99.

Graham, William A. (1987). *Beyond the Written Word: Oral Aspects of Scripture and the History of Religion.* Cambridge: Cambridge Univ. Press.

Grant, Robert M., with David Tracy (1984). *A Short History of the Interpretation of the Bible.* London: SCM; Minneapolis: Fortress Press.

Green, Joel B. (1995). *The Theology of the Gospel of Luke.* New Testament Theology. Cambridge: Cambridge Univ. Press.

——— (1997). *The Gospel of Luke.* Grand Rapids, Mich.: Eerdmans.

——— (1998). "Bodies—That Is, Human Lives: A Re-examination of Human Nature in the Bible." In Brown, Murphy, and Malony 1998:149–73.

——— (2000). "Scripture and Theology: Uniting the Two So Long Divided." In Green and Turner 2000a:23–43.

Green, Joel B., and Max Turner (2000a). *Between Two Horizons: Spanning New Testament Studies and Systematic Theology.* Grand Rapids, Mich.: Eerdmans.

——— (2000b). "New Testament Commentary and Systematic Theology: Strangers or Friends?" In Green and Turner 2000a:1–22.

Grenz, Stanley J. (2001). *The Social God and the Relational Self: A Trinitarian Theology of the Imago Dei.* Louisville: Westminster John Knox.

Greshake, G. (1969). *Auferstehung der Toten: ein Beitrag zur gegenwärtigen theologischen Diskussion über die Zukunft der Geschichte.* Essen: Ludgerus-Verlag.

Guarducci, Margherita (1984). *Pietro in Vaticano.* Rome: Libreria dello Stato.

Gudykunst, William B., and Young Yun Kim (2003). *Communicating with Strangers: An Approach to Intercultural Communication.* Fourth edition. Boston: McGraw-Hill.

Gurevich, Aaron (1995). *The Origins of European Individualism.* Translated from the Russian by Katharine Judelson. Oxford: Blackwell.

Gurr, Ted Robert (1993). *Minorities at Risk: A Global View of Ethnopolitical Conflicts.* Washington, D.C.: United States Institute of Peace Press.

Halbwachs, Maurice (1950). *La mémoire collective.* Paris: Presses Universitaires de France.

——— (1972). *Classes sociales et morphologie.* Paris: Éditions de Minuit.

——— (1980). *The Collective Memory.* Partial English translation of the 1950 French original *La mémoire collective* by Francis J. Ditter Jr. and Vida Yazdi Ditter, with an introduction by Mary Douglas. New York: Harper Colophon Books.

——— (1992). *On Collective Memory.* Edited, translated with an introduction by Lewis A. Coser. The Heritage of Sociology. Chicago: Univ. of Chicago Press. (A translation of large parts of *Les cadres sociaux de la mémoire* [1925] and the concluding chapter of *La topographie légendaire des évangiles en terre saint. Étude de mémoire collective* [1941]).

Haldane, J. J. (2003). *An Intelligent Person's Guide to Religion.* London: Duckworth.

Hamacher, Werner, Neil Hertz, and Thomas Keenan (1988). *Wartime Journalism, 1939—1943, by Paul de Man.* Lincoln: Univ. of Nebraska Press.

———— (1989). *Responses: On Paul de Man's Wartime Journalism.* Lincoln: Univ. of Nebraska Press.

Harris, Murray (1983). *Raised Immortal.* Grand Rapids, Mich.: Eerdmans.

Harris, William V. (1989). *Ancient Literacy.* Cambridge: Harvard Univ. Press.

Hasker, William (1995). "Concerning the Unity of Consciousness." *Faith and Philosophy* 12: 532–47.

———— (1999). *The Emergent Self.* Ithaca, N.Y.: Cornell Univ. Press.

Hastie, W. (1890). *(Friedrich Schleiermacher's?) Christmas Eve: A Dialogue on the Celebration of Christmas.* Edinburgh.

Hays, Richard (1989). *Echoes of Scripture in the Letters of Paul.* New Haven: Yale Univ. Press.

Helm, Paul (1978). "A Theory of Disembodied Survival and Re-embodied Existence." *Religious Studies* 14:15–26.

Hengel, Martin (1985). *Studies in the Gospel of Mark.* London: SCM.

———— (2000). *The Four Gospels and the One Gospel of Jesus Christ.* London: SCM.

Hens-Piazza, Gina (2002). *The New Historicism.* Guides to Biblical Scholarship. Minneapolis: Fortress Press.

Hezser, Catherine (2001). *Jewish Literacy in Roman Palestine.* Tübingen: Mohr/Siebeck.

Hick, John H. (1976). *Death and Eternal Life.* San Francisco: Harper & Row.

Hill, Charles (1992). *Regnum Caelorum: Patterns of Future Hope in Early Christianity.* Oxford: Clarendon.

Hirsch, E. D. (1967). *Validity in Interpretation.* New Haven: Yale Univ. Press.

———— (1976). *The Aims of Interpretation.* Chicago: Univ. of Chicago Press.

———— (1984). "Meaning and Significance Reinterpreted." *Critical Inquiry* 11:202–24.

———— (1994). "Transhistorical Intentions and the Persistence of Allegory." *New Literary History* 25:549–67.

Hodgson, Peter C. (1994). "Editor's Introduction: Strauss's Theological Development from 1825 to 1840." In Strauss 1994:xv–l.

Hofstede, Geert (1980). *Culture's Consequences: International Differences in Work-Related Values.* Beverly Hills, Calif.: Sage.

———— (1991). *Cultures and Organizations: Software of the Mind.* London: McGraw-Hill.

Hogg, Michael A., and Dominic Abrams (1988). *Social Identifications: A Social Psychology of Intergroup Relations.* London: Routledge.

Horden, Peregrine, and Nicholas Purcell (2000). *The Corrupting Sea: A Study of Mediterranean History.* Oxford: Blackwell.

Hsu, Francis L. K. (1971). *Under the Ancestors' Shadow: Kinship, Personality and Social Mobility in China.* Revised edition. Stanford, Calif.: Stanford Univ. Press.

Hübner, Hans (1990–95). *Biblische Theologie des Neuen Testaments.* Three volumes. Göttingen: Vandenhoeck & Ruprecht.

Ingold, Tim, ed. (1994). *Companion Encyclopedia of Anthropology*. London: Routledge.

Inwagen, Peter van (1988). "The Possibility of Resurrection." *International Journal for Philosophy of Religion* 9:114–21.

——— (1990). *Material Beings*. Ithaca, N.Y.: Cornell Univ. Press.

Isaac, E. (1983). "1 (Ethiopic Apocalypse of) Enoch." *OTP* 1:5–89.

Iser, Wolfgang (1974). *The Implied Reader: Patterns of Communication in Prose Fiction from Bunyan to Beckett*. Baltimore: Johns Hopkins Univ. Press.

Jasper, David, ed. (1986). *The Interpretation of Belief: Coleridge, Schleiermacher and Romanticism*. London: Macmillan.

Jeanrond, Werner (1986). "The Impact of Schleiermacher's Hermeneutics on Contemporary Interpretation Theory." In Jasper 1986:81–96.

——— (1990). "Hermeneutical Circle." In Coggins and Houlden 1990:281–82.

——— (1994). *Theological Hermeneutics: Development and Significance*. London: SCM.

——— (1995). *Call and Response: The Challenge of Christian Life*. New York: Continuum.

Jenkins, Keith (1991). *Re-thinking History*. London: Routledge.

Jeremias, Joachim (1971). *New Testament Theology*. Volume 1: *The Proclamation of Jesus*. Translated by John Bowden. London: SCM.

Johnson, Aubrey R. (1961). *The One and the Many in the Israelite Conception of God*. Second edition. Cardiff: Univ. of Wales Press.

Johnson, Elizabeth A. (1998). *Friends of God and Prophets: A Feminist Theological Reading of the Communion of Saints*. London: SCM.

Johnson, Luke Timothy (1998). *Religious Experience in Earliest Christianity: A Missing Dimension in New Testament Studies*. Minneapolis: Fortress Press.

Jonker, Gerdien (1995). *The Topography of Remembrance: The Dead, Tradition and Collective Memory in Mesopotamia*. SHR 68. Leiden: Brill.

Kâgitçibasi, Çigdem (1994). "A Critical Appraisal of Individualism and Collectivism: Toward a New Formalism." In Kim et al. 1994:52–65.

Kâgitçibasi, Çigdem, and J. W. Berry (1989). "Cross-Cultural Psychology: Current Research and Trends." *Annual Review of Psychology* 40:493–531.

Kähler, Martin (1964). *The So-called Historical Jesus and the Historic, Biblical Christ*. Foreword by Paul Tillich. Translated, edited, and with an introduction by Carl E. Braaten. Philadelphia: Fortress Press.

Keck, Lelander E. (1977). "Editor's Introduction." In Strauss 1977:xv–cvi.

Keenan, J. L., ed. (1975). *Formal Semantics of Natural Language*. Cambridge: Cambridge Univ. Press.

Kelber, Werner H. (1983). *The Oral and the Written Gospel: The Hermeneutics of Speaking and Writing in the Synoptic Tradition, Mark, Paul, and Q*. Philadelphia: Fortress Press.

——— (1987). "Narrative as Interpretation and Interpretation as Narrative: Hermeneutical Reflections on the Gospels." In Lou H. Silberman, ed., *Orality, Aurality and Biblical Narrative*. Semeia 39. Decatur, Ga.: Scholars, 107–133.

——— (1994). "Jesus and Tradition: Words in Time, Words in Space." In Joanna Dewey, ed., *Orality and Textuality in Early Christian Literature. Semeia* 65. Atlanta: Scholars.

Kelly, J. N. D. (1972). *Early Christian Creeds.* Third edition. London: Longman.

Kelsey, David H. (1975). *The Uses of Scripture in Recent Theology.* Philadelphia: Fortress Press.

Kim, Jaegwon (1994). "The Myth of Non-Reductive Materialism." In Warner and Szubka 1994:22–310.

——— (1998). "The Mind-Body Problem after Fifty Years." In O'Hear 1998:3–21.

Kim, Uichol, et al., eds. (1994). *Individualism and Collectivism: Theory, Method, and Applications.* Cross-Cultural Research and Methodology Series 18. Thousand Oaks, Calif.: Sage.

Kirk, G. S., and J. E. Raven (1971). *The Presocratic Philosophers: A Critical History with a Selection of Texts.* Cambridge: Cambridge Univ. Press.

Koester, Craig R. (2001). *Hebrews: A New Translation with Introduction and Commentary.* Anchor Bible 36. New York: Doubleday.

Krober, A. L., and Clyde Kluckhohn (1952). *Culture: A Critical Review of Concepts and Definitions.* Cambridge: Peabody Museum.

Kümmel, W. G. (1978). *The New Testament: The History of Interpretation of Its Problems.* London: SCM.

Kuper, Adam, and Jessica Kuper, eds. (1985). *The Social Science Encyclopedia.* London: Routledge.

LaCapra, Dominick (1983). *Re-thinking Intellectual History.* Ithaca: Cornell Univ. Press.

LaCugna, Catherine Mowry (1992). *God for Us: The Trinity and Christian Life.* New York: HarperSanFrancisco.

Lampe, G. W. H. (1955). "The Early Church." In F. W. Dillistone, ed., *Scripture and Tradition.* London: Lutterworth, 24–52.

Larson, E. J., and L. Witham (1997). "Scientists Are Still Keeping the Faith," *Nature* 386:435–36.

Lawrence, Louise Joy (2003). *An Ethnography of the Gospel of Matthew: A Critical Assessment of the Use of the Honour and Shame Model in New Testament Studies.* Tübingen: Mohr/ Siebeck.

Lehman, David (1991). *Signs of the Times: Deconstruction and the Fall of Paul de Man.* London: Deutsch.

Lenski, Gerhard, and Jean Lenski (1987). *Human Societies: An Introduction to Macrosociology.* Fifth edition. New York: McGraw-Hill.

Lessing, Gottholt (1957). *Lessing's Theological Writings.* Selections in translation with an introductory essay by Henry Chadwick. A Library of Modern Religious Thought. Stanford, Calif.: Stanford Univ. Press.

Lewis, Alan (1987). "The Burial of God: Rupture and Resumption as the Story of Salvation." *SJT* 40:335–62.

Lewis, C. S. (1958). *Reflections on the Psalms.* London: Geoffrey Bles.

Lipstadt, Deborah E. (1993). *Denying the Holocaust: The Growing Assault on Truth and Memory.* New York: Free Press; Toronto: Maxwell Macmillan.

Locke, John (1987 [1705]). *A Paraphrase and Notes on the Epistles of St. Paul: To the Galatians, 1 and 2 Corinthians, Romans, Ephesians.* Edited by Arthur W. Wainwright. Oxford: Clarendon.

Longenecker, Richard N., ed. (1998). *Life in the Face of Death: The Resurrection Message of the New Testament.* Grand Rapids, Mich.: Eerdmans.

Lundin, Roger (1999). "Interpreting Orphans: Hermeneutics in the Cartesian Tradition." In Lundin, Walhout, and Thiselton 1999:1–64.

Lundin, Roger, Clarence Walhout, and Anthony C. Thiselton (1999). *The Promise of Hermeneutics.* Grand Rapids, Mich.: Eerdmans.

Macksey, Richard, and Eugene Donato, eds. (1970). *The Languages of Criticism and the Sciences of Man.* Baltimore: Johns Hopkins Univ. Press.

Macmurray, John (1957). *The Form of the Personal.* Volume 1: *The Self as Agent; Being the Gifford Lectures Delivered in the University of Glasgow in 1953.* London: Faber.

———— (1961). *The Form of the Personal.* Volume 2: *Persons in Relation; Being the Gifford Lectures Delivered in the University of Glasgow in 1954.* London: Faber.

Macquarrie, John (1984). Foreword to Grace Jantzen (1984), *God's World, God's Body.* Philadelphia: Westminster, ix–x.

Malina, Bruce J. (1993). *Windows on the World of Jesus: Time Travel to Ancient Judea.* Louisville: Westminster John Knox.

———— (2001). *The New Testament World: Insights from Cultural Anthropology.* Third edition. Louisville: Westminster John Knox.

Marcus, George E., and Michael M. J. Fischer (1986). *Anthropology as Social Critique: An Experimental Moment in the Human Sciences.* Chicago: Univ. of Chicago Press.

Markus, Hazel, and Paula Nurius (1986). "Possible Selves." *American Psychologist* 41:954–69.

Marxsen, Willi (1969). *Mark the Evangelist: Studies on the Redaction History of the Gospel.* Nashville: Abingdon.

McDermott, Timothy (1989). *St. Thomas Aquinas, Summa Theologiae: A Concise Translation.* London: Methuen.

McDonald, Lee M. (1995). *The Formation of the Christian Biblical Canon.* Revised edition. Peabody, Mass.: Hendrickson.

McLuhan, Marshall (1962). *The Gutenberg Galaxy: The Making of Typographic Man.* Toronto: Univ. of Toronto Press.

Meade, D. G. (1986). *Pseudonymity and Canon: An Investigation into the Relationship of Authorship and Authority in Jewish and Early Christian Tradition.* WUNT 39. Tübingen: Mohr.

Meiland, Jack W. (1965). *Scepticism and Historical Knowledge.* Random House Studies in Philosophy. New York: Random House.

Metz, Johann Baptist (1980). *Faith in History and Society.* Translated by David Smith. New York: Seabury.

Metzger, Bruce M. (1987). *The Canon of the New Testament: Its Origin, Development, and Significance.* Oxford: Clarendon.

Middleton, David, and Derek Edwards, eds. (1990a). *Collective Remembering.* London: Sage.

———— (1990b). "Introduction." In Middleton and Edwards 1990a:1–22.

Mills, J., and M. S. Clark (1982). "Exchange and Communal Relationships." In L. Wheeler, ed., *Review of Personality and Social Psychology,* Volume 3. Beverly Hills, Calif.: Sage.

Misra, Bhabagrahi, and James Preston, eds. (1978). *Community, Self and Identity.* World Anthropology. The Hague: Mouton.

Mitchell, Margaret M. (1992). *Paul and the Rhetoric of Reconciliation: An Exegetical Investigation of the Language and Composition of 1 Corinthians.* Louisville: Westminster John Knox.

———— (2003). "Patristic Counter-Evidence to the Claim That 'The Gospels Were Written for All Christians.'" Paper delivered at the Society of Biblical Literature Annual Meeting in Atlanta, November 2003. This essay appears in *NTS,* Volume 51 (2005), in a version that came too late for this volume.

Molina, D. Newton-De, ed. (1976). *On Literary Intention.* Edinburgh: Edinburgh Univ. Press.

Moreland, J. P., and Scott Rae (2000). *Body and Soul: Human Nature and the Crisis in Ethics.* Downers Grove, Ill.: InterVarsity.

Morgan, Robert (1973). *The Nature of New Testament Theology: The Contribution of William Wrede and Adolf Schlatter.* SBT. Second Series 25. London: SCM.

———— (1976–77). "A Straussian Question to 'New Testament Theology.'" *NTS* 23:243–65.

———— (1986–87). "Gabler's Bicentenary." *ExpT* 98:164–8.

———— (1987). "The Historical Jesus and the Theology of the New Testament." In L. D. Hurst and N. T. Wright, eds., *The Glory of Christ in the New Testament: Studies in Christology in Memory of G. B. Caird.* Oxford: Clarendon, 187–206.

———— (1990). "Strauss, D. F." In Coggins and Houlden 1990:650.

———— (1996). "Can the Critical Study of Scripture Provide a Doctrinal Norm?" *JR* 76:206–32.

———— (2002). "The Letters of Paul in the Context of a New Testament Theology." In J. Capel Anderson, ed., *Pauline Conversations in Context: Essays in Honor of Calvin Roetzel.* Sheffield: Sheffield Academic, 240–61.

Morgan, Robert, with John Barton (1988). *Biblical Interpretation.* Oxford: Oxford Univ. Press.

Morrill, Bruce T. (2000). *Anamnesis as Dangerous Memory: Political and Liturgical Theology in Dialogue.* Collegeville, Minn.: Liturgical.

Moxnes, Halvor (1980). *Theology in Conflict: Studies in Paul's Understanding of God.* NovTSup 53. Leiden: Brill.

Mulder, Martin Jay, ed. (1990). *Mikra: Text, Translation, Reading and Interpretation of the Hebrew Bible in Ancient Judaism and Early Christianity.* CRINT 2.1. Assen: Van Gorcum; Minneapolis: Fortress Press.

Mulert, Hermann, ed. (1908). *Schleiermacher's Weihnachtsfeier.* Philosophische Bibliothek, Volume 117. Leipzig: Dürr'schen Buchhandlung.

Munck, J. (1959). *Paul and the Salvation of Mankind.* Translated by F. Clarke. Richmond: John Knox.

Murphy, Nancey (1998a). "Human Nature: Historical, Scientific, and Religious Issues." In Brown, Murphy, and Malony 1998:1–29.

——— (1998b). "Nonreductive Physicalism." In Brown, Murphy, and Malony 1998:127–48.

Newsom, Carol A. (1996). "Bakhtin, the Bible, and Dialogic Truth." *JR* 76:290–306.

Newton, Derek (1998). *Deity and Diet: The Dilemma of Sacrificial Food at Corinth.* JSNT Supp. Series, 169. Sheffield: Sheffield Academic.

Neyrey, Jerome H., ed. (1991). *The Social World of Luke-Acts: Models for Interpretation.* Peabody, Mass.: Hendrickson.

——— (2004). *Render to God: New Testament Understandings of the Divine.* Minneapolis: Fortress Press.

Niebuhr, Richard R. (1965). *Schleiermacher on Christ and Religion.* London: SCM.

Noble, Paul R. (1995). *The Canonical Approach: A Critical Reconstruction of the Hermeneutics of Brevard S. Childs.* Leiden: Brill.

Oberg, K. (1960). "Culture Shock: Adjustment to New Cultural Environments." *Practical Anthropology* 7:177–82.

Odebrecht, Rudolf, ed. (1942). *Friedrich Schleiermachers Dialektik.* Leipzig: J. C. Hinrichs.

Ohmann, Richard (1971). "Speech Acts and the Definition of Literature." *Philosophy and Rhetoric* 4:1–19.

Olding, Alan (1970). "Resurrection Worlds and Bodies." *Mind* 79:581–85.

Ollenburger, Ben C. (1986). "What Krister Stendahl 'Meant'—a Normative Critique of 'Descriptive Biblical Theology.'" *HBT* 8:61–98.

Ong, Walter J. (1971). *Rhetoric, Romance, and Technology.* Ithaca, N.Y.: Cornell Univ. Press.

Palmer, Richard E. (1969). *Hermeneutics: Interpretation Theory in Schleiermacher, Dilthey, Heidegger, and Gadamer.* Studies in Phenomenology and Existential Philosophy. Evanston, Ill.: Northwestern Univ. Press.

Pannenberg, Wolfhart (1985). *Anthropology in Theological Perspective.* Translated by Matthew J. O'Connell. Edinburgh: T. & T. Clark.

Parratt, John, ed. (1987). *A Reader in African Christian Theology.* London: SPCK.

Passerini, Luisa (1988). *Storia e soggettività: La fonti orali, la memoria.* Florence: La Nuova Italia.

Peel, J. D. Y. (1985). "Comte, Auguste (1798–1857)." In Kuper and Kuper 1985:144–45.

Penelhum, Terence (1970). *Survival and Disembodied Existence.* New York: Humanities.

Pennebaker, James W., Dario Paez, and Bernard Rimé, eds. (1997). *Collective Memory of Political Events: Social Psychological Perspectives.* Mahwah, N.J.: Lawrence Erlbaum.

Perham, Michael (1980). *The Communion of Saints: An Examination of the Place of the Christian Dead in the Belief, Worship, and Calendars of the Church.* London: Alcuin Clubs/SPCK.

Peterson, David (1982). *Hebrews and Perfection: An Examination of the Concept of Perfection in the Epistle to the Hebrews.* SNTSMS 47. Cambridge: Cambridge Univ. Press.

Petersen, William L. (1994). *Tatian's Diatessaron: Its Creation, Dissemination, Significance, and History in Scholarship.* Leiden: Brill.

Pfitzner, V. C. (1967). *Paul and the Agon Motif: Traditional Athletic Imagery in the Pauline Literature.* NovTSup 16. Leiden: Brill.

Phillips, D. Z. (1970). *Death and Immortality.* New York: St. Martin's.

Pieper, Josef (1968). *Tod und Unsterblichkeit.* Munich: Kösel.

Pilch, John J., ed. (2001). *Social Science Models for Interpreting the Bible: Essays by the Context Group in Honor of Bruce J. Malina.* Leiden: Brill.

Plantinga, Alvin (1999). "On Heresy, Mind, and Truth." *Faith and Philosophy* 16:182–93.

Plevnik, Joseph (1984). "The Taking Up of the Faithful and the Resurrection of the Dead in 1 Thessalonians 4:13-18." *Catholic Biblical Quarterly* 46:274–83.

Ploeg, J. van der (1947). "L'exégèse de l'Ancien Testament dans L'Épître aux Hébreux." *RB* 54:187–228.

Polkinghorne, John (1986). *One World: The Interaction of Science and Theology.* London: SPCK.

Porsch, Felix (1982). *Viele Stimmen - ein Glaube: Anfänge, Entfaltung und Grundzüge neutestamentlicher Theologie.* Kevelaer and Stuttgart: Butzon und Bercker and Verlag Katholisches Bibelwerk.

Pratt, Mary Louise (1977). *Toward a Speech Act Theory of Literary Discourse.* Bloomington: Univ. of Indiana Press.

Price, H. H. (1953). "Survival and the Idea of 'Another World.'" *Proceedings of the Society for Psychical Research* 50:1–25. Republished in Donnelly 1978:176–95.

Purtill, Richard L. (1975). "The Intelligibility of Disembodied Survival." *Christian Scholar's Review* 5:3–22.

Rahner, Karl (1970). *The Trinity.* London: Burns and Oates.

——— (1971). "Why and How Can We Venerate the Saints?" In idem, *Theological Investigations,* Volume 8, *Further Theology of the Spiritual Life 2,* translated by David Bourke. London: Darton, Longman and Todd and Herder and Herder, 3–23.

——— (1973). "Tod." In Karl Rahner, ed., *Herders Theologisches Taschenlexicon.* Freiburg: Herder, 7:279–84.

Räisänen, Heikki (1990a). *Beyond New Testament Theology: A Story and a Programme.* London: SCM; Philadelphia: Trinity Press International.

——— (1990b). *The "Messianic Secret" in Mark's Gospel.* Studies of the New Testament and Its World. Edinburgh: T. & T. Clark.

Ratzinger, Joseph (1988). *Eschatology: Death and Eternal Life.* Translated by M. Waldstein and edited by A. Nichols. Washington, D.C.: Catholic Univ. Press of America.

Redeker, Martin (1973). *Schleiermacher: Life and Thought.* Translated by John Wallhauser from the 1968 German original. Philadelphia: Fortress Press.

Rhoads, David, and Donald Michie (1982). *Mark as Story: An Introduction to the Narrative of a Gospel.* Phildadelphia: Fortress Press.

Rickman, H. P., ed. (1976). *W. Dilthey: Selected Writings.* Edited, translated, and introduced by H. P. Rickman. Cambridge: Cambridge Univ. Press.

Ricoeur, Paul (1970). *Freud and Philosophy: An Essay on Interpretation.* Translated by Denis Savage. New Haven: Yale Univ. Press.

—— (1974). *The Conflict of Interpretations: Essays in Hermeneutics.* Edited by Don Ihde. Evanston, Ill.: Northwestern Univ. Press.

—— (1976). *Interpretation Theory: Discourse and the Surplus of Meaning.* Fort Worth: Texas Christian Univ. Press.

—— (1981). *Hermeneutics and the Human Sciences: Essays on Language.* Edited and translated by John B. Thompson. Cambridge: Cambridge Univ. Press.

—— (1988). *Time and Narrative.* Volume 3. Translated by Kathleen McLaughlin and David Pellauer. Chicago: Chicago Univ. Press.

Robbins, Vernon (1992 [1984]). *Jesus the Teacher: A Socio-Rhetorical Interpretation of Mark.* Minneapolis: Fortress Press.

—— (1996). *The Tapestry of Early Christian Discourse: Rhetoric, Society, and Ideology.* London: Routledge.

Robinson, H. Wheeler (1981 [1936]). *The Hebrew Conception of Corporate Personality.* Edinburgh: T. & T. Clark.

Robinson, James M., and John B. Cobb Jr., eds. (1964). *The New Hermeneutic.* New York: Harper & Row.

Robinson, Peter, ed. (1996). *Social Groups and Identities: Developing the Legacy of Henri Tajfel.* Oxford: Butterworth Heinemann.

Rohrbaugh, Richard L., ed. (1996). *The Social Sciences and New Testament Interpretation.* Peabody, Mass.: Hendrickson.

—— (2001). "Gossip in the New Testament." In Pilch 2001:239–59.

Rorty, Richard (1982). "Is There a Problem about Fictional Discourse?." In idem, *Consequences of Pragmatism: Essays, 1972–1980.* Brighton, UK: Harvester, 110–38.

—— (1985). "Texts and Lumps." *New Literary History* 17:1–16.

Rosenzweig, Franz (1971). *The Star of Redemption.* Translation by William W. Hallo from the second edition. London: Routledge & Kegan Paul. (The original German edition of *Stern der Erlösung* appeared in 1921.)

—— (1994). "Scripture and Word: On the New Bible Translation." In Buber and Rosenzweig 1994:40–46.

Ryle, Gilbert (1990 [1949]). *The Concept of Mind.* Harmondsworth, UK: Penguin.

Sandys-Wunsch, John, and Laurence Eldredge (1980). "J. P. Gabler and the Distinction between Biblical and Dogmatic Theology: Translation, Commentary, and Discussion of His Originality." *SJT* 33:133–58.

Saussure, Ferdinand de (1971 [1916]). *Cours de linguistique général.* Paris: Payot.

Sawyer, Harry (1987). "What Is African Theology?" In Parratt 1987:12–28.

Schlatter, Adolf (1973 [1909]). "The Theology of the New Testament and Dogmatics." In Morgan 1973:117–66. This is the first English translation to be published of *Die Theologie des Neuen Testaments und die Dogmatik* (Gütersloh: C. Bertelsmann, 1909).

Schleiermacher, Friedrich D. E. (1836). *Schleiermacher's Introductions to the Dialogues of Plato.* Translated by William Dobson. Cambridg: J. and J. J. Deighton; London: John William Parker.

———(1838). *Sämmtliche Werke.* Part 1. Volume 7: *Hermeneutik und Kritik mit besonderer Beziehung auf das Neue Testament.* Edited by Friedrich Lücke. Berlin: G. Reimer.

———(1890). *Christmas Eve: A Dialogue on the Celebration of Christmas.* Translated by W. Hastie. Edinburgh: T. & T. Clark.

———(1958 [1799]). *On Religion: Speeches to Its Cultured Despisers.* Translated by John Oman, with an introduction by Rudolf Otto. New York: Harper Torchbooks.

———(1959). *Hermeneutik, nach den Handschriften neu herausgegeben und eingeleitet von Heinz Kimmerle.* Heidelberg: Carl Winter.

———(1970). *Brief Outline on the Study of Theology.* Translation of *Kurze Darstellung des theologischen Studiums zum Behuf einleitender Vorlesungen* (Berlin, 1830) with introduction and notes by Terrence N. Rice. Richmond, Va.: John Knox.

———(1977a). *Hermeneutics: The Handwritten Manuscripts.* Edited by Heinz Kimmerle and translated by James Duke and Jack Forstman. American Academy of Religion Texts and Translation Series 1. Missoula, Mont.: Scholars Press.

———(1977b). *Hermeneutik und Kritik: Mit einem Anhang sprachphilosophischer Texte Schleiermachers.* Edited by Manfred Frank. Frankfurt am Main: Suhrkamp.

Schneemelcher, W., ed. (1991). *The New Testament Apocrypha.* Volume 1. Cambridge: James Clarke & Co; Louisville:Westminster John Knox.

Schwartz, Barry (1982). "The Social Context of Commemoration: A Study in Collective Memory." *Social Forces* 61:374–402.

Searle, J. R. (1968). "Austin on Locutionary and Illocutionary Acts." *Philosophical Review* 57:405–24.

———(1969). *Speech Acts.* Cambridge: Cambridge Univ. Press.

———(1975). "Indirect Speech Acts." In Cole and Morgan 1975.

———(1979). *Expression and Meaning.* Cambridge: Cambridge Univ. Press.

———(1994). "Literary Theory and Its Discontents." *New Literary History* 25:637–67.

Sherry, Patrick (1984). *Spirit, Saints and Immortality.* London: Macmillan.

Sim, David C. (2001). "The Gospels for All Christians? A Response to Richard Bauckham." *JSNT* 24:3–27.

Smart, J. J. C., and J. J. Haldane. (2002). *Atheism and Theism.* Second edition. Great Debates in Philosophy. Malden, Mass.: Blackwell.

Smart, Ninian, et al., eds. (1985). *Nineteenth-Century Religious Thought in the West.* Volume 1. Cambridge: Cambridge Univ. Press.

Snodgrass, Klyne (2002). "Reading to Hear: A Hermeneutics of Reading." *HBT* 24:1–32.

Stanford, Michael (1998). *An Introduction to the Philosophy of History.* Oxford: Blackwell.

Staniforth, Maxwell (1968). *Early Christian Writings: The Apostolic Fathers.* Harmondsworth, UK: Penguin.

Stendahl, Krister (1962). "Biblical Theology, Contemporary." *IDB* 1:418–32.

———— (1963). "The Apostle Paul and the Introspective Conscience of the West." *HTR* 56:199–215. Reprinted in idem, *Paul among Jews and Gentiles, and other Essays.* Philadelphia: Fortress Press, 1976.

————, ed. (1965a). *Immortality and Resurrection: Four Essays by Oscar Cullmann, Harry A. Wolfson, Werner Jaeger, and Henry J. Cadbury.* New York: Macmillan.

———— (1965b). "Method in the Study of Biblical Theology." In J. P. Hyatt, ed., *The Bible in Modern Scholarship.* Nashville: Abingdon, 196–209.

Stiver, Dan R. (2001). *Theology after Ricoeur: New Directions in Hermeneutical Theology.* Louisville: Westminster John Knox.

Stock, Brian (1990). *Listening for the Text: On the Uses of the Past.* The Middle Ages Series. Philadelphia: Univ. of Pennsylvania Press.

Stone, Lawrence (1987). *The Past and the Present Revisited.* London: Routledge & Kegan Paul.

———— (1991). "History and Post-Modernism II." *Past and Present* 131:217–18.

Stowers, Stanley K. (1986). *Letter Writing in Greco-Roman Antiquity.* Library of Early Christianity. Philadelphia: Westminster.

Strauss, David Friedrich (1977). *The Christ of Faith and the Jesus of History: A Critique of Schleiermacher's* The Life of Jesus. Translated and with an introduction by Lelander E. Keck. Philadelphia: Fortress Press.

———— (1994 [1846]). *The Life of Jesus Critically Examined.* Translated by George Eliot from the fourth German edition (1840; the first edition appeared in 1835 in two volumes, the second of which bore the date 1836). Edited and with an Introduction by Peter C. Hodgson. Ramsey, N.J.: Sigler.

Strecker, Georg (1996). *Theologie des Neuen Testaments.* Edited by Friedrich W. Horn. Berlin: Walter De Gruyter.

Stuhlmacher, Peter (1997). *Biblische Theologie des Neuen Testaments.* Volume 1: *Grundlegung von Jesus zu Paulus.* Göttingen: Vandenhoeck & Ruprecht.

———— (1999). *Biblische Theologie des Neuen Testaments.* Volume 2: *Von der Paulusschule bis zur Johannesofferbarung: Der Kanon und seine Auslegung.* Göttingen: Vandenhoeck & Ruprecht.

Stuhlhofer, Franz (1988). *Der Gebrauch der Bibel von Jesus bis Euseb: eine statistische Untersuchung zur Kanongeschichte.* Wuppertal: R. Brockhaus.

Stump, Eleonore (1995). "Non-Cartesian Substance Dualism and Materialism without Reduction," *Faith and Philosophy* 12:505–31.

Swinburne, Richard (1986). *The Evolution of the Soul.* Oxford: Clarendon.

———— (1994). "Body and Soul." In Warner and Szubka 1994:311–16.

———— (1996). "Dualism Intact." *Faith and Philosophy* 13:68–77.

Sykes, Bryan (2001). *The Seven Daughters of Eve.* London: Bantam.

Tajfel, Henri, ed. (1978). *Differentiation between Social Groups: Studies in the Social Psychology of Intergroup Relations.* London: Academic.

Taliaferro, Charles (1994). *Consciousness and the Mind of God.* Cambridge: Cambridge Univ. Press.

Taylor, Charles (1989). *The Sources of the Self: The Making of Modern Identity.* Cambridge: Cambridge Univ. Press.

Theissen, Gerd (1982). "Social Integration and Sacramental Activity: An Analysis of 1 Cor. 11:17-34." In idem, *The Social Setting of Pauline Christianity.* Edinburgh: T. & T. Clark, 145–74.

——— (1983). *The Miracle Stories of the Early Christian Tradition.* Translated by Francis McDonough. Philadelphia: Fortress Press.

——— (2001). *Gospel Writing and Church Politics: A Socio-Rhetorical Approach.* Chuen King Lecture Series 8. Hong Kong: Chinese Univ. of Hong Kong.

Thiselton, Anthony C. (1980). *The Two Horizons: New Testament Hermeneutics and Philosophical Description with Special Reference to Heidegger, Bultmann, Gadamer, and Wittgenstein.* Grand Rapids, Mich.: Eerdmans.

——— (1992). *New Horizons in Hermeneutics: The Theory and Practice of Transforming Biblical Reading.* London: Collins.

Thüsing, Wilhelm (1981–). *Die neutestamentlichen Theologie und Jesus Christus.* Düsseldorf: Patmos.

Torrance, Alan J. (1996). *Persons in Communion: An Essay on Trinitarian Description and Human Participation with Special Reference to Volume One of Karl Barth's Church Dogmatics.* Edinburgh: T. & T. Clark.

——— (2004). "What is a Person?" In Malcolm Jeeves, ed., *From Cells to Souls—and Beyond: Changing Portraits of Human Nature.* Grand Rapids, Mich.: Eerdmans, 199–222.

——— (2005). "Open Society and the Problem of Closure in Accounts of Human Nature." In Malcolm Jeeves and Stewart Sutherland (eds.) *On Human Nature—Proceedings of the Royal Society of Edinburgh.* Edinburgh.

Torrance, James B. (1968). "Interpretation and Understanding in Schleiermacher's Theology: Some Critical Questions." *SJT* 21:268–82.

Torrance, Thomas F. (1962). "Introduction." In Karl Barth, *Theology and Church: Shorter Writings 1920–1928.* Translated by Louise Pettibone Smith. London: SCM, 7–54.

——— (1968). "Hermeneutics according to F. D. E. Schleiermacher." *SJT* 21:257–67.

——— (1988). *The Trinitarian Faith: The Evangelical Theology of the Ancient Catholic Church.* Edinburgh: T. & T. Clark.

Toynbee, Jocelyn, and John Ward Perkins (1956). *The Shrine of St. Peter and the Vatican Excavations.* London: Longmans, Green.

Triandis, Harry C. (1989). "Cross-Cultural Studies of Individualism and Collectivism." In Richard A. Dienstbier and John J. Berman, eds., *Nebraska*

Symposium on Motivation, volume 37, *Cross-Cultural Perspectives.* Lincoln: Univ. of Nebraska Press, 41–133.

———— (1994). "Theoretical and Methodological Approaches to the Study of Collectivism and Individualism." In Kim *et al.* 1994:41–51.

Triandis, Harry C., and Richard W. Brislin, eds. (1980). *Handbook of Cross-Cultural Psychology: Social Psychology.* Volume 5. Boston: Allyn & Bacon.

Triandis, Harry C., and Vasso Vassiliou (1972). "A Comparative Analysis of Subjective Culture." In Harry C. Triandis, et al., eds., *Comparative Studies in Behavioral Science.* New York: Wiley-Interscience, 299–301.

Triandis, Harry C., et al (1993). "An Etic-Emic Analysis of Individualism and Collectivism." *Journal of Cross-Cultural Psychology* 24:366–83.

Troeltsch, Ernst (1977). *Writings on Theology and Religion.* Edited by Robert Morgan and Michael Pye. London: Duckworth.

Tshibangu, T. (1987). "The Task and Method of Theology in Africa." In Parratt 1987:37–57.

Turner, Max (2000). "Historical Criticism and Theological Hermeneutics of the New Testament." In Green and Turner 2000a:44–70.

Vanhoozer, Kevin J. (1998). *Is There a Meaning in This Text? The Bible, the Reader, and The Morality of Literary Knowledge.* Grand Rapids, Mich.: Zondervan.

Volf, Miroslav (1996). *Exclusion and Embrace: A Theological Exploration of Identity, Otherness, and Reconciliation.* Nashville: Abingdon.

Warner, Richard, and Tadeusz Szubka, eds. (1994). *The Mind-Body Problem: A Guide to the Current Debate.* Oxford: Blackwell.

Warnock, G. J. (1973). "Some Types of Performative Utterance." In Isaiah Berlin et al., *Essays on J. L. Austin.* Oxford: Clarendon, 69–89.

Watson, Francis, ed. (1993). *The Open Text: New Directions for Biblical Studies?* London: SCM.

———— (1994). *Text, Church, and World.* Edinburgh: T. & T. Clark.

———— (1997). *Text and Truth: Redefining Biblical Theology.* Edinburgh: T. & T. Clark.

———— (2000). *Agape, Eros, Gender: Towards a Pauline Sexual Ethic.* Cambridge: Cambridge Univ. Press.

———— (2004). *Paul and the Hermeneutics of Faith.* London: T. & T. Clark.

Weber, Max (1964 [1947]). *The Theory of Social and Economic Organization.* Translated by A. M. Henderson and Talcott Parsons. New York: Free Press.

White, Hayden (1973). *Metahistory: The Historical Imagination in Nineteenth-Century Europe.* Baltimore: Johns Hopkins Univ. Press.

———— (1992). "Historical Emplotment and the Problem of Truth." In Friedländer 1992:37–53.

White, Hugh C. (1988a). "Introduction: Speech Act Theory and Literary Criticism." In White 1988b: 1–24.

————, ed. (1988b). *Speech Act Theory and Biblical Criticism. Semeia* 41. Decatur, Ga.: Scholars.

White, John L. (1988). "Ancient Greek Letters." In Aune 1988: 85–105.

Wilken, Robert Louis (2002). "Sanctorum Communio: For Evangelicals and Catholics Together." *Pro Ecclesia* 11:159–66.

Williams, Margaret H. (1994). "The Structure of Roman Jewry Re-considered—Were the Synagogues of Ancient Rome Entirely Homogeneous?" *Zeitschrift für Papyrologie und Epigraphik* 102:129–41.

Wimberley, Howard, and Joel Savishinsky (1978). "Ancestor Memorialism: A Comparison of Jews and Japanese." In Misra and Preston 1978:115–31.

Wimsatt, William K. (1954). *The Verbal Icon.* Lexington: Univ. of Kentucky Press.

Wimsatt, William K., and Monroe C. Beardsley (1946). "The Intentional Fallacy." Reprinted in Wimsatt 1954:3–18 and Molina 1976:1–13.

Wolfson, Harry A. (1965). "Immortality and Resurrection in the Philosophy of the Church Fathers." In Stendahl 1965a:54–96.

Wolterstorff, Nicholas (1995). *Divine Discourse: Philosophical Reflections on the Claim That God Speaks.* Cambridge: Cambridge Univ. Press.

Wrede, William (1973). "The Tasks and Methods of 'New Testament Theology.'" In Morgan 1973:68–116. The first published English translation of *Über Aufgabe und Methode der sogenannten neutestamentliche Theologie* (Göttingen: Vandenhoeck & Ruprecht, 1897).

Wright, N. T. (2003). *The Resurrection of the Son of God.* London: SPCK; Minneapolis: Fortress Press.

Yandell, Keith (1995). "A Defense of Dualism." *Faith and Philosophy* 12:548–66.

Yerushalmi, Yosef Hayim (1982). *Zakhor: Jewish History and Jewish Memory.* Seattle: Univ. of Washington Press.

Yonge, C. D. (1993). *The Works of Philo: Complete and Unabridged.* New updated edition with foreword by David M. Scholer. Peabody, Mass.: Hendrickson. Original edition published 1854.

Zizioulas, John D. (1975). "Human Capacity and Human Incapacity: A Theological Exploration of Personhood." *SJT* 28:401–48.

———— (1985). *Being as Communion: Studies in Personhood and the Church.* London: Darton, Longman and Todd.

INDEX OF SUBJECTS

Life of Brian, The: 111
literary works, character of: creation of
quasi-autonomous imaginative worlds,
88; NT works as non-literary, 89; the
Bible as literary, 90–91; distinguishing
between literary and non-literary
works, 91–92, 96–97; Gadamer on
nature of art and literature, 94–96;
dissolution of purposive intentions,
95–96; as expository and didactic, 97;
fictional and non-fictional, 97; the
NT "texts" as non-literary writings,
97–98; as performative, illocutionary,
and perlocutionary, 102; fiction as
non-illocutionary, 104–5; "discourse
without illocutionary force," 104. *See
also* authorial intention; intentional
fallacy
Locke, John: 14, 17
Lücke, Friedrich: editor of
Schleiermacher's hermeneutics, 127
Luther, Martin: 12
Man, Paul de: controversy about his
writing activities in World War II,
74–75; defended by Derrida, 75
Marcion: 261–62, 275
martyrdom: Polycarp of Smyrna and
generally, 223. *See also* social identity
meals: *see* communion, interpersonal; the
eucharist
meat: in Greco-Roman sacrifice, 164
memory: role in interpersonal
communion, 41; of people and events
beyond and within our personal
experience, 68–69; impact on identity,
69; Paul's use of Israelite collective
memory, 165; "memoirs" of the
apostles in the second century CE,
181; collective memory and history,
217–18; Mary remembered, 218; the
anonymous but remembered woman
of Mark 14:9, 218; theorizing collective
memory, 218–21; its integration
with social identity theory, 221–22;
collective memory, social identity, and
the early saints, 222–24; memory of

martyrdom, 223; martyrs as prototypes
and "possible selves" of Christian
identity, 223; petitionary prayer to the
saints, 224; anamnesis in the invocation
of the saints, 252; Paul in Romans, 278
Menenius Agrippa: metaphor of the body,
158
Michaelis, Johann: 20
models of the human person: four
broad possibilities, 234–35; reductive
or eliminative materialism and its
problems, 236–37; radical dualism and
its problems, 237–38; the possibility
of disembodied existence, 238;
non-reductive physicalism and its
problems, 239–46; emergent properties,
239; ultimate vindication through
resurrection, 240; existence of the
soul dependent on God, not a natural
quality, 242; identity of the resurrected
person, 242–46; David Brown's version
of nonreductive physicalism, 246–49;
integrative dualism, 249–51; Aquinas
on the immortality of the soul, 250–51;
the God-given knowledge of the souls
in heaven of what passes on earth,
250–51; invocation of the saints in an
actual sense, 251–53
Morgan, Robert: diagnosis of relationship
between history and theology, 31–32
Mother Teresa of Calcutta: 224
myth: *see* Strauss
New Testament: source of Christian
life and identity, 1–3; historical
interpretation, 1; various ways to
interpret, 1; Christian reading of, 2; use
by systematic theologians, 2; historical
interpretation, 7; distinction between
historical features and "universal
truths," 19. *See also* New Testament
writings; New Testament theology
New Testament writings: non-literary
character, 9, 88–118, 97–98; as
"practical messages" (Wimsatt
and Bearsdley), 93, 182–83; their
illocutionary character, 105–6;

INDEX OF MODERN AUTHORS

INDEX OF SCRIPTURE

PHILIP F. ESLER is Professor of Biblical Criticism at the University of St. Andrews, Scotland. Among his publications are *Conflict and Identity in Romans* (Fortress Press, 2003), *The Early Christian World* (editor, 2000), *Galatians* (1998), and *The Early Christians and Their Social Worlds* (1994).